"GETTING BY"

D1028445

"Getting By"

Class and State Formation among Chinese in Malaysia

Donald M. Nonini

CORNELL UNIVERSITY PRESS   **ITHACA AND LONDON**

Cornell University Press gratefully acknowledges receipt of grants from the Department of Anthropology and the University Research Council of the University of North Carolina at Chapel Hill, which aided in the publication of this book.

Cornell University Press gratefully acknowledges receipt of a Subsidy for Publication grant from the Chiang Ching-kuo Foundation for International Scholarly Exchange (USA), which generously assisted in the publication of this book.

First published 2015 by Cornell University Press
First printing, Cornell Paperbacks, 2015
Printed in the United States of America

Library of Congress Cataloging-in-Publication Data

Nonini, Donald Macon, author.
   Getting by : class and state formation among Chinese in
Malaysia / Donald M. Nonini.
      pages cm
   Includes bibliographical references and index.
   ISBN 978-0-8014-5247-5 (cloth : alk. paper)
   ISBN 978-0-8014-7908-3 (pbk. : alk. paper)
   1. Chinese—Malaysia—Bukit Mertajam (Pulau Pinang)—Politics and
government. 2. Chinese—Malaysia—Bukit Mertajam (Pulau Pinang)—
Ethnic identity. 3. Social classes—Malaysia—Bukit Mertajam (Pulau Pinang)
4. Nationalism—Malaysia—Bukit Mertajam (Pulau Pinang) 5. Ethnology—
Malaysia—Bukit Mertajam (Pulau Pinang) 6. Bukit Mertajam (Pulau
Pinang, Malaysia)—History. I. Title.
   DS595.2.C5N66   2015
   305.8951'05951—dc23   2014038677

Cornell University Press strives to use environmentally responsible suppliers and materials to the fullest extent possible in the publishing of its books. Such materials include vegetable-based, low-VOC inks and acid-free papers that are recycled, totally chlorine-free, or partly composed of nonwood fibers. For further information, visit our website at www.cornellpress.cornell.edu.

Cloth printing   10 9 8 7 6 5 4 3 2 1
Paperback printing   10 9 8 7 6 5 4 3 2 1

Contents

Acknowledgments

It is impossible to adequately acknowledge the assistance of all the very kind friends and acquaintances in Malaysia and in the United States who have made the ethnographic and historical research and writing that have taken place over a period of more than thirty years possible. Above all, I must thank the residents of Bukit Mertajam—all ages, classes, ethnicities, and genders—who patiently endured my at times impertinent and insensitive questions, tried to answer them as best they could, and led me to new insights. I have been extraordinarily privileged by their gracious help and teaching over many years, combined with a hospitality that has touched me deeply.

I owe a particular debt to my field assistants during several periods of research in Bukit Mertajam from the late 1970s through the late 2000s, who went beyond the usual tasks I asked of them to become superb friends, informants, and co-ethnographers—Kuan Yew Chieo, Tang Swee Huat, Zhou Jinfu, Lim Hai Long, Ng Wen-Sheng, and Lim Kun Heng. In the United States, Changhui Qi and Elizabeth Jones also served ably as research assistants at various times.

I have a special debt of another kind to those who were my hosts in Bukit Mertajam—Goh Chee Ngoh and his family (in 1978–80 and again in 1985). Mrs. Goh was an exceptional host from whose wise and incisive observations I learned much. Between 1978 and 1980, Clifford and Georgeann Sather and family in Georgetown provided very much needed refuge for an overwhelmed researcher.

I've had the singular good fortune of becoming friends with several residents of Bukit Mertajam who have instructed me brilliantly over many years—Tan Chong Keng for his deep knowledge of politics in Bukit Mertajam, Ang Bak-Kau for correcting my Mandarin and for his insights into local history, and Ng Bak Kee for generously sharing his intimate understanding of Bukit Mertajam social life. In 1985, Guo Zhenming provided me with superb instruction in Hokkien. I can now thank him only posthumously for his patience and keen wit, as he taught a far-from-talented pupil the Hokkien language in its performative as well as linguistic dimensions.

There are other friends, particularly Chinese working men and women, who in the interest of confidentiality I must thank anonymously for indulging my impertinent and often ungrounded inquiries, and reminding me, as a person with working-class origins, of another mode of learning beyond the formal spoken and written word—learning through labor. I will always treasure their generosity and friendship.

My thanks go to the Malaysian Government for permitting me to carry out the research on which this book was based. In particular I wish to thank Mohammed Nor Ghani, director-general of the Socioeconomic Research and General Planning Unit of the Prime Minister's Department in 1978. I am also grateful to Goh Cheng Teik, deputy minister of transport in 1978, for his suggestion that I visit Bukit Mertajam as a potential research site and for providing me with introductions to people there. Other prominent Malaysians offered me academic hospitality and invaluable assistance, including Ungku Aziz, then vice chancellor of University Malaya; Awang Had bin Salleh, then deputy vice chancellor, University Malaya; and Kamal Salih, then dean of the School of Comparative Social Sciences at Universiti Sains Malaysia.

I have been fortunate to make the acquaintance of and learn from superb Malaysian scholars while in Malaysia over many years from the 1970s to 2000s: at the University of Malaya, Raymond Lee, Susan Ackerman, Lim Mah Hui, Tan Chee Beng, and K. S. Jomo (now of the United Nations); at the School of Comparative Social Sciences, Universiti Sains Malaysia in Penang, Francis Loh Kok Wah, Johan Saravannamuttu, Khoo Boo Teik, and Masnah Mohamed; at the School of Humanities, Universiti Sains Malaysia: Soak-Koon Wong, Cheah Boon Kheng, Richard Mason, and Lok Chong-Hoe. I hope that bringing this book to fruition after so many years will repay to some small extent the many kindnesses, insights, and suggestions they have freely extended.

At the last moment, Sin Chuin Peng of the National University of Singapore Library came to my rescue by sending me scans of issues of the newspaper *Guanghua Ribao* from 1979 in the library's collections needed for chapter 7. I gratefully acknowledge his aid.

All too sadly, I must especially acknowledge those many friends, informants, and teachers in Bukit Mertajam and elsewhere in Malaysia who are now deceased. If I have a major regret in the long and circuitous route to publication of this book, it is that it is appearing when they are no longer able to know how profoundly in their debt I am for their contributions to it.

Over a career now extending into its fourth decade, which has taken many twists and turns, I have been extraordinarily fortunate to have a number of intellectual companions from whom I have learned more than I can say: Aihwa Ong, Tom Patterson, Bruce Kapferer, the late Stanley Diamond, Jonathan Friedman, Ida Susser, the late Bill Roseberry, Don Kalb, James C. Scott, Faye Harrison, Nina Glick Schiller, Gerald Sider, Dorothy Holland, Catherine Lutz, Gavin Smith, and many other friends at the Anthropology of Political Economy Seminar at the

University of Toronto. I am indebted particularly to the late G. William Skinner, my dissertation advisor at Stanford University, who originally set me on this path in 1977, although he might well disagree with the route I've taken on the way to this book.

I have many debts, large and small, extraordinary and quotidian, to my colleagues and students in the Anthropology Department and other departments at the University of North Carolina, Chapel Hill, for making my intellectual and personal life more enjoyable and productive: Dorothy Holland, Arturo Escobar, Charles Price, James Peacock, Margaret Wiener, John Pickles, Michal Osterweil, Weeteng Soh, Euyryung Jun, and Marc David. Everyone should be so fortunate!

Despite the best efforts of friends and informants to correct me, I alone am responsible for any errors of fact or interpretation in this book. In all situations in the book that follows I have referred to people living or with whom I have had interactions by pseudonyms.

I have been fortunate to receive funding for research in Malaysia from the National Science Foundation (Dissertation Completion Grant, 1979–80); and from the Social Science Research Council/American Council of Learned Societies Advanced Research Grant on Southeast Asia, 1992. For providing me with time to conduct further research and writing for this book, I thank the UNC Chapel Hill Institute for the Arts and Humanities Fellowships on two occasions, Spring 1991 and Spring 2007, and the Department of Anthropology, UNC-Chapel Hill for time for two research and study leaves.

I have delivered previous drafts of chapters for this book at the National University of Singapore; University of North Carolina, Chapel Hill; University of Bergen; Universiti Sains Malaysia; Duke University; University of California, Berkeley; University of Illinois at Champaign-Urbana; the workshops on "Globalization, the State and Violence" organized by Jonathan Friedman in Kona, Hawaii, and New York City, sponsored by the Henry F. Guggenheim Foundation; University of Puerto Rico; the National Humanities Center; University of Toronto; Murdoch University; York University; Monash University; and the Social Science Research Council/European Social Research Council at Princeton University.

Parts of this book have been adapted from previously published material and are used with the permission of the publishers: "Shifting Identities, Positioned Imaginaries: Transnational Traversals and Reversals by Malaysian Chinese," in *Ungrounded Empires: The Cultural Politics of Modern Chinese Transnationalism*, ed. Aihwa Ong and Donald Nonini (New York: Routledge, 1997), 204–228; "'Chinese Society,' Coffee-Shop Talk, Possessing Gods: The Politics of Public Space among Diasporic Chinese in Malaysia," *positions: east asia cultures critique* 6, no. 2 (Fall 1998): 439–474 (Duke University Press); "The Dialectics of

'Disputatiousness' and 'Rice-Eating Money': Class Confrontation and Gendered Imaginaries among Chinese Men in Peninsular Malaysia," *American Ethnologist* 26, no. 1 (1999): 47–68; "Toward a (Proper) Postwar History of Southeast Asian Petty Capitalism: Predation, the State, and Chinese Small Business Capital in Malaysia," in *Petty Capitalists and Globalization: Flexibility, Entrepreneurship and Economic Development,* ed. Alan Smart and Josephine Smart (Albany: State University of New York Press, 2005), 167–200; "Processes of State, Class and Ethno-Racial Formation in Urban Malaysia: Geo-Spatial Transformations and Regime Shifts 1970–2000," *Anthropologica* 50, no. 2 (2008): 255–268; and "Theorizing Transnational Movement in the Current Conjuncture: Examples from/of/ in the Asia-Pacific," in *Migration in the 21st Century: Political Economy and Ethnography,* ed. Pauline Gardiner Barber and Winnie Lem (New York: Routledge, 2012), 64–88.

I have had the great fortune of a highly enjoyable and productive working relationship with my editors, Roger Haydon, Karen Laun, and Jack Rummel at Cornell University Press, and with Emily Powers and Susan Barnett, also at the Press. I have particularly benefited from Roger's steady and reassuring approach to bringing this book, so long in the making, to publication. No author could ask for a more professional group. I am grateful beyond words.

Finally, I must thank Sandy and Roque, loves of my life, who have been with me during most of the time this book was researched and written, for their affection and irreverence, and for calling me out from my scholar's study to enjoy the rest of life. May it ever be so!

This book is dedicated to the memory of my mother, Rose M. Horton.

"GETTING BY"

A HISTORICAL ETHNOGRAPHY OF CLASS AND STATE FORMATION

This book is an ethnographic and historical study of the cultural politics of class conflict and state formation among Chinese citizens in peninsular Malaysia over a period of several decades. It is based on several years of research in the northern region of Malaysia from 1978 to 2007. In this book, I interpret how the processes of class, ethnic, and state formation all interact in complex ways to constitute the contemporary infra-politics of everyday life among Chinese in Malaysia.

A Request Long Deferred, but Not Forgotten

In the summer of 1985, I was riding with two Chinese men who were driving the truck of a small Chinese-owned transport firm from its headquarters in the city of Bukit Mertajam in Penang state to Kuala Lumpur, the capital of Malaysia. It was a long, grueling, and muggy day of stop-and-start driving as we passed through congested and at times narrow streets of suburbs of Kuala Lumpur, with Ah-Bah and Kou-Kian, continually watchful for other vehicles, pedestrians, and traffic police, in the process making scores of deliveries. During most of the day, both men were either silent, or shouted briefly to each other over the roar of the truck engine. But then, midafternoon: at one point, I was remarking on the small amounts charged as the transport fee for each parcel. Kou-Kian, thumbing through the thick stack of freight invoices attached to the dashboard, said that although such a small amount of money went to the boss, this was fine with the

1

boss, although for the drivers it represented a lot of work and effort to deliver just one piece to another consignee. He then asked, "Aren't you going to write a book about Chinese society? Well, if you are, be sure to write that the boss sucks our blood [*laoban xixue*]. You know, those ghosts, *gui* [and he cupped his fingers together and placed them on his neck] that the Malays call *beh-nan-ka* [*peneng-galan* (M)], 'vampires'?"[1]

This book seeks to honor the request made that day. I attempt to say something unfashionable about the world we live in—or at least that part of it lived in by the Chinese I knew in Malaysia. This is a world in which "the boss sucks our blood" as well as one in which "we just try to get by"—a phrase I heard many times during my research in Malaysia. It is a world of mystery, deep anger, and the fury of an analysis that can rarely be brought into daily life or made real. How many critical scholars and commentators on East and Southeast Asia, rendered weary or cynical by the post–Cold War epoch, by the triumph of neoliberal capitalism, and by the self-satisfaction of successful economic growth arising from globalization, have recently thought to speak of exploitation (but see Lee 2007)? How many scholars write of the way in which a discourse of triumph about the "prosperity and progress" supposedly characteristic of the newly industrialized economies of Asia occludes the realities of the lived experience of Kou-Kian and many others? These realities are part of the story of the Chinese who were born, live, and work in Malaysia, as they are elsewhere.

However, in the case of the Chinese populations of Southeast Asia, most scholars and journalistic pundits tell us that Kou-Kian's experiences are anomalies. Suffused with descriptions of the fabulous wealth of the "overseas Chinese," business school hacks and journalists would find little of interest or note in the daily lives of those described in this book. Indeed, at one level, the entire point of writing this book has been to honor "ordinary" people such as the truck drivers I rode with that day, and many other people I met during my research, even though their lives are largely ignored in the literature of capitalist triumphalism.

Hailings and Entanglements: The Making of Citizens

If nationalist movements are grounded in the representations of an "imagined political community—and imagined as both inherently limited and sovereign" (Anderson 2006, 6), then nationalism for Chinese Malaysians from the late 1970s onward has been deeply problematic. Which nation was one to identify with, to start with, the territory from which one or one's ancestors came, or the territory in which one now lived—China or Malaysia? In the modern period, those who have imaginatively identified with a nation have always had to come to terms, often in tense and troubling ways, with the state that has sovereignty over that nation. In the case of postcolonial Malaysia in 1979, the vast majority of Chinese living in Malaysia saw themselves as affiliated, connected, and loyal to the Malaysian nation, although they were unsure to what extent it was to be defined as *their* nation. Still they imagined themselves as owing loyalty, as Malaysian citizens, to the new nation-state. By 1979, most of the younger generation, born in Malaysia and passing or having passed recently through its school system, having learned the national language, *Bahasa Malaysia* (M), and having been habituated to the government's pedagogy of the telos of national "development" and the *Rukunegara*, or "national ideology," felt they were genuine Malaysians, and not China citizens, even if they were Chinese: they were, they declared, emphatically *not* "China citizens living overseas in Malaysia," *Malaixiya huaqiao*, but "Chinese of Malaysia," *Malaixiya huaren*. Unlike prior generations of Chinese in Malaya before independence in 1957, they were not sojourners but led lives irreversibly etched in the syncretic popular cultures and landscapes of the Malaysian Peninsula: they spoke hybrid languages such as Penang Hokkien with its Malay loan words, and partook of hybrid cuisines that incorporated Malay dishes such as curry and *laksa* into Hokkien or Cantonese repertoires of cooking; they celebrated Malaysia's National Day, as they did Chinese New Year.

Indeed, the political pressures placed on the Chinese population from independence onward gave most Chinese little choice other than to exhibit "loyalty." As late as the 1970s, Malay political leaders accused many Chinese of being "disloyal," thus harkening back to the counterinsurgency of the Emergency period (1948–60), and wielded this accusation against them on any occasion when they exhibited pride in their cultures, their origins, languages, religious beliefs, or sought to exert political power vis-à-vis the Malay majority. The bitter lesson of May 13, 1969, in which hundreds of Chinese were killed by Malays in riots in Kuala Lumpur in what was in all but name a coup d'état (Kua 2008), was still a traumatic collective memory for Chinese—and at times of crisis, Malay political leaders sought to intimidate them by reminding them of what could happen again if they were seen as disloyal, too powerful, or assertive.

At the same time, however, both personal memory and family narratives among Chinese inscribed recollections or stories of arrival from China one, two, or three generations past—often via Singapore, Thailand, or Indonesia—long efforts of ultimately successful struggle in Malaysia through "raising a household with one's bare hands," *baishou qijia*—including, until the Japanese invasion of China in 1937, trips to visit their native places in China. Many families in the 1970s and 1980s still had stories of fathers or grandfathers who had been successful businessmen and married two wives—one in China, one in Malaya—and fathered children in each. Even in the 1970s during the later years of China's Great Proletarian Cultural Revolution, Chinese Malaysians still received letters from southeastern China, often anguished, sometimes entreating for money, sent by long-unseen (and often unmet) relatives—brothers, sisters, fathers, mothers, cousins, nephews, nieces. These were the epistles of family members dispersed and separated by invasion, warfare, revolution, counterinsurgency, and more recently state prohibitions on travel,[2] that marked the four decades from the mid-1930s to the late 1970s. They felt a common fate with relatives living elsewhere in the Nanyang or "South Seas" (i.e., Southeast Asia)—brothers or sisters or cousins living in Java, Bangkok, or Saigon—some of whom they visited, did business with, or fostered children for. The Chinese-language press in Malaysia, even at its most censored (and then self-censored), brought daily news from the other settlements of Chinese in Southeast Asia, from Hong Kong, from Taiwan, and even from China under the Communists. Until the Bandung Conference of 1955, Guomindang and Communist nationalist discourses regarded Chinese residing overseas as *huaqiao*—as citizens of the China state living outside the boundaries of China itself: *jus sanguinis* made all descendants of male citizens of China Chinese citizens.[3]

Not even in the 1970s were nationalist identifications with China merely pro forma—circulated from afar only—from Beijing or Taipei, but instead "hailed" or made subjective claims on Chinese in Malaysia in various ways. Among the oldest Chinese in Malaysia then alive, collective memories resonated with the idea that a new nation had been founded in China in 1949, at great sacrifice by "the people of China," including by Chinese in Malaya who had suffered massacres and brigandage at the hands of the Japanese army during the occupation years of 1941–45 precisely because the Japanese saw them as loyal subjects of China residing overseas. In the 1970s, older Chinese still recalled their participation from afar in the anti-Japanese movement from the 1930s—they remembered friends and acquaintances who were among the many young Chinese volunteers who answered the patriotic call to return to the China motherland to defend it from the Japanese invaders. Others, slightly younger, had experienced the rigors of the Japanese occupation firsthand and were aware that the Japanese sought to collectively punish Nanyang Chinese for their support of the anti-Japanese movement. Middle-aged adults educated in the postwar Chinese-language schools had been drilled in the Confucian classics and taught the glories of five thousand years of literate culture. Only purely English-educated adults who had experienced the years of late British colonial or early postcolonial rule in English language schools, and teenagers experiencing for the first time schooling in Bahasa Malaysia and a new nationalized curriculum centered on Malaysia, were not susceptible. Men, being more highly educated, were more identified with China than were women, everything else being equal. Thus the claims made by their relationships to China weighed differently on Chinese depending on the experiences of their generation, length of residence in Malaysia, gender, and class.

Still, under the circumstances, few Chinese in Malaysia in 1979 contested the sovereignty of the Malaysian state, for to the vast majority of Chinese the Malaysian government was no colonial occupier, and even the most antagonistic held that it was potentially a democratic state, recognized by other countries internationally as free from colonial rule and having legitimate sovereignty over the territory and population of Malaysia. The British colonial rulers, having first defeated the insurgency for independence by the Malayan Communist Party—the only serious challenge to either British colonialism or to the Malay and Chinese elites it cultivated—had twenty-two years previously peacefully ceded sovereignty to the newly independent Malaysian government ruled by those elites.

People in Bukit Mertajam told me occasional stories of relatives who in the early 1950s had "gone to the hills," and more generally of the "hill rats," *shan-laoshu*, Malayan Communist Party guerrillas who were reputed to be in the remote mountain jungles in northern Kedah and Perak, and in southern Thailand. But older Bukit Mertajam people knew that not even the MCP guerrillas called for unity with China, for that would have been outlandish, but rather for an independent and socialist Malayan Peoples Republic. Adults had memories of the early 1960s in which a rash young Lee Kuan Yew had called for a "Malaysia for Malaysians," meaning a Malaysia not for Malays alone, and provided the impetus whose threat to Malay political domination led to partition of Malaysia from Singapore in 1965. They had heard a similar call for "democracy" and "multiracial justice" from the leaders of the Democratic Action Party (DAP), the largest Chinese-controlled political party, one in opposition to the National Front of the United Malays National Organization (UMNO) and its affiliated parties such as the Malaysian Chinese Association (MCA) and Gerakan. Although DAP leaders and many Chinese spoke of their feeling that they were "second-class citizens," *dierdeng gongming*, due to government discrimination in areas of economic, educational, and cultural life, what needs to be emphasized is not only their sense of "second-class" status but also their strong adherence to being "citizens."

The sheer diversity of these experiences among Chinese Malaysians and their implications for citizenship are so great that they deserve a more adequate accounting than the polyvalent and ambiguous term *diaspora* provides (Vertovec and Cohen 1999).[4] Its casual use by some scholars (including, perhaps Nonini and Ong 1997; Nonini 1997; and Ong 1999) to refer to the condition of Chinese in Malaysia has entered squarely into the cultural polemics between indigenist chauvinists and civil society activists regarding the "loyalty" of Chinese, which some careless scholarly characterizations of Chinese as "diasporic" (e.g., "rootless," "cosmopolitan," "transnational," "flexible") have unwittingly contributed to.[5] Suffice it to say that by independence in 1957, it made little sense to speak of Chinese as being in either a social or political diasporic relationship with respect to China. And since the 1980s what has more clearly emerged is a new social and political relationship of diaspora between those Chinese professionals and owners of petty property who have left Malaysia for sojourns overseas, other Malaysians still living in Malaysia, and the Malaysian state—a relationship described in chapter 10.

It is, instead, the long arc of the history of Chinese citizenship in Malaysia that matters here. How the citizenship of Chinese Malaysians in one city in Malaysia has emerged over three decades as a distinctive but troubled condition is the major subject of this book.

Neglect of Class and the Working Class in "Overseas Chinese" Studies

A certain convergence of learned opinion about the "overseas Chinese" has largely read the Chinese working classes of Southeast Asia out of existence. Conventional wisdom produced by business journalists and pundits in the 1980s and 1990s arising from their Orientalist musings about the "business success" of "Chinese entrepreneurs" joined an earlier 1950s–1970s functionalist and adaptationist approach among anthropologists and sociologists that couched Chinese economic values in Southeast Asia as cultural adaptations by those with a longstanding "commercial culture" to new economic opportunities outside of China—the values of thrift, market vigilance, industry, and savings of capital, among other virtues (Skinner 1957; Crissman 1967; essays in Freedman 1979c; Wang 1981, 1991, 2000; Lim and Gosling 1983). Together, these perspectives elevated Chinese businessmen in Southeast Asia to the status of the ne plus ultra figures required for the understanding of "overseas Chinese culture." Although both business pundits and social scientists conceded that Chinese working men and women existed, they were no more than capitalists manqué; what one needed to study, comprehend, and even empathize with was the "Chinese entrepreneur."

Admittedly, both constituencies had different reasons for this obsessive forgetting: whereas business writers sought the key to "economic growth" and "success" in the habits of wealthy Chinese businessmen in Southeast Asia, the Cold War led many social scientists to engage in a liberal apologetics that focused on Chinese "pragmatism" and the desire for wealth as a defense against the accusation by late colonial and early postcolonial rulers that Chinese in Southeast Asia were actual or potential Communist subversives—the standard defense being that most were after all only practical business people, whose commercial activities were "economic benefits" to the newly independent nation-states in Southeast Asia (Freedman 1979b, 21). What is particularly interesting, if the Chinese of Bukit Mertajam are illustrative, is that these learned conceptions of "overseas Chinese" as "commercially oriented," "practical," "having Confucian values," and the like resonated closely with the classed and gendered stylistics of the city's Chinese mercantile elite itself, which apotheosized the "typical Chinese" precisely along these lines. That an economic elite's classist and masculinist vision of the "typical Chinese" should so closely reflect and be reflected in learned opinion suggests much about the sociology of knowledge. In any event, this convergence has provided the hegemonic ground for seeing Chinese in Southeast Asia as essentially always, already bourgeois—as, *au fond*, male, property owning, pragmatic merchants. These ideological representations fill a conceptual space that hides a far more complex set of social relations of inequality in everyday life among Chinese in Malaysia and elsewhere in Southeast Asia.

Class, Gender, and Where Wealth Comes From

What about class? The issue is, after all, where the wealth of capitalist society comes from, and why, in both theoretical and political terms, it matters to the ways in which people live their lives and see themselves and others. If we ask where such wealth comes from, then we must seriously consider Marx's analysis in *Capital*, in which he demonstrated that under capitalism wealth comes from the appropriation of surplus value, that is, the difference between the new value which a wage laborer's labor power creates—more commodities and thus new capital—and the lesser value expended by her employer as wages for her living (i.e., for the "reproduction of labor"). One might think, for example, of the several hundred women garment workers who labored in Bukit Mertajam's garment sweatshops, and what their labor implied for the profits of the owners of the city's garments industry (see chapter 2). Viewed in this light, Marx's argument was that the quantity of value the capitalist appropriated over time from laborers made the difference not only between the capitalist and the laborers he employed, but also between the wealthy capitalist and the not-so-wealthy one, as capital accumulated and concentrated in some hands and not others. Certain quantities "count" in a capitalist society.

On Gender and Familial Economies

It is by now well appreciated that neither all forms of value extraction nor all forms of oppression can be encompassed under the sign of a Marxist class analysis. As feminist theorists have made clear, capitalist societies depend on distinctively gendered household and family economies that are not themselves capitalist but make the reproduction of labor—and much else—possible in these societies (see, e.g., Gibson-Graham 1996, 2006). The dynamics of value appropriation in such domestic economies have been explored by these theorists and by those interested in petty capitalism (Smart and Smart 2005). Malaysia was no exception, and the issue was certainly pertinent to the hundreds of petty businesses of Bukit Mertajam. Nonwaged and ambiguously requited labor by women, daughters, younger men, and children who were family members of the owner was crucial to the day-to-day operation of the majority of the small-scale businesses I studied in 1978–80. Most hired no "outsiders" (people who were not family members of the owner), and two-thirds hired no more outsiders than they employed family members (see chapter 2). Wives "watched over the shop," *kandian*, while their husbands went out to make deals, entertain creditors, or collect bills; unmarried daughters still in high school worked as clerks to keep accounts; younger children ran errands and cleaned the shop (Nonini 2003; Yao 2002).

From one perspective, the male owner—or owners—of such petty businesses engaged in intensive self-exploitation, and this explained all that many informants felt they needed to explain. The conventional stories of self-made men of the older generation who "raised up a family/business with their bare hands," *baishou qijia*, and "worked hard to overcome bitterness," *keku nailao*, figured prominently within the biographical entries of leaders and stalwart members of Bukit Mertajam community organizations (e.g., native-place associations) recorded in the anniversary memorial books, *jiniantekan*, of these organizations from the 1960s and 1970s. These narratives attested to an androcentric fixation on male effort, intelligence, and sacrifice. It was understood that wives and daughters were expected to comply with patriarchal mandates, and otherwise were left out of the accounts in both senses—left out of the dominant stories *and* the public calculations. From a different perspective, this obsession with heroic male labors and the successes these brought within these narratives occluded the heavy dependence of such achievements on the labor of wives, and on unmarried and adopted daughters of the proprietor—labor unrequited or compensated to an unknown degree. Reciprocity or its absence could be reckoned only over the long term. An older woman, after all, could be left penniless and without property or income by a cruel husband or one newly enamored of a "little wife," or mistress. Even as of the late 1970s, I was told that most grown daughters still received no inheritance from the family's business from their fathers, as long as the latter made some effort to educate them and settle them with husbands.

The paradox about family labor is that because it is not accounted for in the market value of wages, it drops out of economic—and therefore social—reckoning: it fails to exist as a social fact. But this paradox crystallizes the androcentric shortcomings alike of classical Marxist class analysis and of conventional neoclassical economic theory, and of the sexist rationalizations by Chinese businessmen in Bukit Mertajam for their economic success. This paradox also occludes the commonalities of exploitation shared by family members and outside employees under the domination of patriarchal and (petty) capitalist power and an ideology that any sacrifice is worth it "for the family" (Yao 2002), as well as the crucial differences.

In this book, although it is not primarily an examination of gender relations, I focus on the ways in which male-oriented class stylistics marginalize gender oppression within families.

Three Approaches to Inequality within the Politics of Malaysian Society

The absence of scholarly attention to class and gender relations and conflicts in the case of the Chinese of Southeast Asia is of particular relevance to theoretical debates about the relative status of ethnicity and class as explanations for political processes. There are three dominant approaches to the relationship between class and ethnicity that scholars have applied to the study of Chinese people in postindependence Malaysia. These can conveniently be referred to as the "China-oriented" approach, the "ideological manipulation" approach, and the "subjective pluralist" approach. Despite the fact that the classic statements of these approaches go back to the 1960s, fifty years later they still set the dominant framework for thinking about the relationship between ethnicity and class in contemporary Malaysia.

The China-oriented approach originated in the research of sinological anthropologists carried out among "overseas Chinese" from the 1950s to the 1970s at the height of the Cold War. It represented a variety of the earlier "pluralist" approach of Furnivall (1939), which argued that colonial societies in Southeast Asia consisted of independent and parallel, largely self-governing ethnic groups, with a functional division of labor between them, whose relationships were made harmonious by the colonial order. One of the major proponents of the China-oriented approach, Maurice Freedman, made its compatibility with the Furnivallian model quite clear in an essay entitled "The Growth of a Plural Society in Malaya" (Freedman 1979a [1960]). The China-oriented approach assumed that the sociopolitical organization of postwar urban Chinese in Malaya, as elsewhere in Southeast Asia, could be viewed as but a variant of sociopolitical organization among sojourners in late imperial China's cities in the late nineteenth and early twentieth centuries. In both settings—as radically different historically and geographically as they were—urban Chinese were organized into a unitary segmentary structure of organizations based on differential speech-group, native-place, and surname ties. Instead of being fragmented by class differences and integrated as subjects into the colonial societies of Southeast Asia, they were organized within a "self-governing" corporate order that stood apart from the rest of society. Through its hierarchical structure, urban "overseas Chinese society" constituted a virtual *imperium in imperio*. Note the ethnographic present tense of the following statement from *1967*:

> The urban Chinese abroad are really in the same situation as was the urban population of traditional China. They must govern themselves without having noticeable governmental institutions, and their solution of the dilemma is the same. They use the organizational superstructure of their segmentary social structure as both a representative political system and a hierarchical administrative system, maintaining a rarely disturbed balance between the two aspects of government. The urban Chinese abroad are nearly autonomous and self-governing and their system of government is peculiarly Chinese. (Crissman 1967, 200)

The China-oriented approach was developed in several studies of urban "overseas Chinese" during the 1950s and 1960s (Freedman 1957, 1979a, 1979d; Skinner 1957, 1958, 1968; Crissman 1967; Willmott 1967). That there was something "peculiarly Chinese" at the level of a culture emphasizing the values of same surname, native-place, and speech-group loyalties—something that made time and place largely irrelevant—and that such values were the basis for the integration of urban Chinese into a unified ethnically based "community," were both assumed. It is provocative that something very similar to this Cold War anthropological theme of a self-governing hierarchical "segmentary social structure" reappears among Bukit Mertajam's mercantile elite in the 1979–80 dispute described in chapter 7.

The ideological manipulation approach put forward by Marxist political analysts arose as a critique of Furnivall's pluralist model, of which the China-oriented approach was a variant. B. N. Cham challenged the pluralist interpretations of several postwar scholars of Malaysian society, including the sinologists Maurice Freedman, Wang Gungwu, and Victor Purcell, all of whom, he claimed, emphasized "the racial division and the differential incorporation of the various communities [i.e., ethnic groups] in the formal political process as their explanatory principles" (Cham 1975, 447, 458n1). He argued instead for the importance of class relations. Cham argued that the Malay upper class, in control of the state, manipulated conceptions of ethnic-based solidarities and indigenism to mystify and divide off different ethnic fractions of the lower classes from one another:

> The principal contradiction in Malaysia is one between the upper class and the exploited masses in all races. This principal contradiction,

however, has been diverted and distorted by the upper class through the strategy of economic and political *bumiputraism* and communal politics. This strategy serves to enable the Malay upper class to maintain a dominant position in the ruling partnership [of communal-based governing parties]. (Cham 1975, 458)

Like Cham, Mullard and Brennan (1978, 349) found fault with earlier models of a plural society applied to Malaysia and also argued that the "image" of pluralism has been manipulated by a Malaysian ruling class as an "ideological tag," a means for the social control of lower classes. The model of pluralism thus "forms a central part of the political ideology of the ruling racial or cultural bloc" (Mullard and Brennan 1978, 350).

The subjective pluralist approach has emerged as the received wisdom on inequality in postcolonial Malaysia. According to this approach, "class" is a concept with little serious application to the study of Chinese or other communities in Malaysia. Instead, it is ethnicity that is the basis for a "'subjective' pluralism" for Chinese Malaysians, as for other Malaysians (Nagata 1975a, 1975b, 1976), and is the crucial determinant of the lines along which power of different kinds was distributed in Malaysian society. Thus consciousness of ethnic differences in wealth, power, and privilege is both pervasive and more socially salient than awareness of any other sort of social division, and any alternative awareness that does in fact exist is extremely limited and inchoate.

A major assumption of the subjective pluralist approach is that although "objective conditions" for the existence of classes among Chinese exist, the "subjective perceptions" of Chinese Malaysians are based on ethnic differences and not on any awareness of these "objective conditions." Although from the point of view of the external observer, Chinese Malaysians can be distinguished from one another in terms of substantial "objective" gaps in wealth and power, these differences do not in any significant way structure social relations among them nor do they lead to the emergence of "class consciousness" among them (Nagata 1976; Strauch 1981; Gosling 1983).

These three approaches to inequality and power in Malaysia are all badly flawed. Contrary to the China-oriented approach, it cannot be assumed that Chinese Malaysian social and political organization is integrated by the common values of Chinese urban sojourner culture. Instead, the existence of community must be taken as problematic, given that economic inequalities among Malaysian Chinese are great, that they are aware of these inequalities and structure their "internal" social relations accordingly, and are divided with respect to their allegiances to the Malaysian state in its postcolonial form of Malay domination. Against the ideological manipulation approach, it cannot be taken for granted that ethnicity is either a surrogate for class or an ideological mystification imposed on lower classes by dominant classes. Ethnicity must be accorded a reality in its own right, as must the role of cultural production, which cannot be reduced to the expression of ideology. At the same time, the ties between the production of ethnicity and state formation need to be taken seriously. Against the subjective pluralist approach, "class" and "ethnicity" cannot be taken to be distinguishable "objective" and "subjective" phenomena; there are cultural dimensions to class and material dimensions to ethnicity. As this book will clearly demonstrate, Chinese Malaysians do recognize class distinctions and class conflict among themselves and with other classes and class fractions of Malaysian society.

This book considers an alternative perspective that attempts to overcome the shortcomings in these three approaches. Such an alternative perspective, however, requires at least two different optics on social inequalities to encompass the temporalities and spatialities this book seeks to confront—the historical view and the ethnographic view.

The Historical View: An Alternative Perspective of Class Struggles and Ethnic Relations

Instead of the assumptions underlying these three perspectives, what must instead be presupposed as fundamental is the existence of class struggles that have shaped the history of Malaysian society.[6] The theoretical status of the concepts of "class" and "ethnicity" then derive from the cultural and strategic implications of this presupposition.

What are class struggles, and why are they central to the history of Malaysian society? Classes are not categories, groups, or "variables" that exist transhistorically or are to be comprehended by sociological indices, such as income, level of income, or some composite of "socioeconomic status." Instead, they emerge *relationally* through concrete, historically specific struggles. These struggles are contentions between groups over the relations of production—conflicts over who is able to control access to the means of production and to appropriate the surplus produced by the labor process by reason of their ownership (or not) of private productive property. As E. P. Thompson has observed,

> classes do not exist as separate entities, look around, find an enemy class, and then start to struggle. On the contrary, people find themselves in a society structured in determined ways (crucially, but not exclusively, in productive relations), they experience exploitation (or the need to maintain power over those whom they exploit), they identify points of antagonistic interest, they commence to struggle around these issues

and in the process of struggling they discover themselves as classes, they come to know this discovery as class-consciousness. (1978, 149)

All class struggles in Malaysia and elsewhere have semiotic or meaning-making aspects that are integral, in Thompson's words, to people who "find themselves in a society structured in determined ways," "experience exploitation" or "the need to maintain power over those they exploit," "identify points of antagonistic interest," and "discover themselves as classes." Conflict over the control of material resources and over radically different discursive definitions and rhetorics that articulate such conflict are therefore two different aspects of class struggle. People engaged in struggle over material resources articulate their experiences, which separate them from the members of other classes, and what they articulate emerges in the course of struggle, which is simultaneously and inextricably material and discursive. Every class struggle is therefore a contest not only over claims to material resources but also over authoritative discourse—over prevailing representations of the conflict. Ambiguities exist about who the members of a class are, who the members of opposed classes are, and who belong to other potentially allied classes. The histories of ongoing, localized class struggles are contested: as relations of production are transformed, what is at issue is who has benefited, who has lost, who deserves to benefit and lose—and why. In other words, as James C. Scott (1985) has shown, persons in opposed classes must share a common discursive frame about conflict in order to be in conflict at all, although this is not the same as saying that the members of these classes have equal standing in the public enunciation of their class positions. It is the emphasis in this book that a major difference exists between the discursive frame that the members of two opposed classes share and the widely disparate chances they have to declare their positions within it that distinguishes this book's contribution to the ethnographic study of class conflict.

Beside the commonalities and differences related to class, there are other dimensions of the everyday experiences of social difference and inequality that organize the social world in Malaysia as elsewhere. These dimensions include group connections arising from face-to-face association ("we are the people of this town") in contrast to other such groups, the shared fate of gender ("we women have it hard around here"), and from self-ascribed commonalities of origin, descent, and shared cultural practice that people see as expressing essential group difference ("we are Malaysian Chinese") (see Barth 1969). Like class, these dimensions of locale, gender, and ethnicity are structured by power relations between individuals and between groups and are thus also, like class, marked by struggles over both material resources and discursive claims seeking to authoritatively stake out moral high ground and offer justifications for respective strategies of struggle. These and other dimensions of everyday social relations interact in complex ways with the experiences of people as members of a class in specific social interactions.

Ethnic conflict in this respect is particularly interesting, because ethnicity is integrally connected to questions of recognition by modern states. The formation and maintenance of ethnic group definitions are invariably connected to recognition by state functionaries and leaders of the legitimate existence, standing, practices, and rights of one ethnic group vis-à-vis other ethnic groups (Williams 1989). One consequence of differential recognition is that certain groups are excluded from or left on the margins of the nation so constructed by the state. These processes of recognition are therefore fundamental in the making of boundaries between ethnic groups—as groups are recognized as hierarchically ranked, unique with respect to one another, and in some situations, essentially different from one another. Invariably such processes of state recognition allow for "self-recognition" and "other recognition" among members of these different groups, who connect certain specific cultural practices, physical characteristics, languages, cuisines, modes of etiquette, and other markers with statuses created by state recognition, which confers differential rights of access to state resources by such groups and coercively sanctions the political and legal privileges that some groups have vis-à-vis others. Viewed over the long term, the processes of state formation are also processes of the differential recognition by the states of these ethnic groups vis-à-vis one another (Williams 1989; Alonso 1994).

It was precisely the exercise of state power in the hands of the ruling-class fraction of one ethnic group, Malays—an artifact inherited from British colonial racism but, after independence in 1957, institutionalized in a variety of ways—which has given class struggles in Malaysia their peculiarly "racial" or ethnic manifestation. A Malay aristocratic-administrative elite, the chosen inheritor of state power by the British, has since independence taken the initiative to aggrandize its economic position through political power. Within the parliamentary political system of independent Malaysia, particularly under the New Economic Policy in effect from 1970 to 1990, this elite in its quest for capital accumulation has entered into a class-based struggle against Chinese merchants—the principal *Asian* holders of wealth in the country prior to 1957—and in the process has sought allies drawn to Malay chauvinism and economic privilege as the basis for state policy.[7] State initiatives that have enhanced capital accumulation among the Malay governing elite and its ethnic clients have included legal seizures of Chinese business property, and the extraction of politically based rent—also known as "corruption" and "graft"—from Chinese merchants. The conflicts between state leaders and functionaries on one side, and Chinese businesses (at a variety of scales) on the other, thus partake of, but are not reducible to, class struggles, because of the different but overlapping dialectics of ethnic group and class formation. Over the same period, the governing elite has adopted even more hostile policies of violent repression against the members of the Chinese working class, whom they have viewed as subversive, criminal, and antisocial. Here also, state campaigns of repression against Chinese working people who have been deemed threats to the dominant economic order involve class struggles, but are not conflatable with them. Over this period, Malay government ministers have called on Malay peasants and urban lower-class Malays for electoral support by employing both economic incentives (e.g., reserving large percentages of entry-level government positions for Malays) and a communalist rhetoric (e.g., proclaiming "Malay culture" and Islam as the foundation for Malaysian "national culture" and "national religion"). How Malay peasants and poor urban dwellers have responded to this call is another matter, depending in large part on socioeconomic inequalities within these groups.[8] These initiatives, combined with prior, longstanding state repression of class-based parties and movements supported by Chinese workers and other subordinate classes, have rendered authoritative a public discourse of fundamental ethno-racial difference, which has displaced that of class (Vasil 1971). The reconstruction of this displacement is the subject of chapter 1. In any event, it is precisely against such state cultural chauvinism and the pro-Malay policies it bolstered that Chinese citizens have responded antagonistically over the last four decades. Over the long *durée* of Malaysian politics, the processes of state formation, class struggle, and ethnic conflict have been intrinsically interconnected.

"Chinese Culture" in Malaysia and the Dialectics of State Formation

The attentive reader will notice that I have little recourse to "Chinese culture" as an explanation for what takes place in the everyday lives of the residents of Bukit Mertajam. Although I follow much critical theorization against the "culture" concept over the last two to three decades that has deessentialized and desubstantivized the concept (Clifford and Marcus 1986; Clifford 1988; Abu-Lughod 1993; Kahn 1995; Gupta and Ferguson 1997), my approach goes much further.

In sinological anthropology, the popular assumption that "Chinese culture" is essentially unchanging and universal wherever Chinese live has long been subject to scholarly critique, although Orientalist stereotypes still endure in xenophobic constructs in Asia and in the West about people of Chinese descent. The stereotypic Orientalist claims that Chinese carry a cultural essence that predisposes them to show a distinctive patriotic loyalty to the "middle kingdom" of China;

have an arrogant, even overbearing pride in their cultural heritage vis-à-vis other cultures; are obsessed with family; adhere to a hierarchical Confucian ethic; display patriarchy; make crafty but untrustworthy businessmen; form social "connections" called *guanxi*; and exhibit "filial piety"; among other things will find no support in this book.

Such (cultural) racist claims—which were particularly invidious in the indigenist discourses of the European rulers of colonial Southeast Asia and those of their indigenous successors—have long been challenged by anthropologists. Maurice Freedman (1979b, 1979d) and G. William Skinner (1960, 1996) were committed to the critique of such essentialist assumptions—a critique that was aimed at reassuring anxious Western Cold War politicians and academics as well as chauvinist indigenous leaders and intellectuals of the relative political harmlessness of Chinese people living in Southeast Asia. Freedman, Skinner, and others demonstrated that "Chinese culture" varied greatly over time and space, was always subject to attrition in the presence of modernizing contemporary values, and contributed to the economic development of Southeast Asian states.

But what if these aspects of variability, attrition, and economic contribution aren't even half of the story? My analysis in this book extends beyond the liberal adaptationist and functionalist arguments of Freedman and Skinner that defended Chinese against skeptical Cold War rulers, intellectuals, publics, and xenophobic Southeast Asian rulers and citizens. It provides evidence for a far more radical position. What have been deemed fundamental "Chinese cultural" characteristics have been the result of the cultural work arising from the dialectical interactions between Chinese Malaysians and Malaysian state formation within the processes of the making of hegemony. To put the matter straightforwardly: these cultural traits do not exist in potentio within the genius of an internalized Chinese culture but have emerged as social facts through the work done on them by Chinese and non-Chinese within the antagonistic encounters between Chinese citizens and the Malaysian state. Thus, for example, I suggest that the arts of deception among Chinese merchants in Bukit Mertajam (chapter 3); their propensity to remain small in scope (chapter 4); truck drivers' reputation as "disputatious" and clever (chapter 6); the "segmentary social structure" (Crissman 1967) of "Chinese society"[9] (chapter 7); and a variety of practices around transnational sojourns, religious processions, and commensality (chapter 9) are not the products of an essential "Chinese culture" taken overseas but the outcome of these dialectical encounters.

Here I draw on Antonio Gramsci's (1971) concept of "hegemony" as recently reworked by anthropologists, particularly in the theorizations of Gavin Smith (1999). In the approach adopted in this book, features of "Chinese culture" were not the *causes* of practices of Chinese citizenship but instead the *effects* of the hegemonic processes of "Malay domination," *ketuanan Melayu* (M), as Chinese citizens have experienced it. Although the hegemonic projects of the Malaysian state have always had an undeniable coercive side as applied to its Chinese citizens, the traits of "Chinese culture" described in the various chapters noted above were local, antagonistic responses to such projects as state transformation of local spaces through megadevelopment projects. These cultural characteristics were the efflux arising from the *history* of the making of state-led hegemonic projects of Malay domination extending over many years of postcolonial rule. Although these characteristics of Chinese "experience" can be studied ethnographically, their origins can only be investigated historically. Put another way: fundamental features of Chinese culture in Malaysia, far from being unchanged and unchanging imports from China, have been transformed by the very making of state hegemony in Malaysia.

The Ethnographic View: Cultural Styles, Class Struggles, Ethnic Conflicts, and "Gender Troubles"

If class, ethnic, and gender conflicts are fundamental elements of Malaysian history, how then are class, ethnicity, and gender to be studied ethnographically? The ethnographic investigation of such conflicts pose a formidable challenge to reigning Euro-American interpretive anthropology. The latter takes little account of the effects of the past on the present. Since prior struggles between groups have been not only over material resources, but also over authoritative discourse, then such struggles whose historical effects frame the present are particularly refractory to an ethnography of the present grounded in the study of meanings as coded in cultural texts, hermeneutic circles, and identity: in presences, not absences, and in a foundational concept of "identity"—a concept I challenge in the next chapter.

The critical point to be made is that due to the outcomes of prior struggles, only members of certain classes can announce a class existence and identity, while the members of other classes cannot. What if, as a result precisely of the history of the making of hegemony associated with the Cold War and postcolonial Malay domination, the *enunciation* of a public Chinese working-class position as such has proven largely impossible? What if the oppressive conditions under which working-class Chinese (men and women) live in Malaysia place them continually in double binds that victimize them by introducing chaos and unpredictability into their everyday lives (Sider 1986, 2003), not the order of patterned meanings that interpretive ethnography best captures? What if class is such a serious matter that only the members of certain classes can authoritatively announce their existence, solidarities, and interests—while those of other classes dare not do so, and are left to do, what? The processes that generate such differential publicness and enunciation among groups go far to explain why the Chinese working class in Malaysia is largely invisible not only in public life but also in scholarly and business literatures, although working-class men and women who identify themselves as Chinese are present in great numbers in contemporary Malaysia.

In this book, to confront this issue I follow recent theoretical developments in cultural anthropology and feminist theory that emphasize cultural styles and the performative dimensions of the semiotics of social inequalities and differences (Hebdige 1979; Butler 1990, 128–141, 1993; Bourdieu 1977, 1984, 1986; Ferguson 1999), but I also find it essential to go beyond these developments in several crucial respects.

What Are Cultural Styles?

Following Ferguson's (1999, 93–110) thoughtful discussion of cultural styles, I propose that cultural styles "signify differences between social categories" (95) and are performed by individuals before others, and often in the presence of a third group. Yet the conditions under which people are able to perform cultural styles require specification.

Second, I hold that cultural styles are semiotic practices that signify social differences along intersecting axes of inequality, for instance, gender, class, ethnicity, and sexuality. Thus "an upper-middle-class style of being masculine" is different from "a working-class style of masculinity" (Ferguson 1999, 95). In the pages that follow, I am most interested in setting out the cultural styles of working-class and petty-property-owning Chinese men—thus situations in which classed, gendered, and ethnic styles cross-cut one another.

Third, a cultural style requires displays of performative competencies, usually multiple: linguistic (e.g., mastering a prestigious language, argot, or lingua franca); embodied (in postures of servility or familiarity, wearing certain clothes, or consuming certain foods); or social (e.g., appropriate etiquette to signal friendship or disdain), or some combination (see Ferguson 1999, 82–93, 111–122). Such competencies or forms of cultural capital (Bourdieu 1977) take time, energy, and effort to acquire, and thus cultural styles are not easily mastered to the point of proficient performances, nor by the same token can one cultural style be easily abandoned and another taken up in performance (Ferguson 1999, 100). However, a crucial qualification is that such competencies must be recognized as such if they are to be the signs of a cultural style, and this does not always occur.

Fourth, however, contra Ferguson (1999) there are more to the cultural styles of actors than just competencies: their performance must be accompanied by actions that offer or deny, or promise to offer or deny, material resources to specific "others" with whom they interact. An otherwise competent performance of a style that does not offer or deny such resources to specific others may be either repudiated as the sign of a claimed social position ("Who is he kidding? He's all talk and no action") or at very least be unconvincing ("He could be a fake"). This follows from the conception of the histories of class (and other related forms of) struggle set out above: the offer or denial of a material resource to others is the hinge between the concomitant and intertwined struggles over material resources (e.g., the means of production) and over authoritative discourse.

Fifth, those performing the same cultural style may among them "have very diverse motives, values or views of the world" (Ferguson 1999, 97) and therefore do not "express" some underlying or essential identity (e.g., gender, class) of the person performing the style (96–97). Failure to note this, as Ferguson points out (96), may lead the observer to see naturalized or essentialized identities where none exist. This is particularly important in the case of classed performances. The fact that stylistic performances of class, gender, and ethnicity can be viewed as expressions of some inner underlying structurally determined state of mind or cultural whole (norms, values, etc.) has made it possible not only for petty capitalists to reify themselves as examplars of timeless Chinese values, but also for outside observers to see them in very similar terms, while ignoring the existence of the Chinese working class.

Last, and most crucial, cultural styles are often performed in response to "a situation of duress" (Ferguson 1999, 99, citing Butler 1990). But, against Ferguson, duress can consist of more than constrained choices about which cultural style to perform and can even extend to making it impossible to perform a specific cultural style at all—or, what amounts to the same thing within social semiotics, impossible for that performance to be recognized at all.

Classed, Gendered, and Ethnic Styles among Chinese Malaysians

In the chapters that follow, I employ these characteristics of cultural style in my ethnographic investigation of specific classed and gendered styles among Chinese Malaysians—to set out, in effect, a stylistics of the ethnic performance of citizenship among Chinese in Malaysia that is cross-cut by classed and gender dimensions. Class conflict, in particular, weighs heavily in this account because it has so often been neglected, and it was ethnographically discernible in the contrasted and antagonistic performance of specific classed styles among the people

I met and came to know in Bukit Mertajam who formed its majority—the owners of petty enterprise property and workers. But such performances were also
gendered, something I could not fail to note because the majority of my informants were men in the ethnographic situations in which I discovered the arts of
deception recounted in chapters 3–6, and because these arts prescribed a degree
of social and discursive separation of local women not only from men of different classes, but also from outside men (such as an American anthropologist) in
most settings connected to public life.[10] And such performances were always ethnic, in that in my presence my informants debated, argued against, and displayed
their suffering from and animosities against state practices and policies that they
saw as harming and discriminating against them as Chinese—and being present,
I was always an audience for such performances.

As I have described the characteristics of cultural style as an ethnographic
entry into the study of social conflict among Chinese in Malaysia, it should
become clear that current existing theoretical accounts of cultural style need to
be rethought because they fail to take into account the fact that asymmetrical
power relations along lines of class, gender, and ethnic difference affect not only
which cultural styles are performed, but indeed what styles can be performed,
and whether they can be performed at all. Yes, stylistic performances must display competencies if they are to be credible, but what if the very existence of such
competencies by those performing them is disputed by other people antagonistic
toward the members of this category? For instance, although men could show
improvisational virtuosity when performing male working-class styles characterized as "crude"—such as the sophisticated use of vernacular language imbued
with sarcasm and irony, the subtle deployment of embodied pedagogies of
"showing how" instead of "showing that" (chapter 6)—what did it mean that the
existence of these competencies were denied by Chinese merchants and Malay
state officials, who defined these men as "crude" solely as a deficiency marked by
wildness and criminality, as shown in chapters 2, 5 and 6? Indeed, antagonistic
social relationships (classed, gendered, ethnicized, sexualized, nationalized, etc.)
are often marked precisely by such denials of the agency, or even existence, of
members of the stigmatized category.

A related point is that competencies as part of a stylistic performance
must moreover be *enunciable*, which requires minimally that they must be
witnessable—visible and/or audible to others—or else they do not exist for
them. What if, therefore, the deployment of certain socially recognized competencies requires that they be performed in certain spaces, before certain audiences? For instance, when groups of working-class men were prevented from
gathering in certain central places in Bukit Mertajam associated with decision
making about Chinese society—specific restaurants, coffee shops, temples,

or school auditoriums whose centrality registered with the journalists of the regional Chinese-language media (see chapter 7). Thus unable to perform their classed and gendered stylized practices, did they have a presence—and if so, for whom?

What if speaking and writing a certain language—Mandarin—were so closely associated with authority and legitimacy that for someone not to be able to speak that specific language—irrespective of the content of what one said—meant that they had nothing worth saying, in fact had said nothing (see chapter 5)? Competencies are already reflexively ranked within fields of social inequalities prior to their becoming elements of the cultural styles studied by anthropologists, and ethnographers must take this into account by paying more attention to the histories of spatiality, language use, and embodied practices that stigmatize and obscure certain kinds of stylized performances, as much as they are elements within them. The tendency among liberal ethnographers accustomed to the privilege of acting as flexibly mobile, all-seeing observers to neglect the contexts that constrain such performances is something we need to be on guard against. Although the arts of deception among Bukit Mertajam residents were the source of much personal angst for me at the time, these arts, central to their "getting by," taught me after a long period of learned stupidity (i.e., blind reliance on positivist research methods) to never to take such mobile omniscience for granted.

Furthermore, if the performance of a cultural style generally requires not only competencies but also the power to offer or deny material resources to others, what if the provision of resources can compensate for the lack of certain competencies? For instance, many of the "older generation" of Bukit Mertajam "celebrities" —merchants who played a central role in the leadership of Chinese society through their financial generosity to associations, temples, and schools—could not speak or read Mandarin but nonetheless held leadership roles in these organizations. Were they looked down on because they were not fluent in this "language of Chinese," *huayu*, like some political party officials and laborers whose only "Chinese" language was Hokkien? No indeed: they experienced no embarrassment when they had proxies fluent in Mandarin compose and deliver speeches in their name that deployed the pedantic and moralizing oratory in Mandarin expected on public occasions—even while they were personally in the audience. The old man had donated twenty thousand ringgit for a new school auditorium as president of the association—who cared if he hired a proxy to deliver his speech? Even more to the point, competent performances, however accomplished stylistically but not backed up by resources, could be declared incompetent or simply ignored—as in the case of the truck drivers association's attempt to gain public sympathy vis-à-vis truck owners in the controversy described in chapter 5.

Turning to a final point, the ethnographic methods of class, gender, and ethnic formation like those for this historical study must always take into account that class struggles, ethnic conflicts, and "gender troubles" (Butler 1990) manifest stylized cultural performances by members of one group who sought not only to achieve material gains but also to attain authoritative representational status (standing or moral high ground) vis-à-vis opposed categories. For this reason, capable ethnography must always situate such performances within the broader class, gender, and ethnic structures that have over time generated asymmetrical powers, which in turn, *constrain* the very viability, legibility (Scott 1998), and authoritativeness of these performances of cultural styles. Thus it is only through a historical investigation of class, gender, and ethnic formation, with their attendant processes of struggle, that the very preconditions for an adequate critical ethnography of the present can be discovered, which have to do not only with what is publicly present to the ethnographer but also with what is sequestered away and even suppressed and made nonexistent. This is the analytical strategy that I refer to with irony as "strategic totalization" (Nonini 1999).

The Chapters that Follow

This book is a historical ethnography of Chinese citizenship and class in Bukit Mertajam as these have changed over a period of almost thirty years (1978–2007). The first chapter recounts the formative years in Bukit Mertajam during the Japanese occupation of Malaya, the return of the European colonials at war's end, and the British counterinsurgency campaign against the Malayan Communist Party. It was during those years that the public articulation of subaltern class interests in forms of collective activism under the sign of socialism—especially among the Chinese working class, but even among most leftist Malay intellectuals and farmers—was definitively quashed by the coercive and rhetorical powers of the counterinsurgency and pacification campaigns of the British and then of the new Malay rulers who succeeded them at independence. It became politically dangerous for Chinese to speak publicly of class interests or class struggle by the end of this period, much less organize around them, while public rhetoric was reorganized around the articulation of interests by ethno-racial groups who were differentially recognized by the postcolonial state.

Part I describes the economic and political contexts of class formation and class relations among Chinese in Bukit Mertajam. Chapter 2 describes the flourishing commercial and industrial activity around which the city's economy was organized, the relationships between the two major ethnic groups living in the area—Chinese and Malays—with particular reference to the role of the Malaysian state in mediating these relationships, and the economic stratification and inequalities among the Chinese residents of the city and the surrounding district of Seberang Prai Tengah (previously Central Province Wellesley).

Chapter 3 sets out the cultural styles as these varied among those who claimed to "do business," and those relatively select few who were recognized as *towkay*—Hokkien for "head of (family) business"—or as "men of position," and the even fewer referred to as "celebrities" among the Chinese population living in the city—the local mercantile elite. I recount the process through which my own naively positivist attempts to determine the distribution of wealth within that elite led to repeated failures—which I only much later came to recognize were the consequence of my ignoring the arts of deception and the performance of the classed and gendered styles of Chinese men who owned substantial business property. One element of these arts of deception was the collective imaginary regarding "those who travelled the dark road" of narcotics refining and trafficking in the city.

Chapter 4 describes the intimate and quotidian relationships that men in business said they had with state functionaries. I believe that "corruption," as the common cover term for these relationships, considerably occludes both the class differences among these men and the formative effects that state formation had on their classed and gendered styles. These differences and effects led to a codification of tactics that allowed these men's businesses to appear small and dispersed, while they showed male authority over the family and its business. I conclude with a description of the quite different forms of state surveillance and policing that marked official interactions with squatters, largely working-class residents of specific "village" (*kampung* (M)) neighborhoods targeted within the city for state repression and discriminatory neglect.

Chapters 5 and 6 continue the analysis of classed and gendered styles but turn to the peculiarly ambiguous condition of collectivities of working-class men and to the marginalized and largely invisible performances of their classed and gendered styles. Chapter 5 points to the profound scholarly neglect of working-class Chinese among scholars, business pundits, and local elite Chinese alike and argues that the neglect arose from the inability of working-class men to *enunciate* their class or ethnic identities in public—in contrast to towkays and men of position. Instead working men, unable in most conditions to gain control over the authoritative means of representation, showed a fugitive cultural style enacted in marginal places. These cultural styles centered on presenting themselves ironically as "being crude." I discuss what happened in 1979 when, exceptionally, a specific group of working men—truck drivers—were able to "go public" by forming a "working men's society" and describe the emergent qualities of working-class cooperation that were manifested when this society came into public conflict with the occupational association of truck transport towkays over the contentious issue of truck overloads. This issue implicated the state and its functionaries as well.

Chapter 6 analyzes the conflict between truck owners and the truck drivers they hired in Bukit Mertajam not only over material wealth but also over authoritative representations of the conflict, and of who won and who lost within it. The reconstruction of this conflict brings forth specific and contrasted features of the stylistic performances of truck drivers and truck owners. Truck drivers displayed a classed style that affirmed the practices that truck owners accused as being "crude," including an embodied pedagogy of learning through labor. But the chapter also points to the collusions that working-class and propertied men engaged in that separated them socially from women and declared them superior to them, thus bringing out the gendered styles of both working-class and propertied men.

Chapter 7 returns to the mercantile elite of Bukit Mertajam and reconstructs a dispute among the leaders of the city's Chinese society from 1979 to 1980. The chapter challenges the contention that the city's mercantile elite formed a semisovereign, "self-governing" ethnic enclave when in the course of the dispute its leaders invoked the China-nationalist rhetoric of Sun Yat-sen to rationalize the weakness of the city's Chinese population in confronting pressures from a state bent on enforcing "Malay domination" through its increased assertions of control over local features of Chinese-based economic and cultural life. I show the imaginary of a self-governing segmentary hierarchical Chinese society, to the contrary, to be the conceit of an economic elite deeply implicated in compromise with and co-optation by state officials and policies in ways consistent with its class character. The dispute and the rhetoric that defined it represented a form of class discipline directed at other, less economically privileged elements of the local Chinese population.

Part II turns to the years associated with the globalization of the Malaysian economy, the full implementation of the government's New Economic Policy and New Development Policy, and the effects of these processes of state formation on class formation among residents of Bukit Mertajam. Chapter 8 follows the process of class formation reconstructed in part I in terms of the experiences of three different classes among Chinese in Bukit Mertajam, as these were affected by state formation in a period of globalization: the class of capitalists (the mercantile elite or celebrities), the working class, and the class of petty capital owners and professionals. I examine this process by considering the ways in which members of the different classes used, redefined, and struggled over urban spaces during these years. In this city located in one of the growth poles for Malaysia's export-oriented industrialization, people of all three classes were affected by growing employment, increased capitalist profits, and a prosperity that came to be defined by an increased standard of living and consumerism. However, during the same years, large numbers of working-class people living in kampung areas within the city were displaced and dispossessed by state-sponsored projects of megadevelopment that transformed the urban landscape. Finally, the chapter reconstructs the increased irrelevance of Chinese society to the cultural reproduction of Chinese residents of Bukit Mertajam.

Chapter 9 describes how Chinese men (and to a lesser extent women) reacted to the new forms of state enclosure and control described in chapter 8. Bukit Mertajam men circulated narratives of transnational journeys as a rehearsal for possible exit themselves, even as they found themselves employing and living cheek-by-jowl with Indonesian labor migrants as one aspect of this period of globalization. Nonetheless, distinctive classed styles came to the fore: whereas men owning productive property strategized over the possibilities of sending their grown children overseas for university degrees and certification, working men envisioned finding well-paying work overseas to escape discriminatory employers. Also working men and women participated in religious processions for Daoist/Buddhist gods that invoked cosmically enjoined sovereignties over the neighborhoods they lived in that challenged those of the state, and Chinese men and women, whether working-class or better off, showed their massed political potential versus the state in their occupation of local coffee shops.

Chapter 10 describes the very different stylized class strategies of transnational travel of men of property and working-class men in Bukit Mertajam. For the former, by far the most hated, adverse, and longstanding effects of Malay domination lay in the ethnically discriminatory quotas that kept many young Chinese adults from entering the government-operated national universities. I point to the petty accumulation trap that faced such older men—such quotas potentially prevented them from successfully maintaining their grown children in the class position that they themselves enjoyed. I describe how they spoke of the transnational traversals in which they sought to transfer their grown children overseas for university training as one antagonistic response to these quotas. The gendered—indeed patriarchal—aspects of such classed strategies were evident in their only occasionally successful attempts to control the careers of their grown children. In contrast, working men had far fewer options and engaged in transnational reversals during which they migrated to Japan, but sought not permanent exit but the accumulation of petty fortunes that might allow them upward mobility on return to Malaysia. Unable by dint of class to leave Malaysia permanently, these men relied on the women of their families to maintain the households left behind in Bukit Mertajam.

The epilogue sketches out changes over the decade from 1997 to 2006 among the residents of Bukit Mertajam that I was able to reconstruct during fieldwork in the summer of 2007 and looks forward to the present.

COUNTERINSURGENCY, SILENCES, FORGETTING, 1946–69

"Doctor, why do we carry ICs [Identity Cards]?"

One afternoon in June 1991, I was taken aback when Tang Ah-Meng, a truck driver, an informant for many years, and by then a good friend, asked me this apparently casual question as we sat drinking tea near the main road leading east out of Bukit Mertajam, Penang state, Malaysia. The question provoked in me the tensions I had long felt between peoples' experiences, practices, and discourse studied in my ethnography, and the events recorded by historians who documented the violence of class and state formation in Malaysia. I was taken aback not so much by the factual issue Tang's question posed, but by my anxieties about what he meant by asking it and by the discomfort it provoked in me.

Perhaps, on one hand, I was surprised by his question about identity cards because I had all too casually come to think of them after several years of off-and-on fieldwork as second-nature attributes of every person I met, although I knew that the government required each resident of Malaysia to carry them, to show their photograph and name, ethnicity, date of birth, and civil status, to police, state officials, and others in authority. Perhaps, on the other hand, it was my knowledge from reading Malaysian colonial history that ICs had first been instituted during the counterinsurgency period of the Emergency from 1948 to 1960 as a measure in large part for controlling the "subversive" Chinese population,[1] combined with the fact that my questions to many people in Bukit Mertajam about what had happened to them, their parents, or family during these years had been greeted with silence or polite refusal, and clearly judged as indelicate, that led me to falter. Was Tang testing me, several years on in our relationship, about my political standpoint or sensitivity to the hard lives of Chinese working people, or was his question an earnest one based on ignorance of the broader events of the Emergency? I did not, and still do not, know.

In any event, after a few moments' pause, I replied, "How old were you when you received one?" He replied "I was thirteen years old." I then responded with a leading question: "You are now fifty-one years old, and you were thirteen years old when you received one. That was thirty-eight years ago, or about 1953. What was going on then? There were the Malayan Communists." Tang commented that, yes, by receiving I.C. cards, other Chinese were distinguished from the guerrillas. In retrospect I find an American academic seeking to teach an older Chinese Malaysian citizen the meaning of his own identity card to have been a profoundly patronizing act but still cannot help but see Tang's question as indexing, in its ambiguity, a suppressed history created by violence, silencing/silences, and collective forgetting over two generations of working-class Chinese life in Malaysia.

Class, class relations, and class struggle among Chinese Malaysians cannot be made sense of solely by means of the concept "identity" so greatly favored by the dominant interpretivist strain within a cultural anthropology based on an ethnography of experience and its distillation or articulation in discourse. Instead, in the place of identity based on a coherent self, a deeper understanding of class societies requires that we turn to an ethnography of position and structure where identity-elements may or may not cohere; where an identity is not a given but instead a contingent achieved position within structures of inequality; and where fragmentation, disorder, and chaos characterize the lives of people who lack power, while it is only those whose positions allow them to possess various kinds of power who can form coherent, stable, and ordered identities. If an identity is such that it can be performed only by those to whom it is ascribed, then an identity is an attribute of those with class, gender, ethno-racial, or other forms of privilege; those who are less powerful often find themselves without an affirmative identity they can perform and are instead left only with identifications—like those which Malaysians were required to display on their identity cards.

Within class societies such as Malaysia, those belonging to dominant classes and to the state organizations they influence, impose identifications of others as essentially inferior, as less worthy of life and security, and as less moral, within the cultural politics of inequality. Such impositions are sedimented in artefacts like identity cards. Moreover, I argue, the construction of identifications of those who are deemed essentially inferior, and thus without identity, is always a process that begins with and is maintained by violence that generates chaos, contradiction, and disorder among the "inferior" members of a population—and because such violence is difficult, and often impossible, to capture pari passu through ethnography, it requires an historical analysis. Violence in turn silences those members of a subordinate group it is inflicted on; silence prolonged over time brings about collective forgetting among members of that group.

It is this history of violence that has generated the silences about the history of class and of other forms of inequality in Malaysia and the forgetting among Chinese Malaysians—exemplified by the question of Mr. Tang—whom I have known in the course of ethnography extended over more than twenty years—that I begin to set out here. It is a history of state violence against Chinese living in Malaysia that has made it impossible to publicly articulate an identity that speaks of class, class relations, and class struggle—even as the existence of all these can be read in everyday life.

The British Return to Order: Repossessing Malaya, Disciplining Wayward "Asians"

The Malayan Emergency was fought in large part to make Southeast Asia safe for British business.

—T. N. Harper, *The End of Empire and the Making of Malaya*

Returning to Malaya after the Japanese surrender in August 1945, British military and colonial officials sought to quell the disorder in the aftermath of surrender and immediately came under pressure from European planters, miners, and industrialists to reestablish the conditions of the profitable and orderly days of the 1920s and early 1930s, which had been interrupted by the years of the Great Depression, Japanese occupation, and war that followed.[2] In 1946–48, the postwar reoccupation of Malaya by British rulers and their efforts to return European-owned rubber plantations, tin mines, and agency houses to profitability, however, not only faced the postwar demands for independence, but also were confronted squarely by Malayan workers' determination through hard bargaining, work stoppages, and strikes to gain some share of the new wealth of postwar recovery after two decades of extreme physical privation and suffering. During this period, and the years of counterinsurgency known as the "Emergency" that followed (1948–60), successive colonial administrations were concerned to establish the order and stability required to overcome the demands of a mobilized immigrant working class of Chinese and Indian laborers and the restiveness of Malay farmers, to destroy the Malayan Communist Party (MCP) and other threats—political and otherwise—to their rule, and return the colony to the superficially placid conditions of enhanced labor exploitation of the status quo ante bellum, but within the new framework of eventual decolonization and "self-governance."

As Harper (1999, 200) states above, the broader impetus behind the colonial government's attempt to subdue "Asian labor," which led to the declaration of the Emergency, was to "make Southeast Asia safe for British business." This charter was of course long-standing. Should it still be necessary after so many decades of critical work by historians of British colonial rule to simply point out that one major raison d'être of British imperialism in Malaya as elsewhere in the empire was enhanced capital accumulation by British and other European colonial corporations and firms on behalf of their owning and managing elites? The influence of British planter, mining, and commercial capitalists on postwar colonial policies were wielded not only through "public opinion" in Malaya itself but also through extensive interconnections with the British government and parliamentary power in the home country.

In the case of the British elite, the period of the first few years immediately after the Japanese occupation in Malaya displayed its own specific variations on this theme, both ideological and political-economic. There were ideological differences among the elite: "liberals" in the Colonial Office and Foreign Office in Britain supported the co-optation of Malayan labor unions by fostering "healthy" and "independent" labor unions; "reactionaries"—planters, agency houses, and other employers, as well as most officers in the Malayan Civil Service—favored outright repression of labor unions (Morgan 1977, 171). The situation was one in which "once the jubilation over liberation was over, some of the official and employing classes began to think of restoring prewar ways, an idea entirely out of tune with conditions in post-war Malaya" (Gamba 1962, 20). Despite these tensions, both sides came to agreement by interpreting the labor militancy from 1946–48 to be due to the actions of outside agitators with "political" goals—for which a response by the government was imperative, to ferret out Communist agitators and reduce their influence in the labor movement.

In terms of the colonial political economy of the late 1940s, there was the geopolitical imperative for the colonial government to press for aggressive and rapid profit accumulation from rubber and tin extraction by British colonial capitalists in Malaya. These profits were to provide *the major* source of value added for the waning British Empire and its sterling area to the sterling/dollar balance of payments that serviced Britain's war debts to the United States (Caldwell 1977, 242–49; Morgan 1977, 156; Sandhu 1964b; Stockwell 1984, 78).[3] Gamba (1962, 193) summarizes what was at stake for the colonial administration in supporting employers in keeping down the wages of workers and maintaining the conditions of labor exploitation:

> It was certainly true that a complete re-examination of the wage rates now being paid in Malaya would have to take place, rather than grudgingly

granting piecemeal concessions. This, however, seemed impossible because of the unwillingness of Government to impose itself upon the large and more powerful group of Colonial employers and because Government itself, and the War Department Services, were employers of labor ... it was also true that Malaya would not have been worthwhile retaining as a raw material producing area if a higher price for labor brought profits down to a more normal rate.[4]

The political militancy and economic vitality of the Chinese working population posed a serious threat to this late imperial project, not least because in their labor unions, Chinese immigrants formed cross-ethnic alliances with Indian ones. Yet for Chinese, there was a distinctive ecology to labor insurrection: as Harper (1999, 94–148) has made clear, Chinese workers' militancy in urban areas and industrial sites was linked to their capacity to fall back on rural cash-crop cultivation on plots they and their family members occupied when they were unemployed or on strike, and these connections between urban "unrest" and "subversion" and a rural subsistence base became increasingly clear to colonial administrators and European employers alike by the late 1940s and early 1950s.

But there were other forms of provocation by Chinese residing in rural areas. Chinese squatters who had fled the Japanese in the cities and towns for the interior during the occupation years and had cleared forest and cultivated cash crops now occupied valuable Forest Reserve lands, whose tree stands otherwise might be licensed for logging for export markets. Moreover, Chinese squatters' clearings often impinged on Malay Reserves, thus distressing nearby rural Malays and their leaders, who feared "takeover" by an "alien race." Furthermore, as one might expect given the conditions of wartime occupation, squatters living in rural areas "upriver," *ulu*, from cities and towns had devised mechanisms of self-governance—or had had such mechanisms thrust on them in the form of informal, often predatory rule by Chinese secret societies, criminal gangs, and ex-guerrillas from the wartime resistance against the Japanese. Squatters and rural small businessmen made payments and bribes—from one point of view, informal taxes that ensured local order and stability in commerce—to various groups affiliated with the MCP, such as ex-fighters of the Malayan Peoples Anti-Japanese Army (MPAJA), or to armed gangs organized by the Kuo Min Tang (KMT), or by the Ang Bin Hui, and other "Triad" secret society groups (Harper 1999, 94–148). Colonial authorities saw such rule as an intolerable chaos and as a challenge to the legitimacy of reasserted British rule, requiring a restoration of "law and order." The dispossession of rural Chinese from the lands they occupied—some of which they had purchased legally (as the quote from Xu Wurong below implies) and some of which they had squatted on since the start of the Japanese occupation—thus appeared to serve several ends: to destroy the rural subsistence base of intransigent Chinese workers and their labor unions, recover Crown forest lands, assuage the anxieties of the Malay elite, and restore colonial state control over daily life in rural areas. Finally, as conditions of labor militancy and signs of disorder increased, the declaration of the "Emergency" in 1948, and the warlike suspension of civil law it allowed—the banning of political parties and labor unions; the detentions, imprisonment, and banishing of Chinese and Indian immigrants; banning of publications; among other measures—also allowed British colonial administrators, who largely sympathized with the Malay elite, to suppress leftist nationalist Malay organizations and leaders. These leftist leaders were against UMNO elite accommodation to British rule, sought immediate independence, and a socialist economic system where redistribution would center on class and override ethno-racial schisms (Funston 1980; Nonini 1992, 112–19).

The allover regressive and revanchist thrust of postwar British policy influenced by liberal ideology grounded in an imperialist project of accelerated capitalist accumulation, and based on superordinate European private property rights, was clear.

Restoring Imperial Profits and Ordering Ethnic Spaces

> [There is] the whole vast racket of black-marketeering, smuggling and commercial corruption that go to make up Chinese business methods. In the countries around us where Communist or nationalist banditry is rampant the Chinese flourish. They finance it, because in the short term it pays and the short-term profits appeal to Chinese philosophy.
>
> —Henry Gurney, high commissioner to Malaya, 1949

The insurgency declared by the MCP in 1948 was followed by the banning of the party and the arrests of its leaders and activists who had played a role in the leadership of the General Labor Unions (GLUs) during the interregnum between Japanese surrender in 1945 and the reassertion of British rule throughout the peninsula from 1946–48. The postwar GLUs and their federations, the Singapore and Pan-Malayan Federations of General Labor Unions (SFGLU and PMFCLU) grew rapidly in strength and members as Chinese and Indian workers, particularly those laboring in its rubber, tin mining, and industrial sectors, undertook widespread resistance to the return of the British and to their reassertion of

prewar private property rights and of the prerogatives of prewar colonial domin-
ion. Moreover, a sense of a common, shared fate created by class exploitation had
emerged between Chinese and Indian immigrant workers:

> The workers of both Chinese and Indian communities were united
> by a sense of common suffering which encouraged the development
> of worker solidarity and, perhaps, in urban areas, a genuine feeling of
> class-consciousness. . . . As a whole, laborers appear to have been un-
> usually aware of their common interests, and their nationalism [toward
> Malaya] therefore expressed itself, for the time, not in separatist move-
> ments led by the wealthy, English-educated leaders of each community,
> but in a unified class-based movement, led by the vernacular-educated,
> and emphasizing the common interests of workers of all races. (Stenson
> 1970, 110)

Class animus and discontent were compounded by anticolonial feelings,
for not only had the harsh labor discipline by British planters and miners led
to hardship and distress among workers during the depression of the 1930s,
but in early 1942 British military officers, colonial officials, planters, and
other civilians had also ignominiously fled Malaya during the weeks of Japanese invasion of the Malayan Peninsula and Singapore. The flight of British
troops and their Australian allies abandoned Malayan Chinese, in particular,
to suffer the agonies of occupation inflicted by the Japanese Imperial Army
and the Kempetai secret police, which viewed Nanyang Chinese as active supporters of the resistance campaign against the Japanese occupation of China
and massacred thousands of Chinese within weeks of the rapid conquest of
Malaya and Singapore. While the British and Australian forces may have had
no other choice than to flee and suffered gravely after surrender at the hands
of the Japanese, the days of their flight toward the south, witnessed firsthand,
were ones that older informants still recounted to me with a tone of disdain
almost forty years later, before going on to describe the cruelty of Japanese
rule during the subsequent occupation. My informants knew also that the
only major armed resistance to the Japanese during the occupation years had
been the MPAJA, a guerrilla force composed almost exclusively of Chinese
organized by the MCP (see Short 1975; Cheah 1979). Given these conditions,
the reassertion of European race/class privilege on the return of the British
to Malaya—for instance, reinstitution by the British of the old racial epithets
for Asians like "boy" and similar insults to dignity and discrimination against
Asian workers by the government in granting its employees restitution for
wartime losses—were particularly bitter blows to those who had endured the
hardships of the occupation.

In 1946 and 1947, as British industrialists, planters, mine owners, and colonial administrators sought to reestablish the brutal conditions of labor exploitation from the 1930s status quo ante bellum, thousands of Malayan workers, fed up with years of deprivation under the Japanese occupiers and now facing a rising cost of living, resisted through scores of strikes and work stoppages the harsh conditions of work and falling real wages imposed on them. The General Labor Unions provided the leadership for these strikes; their most influential leaders were members of the MCP, and the British correctly regarded the state GLUs as MCP "front organizations" (Stenson 1970). Despite the accusation by employers that they were outside agitators, the GLU leaders and the MCP cadres among them sought to ride as much as foment the tide of spontaneous worker discontent based on very serious grievances about wages and working conditions, transformed into militancy against British employers committed to restoring the conditions of prewar exploitation (Stenson 1970, 66, 99; Cheah 1979, 147–148; Harper 1999).

The postwar militancy of Chinese (and Indian) migrant laborers appears not to directly be an economic response to hardship, much less a spontaneous emotionalism or docile compliance with the demands of MCP agitators, but instead can be explained in terms of a moral economy centered on social reproduction. I suggest that their strikes and other actions manifested their outrage against the violation by European and Asian employers of an agreement first proposed in the 1930s by European employers between employers and immigrant workers: that in times of hardship, burdens and benefits had to be shared between the two sides, but in return there would be expanded shares (of wages and profits) once the colony recovered and economic growth resumed—for both. This is consistent with the pattern of labor relations set during the years of the Great Depression, where violation of such an agreement by employers during the late 1930s led to a surge in strikes and other labor actions by workers (Nonini 1993). Revived a decade later in postwar Malaya, this was a moral economy based on a collective anger by immigrant workers induced by the hard memory that while workers-cum-squatters had experienced disproportionately the burdens of war and the Japanese occupation, European and Asian employers had abandoned their workers during the occupation years and had returned only in the years 1945–48 to reassert their private property rights and to try to reimpose a harsh labor discipline (Nonini 1993, 238). Under these conditions in April 1947, the Malayan labor movement "was at the peak of its strength" with a membership of almost 264,000—more than 50 percent of the total labor force (Morgan 1977, 170).

During the years 1948–51, the MCP went underground and sent its armed units into the upland jungles of the northern, eastern, and southern states of Malaya. As the guerrillas began attacks on British plantations and other industrial sites, the British devised a comprehensive counterinsurgency strategy that, much later, became the model for the U.S. "strategic hamlet" program and several subsequent other American and British counterinsurgency efforts. The British referred to their counterinsurgency campaign against the MCP guerrillas as "the Emergency," and it lasted officially from 1948 to 1960.[5]

The British counterinsurgency campaign of the Emergency was successful in attaining its two strategic goals, repressing the Malayan organized labor movement and contributing to a positive balance of trade for the sterling zone vis-à-vis the U.S. dollar. Regarding the first goal, as a result of the government's attack on the labor unions, between December 1947 and December 1949, union membership declined by 78 percent (Morgan 1977, 190–191).[6] As to the second and its broader political-economic consequences, Gamba (1962, 236–237) noted that since the banning of the MCP and the repression of the GLUs in 1948 to

> the [Korean War] boom of 1950–1951, conditions of work and wages had still not improved, yet Government, during the same period allowed the wholesale exodus of private capital assessed to approximately M$920,000,000. If economic development—it was said—had in actual fact been the desire of the authorities, who were well acquainted with the conditions of the people and the needs of the country, they should not have permitted the whole of this wealth to leave Malaya. Thus labor asked, were the employers unable or unwilling to support a higher wages bill? MCP influence was an important reason explaining the industrial unrest prevalent in Malaya during these years, but economic and social reasons were equally important. This view became still more convincing in later years, when, after profits and dividends had been shown to be high, and Malaya was thanked for the part [it] played in helping to solve Britain's economic difficulties, officially accepted reports and statements by local experts described the abject poverty and low standards of the laboring class and of other large groups within the urban and rural population of Malaya.

The Dangers of Talk about Class and Class Domination

"What do you understand by socialism which represents the political creed of your party?"

"We want to destroy this Government and this system. We want to demolish imperialism, colonialism and capitalism and set up in a

society where the State would control the entire economic life of the society. We would have a real government of the people. The workers would secure the full fruits of their labor. The capitalists would not be able to take over the surplus value."

—Dialogue between the scholar R. K. Vasil and forty Chinese members of the Malayan Labour Party, during his visit to a New Village in Selangor, January 1964.

During the decade from the late 1940s through late 1950s, British colonial administrators prepared conservative privileged Malays—members of royalty, colonial service officers, journalists and school teachers, and large landowners—as their successors after independence, and these latter, interconnected by marriage and clientage, became the governing elite as leaders of the dominant party, the United Malays National Organization (UMNO). This elite formed a coalition, known as "the Alliance," with the anticommunist Chinese bourgeoisie, represented by the Malayan Chinese Association (MCA), and together with it formed an emergent postcolonial ruling class (Milne and Mauzy 1977, 29–43; Lim 1985; Nonini 1992, 103–126, 143–145). Within the partnership of the Alliance, UMNO leaders were not only politically dominant but were also adamant that "Malay supremacy" be fought for and attained by conveying preferential rights on Malays with respect to citizenship eligibility, land ownership, and language used in education, while the MCA and Chinese business elites received in return the right to make major decisions over the commercial economy, supplanting the retreating British in this respect.

Among its other diverse effects, the Emergency and its political aftermath in the five years after independence in 1957 made it increasingly difficult for Malaysians to publicly write, speak, or otherwise act in terms of "class" and "class struggle." Not only were cross-ethnic labor unions deregistered and their workers repressed (thus setting a pattern of ethnic segregation in labor organizing that has persisted to the present), but proletarian class ideologies in support of restive postwar labor unions enunciated by Chinese laborers, displaced squatters, and deprived Indian estate workers were also put under public proscription, as the MCP and the GLUs came under state repression in the late 1940s and early 1950s. The dispossession of rural Chinese by the British rulers through the forced urbanization of more than 500,000 Chinese and their resettlement into fortified "New Villages" identified them to conservative Malay leaders and poor rural Malays alike as suspect "subversives" who were enemies of, and aliens in, Malaya (Nonini 1992, 102–119).

What had not been accomplished by overt military counterinsurgency measures such as the New Villages in the 1950s was achieved by state persecution of the leaders and followers of the Malayan Labour Party, the Party Raayat, and other leftist, multi-ethnic parties (Vasil 1971; Tan 2001). The case of the Malayan Labour Party (MLP), especially popular in Penang state in the 1950s and early 1960s, is instructive. Mainstream trade union leaders in the Malayan Trade Unions Council and a few progressive British colonial officials supported the establishment of state Labour parties in Penang and Selangor in 1951. The Pan-Malayan Labour Party, renamed the Malayan Labour Party, was formally established in 1953. Its English-educated leaders conceived of it as a multi-ethnic Fabian socialist party with members from all three major groups, although the majority from the start were Chinese (Vasil 1971, 93–108). It was a party that the British saw as a foil to counter the radical appeal of the MCP, one that could be co-opted by government authorities and guided to act "responsibly" in the years running up to independence. The MLP with the Party Raayat, a Malay-led party committed to independence and socialism, combined to form the Socialist Front (SF) in 1957.

By the late 1950s, however, large numbers of Chinese-educated members of the working class residing in the New Villages and towns had been attracted to joining the MLP in the wake of their disappointment with the compromises made by the MCA within the Alliance, and by the early 1960s they had succeeded in displacing the prior English-educated leaders from power. As their influence within the MLP grew, so too did their electoral victories as a party within the Socialist Front. In the 1961 local council elections across the Federation, the SF, primarily the MLP, gained more than one-fourth of the total vote. Vasil's exchange with Labour Party members at one of its New Village strongholds suggests that many, and perhaps most, held trenchantly anticapitalist, socialist, and anti-imperialist views, and saw the postindependence Malaysian state as the creation of British capitalist interests. Moreover, many MLP state branches had the temerity to support the militancy of those trade unions that had not been deregistered during the Emergency years. Vasil, whose contempt for the Chinese-educated, working-class members of the MLP was barely concealed,[7] referred to them as "Chinese chauvinists"—many of whom, he conceded, still restrained "for tactical reasons" their chauvinism while publicly supporting the idea that rural Malays were worthy of solidarity and respect—indeed were members (albeit in very small numbers) of the Malay-led Party Raayat within the Socialist Front.

It is evident, however, that the electoral successes of the MLP and the Socialist Front, driven in large part by class-based appeals to solidarity with the trade unions and the needs of labor to a fairer share of the national wealth, threatened the conservative elites of UMNO and the MCA in the Alliance. Beginning in the late 1950s and continuing through the early-1960s, scores of MLP leaders, members, and sympathetic trade unionists were harassed, arrested, detained indefinitely under the Internal Security Act, or tortured; during these arrests MLP offices were raided (Munro-Kua 1996, 46–47). Although most of those arrested under the Internal Security Act were released within a month or less, "what the detentions did achieve was a steady erosion of the politically active and dynamic leadership of the Socialist Front," and short detentions "served as a threat and intimidation to the population at large," while the fact that mass arrests of the MLP and similar opposition groups occurred "almost annually in the Sixties served to emphasize the way in which certain individuals were harassed so as to maximize the 'ripple' effects on the community" (47–48).

This repression was in itself still insufficient, and the Alliance government considered that the threat of widespread electoral victories by the MLP and the SF over Alliance candidates for local councils to be so serious that in late 1964 the government suspended all local council elections indefinitely (Vasil 1971, 143). This antidemocratic feature of Malaysian politics has persisted to the present. Such a strategy of state repression of the opposition and the state's procedural-legal management of democracy continued and if anything intensi- fied during the 1970s in the wake of the May 13, 1969, ethnic violence in Kuala Lumpur. It was no surprise that by the time my fieldwork began in 1978, it was no longer safe to speak publicly of class exploitation, class struggle, or even "the working class."

Once talk and political action along the lines of class, class exploitation, and class struggle had been suppressed, political party differences aligned as closely as possible with ethno-racial identifications, allegiances, and symbols. A hege- monic discourse of essential difference and social division between Chinese, Malay, and Indian "races" emerged and was institutionalized through the powers of the late colonial and immediate postcolonial states. Such an accommodation was indeed peculiar, in that while the elites of the two largest ethnic groups, Malays and Chinese, might disagree about which group was superior to the other, and for what reasons in accordance with their respective racialist ideolo- gies, there was an emergent consensus between them that *ethno-racial* essential differences were the lines along which a postcolonial state and polity should be structured.[8] This was the "hegemony" formed by a victorious "historic bloc" (Gramsci 1971) consisting of Malay political elites and intellectuals and Chinese commercial tycoons.

This account emphatically does *not* deny the existence of ethnic tensions between Chinese and Malays during the 1930s or of deep ethnic antagonisms exacerbated by the Japanese occupation and the settling of old scores along eth- nic lines immediately after the Japanese surrender in the interregnum of 1945–46 (Cheah 2003, 170–240). Nor was the social schism between the immigrant work- ing classes and indigenous poor farmers bridged, except under exceptional cir- cumstances, such as those of the Socialist Front during the 1940s and 1950s. Cross-ethnic solidarities evident during the late 1940s between Chinese and

Indian workers in the labor movement were not generalized to include oppressed rural Malays as part of a broader independence movement, with the exception of the followers of the Malay Nationalist Party (Nonini 1992, 109–119). Nor later, after independence, did most Chinese workers and their leaders try to form a pan-ethnic coalition of parties and organizations representing exploited classes across the urban-rural divide—again with the exception of the MLP and Party Raayat in the Socialist Front. However, these exceptions matter and cannot be easily dismissed.

This account *does* assert that state violence during the counterinsurgency and immediate postcolonial years leading to the extirpation, sequestration, or domestication of class-based discourses and institutions—the MCP, the MLP, the Party Raayat, labor unions, and smaller leftist multi-ethnic parties, leftist newspapers, and their journalists—made alternatives to the new hegemony impossible. Indeed, because publicly unspeakable, these alternatives became increasingly unthinkable as well. The suppression through state violence of cross-ethnic, class-based solidarities, combined with the installation of postcolonial arrangements of governing power divided along the lines of ethno-racial political parties, placed the iron hand of state order, media propaganda, prosecution, and legislation on what had been a situation of considerable flux and possibility from the late 1940s through the 1970s, and decreed the new reality of social division along ethno-racial lines and the foreswearing of alternatives to thinking and acting beyond race difference to those of class and class conflict. Public talk about "the working class," "class struggle," or "revolution" could lead one to being detained without trial, tried and imprisoned, banished to China, or during the years of the Emergency—if perceived by the state military or police to be an active member or supporter of the MCP—shot on sight or hung.

Still, as Foucault (1978) reminds us, "productive" discourses—not practices of violence per se—are what allows power to be successfully constructed around cultural difference, but only when, as Foucault neglected to notice, other equally "productive" discourses are sequestered and silenced by violence. Thus the discourse of race and ethno-racial differences articulated by the new state elite of politically dominant Malays and wealthy Chinese, and promoted by the mass media, government-run schools, and other "ideological state apparatuses" (Althusser 1984) they controlled, circulated and firmed up claims of naturalized differences and inequalities between Malays, Chinese, Indians, and the unmarked "other"—the civilized Europeans. Thus ethno-racial elites and their intellectuals (e.g., journalists) put forward contrasting claims, for example, on one hand, that Malays were essentially Muslim, poor, rural, honest yeomen, taken advantage of by unscrupulous alien sojourners from China and India; and on the other hand, that Chinese were essentially able businessmen, practical, industrious city-dwellers crucial to economic development while rural Malays were backward and uneducated. The open-ended political maneuverings between the elites of the two ethno-racial groups over the policies of the postcolonial state through the 1970s dictated which set of claims publicly prevailed—the one based on Malay supremacy, UMNO dominance, and state power—while the other set of claims—the Chinese counterpart—remained the shadow antagonist of the new publicly dominant discourse. Ethno-racial political divisions and the distinctions these represented between groups thus became public candidates for the truths—or myths—that framed the political controversies of the following years.[9]

To look ahead, by the 1970s, Malay political dominance led to the replication of prior British colonial orientalist discourses regarding essential "racial" characteristics of Chinese. For example, Gurney's stereotype of wealthy Chinese prospering from criminality, subversion, and disorder, given in the quote above, became recycled after independence in repeated official claims of an essential Chinese racial difference—and versions of it were evident in both the official pronouncements of UMNO leaders and informal comments made by government officials as I read or heard them during my fieldwork in the late 1970s (see, e.g., chapter 2).

Spatial Practices of Counterinsurgency: Carceral Urbanism up Close in Seberang Prai (Province Wellesley)

How did so many Chinese in northern Malaya become "urban" during the colonial period? From the late nineteenth century to the 1930s, many settled in a few larger towns such as Bukit Mertajam in Province Wellesley and Alor Setar in Kedah, and in scattered small towns that were often no more than ribbon settlements of shop houses located along the main roads. They moved from the entrepôt city of Georgetown (i.e., Penang) across the straits and inland to start small businesses and to live and work as farmers, petty traders, laborers, and rubber tappers in the towns that provided retail and other services to the rural population of the region. During the years of the Japanese occupation of Malaya (1942–45), many fled Japanese persecution in cities and towns for interior jungle areas of the northern states of Kedah, Penang, and northern Perak, where they took up subsistence farming and later rubber tapping, and where many still remained in the late 1940s.

In 1951, the travel writer Xu Wurong (Xu 1951, 54–58) wrote of the town of Bukit Mertajam, the largest in the district of Central Province Wellesley, and of its

Chinese residents—most of whom were Teochews originating from Chaozhou prefecture, eastern Guangdong province, that

> [after the 1880s], fellow countrymen from Puning district moved here
> in droves. . . . Our countrymen struggled early on to buy land and build
> houses. Since then, it has become the most flourishing district in Prov-
> ince Wellesley, with more than 70,000 people. . . . The large and small
> businesses of overseas Teochews number in the hundreds. . . . Every kind
> of business is active there. Traders in village produce, poultry and eggs
> are many, and use the town for distribution and collection. [Businesses
> in] foreign imported goods and textiles appear even more prosperous.

By the early 1950s, however, rural Chinese experienced far less voluntary movement to the towns and cities of northern Malaya, including those in Province Wellesley in the state of Penang. Approximately 11,200 Chinese in Penang state, and an estimated 860,000 Chinese throughout Malaya out of a total population of 6 million people were forcibly resettled ("relocated") from their rural residences to "New Villages" abutting urban areas or "regrouped" into plantations and other industrial sites (Sandhu 1964a, 165, 170, tables 2 and 5H).[10] This episode of coerced urbanization made Malaya "one of the highest urbanized countries [sic] in Asia" in the 1950s (Sandhu 1964b, 144).

New Villages in northern Malaya were set up during the Emergency in the early 1950s as part of the counterinsurgency campaign of the Federation of Malaya government against the armed guerrilla insurgency of the MCP against British rule. Counterinsurgency theory demanded the policing of the population via spatial separation—if rural Chinese could be kept away from their fellow Chinese Communist guerrillas, then the MCP insurgency would be cut off from its civilian Chinese support base, the Min Yuen, or People's Movement.[11] Forced, large-scale resettlement of rural Chinese into New Villages also met other strategic objectives: it deprived urban Chinese workers of their rural land as a resource base during strikes or periods of unemployment, and pushed them out of rural areas claimed by the Crown or by Malay villagers.

In 1951–52, several thousand Chinese in rural Province Wellesley and southern Kedah were suddenly forced from their homes—given ten days' notice, and then awakened at dawn by colonial soldiers who abruptly ordered them to take the few possessions they could muster and quickly mount the backs of trucks which transported them to the fenced and guarded camps euphemistically called New Villages. As a result, they were separated from their rubber stands, gardens, and land on which their houses were built. This move forced many to move several miles away from their rural plots. For the next several years, they lived under curfew in New Villages at night, and during daytime their travel was monitored by police, and at times, in the name of "food control," they were prevented from making their daily travels to work on their plots in "Black Areas" where guerrillas might be contacted and supplied with food. Many of those relocated were unable to travel to tap their own rubber stands or cultivate their gardens, and had to abandon their plots or see them claimed by strangers. Prior community institutions in such Black Areas (e.g., churches, temples, schools) also had to be abandoned (Sandhu 1964a, 1964b).

The mercantile elite and many other Chinese residing in the region of Central Province Wellesley were strongly predisposed against the MCP's insurgency. The anticommunist Ang Bin Hui, a reconstituted branch of the Hongmenhui anti-Manchu secret society, not the MCP, appears to have been the principal extralegal group with influence among Chinese in the area (Gamba 1962, 244; Cheah 1979, 35–42), and it is likely that Ang Bin Hui leaders had local merchant patrons. Nor were the British insensible to the presence of ambivalence and even antagonism against the insurgency among Chinese in the area. Newell (1962) notes that one population of Chinese farmers were allowed to live "freely" outside the New Villages in Permatang Pau, a few miles to the west of Bukit Mertajam, and to rent land from Malay farmers to grow vegetables to supply the town's marketplace. Nonetheless, five New Villages were set up in the periurban areas around Bukit Mertajam—Berapit to the north, Machang Bubok and Sungai Lembu to the east, and Permatang Tinggi and Juru to the southwest, and thousands of Chinese forced to move to them.

Violence, Silences, and Collective Forgetting

Only that historian will have the gift of fanning the spark of hope in the past who is firmly convinced that *even the dead* will not be safe from the enemy if he wins. And this enemy has not ceased to be victorious.

—Walter Benjamin, Thesis VI, *Theses on the Philosophy of History*

The brutality and violence of the British counterinsurgency campaign against the rural Chinese population of Province Wellesley and southern Kedah has never been publicly acknowledged and has been documented, if at all, only in secret colonial military archives. However, it is not merely that the historical "record" is incomplete, but that those who have been the victims of history were caught in its web of silences imposed by violence and reinforced by the personal experiences of humiliation, victimization, and terror. These experiences are difficult, and often impossible to recount, much less affirm as elements of a coherent identity, in this case, that of poor Chinese Malaysians (see Yong 2006 for a similar case in Sarawak). This is even more the case when a dominant hegemony of racial difference displaced this other discordant way—living and thinking class—of framing experience, which had been forcibly silenced. The ambiguity of the *meaning* of Tang Ah-Meng's question that opened this chapter indexed not a discourse of identity, but a discourse of identification that cannot be made into a publicly acceptable identity—and this not due to a theoretical impossibility but instead to the repression of institutions that affirmatively expressed a working-class identity.

There has been no public commemoration of the suffering that hundreds of Chinese families living in the district experienced during the years of forced relocation. No public accounts outside of official sources articulated their experience. What I found when I asked older people in Bukit Mertajam about their experiences of being forced into, and living in, the New Villages in the district, were what appeared to be fragmentary and haphazard recollections and traces of their (and their families') experiences. These were not the narrative expressions of a collective memory. My informants in 1978–80 in Bukit Mertajam still told family narratives of the traumas inflicted and the disorder and chaos their forced relocation caused them.

Chuah Eng Huat (my field assistant, 1978–79) took me one day to interview his father's father, then eighty years old, when we visited Chuah's home in Machang Bubok New Village in late March 1979. His grandfather first thought I was "English," but when Eng Huat assured him I was "American," the old man then spoke to me in Teochew Hakka, while Eng Huat translated:

> In 1952, the New Village here was built and it was surrounded by two fences, and our movements out of and into it were controlled by the British from then until 1957. In between the two fences, the government built a fortification on which they mounted a mortar. The British frequently used the mortar to bombard the Cherok Tokun area [at the base of the mountain] where many Communists were hiding.
>
> Before the Village was set up, the Chinese around here were scattered with our houses right on our rubber plots. The six of us lived in our rubber plot. Then, suddenly one day, we were given warning we would have to move within ten days to the New Village. If we did not, our houses would be burned and our pigs slaughtered. After that our family was first moved to a temporary house in the Village compound near the police station at the entrance. Later, when things improved, we moved to our present house here. Each family received $30 from the government and $100 from the MCA to spend on building their own house.

In the mornings, before going out to our rubber plots, we had to line up about 4:30 or 5:00 a.m. to be inspected by the police. We were only allowed to carry out enough food for ourselves.

When we first came, the New Village compound was covered with grass and big trees, and no latrines at all had been dug. When people met each other, instead of asking "Have you eaten?" they asked "Where did you go to shit?" People just shat everywhere. For the entire village there were five large wells dug where people went to bathe and get drinking water. Two months after our family moved here, my grandson, Eng Huat's older brother, who was just an infant, died because it was so unhygienic here. That's how Eng Huat became my oldest grandson.

Each household had to provide a member to do guard duty in a patrol once a week, and every afternoon, one member of each household had to attend training sessions. At the age of fifty-three, I had to undergo training.

Most of the people living in Machang Bubok New Village were rubber tappers, along with five sundry shop owners. There was one Indian here who operated a barber shop. During the years from about 1955 to 1957, there were still British troops who periodically came through to patrol the village, and to drop off propaganda leaflets. Most of the people here spoke Hakka, but our family spoke Teochew Hakka.

Eng Huat told me later that one of his uncles had fled the New Village and had joined the MCP guerrillas in the hills of southern Kedah; people in Bukit Mertajam called them "mountain rats," *shanlaoshu*. This was the last that his family had heard from him. I never was able to get Eng Huat to tell me more about him.

In yet another story, an informant I interviewed recalled that as a boy he had witnessed the assassination of a Chinese Resettlement Officer in a coffee shop in Permatang Tinggi New Village a few miles away by an MCP guerrilla who had infiltrated the Village. But my informant failed to mention what happened after that, although he almost certainly must have known about it. The sequel to the assassination was one of the most notorious incidents of the Emergency, when in August 1952 Gen. Gerald Templer, the newly appointed "Generalissimo," or military officer in charge of the counterinsurgency, personally visited Permatang Tinggi New Village, and demanded that the assembled sixty-six villagers provide him with the name of the assassin within seventy-two hours. When they failed to do so, he imposed collective punishment on the villagers by ordering his soldiers to raze their houses and forcibly remove them to other New Villages in central Perak, more than one hundred miles to the south. The incident created a scandal that received much critical coverage in the press in Britain (Short 1975; Shukor 1997).

Fathers, brothers, family members disappeared or separated: this was one theme of recuperated individual memory, as in the case of Eng Huat's uncle. Another instance: in early August 1985, I interviewed a seventy-year old retiree, Mr. Yeo, who had been recommended by a mutual friend as someone knowledgeable about the history of Chinese in Bukit Mertajam, and I managed to pry him away from his *majiang* game for an hour to talk with. I asked him about his experience of the Japanese occupation. When the Japanese army invaded Penang, he, his father, and younger brother had fled Bukit Mertajam for the town of Sungei Siput in Perak state to the south. There his younger brother married a local woman, and then entered the MPAJA to fight the Japanese. When the British returned at the end of the Japanese occupation in 1946, his brother "came down from the mountains to surrender his weapon." Yeo himself also returned to Penang state. But later—in 1951—things became "chaotic" or "disordered" and a police inspector in Bukit Mertajam caught his younger brother, who was tried as an MCP supporter and subsequently banished to China. Yeo and his brother in China had continued to write letters to each other for more than thirty years, and Yeo had recently requested permission from the Malaysian government to go to China to visit him, but had not yet heard whether he would be permitted to travel there. Yeo's narrative, for which my 1985 field assistant was present, unexpectedly provoked another. After my interview with Yeo was over, my field assistant said that he had been told that that his uncle had entered the MCP and gone to the mountains, that is, into hiding. To that day, he said, there was still no contact between his uncle and his father's sister, because his father had entered the Special Branch about that time.

Artifacts on the landscape of the Emergency period also bore witness to its history, and people occasionally mentioned them. In 1990, as my friend Mr. Ng and I drove through the small town of Sungai Lembu near the border between Province Wellesley and southern Kedah state, he mentioned that there was an old abandoned Catholic church near the road. We soon came upon it, above us, the building partly demolished, and the grounds covered with undergrowth. He said that this church was older than St. Anne's Church in Bukit Mertajam, which was almost a century old. Ng noted that during the Emergency, Chinese were forcibly moved either to Sungai Lembu New Village, in one direction, or to Machang Bubok New Village in the other, leaving the church without any people nearby who could worship there. The place was at that time in a Black Area where Communists were suspected to be—and probably in fact were—hiding.

Forced silences from the past were reinforced by the silencings of the then present, and they were directed not only at my informants, but also at me. During my fieldwork in 1978–80 in Bukit Mertajam, intimidation and fear framed the possibilities of any discussion I might have with my informants about these years of chaos and violence, as well as about more recent events which led to the forcible installation of Malay "special rights" in the Malaysian Constitution during the year-long period of martial law implemented after the May 13, 1969, ethnic riots. Inquiries about either period potentially called the legitimacy of Malay political supremacy into question and raised the question of the "loyalty" of Chinese to the Malaysian nation. When I pressed my informants about these matters on occasion, they quietly told me that I needed to show great care in asking about the events of either period, since my inquiries could cause the Special Branch—the Malaysian secret political police—to pay me a visit, and by implication, such talk could endanger my informants. These warnings were reinforced personally for me by the fact that the district's Special Branch officer, an Assistant Superintendent Ooi, went out of his way early in my fieldwork to introduce himself at a banquet I attended, and he made sure to greet me (as I did him), when we encountered each other on several similar occasions during the rest of my 1978–80 fieldwork period. My apprehensions about endangering my informants when I recorded their comments about events from these two periods were sufficiently strong at the time to lead me to code my informants' names in my field notes, in case they should be seized during a police raid. At the time, I quite underestimated the subtlety of the social control mechanisms at work.

The experiences of coerced relocation and of violence and brutality by colonial soldiers and police, and their semi-internment in New Villages, created an embittered and resentful new urban population of poorer Chinese, who made the trials imposed on their elders by a hostile British colonial state during the Emergency equivalent to the suffering they experienced and saw as maliciously imposed on them by an anti-Chinese national government embodied in the Malay police and soldiers still garrisoned among them in the 1970s, who harassed and shook them down on an everyday basis. The depth of antagonism was signaled for example by one shopkeeper who remarked that he was grateful for the MCP "mountain rats" in the forests of northern Malaysia and southern Thailand whose caches of arms would be there for Chinese to use in the event of any future race war between Chinese and Malays.

It is not surprising that New Village residents, along with those other poorer Chinese who had moved into and squatted in the kampung areas surrounding the downtown area of Bukit Mertajam, became the most militant supporters of the Democratic Action Party (DAP), the largest political opposition to the postcolonial successor to the British rulers—UMNO and the Barisan Nasional, or National Front, the governing coalition of parties that UMNO dominated, including the MCA and Gerakan Party, which represented the interests of large-scale Chinese capitalists. By the time of my fieldwork, the DAP, over and against the MCA and Gerakan, viewed as compromised by their coalition with UMNO, had become the party that represented "Chinese rights"—the voice of opposition condensed within the new institutionalized framework of politics organized around antagonisms between ethno-racial groups, whose members defined themselves as essentially different from and superior to the members of other ethnic groups.

Ethno-Race Formation and Questionable "Urban" Subjects

Through such means, by the late 1960s hegemonic state projects of ethno-racial recognition and discursive framing had driven any discussions about class, class conflict, and the MCP insurgency and its repression out of the public realm. Instead, government officials came to identify ethno-racial groups with explicit spatial referents. The distinction between "rural" and "urban" became an official metaphor representing the manifold political and cultural differences between Malays—the "rural" populations—and Chinese and Indians—the "urban" populations.[12] Thus, for example, the reports of successive Malaysia plans in the 1960s and 1970s identified the most serious priorities for "development"—particularly the need for preferential provision of infrastructure such as schools, paved roads, and health clinics—with the "rural population," that is, with Malays (Government of Malaysia 1979). While this spatial image partly represented a euphemism adopted by the government to avoid the use of sensitive ethnic labels, it also pointed to the threatening presence of politically suspect "urban" working-class populations and the spaces they occupied. Their presence became a matter of concern to the ruling Malay elite and its Chinese bourgeois allies.

In this sense, the state of Penang was the most "urban," that is, the most Chinese of all states in peninsular Malaysia—with about 50 percent of its population being listed in recent censuses as ethnic Chinese, compared to the percentage of Chinese nationally at about 35 percent. By the early 1970s, the Chinese population of the town of Bukit Mertajam made up more than 60 percent of the district of Seberang Prai Tengah (Central Province Wellesley), with the remainder being rural Malays and a small number of Indians. But there was an even closer association between ethno-racial identity and place, since 80 percent of the population residing within the municipal boundaries of the city were ethnic Chinese.

1978: A Counterinsurgent Logic Inscribed on the Landscape

When I moved to Bukit Mertajam to start dissertation fieldwork in 1978, the town and its surrounding district still bore the marks of the winding down of the successful Emergency counterinsurgency strategy against the MCP and its People's Movement of "fifth column" supporters of Chinese "subversives." The town's police and military buildings were sited in central downtown positions allowing for coordination against guerrilla subversion: the fortified five-story police station barracks surrounded by a chain-link fence dominated, and indeed towered over, the downtown area, and with the encampment of the antiriot police ("red-helmeted soldiers," *hongtoubing*) off of Jalan Cross Street (now Jalan Arumugam Pillai) located across from it, surrounded the town's municipal square, or *padang*, on two sides; the police barracks abutted this road, which led to the north and opened onto Jalan Aston, which led through downtown to the main road to southern Kedah, Jalan Kulim. The district officer's residence was sited nearby on a hill several hundred feet above the downtown area and the railroad station, and in 1978–80 older informants still called it *polizhushan*, the "hill with the office of window glass"—its name from the British colonial period. In 1979, the signal tower on the top of the "mountain," *bukit*, which rose high above the town and for which the town was named, was a prohibited area where trespassers might be shot. I occasionally saw police roadblocks on the main roads leading out of town still set up, which local informants told me were positioned, not to catch criminals or subversives, but to shake down drivers and motorcyclists for "tea money" by citing them for petty traffic infractions. The New Village of Machang Bubok still had a police guard post at its entry gate, although by then it was unmanned. People carrying weapons or even ammunition without a license might still be tried under an inherited colonial statute for the death penalty if it was ascertained that they had borne such weapons in a Black Area like Bukit Mertajam. The resident squatters of the downtown kampung enclaves of Kampong Cross Street, Kampong Aston, Kampong Tanah Liat, and Kampong Kovil to the west, north, and east of the downtown center, along with the three outlying New Villages (Khoo 1966), remained the foci of this state surveillance and policing.

The impress of this strategy of police and military monitoring of specific fortified sites in semi-incarceration, and control over the influx and movement of the Chinese population, thus remained manifest on the landscape even into the late 1970s.

Part I

DEVELOPMENT (1969–85)

COLONIAL RESIDUES AND "DEVELOPMENT"

Between the late 1950s and 1969, Malay, Chinese, and Indian elites came together in the Alliance coalition of political parties made up of the United Malays National Organization (UMNO), the Malaysian Chinese Association (MCA), and the Malaysian Indian Congress (MIC). The Alliance, negotiated under British tutelage, formed a balance of power between these elites based on an "ethnic bargain" (Tan 2001, 959–961) that left Malay leaders in charge of politics, gave legal citizenship to Chinese residents of Malaya, and allowed Chinese businessmen to occupy the heights of the economy (banks, brand-name manufacturers, rubber and tin processors) while the British withdrew from rule, although their corporate investments remained. This arrangement came to an abrupt end in 1969 when the national elections were followed by the May 13 riots in Kuala Lumpur during which hundreds of Chinese were killed by apprehensive Malays who feared the economic power and new enfranchisement of urban Chinese voters who had successfully elected opposition candidates in parliamentary constituencies in several states. A crisis of legitimation faced the Alliance and challenged the preexisting balance of power between the constituent political parties, in particular between UMNO and the MCA.

During the rest of 1969 and into 1970, under the National Operations Council, the UMNO elite was in direct command, with the country ruled by de facto martial law and the suppression of dissent through detention of political opposition and trade union leaders under the Internal Security Act and related measures. In 1970, the UMNO-dominated Parliament passed the New Economic Policy (NEP) as a response to widespread Malay discontent about the Chinese presence and purported Chinese "domination of the economy," and in order to "develop" the rural sector of impoverished Malay farmers. To implement the NEP, the Alliance was dissolved and reconstituted as the Barisan Nasional, or National Front, consisting of UMNO, the MCA, the MIC, and Gerakan—a new Chinese-based party—and several smaller parties, but with UMNO as the dominant, indeed dictatorial partner with its control over government civil ministries, the army, and police.

There were two stated objectives to the NEP—to eradicate poverty and to eliminate the identification of each "race" with economic function, that is, to move Malays into business and the professions, which had previously been populated mostly by Chinese and expatriates from the colonial period (Government of Malaysia 1979, 27–58). While the first objective of the NEP sought to provide economic and educational opportunities to impoverished Malay farmers and urban poor, the second sought to create the legal and institutional infrastructure for the accumulation of wealth among the Malay population. Both objectives were said to be fundamental to the "development" of Malaysia from its "underdeveloped" status to a modern, prosperous nation.

In retrospect, this second objective of the NEP provided the rationale for the economic aggrandizement of the Malay elite fraction of the ruling coalition—UMNO leaders, Malay royalty, and large landowners, and derivatively, those who belonged to the growing UMNO patronage networks in each state. The NEP was a decisive step that put politics in command and, while ensuring the protection of capitalist accumulation in general and the class domination it required (e.g., repression of independent labor unions), dislodged the wealthy Chinese bourgeoisie from its prior position of economic influence over the national economy and imposed a legal and administrative apparatus of control in the name of development that generated state discrimination against Chinese workers, family-operated businesses, small capital, and professionals.

From an historical and national perspective viewed more than thirty years on, it is possible to infer a broad set of processes of class, ethno-racial, and state formation complexly connected to one another through the ethno-developmentalist rhetorics and policies of the NEP. It does not impute a telos to the process to argue that NEP policies and programs that aimed on paper to reduce overall ethnic economic disparities between the "races" in actuality focused on the goal of making prosperous not all Malays, but UMNO leaders, their family members and relatives, the royal families who were their patrons, and the business groups, landowners, and rentiers who were their clients, while UMNO maintained its dominance over elections and the government (Gomez and Jomo 1997).

NEP developmentalism meant massive state intervention not only in the dominant plantation and mining sectors from the colonial period, but also in the most modernized corporate sectors, in ways that systematically favored those groups who by the 1990s came to be called "New Malays," Melayu Baru—a state-connected, ethno-racial transitional economic upper class. The conceptual link between the Malays forming this class and *all* Malays within official NEP rhetoric was the notion of "trusteeship." These wealthy Malays were to manage public enterprises controlled by UMNO as "trustees" for poor rural Malays, who would eventually come to prosper as soon as (at some indefinite future time) they were able to acquire wealth held for them by the trustees.

From the 1970s into the 1980s, the instrument for state intervention was the public enterprise managed by Malays connected to the UMNO elite by family, marriage, and region, and most markedly, political clientage. What was entailed was no less than a process not well articulated in English: "statification" (*étatisation*) of the economy—that is, nationalization and beyond. This transformation took place in two directions: from government department to public enterprise, and from private enterprise to public enterprise. In one direction, what were previously government agencies providing vital infrastructure services (e.g., for provision of water, telecommunications, aviation, and water collection) and the "statutory bodies" that previously employed civil servants in the management of national and state development goals (e.g., the Malaysian Industrial Development Authority, the Urban Development Authority, Petronas, and the Malaysian Rubber Development Corporation) were transformed into government-owned and controlled, for-profit public enterprises. In the other direction, the government required the transfer of substantial private ownership equity to the public enterprises that it established and continued to control.

New public enterprises thus formed joint enterprises with foreign investors, for whom this ownership arrangement became the expected quid pro quo for establishing new subsidiaries, especially manufacturers, to tap domestic and later export markets. These public enterprises acquired equity from privately owned domestic businesses and business owners. Chinese-owned banks, real estate companies, plantation and mining companies were the largest such private businesses, but many smaller firms were also targeted and were compelled to turn over equity as a condition for their continuing to do business. These new economic conditions were the result of the Industrial Coordination Act and related laws.[1] Various "trust" corporations (and their managements), which held large proportions of equity in the new public enterprises as trustees for *Bumiputras*, to use the term coined by the Malay elite for the indigenous peoples of Malaysia, were founded to meet NEP goals of ethnic redistribution.[2] The rise of public enterprises to a central role to the national economy can only be described as hypertropic: 109 public enterprises in 1970 grew to 363 by 1975, 656 by 1980, and 1,010 by 1985 (Gomez and Jomo 1997, 31).

This pervasive statification of the economy aimed in part at claiming the equity of private Chinese capital for redistribution to public enterprises and to the UMNO patronage machine was well underway by the late 1970s. So too were other measures of the NEP that sought to redress what UMNO leaders and their electoral base saw as other kinds of privilege that favored Chinese over Malays, such as the prevalence of Chinese and English languages in commerce and corporate workplaces, advantages Chinese had in being hired by foreign corporations, and the higher test scores of Chinese youths, which assured them greater access to universities and technical schools. These new state policies confronted Chinese with an increasingly suffocating political environment at all levels of the class structure. Behind the legislation and official policies of the NEP, it was clear that UMNO's base of supporters (farmers, small trades people, soldiers, police, teachers, and petty government functionaries) held widely shared notions that Chinese were essentially alien, subversive, dishonest, greedy, and antisocial, and it is undeniable that an ethnic revanchism by those in power targeted Chinese broadly during the NEP period. For Chinese, several forms of social advantage they had become accustomed to were unraveling, yet the effects varied among them by class.

These varied effects resulted from the other objective of the NEP during the 1970s, which was to develop the economy in the direction of export-oriented industrialization so as to eradicate poverty. The new government-owned public enterprises formed joint ventures with Japanese, European, and American investors in factories in the new industrial estates and export processing zones—of which Penang state had two of the largest (Bayan Lepas on Penang Island, and Prai in Province Wellesley). While export-oriented industrialization entailed the widespread proletarianization of poorer rural Malays so that they could access their share of "prosperity," it also provided an advantage to Chinese owners of petty business property and professionals, because however far they were from direct access to the highest levels of the public enterprises, they were still able to find at least marginal opportunities for capital accumulation in the rapidly expanding export economy. In contrast, under the NEP, the state's assault on the prospects of the Chinese working class for upward mobility—via education, access to capital, and private and government employment—was broadly encompassing, although Chinese workers were able to find the wage labor employment they needed to "get by," if not flourish, during these years of active state suppression of trade union militancy (Jomo and Todd 1994, 106–145).

It was therefore state coercion in the form of the implemented New Economic Policy, not a hegemony in the sense of institutions that had secured widespread "consent" among Malaysia's multi-ethnic population, that constituted the basis of class rule by the late 1970s. While the vast majority of Malays supported the NEP, almost all Chinese, unless they were extraordinarily wealthy and well-connected, complied with NEP statutes and regulations only because these were backed up by the state's repressive apparatus of intelligence, army, and police forces, not because they enthusiastically accepted these programs.

"BOOM TOWN IN THE MAKING," 1978-80

Failure, Recalcitrance, and a Town Undergoing "Development"

Enchanted as a Ph.D. student at Stanford with the approach of regional analysis (Skinner 1965; Smith 1976), I arrived to begin fieldwork in Bukit Mertajam in June 1978 with the intention of investigating the organization of the "regional economic system" of northern West Malaysia and the role of ethnic Chinese traders within it. I felt that based in this city, a major node of trade and truck transport in the northern region, I would be well positioned to collect data on the movement of goods and people that structured the hierarchy of central places of that system and to observe and record the trading activities of Chinese businesses within it, allowing me to trace how networks of elite businessmen controlled trade across the system.

However, as my months of residence in Bukit Mertajam passed, I found my efforts to locate and interview local merchants and collect geographic data from them stymied by the sheer scope of the task. I compiled increasingly unrealistic checkoff lists of the merchants in one line of trade after another whom I hoped to interview: the fish wholesalers one month, the vegetable wholesalers, the next month, and the like. So much data to collect, so little time! Even more galling, my efforts to identify, meet, interview, and observe members of the mercantile elite of Bukit Mertajam engaged in trade increasingly foundered, with a receding horizon of hoped-for observations and interviews that never came about.

Merchants I sought out were difficult to find, claimed they had little time free to be interviewed, but most critically if they allowed me to interview them, were, while cordial, nonetheless uniformly unforthcoming with "the facts" about their control of trade that I thought my research design required me to collect and analyze. These practical ethnographic difficulties—arising from my failure to "systematically" collect masses of data disembedded from the meanings, politics, and human agency of my subjects, and from the latters' recalcitrance toward being thus objectified—indexed more profound political and ethical shortcomings to the approach of the dissertation (Nonini 1983a), and ultimately I gave up on the effort as a failed project. This failure, which almost proved disastrous to me professionally (the dissertation was never revised or published), forced me to rethink what my informants' resistance to my inquiries meant and led over many years' subsequent research to the hard-earned if partial insights that form the basis of the four chapters that follow.

Nonetheless, my faltering efforts at a regional analysis and the positivist impulse behind it allowed me to construct the economic profile of Bukit Mertajam in 1978–80 presented in this chapter. As well, while still in the "field" as a dissertation student, my growing discontent and even desperation with my research design impelled me to look elsewhere—to the palpable inequalities of everyday life among the people of Bukit Mertajam that I witnessed, also described here. These experiences began the process of rethinking the premises of my prior "knowledge" about class, gender, and ethnicity among the hundreds of people I met and came to know, many as friends, in Bukit Mertajam in the years that followed.

"Whatever It Is You Want, We Have It!"

One evening during the early months of my fieldwork in late 1978, one of my closest friends and best informants, Mr. Tan, a school teacher at Jit Sin National Type High School, and I were speaking about the enormous volume of trade carried on by Bukit Mertajam business people. After naming some of the many goods purveyed in and near town, he summarized the situation exuberantly, "As they say around here, whatever it is you want—no matter what it is—we have it!" He meant of course: for a price. Indeed, the findings of the 1979 commercial census of the town's businesses that I undertook for my dissertation (Nonini 1983a) amply confirmed his claim.[1] Within the boundaries of this town of 28,675 people in 1980 (Jabatan Perangkaan 1986, 169, table 7.1), the commercial census found 1,271 businesses, employing a total workforce of 7,203 people (Nonini 1983a, 124–125; tables 20, 21).[2]

To start with, there were 906 retailing and artisanal businesses, which made up 71 percent of the total 1,271. They offered a wide array of goods and services to meet every need—food and drink sold at 100 coffee shops and 41 restaurants; groceries at 2 supermarkets, 105 sundry goods shops and confection, biscuit, and liquor dealers. Foodstuffs were sold by fresh vegetable, fruit, pork, beef, fish, and shrimp vendors, and by bulk goods dealers in beans, rice, sugar, beans, and *ikan bilis* (dried anchovies). Barbers, hairdressers, tailors, attorneys, accountants, Chinese medical practitioners, Western-trained physicians, dentists, and opticians; photo studios and photo supply shops; "motor" repair and spare parts (for trucks and cars) shops, bicycle accessories and repair businesses, and household appliances and electronics goods stores offered their services in the city. And jewelers; furniture dealers; textile, crockery, and cookware merchants; stonemasons (e.g., gravestones) and coffin-makers; banks and "finance companies" (for auto and other kinds of loans); hotels and lodging houses (*rumah tumpangan*); petrol stations and government lottery ticket vendors; and many others purveyed their wares. In addition, hundreds of mobile vendors of fast food (which were not surveyed in the census) made Chinese, Indian, and Malay food and drink available throughout the coffee shops and street sides of the downtown district, in the kampungs surrounding downtown, and on the main thoroughfares leading from it to west, north, and east.

The association of the town's Chinese population with the markets for these goods and services was strongly marked. As one walked the streets of town, it was evident that the vast majority of businesses were Chinese-owned, because almost all the signs mounted over the bottom-story shop fronts of the shop houses that lined downtown Bukit Mertajam's streets and the roads leading out of it carried Chinese characters along with Bahasa Malaysia, the latter being legally required. The shopkeepers and vendors in sight spoke Hokkien or Teochew, the two Chinese lingua francas for the region, with almost everyone they encountered, and only rarely Malay with a few customers. A large proportion of shops had altars to Tiangong, the God of Heaven, mounted on their walls or pillars on the "five-foot ways" in front.

But beyond the sensually evident, I ascertained through a commercial census in 1979 that 1,116, or 88 percent, of the total 1,271 businesses within the boundaries of Bukit Mertajam were owned by Chinese, while only 52 or 4.1 percent, were Malay-owned, and 59, or 4.6 percent, were Indian-owned (Nonini 1983a, 131, table 22). Moreover, these 1,116 Chinese-owned businesses employed 6,582 persons, or 91 percent of the total commercial workforce of 7,203 people (131–132, tables 22, 23). Among the 4,051 waged or salaried employees of these Chinese-owned businesses, that is, persons who were "outsiders" (not family members of the owners) working for a wage or salary, 89 percent were ethnic Chinese (135, table 25).

Mr. Tan's act of repeated speech that "whatever it is *you* want, we have it," *ni yao shenma, women you shenma*, referred not only to the town's residents, or even the people living in the district of Seberang Perai Tengah and beyond throughout the Penang region,[3] but also to people from places as far away as southern Thailand, Kuala Lumpur, and Singapore. In part, the phrase alluded to the social and commercial vitality of a town where large numbers of people continually came in to shop and enjoy the enticements of the town's trade (its snack food vendors, fresh fruit and drink stalls, cinemas, restaurants, coffee shops), and where shop house merchants displayed their wares to all who passed by, vendors and hawkers engaged in frenetic roadside business, and everyone, whether in cars, trucks, small motorcycles, bicycles, or on foot, was on parade in downtown streets filled to overflowing with goods, people, and vehicles. Compared to most places elsewhere in the Penang region, and indeed elsewhere in Malaysia, Bukit Mertajam was, *renao,* "bustling," "lively," "active" in the level of its commerce, and this was a source of local pride and distinction.

Mr. Tan's repeated utterance alluded not only to shoppers, but also to the merchants, dealers, brokers, salesmen, and transporters drawn to the town's hyperactive wholesale trade. In short, it invoked the seductive flux of commercial possibilities and the generation of wealth that the town's Chinese businesses made possible. Bukit Mertajam people spoke of the town as a "transfer center," *zhuankou zhongxin*, or "transfer point," *zhuanxin dian* or *zhuandian*, within the Penang region. This became manifest to me as I lived in Bukit Mertajam from 1978 to 1980 and witnessed on a daily basis the sheer volume of goods being moved—usually by truck—into and out of the town on a daily basis to provision the local population and urban populations elsewhere. People living in Bukit Mertajam spoke of the town's regional position as a thriving wholesale center. One reporter in the national English-language daily, *New Straits Times*, observed that it "has established itself as the 'clearing house' for lorry transport firms. This [is] because of its 'strategic position' lying as it does just off the main truck road." When traveling outstation from Bukit Mertajam, I met many people who knew of the town by its reputation. The author of the same article described it as a "growing town with hardworking people and an enterprising business community"— as a "boom town in the making on the mainland" (Ahmad 1978).

The town was a busy wholesale center and had more wholesale businesses per capita than any other urban area in Malaysia (Nonini 1983a, 99, table 13). (My commercial census of 1979 found that 172 of the 1,271 businesses, or 13.5 percent, engaged exclusively in wholesale trade and had a workforce of 967 people, or 13.4 percent of the town's total business workforce of 7,203 persons (157; 374, table 41). Of these 172 wholesaling businesses, 160, or 93 percent, were owned by Chinese, and Chinese made up 92 percent of all employees (157). Fifty-three, or about one-third, of these 170 businesses engaged in wholesaling of fresh foodstuffs—fish, shrimp, vegetables, poultry, pork, and fruit (374, table 41). Another major component (35 businesses) were wholesalers of nonperishable foodstuffs—bulked goods like rice, beans, and sugar; and canned goods, liquor, soft drinks—which sold to local sundry goods shops and other retailers in the town, as well as to retailers far beyond Bukit Mertajam. The remainder of the town's wholesale businesses traded in a wide variety of goods servicing the district's industries (e.g., textiles for garment factories; truck spare parts, tires, and batteries for the truck transport industry); purveyed electronics goods and appliances to supermarkets and electronics outlets; and sold agricultural chemicals, fertilizers, and pesticides to agricultural goods retailers (374, table 41).

For instance, consider the thirty-one fish and shrimp wholesalers. Behind the downtown public market, every evening from 7:00 p.m. onward, with the exception of two or three days during Chinese New Year, trucks heavily laden with crates of fish on ice lumbered through this deeply pitted, dirty, malodorous, and short street (perhaps hopefully named Jalan Bunga Raya, or Hisbiscus Street) to pull up in front of the shop houses of fish wholesalers on either side of the street, or to stop before an open concrete square directly behind the public market. Most of these trucks came from the ports of Haadyai and Songkla in southern Thailand, while a few others came from the coastal fishing villages of Kedah and Perlis states. Every night, twenty to thirty trucks arrived, carrying a total of anywhere between 50 and 160 tons of fish and shrimp. Men struggled with crates that weighed as much as 200 *katis* (about 260 pounds) in the backs of these trucks—and drivers and laborers lifted some of the crates down to the concrete square for the fish they contained to be sorted and graded by the fish wholesaler and sold at the public market the next morning, but most of the crates remained in back. Within an hour or two, these trucks left on their way south and west to the fish auctions held between 3:00 a.m. and 4:00 a.m. the next day in the wholesale marketplaces of Kuala Lumpur, Georgetown, Ipoh, and even Singapore. A small and close-knit community of fish wholesalers, all of whom were Teochews like their counterparts in southern Thailand,[4] carried out the intricate and complex logistics of setting prices and quantities for the different species and grades of fish sold, made deals over the telephone to their Thailand suppliers and vendors on credit, and allocated the day's catch between dealers in these urban markets separated from one another by hundreds of miles on the basis of market conditions of supply and demand on a daily basis.

Thus the seduction in Tan's repeated speech, "whatever *you* want, we have it," was targeted not only at the shoppers who flowed into the public market, supermarket, department and sundry shops of downtown Bukit Mertajam every day but also—and most compellingly—at the many merchants and others (distributors, brokers, supermarket managers, sundry shop proprietors, garment industrialists, street vendors, motor works and repair shops proprietors, salespeople on circuits, feed mill agents, farmers) who had reason to come to Bukit Mertajam and "do business" with its merchants—in search of deals and trading profits to be made, and offering them in turn. Whereas "we" were the merchants of Bukit Mertajam, "you" came from not just the town itself or its district, but also from other places far away—"you" were not only a housewife on her "moto" coming in from outlying Berapit New Village to buy the day's vegetables in the public market on Jalan Pasar, but also a department store agent from Butterworth seeking bargains in textiles from a Bukit Mertajam wholesaler; a restaurant owner from Kulim in Kedah wanting to buy cold-weather vegetables grown in the Cameron Highlands in Pahang state offered for sale by a Bukit Mertajam vegetable dealer; or a fish wholesaler with a stall in the huge wet market outside Kuala Lumpur who sought pomfret and other choice fish for banquets from the waters of southern Thailand, harvested by Thai fishermen, sold to a Haadyai dealer, and traded in turn to a fish wholesaler in Bukit Mertajam. It was therefore not merely goods that moved into and out of town through such connections: traders from other cities and towns came to Bukit Mertajam in search of goods to buy or sell and to collect bills owed on credit; just as, in turn, traders residing in Bukit Mertajam traveled to many cities and towns outstation—to Kuala Lumpur, Malacca; to Johor Bharu and Singapore; to Alor Star in Kedah, Haadyai, and Songkla in Thailand; or to Ipoh in Perak in pursuit of business and to collect bills for credit extended for past business done.

It was this constant movement of people in the course of a month, during which hundreds of out-of-town traders visited Bukit Mertajam even while scores of local merchants ventured throughout West Malaysia to trade and deal, that gave Bukit Mertajam its buzz, vitality, and attractions as a "transfer center." I experienced this firsthand as I came to be acquainted with local merchants who, in the course of an afternoon's visit to their shops, introduced me to traders and salesmen who had come from Kuala Lumpur or other cities and towns, and often took me with them and their visitors to coffee shops or restaurants downtown, to "entertain," *yingchou*, the latter, that is, to treat and charm them leading up to an advantageous deal or to a discreet request to defer payment of a bill on credit, to gossip, and to see and be seen by other men "of position" (see chapter 3).

Finally, it should be noted that Tan's repeated utterance no doubt referred not only to the attractions Bukit Mertajam offered in terms of licit goods and services but also to other less socially approved temptations arising from its longstanding reputation as a center for smuggling—to prostitutes working in the *rumah tumpangan* whose services could be bought by the hour; to "bar girls" trafficked in from rural Thailand; to illegal gambling halls and the "four-character" *ekor* lottery sales run by secret societies; to traffickers who brought in narcotics from the Golden Triangle and to the hidden heroin refineries that "hung out the name," *kuaming*, of a legitimate business on the signs on their shop house fronts; and to illegal *samsu* (moonshine) stills that operated up on "the mountain" behind the downtown area and were guarded by ferocious dogs. After all, "*whatever it is* you want, we have it": as long as you were willing to pay for it.

The Work of Laboring Women

In 1978–80, the neighborhoods of Tan Sai Gin and Taman Betek, not far from the downtown business area and set back from the thoroughfares leading west out of town, consisted of several hundred "semidetached" two-story brick and tile houses built in the late 1960s and early 1970s. Walking along the streets of these two neighborhoods, I saw signs mounted on the second-story fronts of many such houses written with Chinese characters and English and Bahasa words for "Garments," "Clothing," and "Lady Garment Maker" as part of the company name whose factory was inside. Posted on the front fences of some of these houses were white paper banners with Chinese characters soliciting "garment workers being hired." I could see the front paved courtyard of such a house filled with parked bicycles and motorcycles underneath the jutting roof that covered the first story and extended out to the road, and behind it the steel mesh sliding front door and open slatted windows of the house. If I stopped, found the front gate unlocked, and was brazen enough to step uninvited through the covered courtyard, and peer in through the open front doors of such a house, I could see anywhere from four to fifty or more women hunched over sewing machines and sewing furiously at parts of pants, dresses, brassieres, or underwear to add to the piles nearby, or standing next to tables on which were laid out the textile patterns that they cut out or trimmed. A veritable sweatshop of industry in Malaysia's humidity and heat, each such lower-level room with its rows of workers had behind it a walled-off, air-conditioned back office with a broad window facing outward, behind which sat the "boss," *laoban*, at his desk, overseeing the room before him, with one or two female clerks. These two neighborhoods represented the largest concentrations of the sixty garment manufacturers that my census (Nonini 1983a) found in Bukit Mertajam in 1979.[5]

Altogether the garment industry employed 984 workers, or 23 percent of the total waged labor force of 4,339 persons in the town (Nonini, 1983a, 133, table 24, 170). Garment factories in Tan Sai Gin, Taman Betek, and elsewhere in town produced Western-style shirts, dresses, jeans, and men's and women's underwear at a furious pace. Much of what was sold were knock-off copies of brand-name apparel. The vast majority of employees, 862 people, were Chinese women. Almost all such women were young, between the ages of eighteen to twenty-five years, and had begun sewing garments a few years after having dropped out of middle school. They tended to stay in such factory work, if not with the same employer, from the time they left school until the time they married, or until they had their first child.

Referred to as "women workers," *nugong*, they began working in the garment factories as "monthly workers" for about $MR 100 per month, or $MR 4 per day; if they were ambitious and worked hard, they might become "piece workers" whose fast pace of work would earn them as much as $MR 300 per month, but most leveled out at between $MR 150 and $MR 200 per month by the time they quit.

Those in authority over women workers on the shop floor were all men—the boss and his partners, when he had them; the production manager who set the shop floor work pace; and perhaps one or two men who were packers, transporters, or did other miscellaneous labor. I found subsequently that for most such young women there was a shift in the site but not in the relationships of asymmetrical power in which they had found themselves all their lives, from older men of their families—their fathers and older brothers—to older men in the factories—bosses, production managers, and a few older male workers. All the same, most female workers, unmarried, lived with their parents and younger siblings in town, for they could not afford to live on their own, even if parents had permitted them to. This effectively lowered the cost of their wages to their employers, while it provided them with support for their livelihood if they were laid off from work (say, due to slackened demand) or changed employers.

To introduce the regime of production that encompassed the working days of these several hundred working women and to understand the social conditions within, I present briefly two different perspectives on the local garment industry. One came from a Mr. Yeoh, whom I encountered one day in May 1980, and who invited me to tour his garment factory during its very first day of production. Actually, he said, he was glad to see me because he and his partners, who had just formed a new company to manufacture childrens' and infants' garments hoped to "systematize," *xitonghua*, production, but because he was originally "not in this line" of business, *bu neihang*, and was inexperienced in garment production, he wanted me to tour the production line in order to "criticize" it so that it could be improved. Taking me to a house in Tan Sai Gin, he showed me the workroom where there were thirty new sewing stations, with twenty seamstresses already hard at work, along with five packers and pattern cutters, two men and three women. There he told me what he meant by "systematization":

> We give each garment worker a small task to do on a part of clothing, and then she is expected to do this and only this, repeatedly all day, but most important is that she has to work as fast as possible, to sew as many pieces of this part of a garment as she can during the work shift. If she works beyond eight hours, we have to pay her the overtime rate. So it is necessary to pressure her to work as fast as possible, because the length of each working day is fixed by Malaysian law and we have to get as much done as possible.... We want to pay our workers by the month, instead of by the day, because if they are paid only by the day but do not wish to come to work, they don't have to, while workers paid by the month have to come to work every day, and only in this way can a high level of daily production be set and maintained.

Yeoh then proceeded to describe his and his partners' aspirations—to secure a contract with a local supermarket chain to manufacture childrens' and infants' clothes for its outlets throughout Malaysia—and his anxieties about expanding their market. Because local garment factories like his were small-scale and limited in capital, they could manufacture only for the domestic market; they could not afford to produce and export large lots of garments on the international market. For the same reason, they were relegated to using the cast-off sewing machines and other specialized machines (e.g., buttonhole makers) no longer in use in Japan, Taiwan, and South Korea. They were subject to being cheated by the Japanese suppliers who provided them only with less expensive "second grade" textiles. Many local factories had "become westernized" and used only English words and not Chinese characters on their trademarks and logos, because Malays, if they saw a product with a Chinese character on its label, believed that the product came from China, was made by "Chinese people," *orang cina*, and not by Malaysians—or simply did not distinguish between the two.

A second perspective on the garment industry was that of Miss Tan, who was employed in October 1979 as a clerk for Tai Heng Clothing Factory, the largest garment factory in Bukit Mertajam, which employed ninety workers in its factory downtown, and another thirty in a branch factory in a town thirty miles to the south. Almost all female workers she said were Chinese, and there were only a few Malays and Indians who were in the packing department. When Labor Department inspectors came and asked why so few Malays were employed, a manager replied that Malays were unsuited to the work, and did not want to do it, and the inspectors accepted this answer. Miss Tan stated that "Malay girls only work until they marry, and they don't work very diligently. Many but not all Chinese girls are conscientious and very productive, and quite a number work for Tai Heng after they marry." Still, Miss Tan went on, "factory turnover is very high. Often girls stay only for a few months before leaving for another job. This is possible because there are many clothing factories nearby and a high demand for workers. Female workers at Tai Heng often complain about their work to management, well, really to me or another clerk, and we are caught in the middle between the two sides. The workers are very articulate about their grievances."

Miss Tan recounted the recent mid-Autumn festival banquet which Tai Heng had recently held, an important occasion for the company, she noted, because it fell just prior to the onset of the factory's busiest period leading up to Chinese New Year. "There was separate food for the honored guests, *guibing*, and for the female workers and clerks. The honored guests were members of Tai Heng's board of directors, a police inspector, and an assistant superintendent of the Special Branch (political police). The honored guests sat at a table, while we employees ate our food sitting on chairs. Many of the female workers did not even attend the banquet—they didn't want to." When I asked why the honored guests and employees had been separated with different seating, she replied, "Many of the female workers speak crudely [*jiang culuhua*]. If they were with the honored guests at the same table, they would not know what to say or do. Some would be quite shy. So it's better that they were separated." When, where, and with whom workers were "crude" or articulate was thus a matter of class and context—a matter I turn to in chapter 6.

Truck Drivers "On the Roads in a Great Hurry": Time's Duress and the "Gangster" Question

> When you are talking about the Penang lorry transport industry, you are talking about Bukit Mertajam.
>
> —Mohamad bin Bakar, road transport official, Ministry of Transport, 1980

> We in the transport industry compete with time. Otherwise, it would not be profitable.
>
> —Mr. Oon, transport company towkay (owner or "head of family/business")

What made possible the hyperactive trade and manufacturing for which Bukit Mertajam people were nationally known was the flexible and time-driven work performed by the town's truck transport industry. This industry had originally arisen in the 1960s to supplement but then came to replace the town's railway junction as a transshipment node that connected Kuala Lumpur and cities south to Butterworth and Georgetown to the West, and to Kedah, Perlis, and southern Thailand to the north. By the late 1970s, the local transport industry had become central to the town's competitive position within Malaysia's flourishing export-oriented industrializing economy marked by the speed-up of time and a new urgency in delivering goods to faraway destinations in accordance with precise schedules tied to fluctuations in market demand.

It makes sense to speak of a new episode of time-space compression (Harvey 1989) occurring relative to the far less frenetic years of the late colonial economy. Transport towkays and the truck drivers they hired undertook to haul the commodities that allowed Bukit Mertajam's retail and wholesale merchants to be well supplied yet flexibly and rapidly responsive to market opportunities. They also provided its factory managers with the timely inputs they required to keep their laborers at work and allowed them to be able to promise the delivery of their products to customers in distant cities in accordance with pressing contract deadlines. The flexible and inexpensive transport provided to dealers like the fish and shrimp wholesalers described above was critical to the reputation of Bukit Mertajam as having the lowest prices and freshest seafood in the entire north Malaysian region, a reputation ritually invoked by local people over lavish meals in the town's restaurants as a sign of its distinction relative to other cities in the region. Trucks, their drivers, and the freight they carried were omnipresent. During the hours of daylight and into the evening, I found it impossible to pass through the congested streets of the town's downtown business area or along the roads leading out of town to the west, north, south and east, without noticing trucks of diverse sizes and types in motion carrying goods piled high in back under tarps, or stopped, often double-parked blocking a lane of the street, their drivers hurriedly loading or unloading freight outside the shops of local merchants.

But the scope of the local truck transport industry was actually much greater, for as I found out through my interviews with owners and drivers in the industry, drivers in trucks from Bukit Mertajam passed through the cities and towns of Malaysia every working day of the year. It was, after all, Bukit Mertajam's status as a truck transport center that mattered in the national scheme of things. The town's truck drivers hauled manufactured goods from the major industrial region of the country—the Klang Valley (Kuala Lumpur and satellite cities)—and from Singapore hundreds of miles to Penang state, and then dispersed these goods to the cities and towns of northern Malaysia. On the return trips south they carried manufactured goods from Penang state industrial estates to the dealers, wholesalers, retailers, and consumers of the metropolises and towns of central and southern Malaysia. Drivers also carried the fresh and processed foodstuffs from the north (as in fish from southern Thailand, rice from Kedah, refined sugar from Perak) and the central region (vegetables of the Cameron Highlands of Pahang) to merchants throughout the Penang region to the north in one direction, and to the south (as in fresh fish and poultry to Kuala Lumpur) in the other (Nonini 1983b).

Some 105 people, 102 of whom were Chinese and 3 Malays (97 men and 6 women), owned and managed 53 truck transport companies with their home offices in the town and its district. Altogether these 105 towkays employed 1,100 drivers, clerks, office managers, truck attendants, and general laborers—the majority being Chinese men (Nonini 1983b)

Transport towkays and their hired managers and drivers I interviewed during 1978–80 spoke often to me of the press of time imposed on them—with the difference for each being exactly who or what generated this pressure. Towkay Oon said he faced pressure "to keep my trucks constantly in motion" to meet the constant demands of consigners for precise and timely transport, and to pay the fixed costs of drivers' salaries, road tax, and insurance. Here was the cycle that Towkay Oon outlined for me for his trucks, which carried fish on ice from southern Thailand to Kuala Lumpur via Bukit Mertajam:

Day 1: 5:00 a.m. to 10:00 a.m.: Bukit Mertajam to Songkla
10:00 a.m. to 12:00 p.m.: load fish in Songkla
12:00 p.m. to 6:00 p.m.: Songkla, clearing Malaysian customs at Thai border, to Bukit Mertajam
6:00 p.m. to 3:00 a.m. (Day 2): Bukit Mertajam to Kuala Lumpur fish wholesale market
Day 2: 3:00 a.m. to 11:00 a.m.: Kuala Lumpur back to Bukit Mertajam (change drivers in Bukit Mertajam)
11:00 a.m. to 4:00 p.m.: Bukit Mertajam to Songkla
5:00 p.m. (or so) to 10:00 p.m.: fish loaded in Songkla, clear customs, return to Bukit Mertajam
10:00 p.m. to 12:00 a.m.: unload fish for Bukit Mertajam wholesale market
Day 3: Start new cycle

For office managers, this meant incessant demands from the towkay to find new consigners and to quickly oversee the process of batching different consignments of freight together for the same destinations and have drivers load them and get underway according to schedule. For driver and truck attendants, the situation was one of unrelenting pressure from the towkays, which to drivers took various forms, characterized by one driver as "being on the road in a great hurry," *zai daolu benpao* (see chapter 6). One driver spoke of his experiences accompanying two other drivers on their trips hauling crates of fresh fish on ice from Bukit Mertajam to Malacca approximately four hundred miles to the south:

> We [drivers] are under great pressure from the boss . . . to make the trip as quickly as possible within 24 hours, and immediately set off again as soon as we arrive back in the evening [in Bukit Mertajam] after completing the trip. As a result, driving south is quite dangerous. We must drive very fast, and we are also overloaded with fresh fish. Because of this, we have had no less than seven accidents this last year.

In contrast to these accounts by transport towkays, their managers, and drivers, which pointed to the constant pressure of time, even if discordant about the sources of such pressure, Mohamad bin Bakar, an official who worked for the Road Transport Department in Penang, whose bureau licensed and inspected trucks, had an altogether different view of the truck transport industry and its pressures:

> The people in the lorry transport industry . . . are a bunch of gangsters. Many drivers are gangsters. I've been out with my officers and stopped fish lorries, and there sitting up in the lorry are two or three heavy-set gangsters, Chinese, and they've threatened my life if I stop their lorry and refuse to let them pass. You know, in the past they even carried guns from Thailand under the fish they transported, and who knows what they might do?

In my interview with Mohamad bin Bakar, he described what he saw as the many morally reprehensible and certainly illegal characteristics of those who participated in the Bukit Mertajam truck transport industry. Drivers were gangsters, intimidating, unruly, violent. They disobeyed legal orders, threatened enforcement officers with mayhem, drove too fast, and too dangerously. He knew this from his own experience and was prepared for the worst: "I have received anonymous notes threatening me and phone calls threatening me with death. I've told my wife what may happen to me some day. . . . They have a social attitude . . . they sit high up in the lorry and act superior to other drivers." Who knew what they might do?

If drivers were gangsters, truck owners were, in Mohamad's estimation, not much better. They were "involved in smuggling, particularly of goods from Thailand." He was alluding to narcotics and to other goods that escaped customs duties, like sticky Thai *pulut* rice. They allowed their trucks to be overloaded, thus posing hazards and the risk of injury or death to other road users as well as to their own drivers. They forged trailer permits, which allowed them to put trailers on the road illegally, thus avoiding the road taxes they were required to pay in return for their use or rather abuse—given their overloads—of Malaysia's roads. They "abused their permits" when they had their trucks carry unauthorized cargo—if their permits allowed them only to carry their own freight, but they carried the freight of others for profit—this was a violation. They also abused their permits by having their trucks operate outside the states to which they were limited by their permits. "They have even tried to corrupt my officers, but I've been able to put a stop to it." But truck owners were not gangsters, unlike their drivers: "When we stop their lorries, they give us no problem. They smile and act like real gentlemen, and pay their fines without argument. They're very rich, after all. It doesn't mean much to them."

The animosity felt by Mohamad bin Bakar was strongly felt yet directed against Chinese as a population, although embodied most specifically in the figures of threatening "gangsters" and criminal "gentlemen." Such an animosity was common among government officials, particularly if they were Malays. But the animosity was more than personal, for it was deeply encoded within the development policies of the postcolonial Malaysian state.

Development Comes to Bukit Mertajam: The New Economic Policy

Chinese merchants are always complaining, aggressive, and always looking out for themselves. This is especially true of their dealings with Malays. Chinese merchants allow other Chinese to use credit to pay for the time being, but always demand cash from Malays. They always offer very poor prices for the agricultural products of Malays, and so kill the market for the Malays, and discourage Malay participation in the economy. . . . Malays have actually been patient with this kind of behavior from Chinese. They have had to tolerate it for so many years.

—Balasingam, clerk in a local government office, 1978

Ooi [a sawmill owner and land developer] is unlike other Chinese because he deals fairly and openhandedly with Malays. Most Chinamen are not worth anything, in contrast.

—Hamzah, Malay landowner, living near downtown Bukit Mertajam, 1979

How are the Malays going to reach the 30% goal of the NEP by 1990? Especially when the Chinese already have the money, but the kampung people have little or none [of capital] to buy the shares of enterprise that the government is going, under the NEP, to allocate to them?

—Ahmad bin Hussein, technician in District Office, Seberang Prai Tengah, 1978

By the late 1960s Malays, the largest ethnic group in Malaysia, whose identities were based on being Muslim, being loyal to their rulers, the *raja*, following Malay *adat* or "custom," and being native speakers of Malay, were obsessed with the question: "What to do about the Chinese?" To many Malays, Chinese had proven unworthy citizens—unwilling to share the economic proceeds of the postcolonial economy, selfish and acquisitive, narrow-minded, and ambitious in their political claims to power: always wanting more. The residue of ethno-racial antagonisms from the Emergency, the colonial government's campaign against the insurgency of the Malayan Communist Party during the late colonial years of 1948–60, led many Malays to remember that most of the Communist "terrorists" and almost all their civilian supporters were Chinese.

Many Malay men who had served in the colonial government's army and police had bitter memories of combat against Chinese guerrillas and of suspicion of their supporters who, they were convinced by British propaganda, backed an alien and subversive movement that had it been victorious would have aligned Malaya with an atheist Communist China. Moreover, the fact that Chinese were not Muslims, ate pork, drank alcohol, and worshipped many gods, and refused to learn to speak and write Bahasa Malaysia and thus make themselves understood, and instead were satisfied to speak either the colonial master's language of English, or Mandarin, the national language of an alien China, made them appear even worse in the eyes of Malays.

The statement by Balasingam, an ethnic Indian, English-educated and a devout Hindu, who served as a clerk in a local government office and was one of my closest friends and most articulate informants, summarized much of the case against Chinese merchants like those of Bukit Mertajam in their treatment of Malays. Whereas Chinese merchants extended other Chinese credit, they demanded cash from Malays. They depressed prices they offered for the commodities that Malays, predominately agrarian in their livelihoods, produced—for their padi (rice), their rubber, their coconut oil, and fresh fruit. They drove out Malay competitors when the latter did start up businesses. Moreover, Balasingam complained that Chinese preferentially hired other Chinese even for menial or common labor. They also, others alleged, overcharged Malays for goods they sold them, and at times, sold them adulterated goods.

Not all Chinese, of course: there were the exceptions of the good Chinese. As in Hamzah's statement above that a few Chinese like Mr. Ooi, a developer who had formed partnerships with Malays in business, dealt fairly and openhandedly with Malays, the premise was still that "most Chinamen were not worth anything."

By the mid- to late 1960s, animosities between Malays and Chinese had mounted throughout Malaysia, including Bukit Mertajam. The principal strategy to avoid conflict was to avoid any contact at all to the extent possible.

Nonetheless, in Bukit Mertajam there were incidents of ethnic violence. Accord-ing to Mr. Lok, a retired school teacher who lived in Bukit Mertajam at the time, in 1964 a Malay market sweeper had beaten a misbehaving Chinese child at the public market in downtown Bukit Mertajam. Several Chinese in the marketplace had beaten the Malay man in turn; he ran back to call on neighbors from his kampung to retaliate and they returned to the marketplace to attack. Chinese there fought back; "chaos broke out," several people were killed, and Chinese shops nearby were looted and burned, and the violence continued until the gov-ernment instituted a curfew that put an the end of the violence.

Such violence was a prelude to the much greater trauma for Chinese of the May 13, 1969, violence in Kuala Lumpur and elsewhere, primarily involving non-Chinese perpetrators attacking relatively larger numbers of Chinese victims (Von Vorys 1975). A year after "May 13," the New Economic Policy (NEP) was passed by the Malaysian Parliament, which placed Malay "special rights" within the Malaysian Constitution as the foundational concept defining essential group membership and the privileges of one specific ethnic group over others within Malaysian society.

Ethnic Complaints (At a Discount)

I arrived to do fieldwork among Chinese in Malaysia eight years after the incep-tion of the New Economic Policy. Without at this point entering into the debate about the merits of the NEP for Malaysia as a whole, or for its Malay population or its Chinese population,[6] what I want to describe are the responses to it by Bukit Mertajam Chinese as they interpreted their experiences of it during 1978–80. Their interpretive claims represent a hegemonic semiotics of argument about the processes of social and cultural reproduction, and about the ways in which constraints on these processes arose from ethno-racial relations, that is, relations between hierarchically ranked and essentially different groups. After my arrival in Bukit Mertajam in late 1978, I eventually became inured to hearing what, from sheer repetition, I came to take as a standard inventory of resentments and complaints from Chinese residents about state policies.

The list of recounted injustices was long and came from people diversely situated in the local economy. People told me that the Malaysian government discriminated against Chinese because it required their children to pass examina-tions in Bahasa Malaysia (the national language, a standardized Malay) instead of in English or Mandarin in the Form 5 high school year that determined whether they would go on to the universities. They said it set quotas for the number of

Chinese who could enter the government's universities, severely limiting their intake, while it forbade Chinese from setting up their own Chinese-language university, Merdeka University. They stated that almost all government officials were Malays, who were suspicious, vindictive, and mean toward Chinese, and "corrupt" and hungry for bribes. They claimed that the government took away hard-earned equity from Chinese business owners without adequate compensation under the Industrial Coordination Act of 1975.

My informants told me that government policies excluded Chinese from being hired for the burgeoning civil service, the police, and the military—and people noted that the government after all was the country's largest employer. Businessmen told me that the government's Ministry of Public Works discriminated against Chinese businesses in handing out large government contracts, but rewarded them instead to influential Malays, friends of UMNO leaders, who allotted contracts to their co-ethnic clients until the latters' businesses failed, and only then subcontracted out to Chinese firms to do the work for a small fraction of the total contract. People said to me that the Special Branch police threatened Chinese dissidents and opposition leaders when they spoke out against Malay "special rights," *tequan*, with preventive detention (and had detained some)—and on and on.

Informants made these complaints to me discreetly, as over time they came to expect that I would listen sympathetically, since my ability to speak and read Chinese indicated that I honored "Chinese culture." They said they dared not utter such words in public out of fear they might come to the attention of the Special Branch. What I want to emphasize is that while this catalogue of felt injustices rehearsed the ways in which Bukit Mertajam residents felt they were being treated "unfairly" as "second-class citizens" by "their [Malays'] government," at the same time my informants stated unequivocally that as citizens of the Chinese "race" they recognized the legitimacy of the independent Malaysian state. Their home was Malaysia where many had lived for generations, and they knew little about China, never having visited there but, at most, if they were old enough, might have received letters from remote relatives there.

Although almost all my informants saw the NEP as an assemblage of vindictive, punitive, and capricious abuses imposed on them by "their [Malays'] government," NEP policies underwrote capital accumulation for all ethnic fractions of capitalists—the development aspect of the NEP—even as they furthered the economic and social and political status of Malays—its redistributionist aspect. First, the industrial growth spurred by the NEP by no means harmed the economic interests of all Chinese in Bukit Mertajam. The export-oriented industrialization development policies of the NEP, which promoted major foreign investments in nearby export processing zones (EPZs) in Penang state, provided owners of local industrial subcontractors and small factories many opportunities for enhanced capital accumulation. These included garment factories like those described above and others producing small consumer goods. Construction contractors, labor recruiters, bus company owners, and others providing ancillary services to the large factories in the EPZs also found chances for private enrichment. Such examples of local petty capitalist enrichment provided a pedestrian rationale for the image of a "constantly expanding pie" proffered by leaders and party stalwarts of the local MCA and Gerakan Party chapters. In this presumed least bad of all possible meals for Chinese, even though the Chinese "slice" might be smaller than the Malay "slice," the pie for everyone was growing rapidly under the government's export industrialization programs, and thus no one suffered unduly, while political stability and civil peace prevailed.

The second tension between the developmental and redistributionist aspects of the NEP arose in relation to Ahmad bin Hussein's plaintive question in 1978—how to make Malays more prosperous when "the kampung people have little or none [in capital] to buy the shares of enterprise that the government is going, under the NEP, to allocate to them?" This question remained relevant through the 1980s and 1990s, when economic inequalities among Malays, particularly the divisions between the Melayu Baru, or "New Malay," technocrats and corporate managers and poorer rural Malays continued to widen.

Despite examples of Chinese who prospered during the late 1970s into the 1980s, from my ethnographic evidence it is difficult to escape the conclusion that NEP policies and programs stifled the prospects for upward mobility of Chinese workers and students and the social and cultural reproduction of Chinese professionals, artisans, and those self-employed in small businesses. While some prospered, the NEP held back many other Chinese by restricting or denying them access to university education, capital, government and corporate employment, and to Chinese (Mandarin) language education in state-supported schools, while Chinese merchants were deprived of equity in their firms when it was appropriated by government agencies. These barriers led many better-off Bukit Mertajam residents to consider emigrating from Malaysia to the Anglophone nation-states of the Pacific Rim—a theme I turn to in chapter 10.

For poor Chinese in Bukit Mertajam, features of the state's carceral counterinsurgency regime persisted. Police continued from the 1960s their violent repression and dispossession of working people who did not have the option of permanent flight—putatively "subversive" workers, "gangsters," and "secret society elements" among the estimated one-fourth of the town's Chinese population who lived in the squatter settlements surrounding the downtown area and among the impoverished residents of the surrounding New Villages.[7]

Many Labored, Petty Property Prevailed, and There Were a Few at the Top

This book arises from my critical but engaged and supportive partiality toward the many people I have come to know from fieldwork in Bukit Mertajam over the last thirty years. When I visited him in 2007, Mr. Lau, a long-time acquaintance and a retired school teacher and by then a travel agent, pleaded with me that it would be crucial above all in this book for me to demonstrate the falsity of the claim that "Chinese dominate the Malaysian economy." Although this book cannot be such a demonstration, his request is worth addressing. Much of the political controversy surrounding the NEP has taken the form of an argument between NEP advocates—scholars (e.g., Faaland et al. 2003) and UMNO leaders and supporters—and their opponents about whether Chinese were "wealthy" and/or "dominated the economy." As I observed above, NEP advocates frequently also saw Chinese as "clannish" and biased against Malays, particularly in the economic sphere.

As I argue in chapter 1, political conflict in postcolonial Malaysia has manifested the deflection of class-based antagonisms into ethno-racial ideologies and practices of struggle. As I note above, the counterinsurgency campaign during the Emergency made it politically dangerous for Malaysians of any ethno-racial group to even "think/speak/act class." For anthropologists, these ideological deflections must simultaneously be accepted at face value as real in one's ethnography, even as they can be challenged analytically—and also in one's ethnography—by a critique in terms of class and class relations. Moreover, because of the oppression of women under conditions of patriarchal power within the family business, any critique must also consider the interactions between class and gender relations. In the chapters that follow, I seek to engage in this double-sided intellectual task as it bears on class, politics, and citizenship. It is therefore helpful to open to scrutiny the claims about putative Chinese wealth, economic dominance, and clannishness by examining the case of the Chinese of Bukit Mertajam as I came to know them from 1978 to 1980 through my ethnographic and statistical research. Following this analytical trail of numbers gives broad insight into the question of wealth, and who controlled it and who did not in Bukit Mertajam—a finding which, I hope, simultaneously addresses and deconstructs the claims made by NEP advocates. (I present only my principal findings here; the analytical argument an evidence are set out in detail in the appendix.)

Most adult Bukit Mertajam Chinese in the late 1970s had either or both of two sources of livelihood. First, they depended primarily on their wages and salaries paid in return for their labor. An estimated one-third were hired by Bukit Mertajam employers (e.g., as garment workers, truck drivers, shop clerks, stonemasons), the remainder by corporate and government employers in Penang state and southern Kedah, and by small businesses in nearby cities and towns. Insofar as their wage incomes formed the major source of their social wealth, such residents could be said to be working class, in the broadest sense of having to sell their labor power to survive economically. People of Chinese descent belonging to the working class like this relatively large population can be found in any major city or town in Malaysia or in other Southeast Asian countries, and their existence, daily lives, and crucial economic contributions are ignored and passed over by the mainstream business press on "overseas Chinese," and by many anthropologists of the "Chinese diaspora." I examine their condition more closely in chapters 5 and 6 below.

Second, and by no means completely separate from those who worked for wage incomes, a large number of Bukit Mertajam Chinese relied on what they called "doing business," *zuo shengyi*, most in small and barely profitable endeavors for their livelihoods—not dependent on accumulated capital. A very large number of residents saw themselves as "doing business" and acted accordingly. For example, there were street vendors and public market stall vendors, like the married couple serving up Hainan chicken rice from a stall in a coffee shop, or the man working with his adolescent son vending fruit from a roadside stall—and there were hundreds of such small enterprises. The means and mechanisms by which they did business were ingenious and multiplex, in a word "entrepreneurial." They were self-employed, and often but not always owned small amounts of productive property, which they used for their own employment, and could be said to be petty commodity producers. A man worked for his father's electronics retail shop but also had a sideline business selling insurance; a woman labored side-by side with her husband at their *guitiao* (fried noodle) stall at an open-air coffee shop in the evenings, but could be found at home during the day laboring on a piecework basis to sew parts of garments on a sewing machine she owned, while overseeing her two daughters also sewing by the piece as part of a "contracting out" arrangement with a local garment factory; an acupuncturist operated his own clinic in town while acting as a small-scale land speculator; a rubber estate manager operated his own small rubber estate on the side, using family labor. Resourcefulness, flexibility, and the continuous search for new sources of profit from exchange were characteristics shown by a large proportion of the town's population.

When a person said he was "doing business," he was using this highly elastic term to stake a broad claim to a valued social identity. Perceptions by Malays that Chinese "dominated" the Malaysian economy may have been cued by the fact that so many Chinese in Bukit Mertajam, as in other cities and towns, were constantly, visibly, and busily engaged in some form of doing business, but whether this fact was equivalent to "domination" of the economy is certainly subject to debate. What is less debatable is that certain kinds of performance, manifesting specific cultural styles identified as "Chinese" were on public display—and these are the subjects of chapters 3 and 4.

Only a minority of Bukit Mertajam Chinese who claimed they "*did* business" also *possessed* substantial business capital through which they set others to labor for their firm's profits. Among Chinese who owned businesses, more than one-half of the 1,116 businesses they owned depended solely on family labor, and approximately two-thirds of all businesses employed more family labor than they did hired outsiders (Nonini 1983a, 136). These 1,116 Chinese-owned businesses were operated by 2,531 proprietors and their family members, with 4,051 hired employees (outsiders) (133–135, tables 24, 25). Thus a large majority of towkays in Bukit Mertajam engaged more in self-exploitation and in the (unaccounted-for) exploitation of their wives, daughters, mothers, and nonadult sons than they did of outsiders—whether Chinese or non-Chinese. There was thus the prevalence of petty property among Chinese business people. This was a situation founded on patriarchal power in which towkays declared the hegemonic view that the business was coextensive with "the family"—a viewpoint at times challenged covertly by wives, daughters, and other family members.

What about those business owners with significant class power as owners of the means of production and employers of a large labor force? From my 1979 census, I found that only 108 businesses, or 8.7 percent of the total 1,271 enterprises, employed ten or more hired employees. Those hired by these 108 businesses numbered 2,792 persons, or 64 percent of the town's total hired labor force of 4,339 persons (133, table 24, 186). Altogether, only 294 Chinese individuals (93 percent of them men) living in Bukit Mertajam owned these 108 large businesses plus 26 other businesses with ten or more employees or with relatively large capitalization (at least $MR 100,000) elsewhere in the district—a total of 134 businesses (198, 202).[8] These 294 individuals were supermarket chain magnates; the owners of large garment factories; proprietors of truck transport companies with scores of long-distance trucks on the road; proprietors of rice, tapioca, and oil mills; exclusive regional distributors of brand-name petroleum products, alcohol, and foodstuffs; real estate and housing developers; and owners of rubber estates hundreds of hectares in area (194–202).

These (mostly) men formed the mercantile elite of the Chinese population of Bukit Mertajam. They were "persons of position"—that is, they owned and controlled amounts of wealth that made their presence and actions socially significant and important to Chinese residents of the town and its surrounding district. When these individuals sought to use their wealth to make contributions to certain political parties, they were bestowed feudal titles (e.g., "justice of the peace," or J.P.) by the government, and received inside information on official

development plans. When they made contributions to "Chinese society" composed of community organizations, they were "celebrities" who became these
organizations' esteemed presidents, treasurers, and members of boards of trustees. When they gave "gifts" to prominent government officials and police, they
became their friends.

However, not all large businesses in Bukit Mertajam were owned or controlled
by Chinese residents. Another 154 men who did not live in Bukit Mertajam controlled thirty-seven large businesses operating in town—including thirteen businesses which were among the largest corporations in Malaysia, most of them
government-owned. Of these 154 men, 116 were Chinese, and 27 were Malays
(Nonini 1983a table 30, 199–200). The fact that approximately one-sixth of these
men were Malays point to a shift in the composition of Malaysia national economic elite with the creation of a new ethno-racial fraction, the New Malays,
Melayu Baru—precisely an outcome of the NEP underway by 1978.

To summarize, most Chinese living in Bukit Mertajam worked for wages and
salaries and/or engaged in very small business ventures ("did business"), while
petty property prevailed among the vast majority of business families. In contrast
only a relatively very few individuals owned or controlled large concentrations of
property—and not all of those who did were Chinese or lived in Bukit Mertajam.
It was this remarkable presence of a large number of working people combined
with a dispersion of business property for the majority of local Chinese businesses, compared with the concentration of wealth among a relatively very few,
that provided the economic backdrop against which Chinese in Bukit Mertajam
sought and at times fought to create their identities as citizens of the nation-state.
The chapters that follow set out the processes through which Chinese in Bukit
Mertajam came to act as citizens.

Coda: Worshipping the King of the Ghosts

It is fitting that Bukit Mertajam people should have the last say in this chapter introducing their town and their lives as I encountered them from 1978 to
1980. I conclude this chapter with a translation of and commentary on a newspaper article published in the "Local News" section of the Chinese-language daily
Xingbin Ribao by a journalist who lived in and was/is well known in Bukit Mertajam (*Xingbin Ribao* 1979a; August 28, 1979). This article was therefore written
from the perspective of a Chinese-educated resident, but given his position, one
that could be taken to be a more general representation acceptable to Bukit Mertajam Chinese-educated people. It describes the largest Daoist/Buddhist festival
in Bukit Mertajam, widely known as "Festival of the Hungry Ghosts," or more
formally as Yulanshenghui or Zhongyuanjie, which took place during the Chinese

seventh lunar month in August 1979. I offer it here not only because it provides a representation of Chinese society in Bukit Mertajam that few Chinese residents would argue with, but also because it suggests much about the varieties of power, cultural styles, and claims of citizenship from a local perspective, discussed in the chapters that follow. The political dimensions of the festival are specifically addressed in chapter 9.

In what follows, the principal god being honored, the "king of the ghosts," was addressed as Dashiye; the five gods of the Fudezhengshen or Dabogong Temple—Bukit Mertajam's oldest and best known temple—were also being honored (see chapter 7). I was told by informants that one source of local pride was that Bukit Mertajam's nineteen-foot high statue of Dashiye, sitting in majesty with its lap piled high with "spirit money," and facing the tables covered with overflowing offerings, was the tallest and largest in Malaysia. The article states:

> Bukit Mertajam's annual celebration of Yulanshenghui began from today (the 27th) and will go through September 12 for seventeen consecutive days in the courtyard area of the Dabogong Temple on Jalan Pasar, and it will be warmly attended. It is anticipated that this grand occasion's expenses will be $MR 100,000 at the very least. This Yulanshenghui is one of Bukit Mertajam's four magnificent events each year, the other three being the Hindu temple's firewalking ceremony, the Catholic St. Anne's festival, and the Nine Emperor Gods festival of Doumugong Temple lasting nine successive days.
>
> At this year's Yulanshenghui, in addition to inviting Teochew opera troupes to perform [for the gods] for seventeen days, devotees will piously offer in worship dragon joss sticks, pigs and goats approximately 1,000 in number, an estimated 10,000 chickens and ducks, countless pieces of fresh fruit, and cakes in such numbers the eyes cannot believe them.
>
> Tonight at 9:30 p.m., as a prologue for the ceremony of this great occasion, this year's incense urn master, Ong Lien Tuan of Krian Lorry Company Ltd., will lead the festival committee members from his place, respectfully bearing the incense urn to the palatial platform at the Dabogong courtyard for Dashiye.

Comment

Dashiye, the "king of the ghosts," is also known in Mandarin as Dalaoye, and most intimately among Bukit Mertajam people in Hokkien as Podogong. As the presiding god and leader of the band of ghosts of the unknown dead who died violent deaths and come up from the underworld during the seventh lunar month to visit the living, Podogong is a ravenous and gluttonous god with a ferocious temper whose power over his ghostly followers is also the power to cause chaos and disorder in the lives and fortunes of human beings during this month's visit to the phenomenal world. One might think of Podogong as the mafia don or brigand chieftain of the underworld. Human beings therefore are expected to treat him with reverence and honor him and his followers with bountiful offerings—food, liquor, incense, and money, and the opera performance—during the period that his visit, dangerous to humans, is underway. The incense urn master, *luzhu*, was [almost always] a wealthy towkay chosen by Podogong through divination to manage the festival, and the festival committee members, *xieli*, also so chosen, were towkays or men of position drawn from the downtown area, from five neighborhoods within the town, and from four outlying small towns and New Villages.

Moreover the incense urn master has invited a Daoist priest to chant sutras and open the light [to awaken Dashiye] and to call in all the lonely ghosts. This is a very extraordinary and important ceremony.

The incense master and his festival committee have passed on each of the following matters related to the period of the festival:

1. This year's celebration of Yulanshenghui . . . will have the following Teochew opera troupes performing during the period from the 5th day through the 21st day of the seventh lunar month, in order to respectfully honor the gods. . . .
2. Each group which will honor the gods by sponsoring the opera are as follows:
   —5th to 7th day: three days for the public
   —8th day: fish retailers
   —9th day: fish wholesalers
   —10th day: fruit vendors
   —11th day: vegetable retailers
   —12th day: taxi drivers
   —13th day: chicken and duck wholesalers
   —14th day: the 18 trades associates
   —15th day: lorry owners association
   —16th day: roadside hawkers
   —17th day: textile wholesalers, tailors and garment manufacturers
   —18th day: Yufeng Bak-kut-teh [food vendors of "meat/bone tea," a popular Hokkien dish]
   —19th day: Chuah Seong Joo Transport
   —20th day: the devotees of Sungai Rambai [a neighborhood west of downtown]
   —21st day: this year's incense urn master, Krian Lorry Company

Comment

When I asked businessmen why they worshipped Podogong, they replied this was to help them "make money," *zhuanqian*, and to bring them "peace" (*pingan*) and "ease" (*shunli*) in business. After the day's worship of Podogong, the group sponsoring the day's worship and opera assembled in their association hall or some other large space, divided what remained (i.e., the mere material) of the offerings made to the god, butchered and cooked the carcasses of the animals sacrificed, and ate a feast together. The article goes on:

3. The dragon joss stick of every devotee offered in respectful worship must, in accordance with regulations, not exceed 8 feet in height, and moreover must be inserted into a mound for its support [upright].
4. The dragon joss sticks for every day, whether burned down or not, must in accordance with regulations be moved at 12 midnight, and it is hoped that every devotee will abide by this.
5. This year's festival committee members from every neighborhood must come out to assist during the period from the 5th day to the 7th day, the three days for public worship.
6. No one is invited to act like a wild child [go into trance] in front of the platform of Dashiye for the sake of divining lucky lottery numbers from the god.

Comment

Residents told me that in the past the length and size of the "dragon joss sticks" had been the subject of tense negotiation between the police, the incense urn master, and a local leader of the MCA. According to the police, these joss sticks posed a fire hazard, while to local worshippers, their size was a sign of the freedom of religious expression guaranteed them in the Malaysian Constitution.

People being possessed by Podogong posed a social order problem for all authorities.

One might ask: Why would Bukit Mertajam's merchants find it so important to sequentially organize their collective worship of the otherworld's bandit war-lord around their principal lines of business?

"GETTING BY"

The Arts of Deception and the "Typical Chinese"

There is a general assumption in the case for long-term ethnographic work that progressive insights emerge over time, and that the intellectual disorder, the conceptual dead-ends, and many personal frustrations experienced by the anthropologist during an earlier period of fieldwork will eventually give way to these insights—even if much later, when one "understands what our informants are trying to tell us." Long-term ethnography thus has pretensions of revelation to it.

In this book, I cannot claim for my own any such revelations in the case of the Chinese mercantile elite of Bukit Mertajam whose activities were my original object of study in 1978–80. I can infer that during that fieldwork I asked informants questions they considered to be impertinent and indelicate, whose very framing and posing they rejected through evasion, indirection, and refusal to answer. With very few exceptions, whenever I asked them what their business's profits were, the volume of the goods they sold, or what their annual net incomes were, or even posed what I thought was a general, less sensitive question, such as "how is your business doing," I encountered these tactics of resistance. More often than not, this question led to the immediate response, "We're getting by" (*guoliao*), "We can get by" (*keyiguo*), or "We can only get by" "(*zhi guoliao* or *zhi keyiguo*), usually followed by a qualifying phrase like, "but business is difficult" and an elaboration of what made business so hard to do. Thus, for example, the business of a truck owner allowed him to barely "get by" because truck drivers demanded wages that were too high, fuel prices were too high, competition was too severe, or police stopped too many trucks for inspections. (The lack of such a segue into a qualifying clause I came to eventually interpret as—perhaps—the merchant "really doing well.")

I cannot claim revelation because I am not sure whether I could ever have asked the "right" questions in my ongoing and continued efforts in 1978–80 to gather and then aggregate quantitative data on the regional economy of Bukit Mertajam. Did I fail because I had not developed sufficient rapport with specific informants to receive honest or frank answers from them? (And how many trusting informants would I have needed such specific answers from to meet my research objective of rigorously inventorying the level of regional trade passing through the town?) Were the questions I asked ones that—for reasons I did not understand—informants knew the answers to but were unwilling to tell me? And if so, why? What were they hiding—if they were hiding something—and what could *almost everyone* be hiding? Were some being ethnocentric, even xenophobic toward Americans or Westerners—but then what about the others? When people came to trust me, a few spoke candidly, commenting: "The questions you are asking concern somebody's private affairs," *tamen ziji de shiqing*, and thus it was quite understandable that they would not tell me about them. For many months during 1978–80 I persisted in this line of inquiry. What I can say is that, like repeatedly hitting one's head against a hard wall, through my frustration I started to be less obsessed by the question of why the impediment had been erected and became more interested in the nature of the structure of that impediment—to extend the metaphor, a wall of speech based on evasion and indirection. I eventually came to situate it within a class praxis based on the arts of deception, of which the performance of "getting by" was only one element. And this is the major claim of this chapter: that there is a such specific class praxis—that of the small-scale petty capitalist of Bukit Mertajam.

To initiate the inquiry, one must begin by asking what the social field of classes was in Bukit Mertajam? As I note in the previous chapter, there was a classed and gendered identity called *zuo shengyi*, or "doing business," that a very large proportion of Chinese men claimed, whether they were soy-bean drink peddlers or supermarket chain managing directors. "Doing business" was any activity seeking to make a profit from the exchange of commodities. And, whether peddler or manager, when I asked a man whom I had just met about what he did for a living, this was a frequent response, often prelude to saying he was merely "getting by" and then inventorying the many causes of this unhappy condition.

Among those doing business, there was a much smaller subset of men in Bukit Mertajam who were addressed by others (rather than using it to refer to themselves) as *towkay*.[1] Towkays were male business proprietors who were simultaneously the principal legal owners of businesses and the legal heads of the families whose members managed and operated these businesses. Within the municipal boundaries of Bukit Mertajam in 1979, I found approximately 1,300 such businesses operating, and so would estimate, for those interested in counting, that there were between 1,500 and 2,000 people owning them who might be addressed in everyday speech as "towkay." To address someone as towkay who did not own a business was a caricature and insult, and I heard it only rarely, by, say, a man spoofing a close friend for his pretensions. The businesses a towkay owned "stood for" him, and on public occasions and in the Chinese-language press, a man was at times referred to not by his own patrilineal surname and given names, but by the name or names of the firms he owned. More specifically, towkays' ownership of property and their authority over family members meant that they were "persons of position," *you diwei de ren*. I argue below that towkays as persons of position engaged in certain stylized performances that identified them as such not only toward other Chinese—particularly to an audience of working-class Chinese toward whom they held the commanding role in the labor process—but also to a predatory Malaysian state embodied in state officials and police. To be blunt, it was not essential Chinese cultural characteristics that shaped towkay identity-performances before others, but their dialectical responses to people who were not "persons of position" and to an intrusive monitoring tributary state.

An even smaller group of merchants—two hundred to three hundred men (and a very few women)—among these "persons with position" were known as "celebrities," or "persons of renown," *wenren*. Celebrities were not only wealthy—and by common agreement were among the most wealthy property owners living in the town or nearby—but also those who spent their wealth in acts of conspicuous public benevolence to support the institutions of "Chinese society," such as the local Chinese-language schools and native-place associations (figure 3.1; and see chapter 7.) They were therefore socially identifiable among Bukit Mertajam people because of the public ways in which they spent a portion of their wealth. However, one could be extremely wealthy, but if he did not engage in such acts, he would never be regarded as a celebrity.

Finally, at the apex of the class system, there was a very small, very well-known number of extraordinarily wealthy tycoons, *qianwan fuyou ren*, who were renowned because of their wealth and control of corporate business empires in and beyond Malaysia, but to my knowledge, none lived in Bukit Mertajam. They were known because of their national corporate holdings, such as banks and finance companies, with branch offices in Bukit Mertajam, and Bukit Mertajam people "knew" them through the presence of such businesses in town. They were the heroes of the English- and Chinese-language press, the *Wall Street*

Journal Asia, and similar media sources, with their business exploits recounted far and wide.

The Arts of Deception, the Arts of Modesty

One way that rich Chinese try to hide their wealth here in Bukit Mertajam is by looking poor. There is one man who owns the new theater just opening in downtown Bukit Mertajam. He rides around in an old car, wearing just shorts and shirt like everyone else.

—Balasingam, clerk in a local government office, June 18, 1978

DMN: When I first came to Bukit Mertajam I compared the Fudezhengshen temple to the Kuan-yin temple [on Jalan Arumugam Pillai]. I thought the former was very drab and dirty—and never imagined it had so much money.

Yeoh Bak Nam (reporter, *Nanyang Shangbao*): You can't tell from external appearances, *renbuke maoxiang*. Thus, many wealthy Chinese dress very shabbily. Teh Cheok Sah dressed like a beggar, although he owned many pieces of property near the Butterworth ferry, which are now his sons', and was very wealthy.

—Conversation, September 11, 1979, Bukit Mertajam

People in Bukit Mertajam often told me stories about legendary businessmen like Teh Cheok Sah—whose position as one of the town's wealthiest men you could not "tell from external appearances." Here is one about Teh—set in the now-remote 1950s:

A salesman from another state came into downtown Bukit Mertajam one day seeking one of the wealthiest men in the town, Teh Cheok Sah. As he was driving down Jalan Pasar in his car, he spied an old man laboriously pushing a large cart laden with heavy cargo. The old man was dressed in a dirty and drab undershirt and shorts and wore sandals. He abruptly called out to the old man, "Ah-Beh, where is the business of towkay Teh Cheok Sah?" and the old man proceeded to tell him to continue up Jalan Pasar to the towkay's shop house. When he arrived and entered the shop of Cheok Sah, a clerk came out to greet him. "I'm looking for Towkay Teh." The clerk replied: "Well, you must have passed right by him. He is pushing a cart with some goods all by himself down Jalan Pasar, and wanted to save the expense of hiring someone else to do it."

Despite his stinginess at business, Teh was nonetheless a celebrity, for after the Japanese occupation he and several other Teochews came together to rebuild the hall and restart the activities of the Teochew Association, and he was distinguished by his arduous work and his "eminent contribution" of a large sum of money to the effort (Hanjiang Gonghui 1965).

Such stories were not all from the past. One day, I was visiting Mr. Ng, owner of Heng Ee Agricultural Supply, at his small store front located downtown. He, two of his friends, Mr. Lau and Mr. Fong, and I were sitting on stools ringed around his desk where he held court, looking out across his stacks of imported fertilizer bags and bottles of herbicides to the street beyond. Mr. Teow, an old man who owned a large parcel of land in the eastern suburb of Kampung Bahru came by briefly. When I had seen him previously at Heng Ee, like this day, he was dressed in shorts, shirt and a rumpled old hat, and came up riding a bicycle which (I was later told) he had ridden all the way in from his landholdings to the downtown district instead of driving a car. He spoke Hokkien but no Mandarin, so we had little to say to each other.[2] After he left, the talk focused on him.

Mr. Lau, the owner of a small apparel factory, first observed that Teow owned 2 to 3 million ringgit worth of property: rubber estates, houses, and orchards with durian and rambutan, among other things. Mr. Fong, a land broker, then went on to say that Teow was a "typical Chinese," *dianxing huaren*. Fong explained: "Teow began his life poor, with his father having very little property, but by using his bare hands he established his own family/business [*baishou chengjia*]. He still works every day, he acts as if he is still poor and doesn't give himself any special comforts. He rides everywhere on a bicycle, and sometimes does physical labor." Lau said, "If Teow didn't work every day, he would fall sick." Fong went on, "Although Teow is very rich, he is a good man. For example, he lets people live on his land without paying rent. In fact, my younger brother has built a house on his land but pays him no rent." Ng was listening. Hearing this, he laughed and interjected, "Perhaps Teow lets people only live without rent on the parts of his land that have no development potential [*mei you fazhan jianzai*], while he builds his own houses on parts of his land with more potential!"

Lau and Fong then compared Teow to Teh Cheok Sah. Lau said, "Teh owned about [MR$] 10,000,000 in property in Bukit Mertajam, and one street of the town was named after him, Jalan Cheok Sah, where he and his descendants since his death ten years previously owned most of the buildings, including the Cheok Sah Cinema. He was a legend for being stingy [*linse*]. He rode about in a very old car, he never ate anything more than salted fish. He started out his life a very poor man who drove a hand pushcart, *renliche*, and delivered goods. This was before he became rich." Fong commented, "The sort of Chinese like Teh Cheok Sah and

Teow belong to the older generation. Things are different today. All people like myself do is to sit around all day."

Teh, who died in the 1960s, and Teow were by no means "typical" statistically in the sense of falling anywhere near the mean of the distribution of accumulated wealth and income held by towkays—they were conspicuously at the high end, and in fact towkays I talked to were consistent in that they counted Teh, his sons, and Teow as among the most wealthy merchants in Bukit Mertajam. However, the stories told about Teh and Teow were narratives that did not describe but instead *prescribed* the "typical" behavior to which towkays and men of position were to aspire: these stories made simultaneously moral and aesthetic claims. Moral, in that these stories exemplified traits that were highly esteemed; aesthetic in that they prescribed a class sensibility or style associated with these traits. This Mr. Fong conceded straightforwardly in noting that "things are different today," and that he himself, unlike either Teh and Teow, failed to live up to these claims by "sitting around all day," although like them he dressed in shorts, short-sleeve white shirts, and sandals. What truths do stories like these set out within the broader moral economy of Chinese petty capitalism?

To be a "typical Chinese" was to be a man who started out poor, and worked hard while learning a business as an employee. Such a man was unpretentious even as he accumulated capital, and eventually through his own efforts, including his physical labor, managed to start a flourishing business and raise a family (using his "bare hands," *baishou*; "to make a family/business," *chengjia*; or "raise up a family/business," *qijia*). He was usually an immigrant from southeastern China, and more likely than not, poorly educated with little or no Chinese schooling, and thus spoke only Hokkien, Teochew, or some other "dialect." Once economically successful, this man still dressed in the unpretentious clothing of a worker, wore the distinctive colonial apparel of undershirt, shorts, and sandals, and like a worker, performed physical labor and deprived himself of physical comfort, even as his business continued to flourish. Although he might personally be "stingy," the typical Chinese was still "a good man" because, like Teh (who not only contributed to the rebuilding of the Teochew Association after the war, but was one of its founders in 1926),[3] he was generous in his financial support of Chinese society, or like Teow, provided generously for less wealthy persons, like Mr. Fong's younger brother. He was a celebrity.

The typical Chinese, it was said, was generous to all the associations of Chinese society, but above all in his contributions to Chinese schools because they afforded later generations the opportunities for Chinese-language schooling that he himself had forgone by dint of his childhood poverty and having to "come out" early in life into the world of work and commerce. The biographical entries for leaders and prominent contributors to the associations of Chinese society, as recorded in their "commemorative books," *jiniantekan*, published on the occasion of their anniversaries, were larded with formulaic ascriptions of worthiness. For example, taking two entries from the Golden Anniversary Commemorative Book of the regional Hokkien Association, *Hokkien Hoay Kuan*, one prominent member "has a natural temperament of honesty, is a person who is easy to approach because he is both just and easygoing, and in all cases does his utmost to support projects of general interest to society" while another is described as, "beyond his business, being enthusiastic for the general interest of society, focusing on Chinese education, unstintingly contributing money and effort to it" (Hokkien Hoay Kuan, Seberang Perai, 1976, 147, 145).

These stories about typical Chinese—the "older generation," *lao yibei*—must be understood within a two-dimensional imagined social field that diacritically differentiated such self-made men of "the older generation" from towkays of the current generation of thirty to fifty years of age (who formed most of my informants), that differentiated Chinese-educated towkays from those who were English educated, that distinguished people in all three positions from Malays, and that contrasted all these from the unmarked position of the Chinese working class (see figure 3.1).

What I argue in the rest of this chapter is that men of position located themselves within this imagined social field that positioned people differently in terms of their moral worth, and that this envisioned social field and the set of practices it framed were linked in the late 1970s to the contradictions and tensions in the social reproduction of Chinese petty capitalists—with respect to one another and to the predatory logic of the Malaysian state.

In one respect, one either had wealth due to one's business abilities—one's cleverness, resourcefulness, hard work, capacity to save money—or one did not. In another respect, one either appeared to "just get by" or one did not, but acted instead like a "big shot," *dapai*, that is, a person of high position. "Typical Chinese" occupied the privileged place in this moral landscape: they were said to have great wealth due to their abilities as businessmen, yet they appeared to just "get by." They dressed modestly, even shabbily, they spoke only dialects, they could be crude in speech. Their homes and shop houses were messy, old-fashioned, unpretentious—although they might have two, three, or more wives with children by each set up in separate households. To act as if one was just "getting by" was to put on a public performance of poverty, smallness, and thrift, because there was so little to go around, doing physical labor oneself to save costs, being industrious—but this was also a performance of desirable modesty and lack of pretentiousness which the big shot was incapable of. This was a performance on the stage of public (visible) practice, set before an audience of other Chinese merchants and of predatory state functionaries.

There were others who in appearance were much like typical Chinese but had no wealth. Those others belonged in the un(re)marked category—they were "workers." Workers did "just get by." But could their appearances not also sometimes deceive? Who was a worker and who might not be was at times unclear: external appearances might deceive. Thus, for instance, towkays repeatedly told me that the fried *guitiao* (noodle) vendors who rented space on the edges of coffee shops were often secretly wealthy despite their drab appearance and unprepossessing stalls because they pocketed income without paying taxes to the government. Still guitiao vendors "did business" and were self-employed. Workers might be better off than their physical labor, low wages, simple clothing, crude speech, and body movements suggested because of their varied ways of making illegal "outside income," *waikuai*—coming from the bag of Thai *pulut* (sticky) rice that

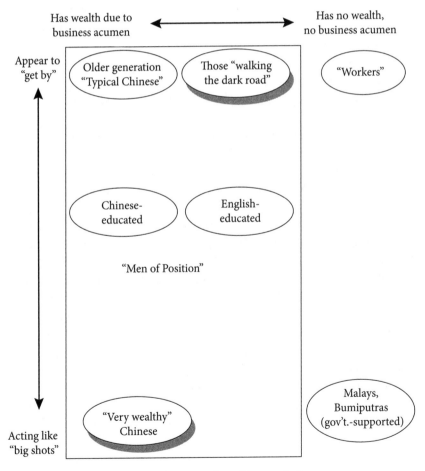

FIGURE 3.1 A moral topography: men of position, and others

drivers smuggled in across the border in the back of a truck, or from the pilferage of goods of "the boss" from his warehouse, and from many other sources. Even if they were what they presently appeared to be, they might well be aspiring to finding sources of waikuai. Their ambiguity thus made them dangerous. Even more vaguely positioned within this envisioned social field of value were those who "walked on the dark road." These were petty businessmen or working men who might appear just to be "getting by" but who were amassing large fortunes by engaging in illegal narcotics or distilled liquor smuggling and sales, and I turn to them and to the rumors they generated at the end of this chapter.

"Just getting by" performed by men of position thus represented a stylized performance of poverty, earnest effort and modesty not only before one another but also before the monitoring eyes of state officials (and other outsiders). Getting by was approved of as in part the practice of the art of deception aimed at the state, but also in part as the style of male self-presentation in "doing business" aimed not only at cultivating the self but also at enhancing one's reputation, *mingyu*, among other men of position.

This envisioned social field with the identities/identifications of people located on it in terms of their moral worth was a hybrid one in that it not only situated the class positions of "men of position," but also because it indexed socially important and simultaneously generational ethno-cultural and concretely spatial differences. The "older generation" made up of typical Chinese were uneducated with a few years of schooling in China or Malaya that allowed them, at most, to recognize some written Chinese characters. In contrast to this "older generation," "our generation," *women de yibei*—most of the men I interviewed—were the grown sons of the older generation who had inherited their fortunes, not founded them by their own efforts. Or they were professionals—accountants or engineers, say. They were either "Chinese-educated," *shou huawen jiaoyu de,* or "English-educated," *shou yingwen jiaoyu de.*

Differently positioned were the "Chinese educated" of "our generation," men like Mr. Fong, Mr. Lau, and Mr. Ng. They had finished not only primary but also secondary school where Mandarin was the spoken language of instruction and written Chinese the language of texts. These schools were those supported by Chinese society, for they inculcated Confucian values of propriety, manners, and respect for authority, that is, for elders by juniors and for men by women, by means of memorization of the China classics and related texts from Taiwan and pre-Maoist China. In these schools, the ideal form of learning came not from seeking general mastery over a subject, *xue*, but instead from taking to heart through memorization a text such as one of the Confucian classics, that is, to "read" books, *dushu*—to be able to recite, standing before the teacher, passages from the texts accurately recalled from memory. Even technical and "modern" knowledge such as mathematics and physical sciences were acquired by a similar pedagogy based on rote memorization. The Chinese-educated, unlike the older generation, spoke Mandarin fluently and could thus read and comprehend the articles appearing in national and regional Chinese-language newspapers like *Nanyang Shangbao, Guanghua Ribao*, and *Xingbin Ribao*, which simultaneously reported on Chinese business in Malaysia and beyond, and on the "local news," *difang xingwen*, about Bukit Mertajam's Chinese society. Although these men had acquired the benefits of Chinese-language education, it was unclear whether they possessed the virtues of the "older generation" who rose from being impoverished immigrants to men of position by appearing to "just get by," by being industrious, clever, stingy, yet committed to Chinese society. In contrast to the older generation, Chinese-educated men were deemed more likely to dress "smart," (e.g., wear tailored batik shirts and trousers, an expensive watch and gold ring, and imported Italian shoes) and drive expensive cars like Volvos and Mercedes-Benzes, and spend their money freely, and thus less likely to accumulate wealth.

"English-educated" men had studied in "English-language" schools, but these were government-controlled, and thus such men were morally ambiguous. This presumed among other things that such men could neither speak Mandarin taught in the Chinese-language secondary schools, nor could they read the Chinese-language newspapers. They were thus cut off from the broader ecumenium of culture and commerce accessible to the Chinese-educated. Despite their family backgrounds in businesses or their degrees as accountants, engineers, attorneys, or other professionals, they had to speak to other Bukit Mertajam people either in a dialect like Hokkien if the others could not speak English, and were thus cut off from the rhetorical competence associated with Mandarin speech that defined men of position in Chinese society. Their capacity to accumulate capital was particularly suspect. A young man on leave from studying sociology at the Australian National University diagnosed the problem of the professional employed by others through the words of his father, one of the most wealthy towkays of Bukit Mertajam: "Chinese will always try to employ labor rather than being employed by others. When I returned here from Australia where I was working as a research assistant, my father asked me, 'Why do you want to be employed in Australia when you can employ people here in Bukit Mertajam?'" The English-educated of "our generation" who had not acquired the values instilled by Chinese-language education were seen as most subject to the blandishments of the English-language media and the government to dress smart, spend money freely and conspicuously, and try to act like "big shots."

I want to suggest that how towkays saw themselves and others within the envisioned social field of petty capitalists in Bukit Mertajam was grounded in the distribution of values centered on an articulation of the acquisition of wealth with the arts of deception, and that, for the class to which these men belonged, this formed a specific ideology that also represented a grander hegemonic project with respect to other Chinese. No matter that "our generation" of men of position might also wear T-shirts, shorts, and sandals while doing business; no matter that a Chinese-educated towkay might dress smart and drive a late-model Mercedes-Benz sedan while speaking of his early "bitter struggle and hard labor," *kekunailao*; no matter that a wealthy man in the "older generation" might not be able to speak Mandarin but had to call on better-educated employees to read out their ghostwritten speeches for them at association banquets; no matter that a rare working man might accumulate wealth from waikuai, smuggling narcotics or winning the *ekor* "four character lotteries" and turn into a man of position overnight. The accumulation of wealth, even as one averred that one was just "getting by," pointed to a practitioner of the art of honorable deception, which provided the everyday standards of value against which men of position in Bukit Mertajam were judged—the extant moral order. This provided the unquestioned distribution of values with respect to which certain practices stood out—like honorific addressing (e.g., calling a wealthy young man "towkay" to his face followed by the latter's jovial denial that he was such), transmitting rumors (e.g., about why a guitiao vendor suddenly appeared wealthy), demonstrating polite indulgence (toward an uneducated man of position who dared to give his association's banquet speech in Hokkien), making a caricature (e.g., of a truck driver or hawker who contributed too much of his money to an association fund-raiser), or making behind-the-back criticism (e.g., of a wealthy towkay of the older generation who refused to donate to Chinese schools).

This envisioned social field among men of position was, as well, a representation of people's positions in social space. The older generation and "our generation" of the Chinese-educated and English-educated men of position all belonged to local Chinese society. Workers and those walking the dark road were on its edges. But beyond the locale of Bukit Mertajam there were also those men who were very wealthy Chinese with "thousand ten-thousands," *qianwan*, ringgit in wealth, who all men of position "knew of" through either news in the Chinese-language or English-language media and by rumor—but who lived elsewhere—in Penang, Kuala Lumpur, Singapore. Few local men of position, except for a very few "celebrities," could say that they "knew" these tycoons personally. They were known as not only extraordinarily wealthy but also as well-connected politically to the ruling Malay elite who led UMNO, the party in power, and this was exemplified in the feudalist titles they received from Malay royalty, such as Tan Sri and Datuk.[4] There was for instance the fabled Datuk Loh Boon Siew, "the motorcycle king" who owned the franchise for distributing Honda motorcycles in the northern region of West Malaysia, who lived in Penang. These men were the economic elite of Malaysia—the big bankers, the hotel owners, those who held national monopolies. Undeniably men of position, these thousand ten-thousand men were "big shots," but they were absent from the town's Chinese society.

In contrast, in this envisioned social field whose positions indexed moral worth, Malays occupied the position furthest both in wealth and appearance from the older generation. According to towkays, they had neither wealth nor business acumen, and instead of "just getting by," they acted in unseemly ways like "big shots." They relied solely on the wealth and power of the national government to get ahead. I describe how they were viewed later in this chapter.

"Getting by" performed by men of position required a stylized performance of poverty and smallness before other towkays—before whom, after all, it conveyed an attitude of modesty and propriety—but more than that, the monitoring eyes of state officials. Getting by was a performance based on the presumed deception of representatives of the state and hostile others but was also a style of male self-presentation of "doing business" aimed at cultivating not only the self, but also at enhancing one's reputation, *mingyu*, among other men of position.

"The Passions and the Interests": War by Other Means

The problem with Chinese in Malaysia is that they are Chinese. They are throughout Southeast Asia the waste. Nobody wants them. They can't unite. They need a change of heart. Always, if they are with someone richer or better off than themselves, they try to bring him down, rather than thinking his success reflects favorably on all Chinese.

—Ooi Tiam Hooi, English-educated municipal councilor, Seberang Perai, 1979

In their discourse, towkays displayed the anxieties of a condition mediated by two strong desires: first, to avoid falling into the condition of the wage laborer whose labors were governed by someone else, and second, the desire to accumulate capital to the point that the process became self-perpetuating, and thus to move up into the ranks of the wealthy businessmen who were "celebrities."[5] Most towkays did not hire wage laborers but employed only the unpaid labor of their family members—particularly that of their wives and daughters.[6] For these men, capital accumulation arose primarily from self-exploitation, the exploitation of family members, and the volatile profits derived from mercantile exchange. The prospects for most towkays for expanded capital accumulation were tenuous at best. They recognized that their prospects depended not only on their own efforts, but also on factors external to the local sphere of circulation, such as the international demand for primary-product exports (e.g., rubber, palm oil, hardwoods) marketed by local merchants, monopolists' control of imports, and the global business cycle. In short, local businessmen in their pursuit of wealth faced conditions of great uncertainty and insecurity. It was from these that their obsessive concern with the processes of what can be called the "production of production" derived.

Local Chinese businessmen spoke of their relations to their competitors, customers, suppliers, and employees in business, like politics, as war by other means. A kind of backstage talk (Scott 1985) among towkays that I was privy to contrasted strongly with the face-to-face, cordial interactions between businessmen in public. Told between friends sitting together over tea around shop house desks or over lunch in nearby restaurants, their stories assessed the pragmatic ethics of the businessmen not present—tales implying that what was given to one was taken from someone else—an advantageous price, business patronage, a higher quality of product sold, and so on. Men spoke of bitter and intense competition, breaches of trust between trading partners, the theft of patronage, disputes between sellers and buyers over prices and the qualities of goods sold, and of deep antagonisms and distrust between merchants and their employed clerks and laborers.

Merchants characterized others in the same "line of business," the *hangye*, whether fish wholesalers, truck transporters, or whoever, as persons to view with caution and even distrust, for the speaker envisioned them as committed to "stealing" his own customers or his production and marketing techniques, in the course of doing business. The owner of a small basket manufacturing enterprise drew a contrast starkly:

> We Chinese are less hesitant to share with outsiders our secrets and indulgences such as visiting prostitutes together, or going out to bars, than we are in taking outsiders into our confidence about how we make baskets and other techniques, or our marketing. We fear that outsiders will become our competitors after they learn our techniques and find out who our customers are.

The older male voice here can be noted and, again, it is consumption—even where illicit, as in visiting prostitutes—which is open to view to the (male) outsider, not the esoteric arts of production, or Marx's "hidden abode." A discourse of reserve and distrust extended not only to those merchants already in the same line of business as one's own but also to all others who could, potentially, become one's competitors. One potentially had enemies everywhere. The sphere of technique, the organization of labor, the physical composition of commodities produced, and the sphere of exchange, of prices offered, credit arrangements made, and so on: these were shrouded from the in-looker's gaze and inquiries of those who were not family members.

Towkays spoke of suspicion and distrust between sellers and the buyers of their products. Each spoke of reasons to lack trust in the other side. Sellers offered assurances to potential buyers that the quality of their commodities would be of a certain level (e.g., fertilizers would have a balanced chemical composition and contain specific chemicals suitable to local soils). Buyers made promises about the amounts of money they would pay for set quantities of goods sold and when they would make payments under credit terms. Still, accusations of bad faith and sharp practice passed in both directions in the form of backbiting gossip, but occasionally this was spoken about overtly. For example, one of my field assistants later became a salesman of motor oil additives marketed to truck owners. At one point, he told me that although he made oral assurances to owners that his product would protect truck engines from frequent breakdowns and the need for overhauls, nonetheless he never provided certain owners with written guarantees—mentioning them by name to me—for he knew that they overloaded their trucks with freight, which shortened their engine life. These truck owners, he said, distrusted his unwillingness to make written guarantees and, claiming that his product was unsatisfactory, held back a certain percentage of payments promised to him.

Although firms with (nonfamily) employees constituted a minority of all firms, owners and employees spoke of tense and often overtly hostile relationships that existed between those on each side—people often called their counterparts "disputatious." Towkays indicated that, when they could, they kept back information about production techniques or customers from their employees because they feared that the latter—once they had saved some money—might establish themselves as competitors. A man who had previously been an office manager in a truck transport firm told me that many truck owners refused to allow "outsiders" (i.e., not family members) to become the managers of their companies' outstation branches, because they feared workers would "steal" or "drag away" their consigners and start their own rival transport firms. Merchants attacked the honesty of their employees, whom they accused either to their face or indirectly of stealing goods and other property, while in the case of the truck transport industry, drivers said that their bosses' lack of confidence in and hostility toward them led to stealing, although they also gave other reasons for their pilferage.

While talk about one's potential and actual adversaries was common, who one's allies were was mentioned only in passing in the specific context of a relationship with them. Despite talk about generalized animosity, business-men formed long-standing alliances among trading partners and those who did each other favors in commerce. These relationships even crossed genera-tions for those whose fathers traded with each other. Among truck owners in the case of the industry I knew best, one's adversaries were competitors, that is, owners whose trucks carried similar kinds of freight (either "miscellaneous" or "bulk" freight) along the same routes as one's own trucks—and thus competed with one for the same consigners; allies were truck owners whom a truck owner would contract with to carry freight to pass on beyond one's own routes in return for a "commission" (Nonini 2003). Truck towkays mentioned that such contracting relationships lasted for years and could lead to strong friendships between truck owners.

However reliable and trustworthy business counterparts might actually be, towkays spoke of commercial life as war by other means. There was the proverb about knowing one's competitors: *zhici zhibi, baizhan baisheng* ("if you know the situations of both sides, in a hundred battles you will always emerge victori-ous"). Of one's business partner, you must always attempt to discern his fun-damental interests if you were to realize his intentions: *duming zhixin* ("if his stomach is clear to you, you will know his heart"). And one must never adopt a vulnerable stance toward those you have to trust, like employees, but one must not be hostile either: *hairen zhi xin bu ke you, fangren zhi xin bu ke wu* ("you can't intend to harm someone, but you can't do without seeking to protect your-self from him")."

Ooi Tiam Hooi's assessment of Chinese in Southeast Asia as "the waste . . . [who] can't unite... [who] try to bring down" someone more successful, reflected the broad sense among owners of petty capital of the profound risks associated with their class reproduction vis-à-vis one another, and this sense of insecurity threaded through the everyday performance of their class praxis.

Huānà Tales: "After All, Isn't Cheating Someone a Matter of Making Money?"

Huānà—Foreigner, non-Chinese (used by Chinese in Malaya when referring to Malays)

—N. C. Bodman, *Spoken Amoy Hokkien*

The semipublic list of complaints enumerated by Bukit Mertajam merchants and other residents against the Malaysian national government and Malays in general was an argument about rights denied and citizenship marginalized—an argument about the rights of Chinese citizens within the Malaysian nation-state.[7] State laws and policies that excluded Chinese from universities and government employment, prohibited them from setting up their own universities, and seized their property through the Industrial Coordination Act, were "unfair," *bu gongping*, and made Chinese into "second-class citizens," *dierdeng gongming*. The recital of the list of complaints was, for all that, a claim for inclusion and recognition in the Malaysian nation-state. But as I note in the next chapter, to Bukit Mertajam Chinese the Malaysian state took a highly personalized form—specific Malays, whether police constables, utility inspectors, or high-level ministers, stood for a national government which, in all its hostile policies and programs, was a government of, by, and for Malays against Chinese. And according to my informants in Bukit Mertajam, how undeserving these Malays were! Towkays told me repeatedly that most Malays were poor, but this was only because they were lazy. Malays expected the government to do everything for them, and showed no initiative or independent effort to get ahead by establishing their own businesses. Malays who, encouraged by government loans and training programs, entered business invariably failed because of various weaknesses in their character.

The critical characterizations of Malays in business took the form of an extended morality tract on how *not* to succeed in business, and on the ways in which Chinese were successful because they were unlike Malays. Malays just starting out in business wasted their capital on buying new cars, new clothes, and other expensive items instead of spending their money on suppliers in order to establish a line of credit, as Chinese would. Malay businessmen dressed in new clothes, acted like "big shots," and thus did not encourage others—that is, Chinese businessmen—to assist them by providing patronage, unlike Chinese businessmen who dressed far more plainly. Malays, unlike Chinese, did not understand the importance of keeping their capital "turning," even if at a loss: as Mr. Lau, a schoolteacher put it, "And, when they do business, Malays cannot accept or are not aware of why to sell at a loss, while Chinese do this often. Chinese do this to keep their capital turning, but Malays cannot understand the value of buying a cup at one ringgit and then selling it for [MR$] eighty cents." Malays were also troublesome as business partners, because if disagreements arose, they would immediately report or threaten to report their complaint to the government, while Chinese partners working with one another would attempt to talk the matter over and settle it among themselves.

Bumiputras were thus depicted as exemplifying the antithesis of the most advantageous traits of Chinese businessmen. But this is not to say that such contrasts always glorified Chinese businessmen, for at times they actually revealed a more ambivalent stance toward Chinese business practices, one reaffirming a racialist imaginary. As Mr. Lau, a man who claimed close friendship with one of the town's wealthiest towkays, expatiated:

> LAU: Malays don't realize how difficult it is to do business. So much depends on bitter and patient labor, *keku nailao*. They also don't appreciate how competitive business is here in Malaysia, and they don't know how often Chinese companies go bankrupt.
>
> DMN: I recall asking one Malay why Malays did not grow their own vegetables to market and he replied that he feared that when it came to marketing their vegetables, Chinese merchants would cheat them.
>
> LAU: Well, if Malays attempt all on their own to market their own vegetables, Chinese middlemen would most likely cheat them by taking advantage of their ignorance of prevailing market prices, and so set a very low price for their produce. But after all isn't cheating someone a matter of making money? [*Pian ren jiu shi zhuanqian, duibudui?*]

Towkays told stories of strategies by Chinese merchants aimed at taking advantage of Bumiputras or resisting government practices against them. Among acquaintances they trusted, merchants recounted these with a mixture of pride and scornful glee. These strategies were both individual and collective. As to the former, Mr. Ng described the existence of what he called "trolling for money companies," or *laoqian gongsi*. These were companies that Chinese brought into existence with the sole aim of cheating someone else, and which the proprietors then allowed to go out of existence or become bankrupt. He gave as an example a friend of his who had cheated a Malay-owned company of several hundred thousand Malaysian ringgit worth of goods extended to his company on credit and had then disappeared. Being aware of the stated importance of trust among Chinese merchants, I was somewhat taken aback by this and asked him about it. His reply was that "the trick is to cheat the international companies or Malay-owned companies," and not locally owned Chinese businesses.

Narratives of collective resistance described moves of opposition to the Malaysian state and to the large-scale corporations it controlled as public secrets among local Chinese. In one instance, a large cigarette manufacturer, the Malaysian Tobacco Company, owned in part by the Malaysian government, had refused to make a contribution to the fund for the proposed Merdeka University. Local merchants joined other Chinese in a widespread consumer boycott of the cigarette brands produced by this company, in combination with similar actions elsewhere in urban Malaysia. Members of neighborhood gangs or secret societies helped convince recalcitrant merchants to go along. As a result, the company's sales fell drastically despite government denunciations of the boycott.

In each of these instances, Chinese merchants resisted actions sponsored by the government in ways it considered illegal, although the forms of resistance taken were quite different: commercial guile for personal benefit in the first example, widespread passive resistance in the second. In each instance, however, actions adopted against Malays or the Malaysian state were sanctioned more or less enthusiastically by local Chinese merchants.

Public Benevolence and Meritorious Consumption

Take from society, but use for society [*Quzhi shehui, yongyu shehui*].

—Common Bukit Mertajam merchants' expression

In the contrast between local Chinese society (represented by its paradigmatic exemplars, its wealthier businessmen) and the Malaysian state with its encompassing and hostile population of Malay peasants, petty bureaucrats, policemen, and army officers, it is not difficult to see how the definitions of legality put forward by that state were rejected by the moral economy of Chinese in Bukit Mertajam. And yet the moral economy was deeper still: it extended beyond a negation of the Malaysian state and of Malay society to a negation of one of its own silences. That is, citizenship in local Chinese society was defined in terms of public benevolence and meritorious consumption, but in this definition, there was an oversight, a silence, for above all something was being left unsaid. This silence stated: it matters little how one acquired capital *once one has it*, but instead it is how one *distributes* and *consumes* one's capital for the benefit of local Chinese society that is esteemed. In the words of a Chinese saying I was told: "Take from society, but use for society." And in the sphere of public benevolence and meritorious consumption, the rules and the strategies for establishing one's position and level in local Chinese society were straightforward, conventional, and almost awkwardly unambiguous, known to all Chinese small-scale capitalists in the town.

If sufficiently large, wealth spent by a businessman on donations to any one or more of a variety of Chinese associations led invariably to invitations to become an officer of these associations. In this town with some twenty-five thousand to thirty thousand Chinese in 1980, there were a large number of such associations and groups, such as temple management committees, native-place associations (e.g., Hokkien or Teochew associations), surname halls, school old boys' clubs, religious festival committees, school boards, occupational and professional organizations (e.g., fish wholesalers association), sports groups, and neighborhood development councils. A towkay making a generous donation eventually would be invited to become an officer of these organizations and his later donations for association activities would be recorded faithfully and with much fanfare in articles appearing in the three regional Chinese-language newspapers. Even the size of the photographs of officers and prominent members mounted on the walls of association meeting halls varied depending on the amounts of the monetary contributions made by their subjects. Less prominent members had the amounts of their contributions scrupulously recorded below their same-sized photographs lining the walls.

Conspicuous public benevolence by businessmen, in the form of money contributed for the welfare of local Chinese, took many forms, some of which can be listed here to illustrate the point: donations to building fund drives for local schools or Chinese-owned hospitals; subsidies to sponsor a religious festival on a birthday of a god in the Daoist/Buddhist pantheon; purchases of land for temples and parks; donations to send aid to Cambodian refugees; payments to funds for poor Chinese needing expensive surgery; and much more. Such forms of largesse for the public weal were almost invariably celebrated and praised in banquets held in honor of contributors and were listed by donor and amount in articles in the regional Chinese-language press on the occasion in question for the consumption of local readers. If a businessman wanted to develop a reputation as a "celebrity" or "man of renown," a wenren, within the district, then he made such contributions, and they invariably brought him this reputation.

Within this moral economy of philanthropy, it mattered little how towkays accumulated capital—for, within their families and their businesses, this was "their affair," *taman de shiqing*. And whose business could bear up well against outsiders' scrutiny?—and why, as I described above, allow it anyway? Towkays whose wealth when viewed from outside as ill-gotten were as eligible as any other businessmen to acquire positions of formal leadership in associations, or to become "men of renown." No reproach about their characters or their actions prevented their participation, and the only criticism that one could make, if any, had to do with whether the amounts of their contributions to Chinese associations, schools, and temples were as generous as they could and should be. The implicit message was quite clear: ask not how or from whence the towkay accumulates capital, but ask instead that he expend it in such a way as to benefit Chinese society—for this he will receive his reward of prestige and social influence.

The Crypto-Geography of "Traveling the Dark Road": Representational Spaces that Represent What Cannot Be Spoken Of

Assistant Registrar of Companies, Penang: Occasionally the Commercial Crime detail of the police asks me for names of directors of companies and other details in my files of documents, like the memoranda of association. These files cover the entire northern region of Penang, Kedah and Perlis states. About 80 percent of these inquiries concern Bukit Mertajam.

DMN: What kind of illegal activities?

ARoC, Penang: Mostly smuggling of drugs, padi, and other goods. Some companies are incorporated as limited companies only as a front for other, illegal activities. You've clearly picked a difficult place to do research on Chinese business in.

—January 11, 1980, at the Registry of Companies, Penang

Businessmen here in BM take risks. They prefer to, in order to make money quickly. Thus, they indulge in illegal activities such as local manufacturing of morphine. That way, they can turn their capital, and take [MR$] 1,000 invested in drugs to do [MR$] 10,000 worth of business.

—Booi Loi-Fong, insurance agent, March 18, 1979

In the past Bukit Mertajam business people used their heart, *yongxin*, to get ahead. They learned how to get along with others and ways of working with others to make money. Now, instead, businessmen here use their guts, *yongdan*. They take big risks to become wealthy through drug smuggling and other dark means. Whenever some businessman becomes wealthy in only a few years, people believe this is because he has engaged in drug smuggling or something like it.

—Sim Kim Nan, retired primary school headmaster, November 14, 1979

The first day I arrived to visit the town of Bukit Mertajam in April 1978, I discovered that it and its surrounding area possessed a certain international notoriety. One of my first conversations was with Mr. Ng, proprietor of Heng Ee Agricultural Supply, who became one of my closest friends. He was among the Gerakan Party stalwarts who greeted me when I stepped out of the taxi that had brought me over from Penang. A few hours later, Mr. Ng, two other men, and I were sitting around the table in the back room of the textile shop of a friend of his. He asked with a sly smile, "Have you ever heard of Bukit Mertajam before coming to Malaysia? Do you know it's famous internationally, and even well known in Holland?" I demurred, saying that I knew where the town was in Malaysia, and a few other things, but I was not aware of its international reputation, and could Mr. Ng tell me more? "Well, in Amsterdam, the police recently arrested someone from Bukit Mertajam, whom they caught there for transporting and selling heroin brought from Malaysia. So Bukit Mertajam is well known there as a heroin distribution center." I asked them why the town was so favored with this reputation? "The transport facilities here are excellent, because of Bukit Mertajam's place in wholesale trade. Also, all sorts of contacts have been made by Bukit Mertajam people in the course of their trade. If a shop house appears all closed down, nothing going on, it is possible that heroin is being refined there. And if someone who you thought was poor suddenly starts driving a Mercedes or shows a lot of money, then people suspect he's involved in drug trafficking."

Bukit Mertajam was indeed notorious—at least among government officials, as my conversation with the assistant registrar of companies repeated above makes clear. To officials there were a set of equivalences: the residents of the town were Chinese, they were greedy for wealth and would do anything to gain it, and their antisocial activities harmed the nation as a whole. Thus their smuggling, refining, and sale of heroin and morphine were only the most egregious of many such practices, with the illegal distilling and sales of unrefined *samsu* liquor following as a distant second. But what did Bukit Mertajam residents say to respond to this condemnation, or perhaps better put, how did they respond to it without speaking of it?

Wittgenstein wrote in the *Tractatus Logico-Philosophicus* (Wittgenstein 1933) that "that which we cannot speak of, we must pass over in silence," but in daily life, as distinct from philosophy, silence is often highly eloquent. Here I want to suggest that even as state encompassment of Chinese spaces in Bukit Mertajam proceeded in the name of the NEP, not only did a new antistatist sensibility among Chinese emerge to thwart the claims of the state, but it did so without announcing its name. It was radically different from the list of complaints about the Malaysian government's discriminatory policies which I described above. At the level of discreet speech, the latter was a discourse about "unfairness" in how Chinese citizens were treated by the governing Malay majority, adjudicated through a notion of citizen "rights" which the government ignored. Working within the frame set by the state's recognition of group rights, one might take this discourse to be a very model of discursive encompassment of citizens' subjectivities: Chinese were "second class citizens" but still citizens.

However, if this was encompassment, for many Bukit Mertajam residents it was only superficially so. I wish to argue that in strong contrast to it were rumors and telltale spatial signs regarding residents who "traveled the dark road," *zoule heian de luxian*. A metaphor of mobility interesting in its own right, "traveling the dark road" referred to persons who sought to gain wealth through illegal and admittedly antisocial means, especially narcotics trafficking and processing. Narcotics trafficking, people told me, shadowed the transnational connections that businessmen in the Bukit Mertajam truck transport and fish wholesaling industries had established with Chinese merchants trading out of the fisheries of southern Thailand. Both groups shared China native-place and linguistic affinities as Teochews and in some cases had actual kinship ties. People thus speculated about the smuggling of narcotics from the Golden Triangle through southern Thailand based on these connections, or the opportunities for trafficking (e.g., by employees) they provided.

Traveling the dark road constituted a circulating message based on improvised signs that set apart specific features of the everyday landscapes of Bukit Mertajam with the stamp of an antistatist imaginary of capital accumulation—an imaginary that repudiated being stuck as a Chinese business family constrained by smallness, corruption, and state predation. These rumors did not dispute outright so much as displace the moral narrative of the New Economic Policy, which was that Malay economic betterment would develop the whole nation, even if some (i.e., Chinese) had to suffer for the nation's good. At the same time, traveling the dark road, something never declared yet continually alluded to in these rumors, also undermined the conventional trope of Chinese rags-to-riches-and-fame featured in the standard biographies of successful businessmen in the association commemoration books and newspapers—"raising up one's family with one's own bare hands," *baishou qijia*, through hard work, thrift, and intelligence, and then, once having made one's fortune, "enthusiastically supporting Chinese society" through one's philanthropy.

A range of features of the built environment and more broadly of the humanly transformed spaces in Bukit Mertajam coded this alternative moral economy of "traveling the dark road." This moral economy could never announce itself as such in public. Instead, stories and rumors circulated around and invested certain places and spaces—shop fronts, bank offices, plots of land, truck depots, even the mountain behind the town itself—with passing and improvised meanings that pointed to a dangerous path of capital accumulation. Local residents showed great ambivalence about this path. Conversely, local spaces and places were mnemonic placeholders for the stories and rumors that carried the marks of this alternative economy.

One such representational space (Lefebvre 1974) that pointed residents to the possibility that someone living or doing business among them was traveling the dark road were certain two- or three-story shop houses in the downtown district or in outlying commercial ribbons along the roads leading into Bukit Merta-jam, when evaluated in the context of local knowledge and rumors about sudden changes in the financial condition of their owners. Mr. Ng of Heng Ee Agricul-tural Supply, had this to say, at one point,

> People are suspicious of me because I have such a small downtown office on Jalan——, yet I am able to do such a large business. When I first met Mr. Ooi See-Huat, the assistant manager of the OCBC Bank in town, he was very suspicious of me because he knew that my monthly turnover was very high. How could I do this from such a small office? I said that it was due to the convenience of transport in Bukit Mertajam. I can take orders at my shop, and then have the fertilizers and their components transported to and from my *godown* [warehouse] elsewhere a few miles outside of downtown, in Alma. So some people have been suspicious of me because of the smallness of my office, and have assumed that I am smuggling drugs instead.

As his wife Mrs. Ng put it to me on another occasion, "Many Chinese business-men hang out a sign in front of their shops, but do a different kind of busi-ness inside, as in the case of heroin manufacturers—they become rich and no one knows it." "Hanging out a sign," *kua zhaopai,* either on one's shop house or other business property (e.g., on truck cabs or work sites) was a common phrase applied to anyone whose business's public appearance—through its signs and advertisements—disguised illicit or illegal activities that took place within. On another occasion, a friend and I were driving past a row of shop houses along the road heading east out of Bukit Mertajam. I asked him about one truck transport company located in one of the shop houses that served as its office and storage depot. My friend observed that the company was owned by a Mr. Tan, who had recently risen in prominence through his business success and recent public gen-erosity to Chinese organizations, so it only made sense, my friend said, that Tan was currently under investigation by the police for possible narcotics smuggling. Owners and drivers of truck transport companies were among those most sus-pected of making such ill-gotten gains. Balasingam, a clerk employed in a local government office, told me one day:

> Yes, police have discovered two drug refineries here in Bukit Merta-jam. But most of the traffic is in drugs from Thailand. I suspect these

are carried by lorries transporting fish from southern Thailand here for further distribution. Many lorry companies that started small have become phenomenally successful in a very short period of time. You can't account for their wealth only by the economic opportunities around here. They have to be involved in drug traffic. YY Lorry Company, whose office is down the road, started out very small and has become very successful.

Another representational space associated with traveling the dark road were plots of land that someone acquired when their legitimate source of income to purchase expensive land in and near the town was not in evidence. One evening in late January 1980, as Mr. Chooi was driving me out of town, and we were passed by a cemetery, I saw that an area near it had been planted in oil palms.

> DMN: Who has planted oil palms on such valuable land which is road frontage and immediately adjacent to the cemetery?
> CHOOI: Eng Huat Company [pseud.] owns this land. The idea is to plant oil palms and hold onto the land until it can be developed into housing estates and sold at a high profit. People expect that eventually Bukit Mertajam's housing development will even extend as far as out here. This company is also involved in drug trafficking. Recently the son of its owner has been seized by police for drug trafficking. He's only been released after paying a very high bribe of several hundred thousand ringgit to certain people. After he was released, he fled to Taiwan and lives there now. Many of Bukit Mertajam's very wealthy people are involved in drug trafficking and in other illegal ways of making money, like smuggling and manufacturing samsu. But some people trafficking in drugs are not yet wealthy, and both workers and bosses are involved.

The north and west sides of the mountain, *bukit*, which loomed over the downtown area and from which the town derived its name were other spaces associated with traveling the dark road, but in this case through the distilling of samsu—which was illegally produced and had a reputation for often being poisonous to the ethnic Indian workers who were its principal consumers. Abutting the north and west sides of the mountain were the squatters' settlements of Kampung Aston and Kampung Tanah Liat whom outsiders said were patrolled by secret society gangs and which they feared entering unless they knew someone there. In the same conversation, Balasingam said to me,

> As to samsu making, up in the hills above town they, the police and everyone else, know that there is illegal samsu distilling, but it's very

difficult to catch who is doing it. The distillers leave packs of hungry dogs on guard near the stills, and as soon as anyone comes up, they make a lot of noise barking, and discourage further investigation with their ferocity. By the time the police get to the stills, which are located in the many caves in the side of the mountain, all the equipment and people have disappeared and there is nothing left but the mash.

Bank offices were yet another space in which a resident might make known his illicit gains from traveling the dark road. As an officer of one of the town's banks put it, "If someone who you knew before to be poor, appears suddenly with a lot of cash to deposit in our bank, you can be fairly certain that he is involved in some 'dark' activity, but from the bank's point of view, 'it's none of our business.'"

Residents of the city might be said to be divided over this alternative moral economy if it were possible to assess the presence of diverse opinion on the morality of such activities as heroin manufacture, sales, or smuggling, but the articulation of opinion would have required the existence of a field of public debate. Such did not exist, and one could not do an opinion survey. The state promoted its antinarcotics campaign vigorously and unopposed in schools and throughout the electronic and paper media. Government officials spoke of narcotics trafficking as the gravest injury to the Malaysian, and especially Malay, nation in a tone that brooked no discussion of alternative views. Residents told me that most heroin addicts were not Chinese, and when it came to the local government-run drug rehabilitation center, noted that most inmates were young Malay men. Narcotics manufacturing and trafficking were hanging offenses, and in this connection local Chinese had been convicted and hung for engaging in them. Still, the Malaysian government showed no racial favoritism, having hung Malays, Chinese, and Europeans with an equal rope—although class favoritism prevailed, as in the example of the rich man's son successful flight to Taiwan.

Thus no one I spoke to in Bukit Mertajam publicly promoted the idea that narcotics manufacture, smuggling, and trafficking were acceptable practices. Nonetheless, these stories and rumors attached to places suggested that while some disapproved outright, others were ambivalent. Some people displayed a waggish black humor in mentioning Bukit Mertajam's notoriety as a purported center for heroin smuggling in north Malaysia, transparently extolling the town's reputation as a matter of local pride, as Nr. Ng did in bragging of the town's notoriety in the Netherlands.

Others, if pushed, said they deplored these practices but spoke of those who committed them and got away with doing so in terms of moral neutrality or even of backhanded admiration. When I asked Mr. Chooi what residents thought of persons who traveled the dark road, he replied, "To them, it is just a matter of making money, and if people are able to get away with drug trafficking and so become rich, it is acceptable to them. But I myself feel this traffic definitely hurts people, and perhaps such men will find out that in the future they have harmed their own children." Informants like Chooi spoke as if it was inevitable that local people would engage in these practices because of the huge profits to be made, naturalizing what they saw as a trend in business more broadly toward "traveling the dark road," as when retired Headmaster Sim spoke of the change from an older generation of Chinese who "used their hearts" in doing business to a younger generation who "used their guts" by smuggling or manufacturing narcotics. All the same, "take from society, use for society": rumors circulated that several of the town's most wealthy "celebrities," noted for their philanthropy to local Chinese institutions (e.g., Jit Sin Independent High School) and for holding high office in community associations, had begun their journey toward successful capital accumulation by traveling precisely along this "road." After all, even if one "took from society" in this way, as long as such a man's money was also "used for society"—that is what ultimately mattered.

Although Chooi stated that some of those in narcotics trafficking were "bosses" and others "workers," the prevailing rumors suggested a kind of alternative morality that had its own class character deeply inscribed in the circulating stories and rumors of people traveling the dark road, and in the spaces of shop house, land plots, mountain side, and bank offices that were marked by them. Those who were wealthy had the greatest chance of surviving the hazards intrinsic to traveling the dark road. Whereas, as Chooi notes, a rich man's son might pay a heavy bribe to an official to be allowed to flee to Taiwan, such an option did not exist for people without "position," that is, people who labored for their livelihoods. Mr. Tng was a fisherman living in a riverside kampung to the west of town who reared pigs on behalf of Saw Kim Aik. Saw was an English-educated partner in a downtown business, and a small oil palm estate and pig farm owner. When Saw and I visited Tng and his wife and two or three children in 1979, they lived in a squalid shed attached to the pigsties. It was filthy inside, flies everywhere, with very little present in the one- or two-room shed in the way of the usual furnishings found in even poor Chinese houses, such as a cabinet in the front room on which statues of gods, *shen*, curios, family heirlooms, etc. were usually placed, although there was a poster or drawing of *Dabogong* or of some other god, *shen*, on the walls. The children too were very dirty, and one—a small child—cried continually. Mrs. Tng also seemed to be in a bad temper toward them. Rarely in Bukit Mertajam had I seen such a depressing or grubby scene. When I returned in 1985 to Bukit Mertajam and located Saw in the shop house whose business he shared with two of his brothers in the town, he told me that Tng and several other men had recently been arrested for heroin smuggling and sales, and were currently awaiting trial, and would probably face the death penalty for heroin smuggling. I still do not know what happened to Tng but fear the worst.

Far from being discursively encompassed by the rhetoric of citizenship promoted by the Malaysian state, and separate from their discreetly spoken inventory of complaints which were, after all, predicated on the possibility of Chinese being "fairly" treated by the legitimate state, those residents who alluded to the crypto-geography of traveling the dark road cultivated an antistate imaginary that placed them potentially outside and beyond the moral community of the Malaysian nation. This imaginary challenged the conventional rags-to-riches-and-fame account of Chinese achievement: there were ways to become rich and well-regarded, as dangerous and antisocial as they were. This imaginary pointed not to the dangerous "voice" option some residents took in publicly opposing the state, as in the case of those who participated in opposition party politics such as the DAP, much less to the "loyalty" option adopted by some residents who joined and were active in parties allied with UMNO like the Gerakan Party and Malaysian Chinese Association—but to the option of "exit" from the Malaysian nation-state itself (Hirschman 1970). Although some residents were discursively encompassed by the two options of citizens—loyalty and voice—others repudiated this encompassment entirely through imagining the possibility of exit. What I am suggesting here is that this imaginary preceded and facilitated the physical move offshore by many Chinese petty capitalists and professionals in the years that followed.

BANALITIES OF THE URBAN

Hegemony or State Predation?

In this chapter, I seek to set out what happens when two contested hegemonic projects—one, identified with the postcolonial state and a majority ethnic group, waxing; and another, identified with a minority ethnic group showing some degree of economic privilege and tied to a declining Chinese diaspora, waning—come into collision. Gramsci (1971) in his years in prison reflected on the relationship between state "domination" through coercion and a broader "hegemony" involving "common sense" in civil society within Italy of the 1920s and 1930s, and saw each as reinforcing the other to shore up capitalist rule. But in some respects similar to the "Southern question" in the case of Gramsci's Italy, in postcolonial Malaysia class fissures combined with ethno-racial differences associated with spatial position to generate a major social fault line that made the ascent to power of a unified "historical bloc" of class interests impossible. This precluded the emergence of a dominant "common sense" and instead led to contestations between two hegemonic projects that were, ultimately, only resoluble by state coercion. Although in Malaysia both "sides" defined by overlapping class, ethno-racial and spatial characteristics might in some sense be "capitalist," this is too simplistic a view, for capitalism is a highly differentiated process fractured along social and cultural lines.

In this chapter, I delineate the construction of the hegemonic, or "default," classed-gendered identities of men "doing business" and "having position" who, unlike Chinese laboring men and women, commanded the culturally authorized modes of representation associated with declarative speech, the printed language, "being polite," and occupied spatially central spaces in Bukit Mertajam. To demonstrate that the classed-gendered identities of towkays were hegemonic cultural formations arising from Chinese encounters with Malaysian state formation, and not from the purported essences of "Chinese culture," I find it necessary to trace the postcolonial emergence of the predatory governing logics of the Malaysian state, and how the persons I came to know in Bukit Mertajam experienced them.

Postcolonial Malaysian Urban

> Over there in Bukit Mertajam they do a lot of evil things. Smuggling goods in from Thailand. Opening factories making imitation goods. Breaking the traffic laws by having unregistered trailers in their yards or by not having paid road tax. You see, they are all grouped together, concentrated together in a very small area, some twenty to twenty-five thousand of them. Therefore, they let one another do all sorts of illegal things without reporting them to the government. There are also Communists over there. They [Chinese] will do anything to make money. . . . [They are] doing anything they like, with nobody to stop them.
>
> —Mohamad bin Bakar, Road Transport Department official, 1980

Chinese—civilly marked as such by language, dress, and identity cards—in Bukit Mertajam encountered the Malaysian state in a variety of transactions with state functionaries,[1] the vast majority of whom were Malay men. These transactions, despite their variety, shifted between the registers of being instrumental and being antagonistic during which these functionaries took money from persons identified as Chinese in exchange for the favors, services, permits, and licenses essential for the latter to earn wages, carry out business, and accumulate capital. I argue in this chapter that the cultural production of tributary or predatory relations between Chinese and state functionaries created, from the perspective of the former, an antagonistic personalized state. At another level, however, these relations created a dialectics of proliferation in the number of small Chinese family enterprises thereby set into invidious competition with one another.

The urban spatiality of the Chinese population of Bukit Mertajam described in the previous chapter and this population's association with business and wealth—inscribed in the Malay official's comments quoted above—was no accident. There has long been an association in Malaysian state rhetorics between Chinese ethnicity, petty capitalism, and urban spaces. Chapter 1 describes what underlay this association—the violent history of the years of the Malayan

Emergency (1948–60) when 500,000 persons of Chinese descent were forcibly urbanized (i.e., resettled) into New Villages (Sandhu 1964a, 1964b; Harper 1999). Most New Villages, particularly those sited near larger towns or cities, had in fact become geographically "urban" through settlement and population growth in the intervening years since 1950. Berapit New Village on the edge of the municipal boundaries of Bukit Mertajam was one such, as were Permatang Tinggi New Village sited a few miles from downtown on the main north-south trunk road,[2] and Machang Bubok New Village located three miles away off the road from Bukit Mertajam to Kulim in southern Kedah.

Official New Economic Policy discourse through the 1960s and 1970s treated Chinese—even the minority who remained in rural poverty in New Villages in specific regions such as central Perak state (Loh 1988)—as essentially "urban" in more than a locational sense: they belonged to an ethnic group this discourse cast as urban, as being in business, and as wealthy, and they served as foil to the envisioned ethnic community of impoverished rural Malay farmers to be targeted by government projects for improvement and uplift (Government of Malaysia 1979). This was the case despite the persistence of a large number of Chinese workers among the Malaysian population (36.5 per cent of all employees, and 22.4 percent of the Malaysian labor force in 1980; calculated from Jomo and Todd 1994, 8–9), despite the existence of known concentrations of Chinese living in rural New Villages (Loh 1980; Strauch 1981), and despite the fact that the vast majority of Chinese either worked for wages or engaged in "doing business" by operating small-scale, family-based enterprises with no employed, nonfamily labor—hence petty capitalist, as described in chapter 2. In short, Chinese became identified in Malaysian official discourse as pragmatic, economizing, self-aggrandizing agents, and localized by their metaphorical association with cities and towns, irrespective of where they actually lived. Thus when Mohamad bin Bakar said, "They are all grouped together, concentrated together in a very small area, some twenty to twenty-five thousand of them. . . . doing anything they like, with nobody to stop them," his statement arose from an official discursive history that identified Chinese with immoral capitalist behaviors concentrated in urban spaces.

In this light, the history of Chinese identity formation from the 1970s through the 1980s centered on shifting but increasingly routinized tributary or predatory relations between a multiplicity of state agents and a subject population of Chinese treated as owners of illicit wealth. Tributary relations between government functionaries and Chinese petty capitalists—characterized from afar as "corruption"—were not distinct from, but rather deeply implicated in the disciplining rationalities of state governmentality (cf. Smart 1999). These rationalities shaped within broad limits many of the specific features of Chinese petty capitalist production and exchange, and the social relations in which these were situated.

During the same time, working-class Chinese received a very different and far more brutal treatment at the hands of state bureaucracies and police.

"Corruption" or Predatory Governmentality? Constraints of Smallness and "Getting By"

Any history of Chinese in Malaysia must incorporate at its core the shifts in these tributary rationalities that made Chinese into governable, nominally pliant, if at times elusive, citizen-subjects. I make this point in this chapter by examining the relationship between state technologies of regulation aimed at petty capitalist enterprises that kept them petty and generated their proliferation, but defined them as Chinese. These technologies also created a force field for the reproduction of masculinist cultural stylistics among towkays. However, these technologies of regulation—and here I part company with Foucault—were neither all encompassing, nor did they construct subject-positions or identities that were distinctively Chinese. Instead, they engendered a habitus of androcentric, antistatist, and anti-Malay discourse and practice that constituted the classed cultural style of towkays that I examined in the previous chapter.

In August 1985, I interviewed Mr. Ang who was then working as a hawker selling fried fish in a nearby public market on the fringes of the town of Bukit Mertajam. For several years previously, he owned and drove his own small truck, but in 1984 went bankrupt. In that business he drove sundry goods between Bukit Mertajam and Georgetown, and back, delivering them at multiple stops in the city of Georgetown. The entire trip, as the crow flies, was about thirty miles. In meticulous detail, and with great bitterness, he told me of his experience of driving during a typical round trip, which—despite its short distance—required a full day's work:

> My highest costs were the police, who always wanted coffee money. Leaving Bukit Mertajam, by the time I arrived at Prai, I would have encountered at least one police roadblock, and the policemen would not be satisfied by less than 4–5 ringgit. At the wharf, before entering the ferry, my truck would have to be weighed, and if it was overloaded, I would have to pay money to the scales attendant, which would come to perhaps 6 ringgit. On the ferry, the attendant who directed me to park demanded twenty cents. Once I got off the ferry in Penang, there would be another roadblock outside the ferry building. This one would have 4 to 6 policemen, each of whom wanted a sum of money. I would pay between 20 and 25 ringgit to them, which they would divide up among

themselves. In Georgetown, I often had to double-park and each time I did so other policemen would threaten me with a summons if I didn't pay coffee money, so each one I might pay one ringgit. . . . And on the way back I might be stopped by a police roadblock between Butterworth and Bukit Mertajam, and would then have to pay yet more coffee money . . . I would earn a total of 110 ringgit in transport charges for the day, but might spend up to 40 to 50 ringgit in coffee money per trip.

Such a narrative was in no way remarkable—in fact what marked it was its sheer pedestrian quality, both in the sense of its repetitive everydayness for this man, and the great frequency with which stories like it were told me by the people whom I interviewed in 1985, and earlier during my first stay in Bukit Mertajam from 1978 to 1980. The person in question might be a truck transporter like Mr. Ang, or a vegetable wholesaler (a "Baba") who provided a rent to a Malay partner (an "Ali") for the use of the latter's government permit to operate his business, a downtown shopkeeper speaking of monthly visits by a police constable seeking coffee money, a wealthy supermarket owner providing his "friend" the OCPD (the highest police official in a district) with a fat "red packet," *angpow*, stuffed with cash on Chinese New Year day, a man attempting to have electricity extended to his cold storage room and having to pay money "under the table" to installers from the government-owned electrical utility, or a truck driver being shaken down for coffee money by police for driving an overweight truck. As with innumerable other persons, such transactions with state functionaries were the essence of the quotidian. What varied instead was the extent to which these exactions actually affected the viability of a business or of livelihood—Mr. Ang claimed with great bitterness that they had driven him out of the truck transport business and back into the petty hawking his parents did—or merely became a source of recurrent, predictable inconvenience for those with greater financial resources, who were resigned to treating them as part of the inevitable costs of doing business if one were Chinese.

These exactions and the pervasive tributary relations that underlay them were actually much more. Such exactions were called "corruption" (*tanwu*) by towkays and other Chinese, and whether rich or only middling in income, towkays referred to them as harassment—accompanied by implicit or explicit threats of force—something negative that detracted from the processes of their doing business and accumulating capital. Towkays told me that the demands of government officials, police, and other employees for gifts and coffee money had to do with the fact that "we Chinese" suffered at the hands of "them"—meaning Malays, the government, the UMNO party—who held power. Although these exchanges should be viewed as not arbitrary, capricious, or idiosyncratic but as the systematic manifestation of tributary relations connected to state authoritarianism and the consolidation of the economic base of a new ethnic-based ruling class, they can be viewed in another way as well—in terms of cultural formation. What were the effects of numerous, repeated, and predictable tributary exchanges such as those described by Mr. Ang between petty capitalists and persons directly or indirectly associated with the state? Is there a way of conceiving of a social and political order underlying these exchanges that was positive and culturally formative for towkays—instead of solely destructive as they most often depicted them?

The varieties of everyday predation by direct and indirect agents of the state on towkays and the small businesses they owned were so prevalent a feature of Chinese doing business or earning wages that it is hard not to see the workings of such predation and the market-oriented behavior of the petty capitalist populations of urban Malaysia as internally related to each other. Indeed, from the point of view of many Malays, the practices by state agents of demanding coffee money, personal fees for the uses of licenses, and the like were not predation but rather facilitated a just and balanced relationship of "mutual help," *tolong menolong*, in which the Chinese towkay prospered only if the Malay with state connections did, and conversely. What was surprising was that, despite extensive complaints by towkays and other Chinese, many conceded that such relationships did, when all was said and done, still allow them to "get by," *guo shenghuo*. Malay clients made business possible, at times became customers themselves, and served as intermediaries who introduced towkays to other Malay patrons such as government officials who could facilitate new business deals, among other things. What the differential response by towkays to these exactions traversed was their movement within the shifting class relations of Malaysian society—while, for instance, Mr. Ang saw the predations by police and others on his small truck transport business as driving him back into the working class from which his parents came, to other towkays more felicitous outcomes were possible.[3]

The shadow political economy grounded in everyday tributary relations had a certain underlying logic: the more capital held by the business in question—and by the family owning it—the more eagerly state officials sought to extract capital from it. Among more powerful Malays closely connected to higher levels of the state bureaucracies, state police, and the governing UMNO party, the greater was the tendency to seek a significant share of the profits of the business through forceful, if legal, methods. The net effect of operating in the shadow economy was therefore to pressure men owning businesses to depress the visible size of enterprises, that is, to appear to be "poor," for them to say, as they did, "I'm just getting by." This phrase, "just getting by," was by far the most frequent response towkays made to my question about how their businesses were doing.

In addition to everyday, off-the-street forms of predation, the differential monitoring by government ministries of large versus small enterprises with respect to their ethnic ownership was a structural constraint that encouraged towkays who successfully accumulated capital to aspire to own several smaller and spatially dispersed enterprises instead of one or two larger and concentrated ones. Towkays repeatedly stated that smaller enterprises remained largely beneath the surveillance horizons of regulatory officials, while the owners of larger enterprises—owners of large factories, supermarkets, wholesale distributorships, large-scale transport companies—found themselves the object of unwelcome attention by the Ministry of Industry in its extended efforts to increase Malay equity in Malaysian businesses.

The Industrial Coordination Act (ICA) of 1975 served as the foundational legal text guiding tributary relations between the state and the petty capitalist sector. It stipulated that if a private industrial enterprise had a capitalization of more than MR$ 100,000 and employed more than twenty-five employees, it was required to sell no less than 30 percent of its equity to partners who were Bumiputra (i.e., members of indigenous groups, the vast majority of whom were Malay), and offer 30 percent of its jobs to Bumiputra, and that, moreover, the capital required to purchase this equity was to come out of profits from the firm after its acquisition by Bumiputra shareholders instead of being paid beforehand to the current non-Bumiputra owners (Crouch 1996, 207).[4] Towkays told me that the ICA and the monitoring that accompanied it discouraged the growth of their enterprises by increasing the probability that the larger they became, the more they would be seen by Ministry of Industry as an appropriate target for takeover. The most bitter denunciations of ethnic discrimination by "their government" (the government of and by Malays) were made by towkays who themselves felt pressure from the ministry to find Malay partners to whom they would be required to sell equity or who knew others who had experienced such pressure. Consider what a son of a brand-name Chinese medicine manufacturer with more than fifty employees said to me in 1979:

> Chinese secretly resist it [the ICA]. It impedes economic progress since it discourages the larger companies from expanding to the point they will be subject to this law. Not only is the law unfair but it is a kind of robbery. It's one thing to share capital with a Malay if you and he have been partners from the beginning. It's something else entirely for the government to force owners of a business which they have started from scratch to share ownership and profits with a Malay who has contributed nothing to the company's growth.

The constant surveillance by state officials encouraged towkays to remain small or, putting it more accurately, to continue to *appear* small to official eyes by growing through dispersion—by incorporating multiple businesses, in different lines of trade often in more than one city or town. Business owners registered such businesses as separate legal entities with the government; although they had shareholders in common, they thus appeared to state officials as independent enterprises.

This was quite evident in the faddish proliferation of registration of new private limited liability companies among Chinese business families from the mid-1970s onward. When I was in Bukit Mertajam from 1978 to 1980, businessmen seemed eager to register their businesses as private limited liability companies.[5] Informants explained that previously Chinese businessmen registered their businesses either as individual proprietorships or partnerships under the law, legal statuses that allowed their owners to avoid filing annual accounts or to list specific shareholders with the government. People said that the wealthier a businessman became, the more inclined he was to register a new enterprise as a private limited liability company rather than as a proprietorship or partnership because of the tax advantages (a flat 40 percent business income tax rate), and the possibilities for raising capital from banks which this made possible.[6] Although the Companies Act required private limited liability companies to file their annual accounts and declare their legal shareholders (with amounts of shares owned by each shareholder) with the Registrar of Companies, registration also formalized the autonomous existence of many small businesses vis-à-vis the government.

Towkay Stylistics: "Better to Be the Head of a Chicken than the Ass of an Ox"

This eagerness to reveal one's business organization to the state makes sense only when it is connected to the cultural stylistics of towkays as men with position, where they associated prestige with the proliferation of names and entities. It was indeed "better to be the head of a chicken than the ass of an ox"—to be an independent owner of a small firm rather than a partner or manager of a larger enterprise. Moreover, the new degree of public visibility also encouraged wealthier towkays to multiply the enterprises they started. When they registered their businesses as private limited liability companies (either with family members or partners), men of position with considerable fortunes in Bukit Mertajam chose to register two or more smaller enterprises (which were in fact in related or even same lines of business), rather than one larger, more concentrated business that was more visible to government scrutiny. Such men were the minority of business owners discovered in the commercial census in 1979 whose businesses hired ten or more employees. Thus it was not unusual for such a towkay to list himself as "managing director" or "director" of three, four, or sometimes more enterprises on his business card (see figure 4.1).

南發貿易公司（經理）
Nam Huat Trading Co., (Proprietor)

大山脚印刷有限公司（董事副經理）
B. M. Printing Sdn. Bhd. (Asst. Managing Director)
五洲食品工業有限公司（董事）
Continental Food Industries Sdn. Bhd. (Director)

NO. 149, JALAN TEMBIKAI, TAMAN SRI RAMBAI,
BUKIT MERTAJAM, SEBERANG PERAI.
TEL: 515278, 511598, 517818 & 518352

聯和羅哩運輸公司
聯和運輸貿易公司
泰祥棧（無比）油站公司
Syarikat Pengangkutan Bersatu,
Lian Hua Transport Trading Co.,
Thye Siang Chan (Mobil) S/S & Co,

Office: 93, Station Road, Bukit Mertajam, P.W.C
Tel: 513624, 515204, 510772
Res: 11A, Lorong Aman, Taman Shaik Adam,
Bukit Mertajam, P.W.C. Tel: 515663

Weng Hiang Biscuit Factory (Prorietor)
Weng Hiang Wine Dealers (Prorietor)
B'Worth Textile Sdn. Bhd. (Executive Director)

Office: 19, Danby Street, Bukit Mertajam, P. W. Penang.
Residence: 1006, Kulim Road, Bukit Mertajam, P. W.
Tel: 511896

FIGURE 4.1 Business cards—multiple businesses owned

Was it, however, only a matter of *appearance* of smallness, or of "getting by," belied by a patriarch, who would work like the *dalang* (M), or shadowy puppet master,[7] seated behind the stage screen to pull the strings of all his businesses before the public eye, in order to avoid government attention to his property holdings in this new period of visibility and purportedly grasping Malays? To put it another way: could these everyday tributary relations (formalized at their extreme by the ICA) be seen instead not only as limiting but also as formative for oppositional towkay identities? What I want to point to is the existence of a Chinese patriarchal cultural style that arose dialectically from Chinese encounters with state predatory governance without in any way being merely subsumable to it as a structural constraint. For towkays, establishing new businesses was a matter of male pride, of busy-ness, for a man multiplied his reputation as each new business name became identified with him and the family he headed. Wealthy towkays were often addressed in public by other towkays not by their surnames but by the names of the most prominent and successful business each owned: it wasn't wealthy "Mr. Yeap" someone asked for or alluded to secondhand, but "Ban Chuan." The listing of many enterprises on a business card, although this was part of a performance designed to avoid official scrutiny and limit the take of perceived greedy Malays, also signaled a man of wealth and position. Although a man who set up businesses in different (if often related) lines of commerce diversified his investments and so lowered his risks of complete failure, this was primarily from a motive as much dramaturgical as economic: by establishing more than one business, particularly if they were private limited liability companies certified by the state, he displayed to an audience of other men of position in Bukit Mertajam his capacities for multiplexing, for being a deal maker and player in more than one line of profit making. He displayed his industriousness, resourcefulness, and willingness to risk and to put his capital to work by keeping it, as local usage went, continuously "turning," *zhouzhuan*—always in motion and never idle. The performance of solvency, growth in wealth, and reliability thus converged with the proliferation of small enterprises—one consistent with but not reducible to the tributary rationality of government. Delbert Tan, a manager for a local diversified trading company, told me over lunch in 1979:

> Many downtown merchants are now investing in rubber or oil palm plantations or in housing construction, and have made lots of money from these, but their [other] businesses barely get by. For example, my boss has made a great deal of money from the rubber plantations and housing developments he is involved in. Business has been so bad in Bukit Mertajam only recently. Previously, five to ten years ago, there was a lot more money to be made than now by local businessmen. This is due to the government requiring that Malays be given a certain percentage

of business activity in one form or another. This sets definite limits on the expansion of local businesses. . . . Presently the government is putting pressure on many Chinese businessmen to accept Malay partners. It forces them to give a cut to Malays, to give 30 percent of their capital as a gift to them. Presently my boss is under pressure by the government to do this for his supermarket chain, although the matter's still up in the air.

What was also being performed for audiences like Delbert Tan (who collaborated on the "script") were not only the towkay's display of his business talents (as shrewd, penny-pinching, and hardworking), but also the capacities of his family members and his management of them, signified in his ability to deploy them across the different businesses (and branches of businesses) that he founded: for them to work together harmoniously in the making of profit redounded to the reputation of their father, brother, husband, or father-in-law.

> Mr. Ng or "Heng Huat Transport," about seventy years old when I interviewed him, told me he owned a truck transport company with twenty trucks that hauled sundry cargo between Bukit Mertajam and Johore Bharu and Singapore to the south. He detailed the division of labor in his company. His eldest son managed the Johore Bharu branch of the company, while also acting as a partner in another truck transport company headquartered in Bukit Mertajam. Another son worked for him at the Singapore branch of the company, dealing with consigners and freight for the return trips to the north.

Management failures were dealt with discretely, and otherwise passed over silently in public. I only found out from an ex-employee of Mr. Ng that a third son who had worked at Heng Huat had embezzled funds to pay gambling debts, that when Mr. Ng discovered this he had disinherited this son from his shares in Heng Huat, and subsequently the man had left to start his own transport company nearby. The cultural style of the towkay, which I described in the previous chapter, was grounded in a colonial amalgam of British common law and China "customary" law that privileged the rights of male bourgeois heterosexual subjects in the control of family property and family members, a subject I cannot go into here (see Buxbaum 1966; Hooker 1969; Siraj 1994).

Everyday Practices of State Formation, in Two Optics

Tributary relations between Chinese business families and the petty government officials, police, and employees of state-owned enterprises simultaneously ethnicized and personified the state. Towkays spoke of a multitude of dyadic ties between very large numbers of Malay men—petty officials, state employees, policemen—and themselves. These everyday relationships based on tribute taking and the exchange of petty favors (e.g., the policeman who dropped by for his monthly tip), were one of the few ways in which individual Malay and Chinese men had an opportunity to individually interact with one another outside the framework of spatially and socially segregated ethnic groups whose interests were defined as antagonistic. The Malay Ali who owned a business license rented out by a Chinese might become a problem solver, a "fixer" with state officials, for the Chinese Baba he paired with. These personal ties between individual men developed as the basis for comity and at times even friendship. Malay friends were invited to the weddings of Chinese, and vice versa, for instance. Towkays indicated to me that their relationships with such Malay partners were proprietary, like other business secrets in the "war by other means" described in the previous chapter. I discovered in my interviews, however, that among those who were the most wealthy men with position, particularly the elite of "celebrities," that where their ties were with highly placed officials such as the district officer (D.O.) or OCPD, the public acknowledgment of such ties (e.g., having the D.O. or OCPD as guest of honor at one's son's wedding banquet) enhanced a man's reputation. Such officials themselves had a high "position," or rank, *pangkat*, within state bureaucracies or state-connected political parties. At the same time, towkays redefined their experiences of repeated exactions of tribute by less-prestigious, state-related Malay patrons (e.g., the Malay Ali holding their business license) or by petty Malay clients (this telephone lineman, that police constable)—exactions rationalized by a hostile public indigenist narrative of Malays who had been cast into unjust poverty by greedy Chinese—as transactions with "the government" as such. It was, as towkays complained, "*their* government," *tamen de zhengfu*, not "ours."

A state rationality that exacted tribute from Chinese all the way down the line, while putatively encouraging increased business opportunities among Malays, had its ironies. Towkays observed that the government practice of allocating business licenses in great profusion solely to Malay supporters produced via the Ali-Baba arrangement an increase in the number of Chinese enterprises in the same line of business, and thus exacerbated competition among them.[8] In 1985, one truck transport proprietor observed that

> since 1980 or so, the [truck transport industry's] situation has started to become worse, because of the intensified competition. This is because Malays have received too many truck permits, and what with the Ali-Baba arrangement, too many Chinese truck transport companies have come into existence. If one wants to carry freight only for 30 ringgit

per ton, but another transporter is willing to charge only 22 ringgit per ton, then over time, this depresses revenues from transport charges, and decreases profits. The result has been the present "cold" situation where many companies have failed.

This was one source of the rhetoric by truck owners that blamed the government for the invidious "price-shaving" competition they claimed had afflicted the truck transport industry from the 1970s onward. Similar Ali-Baba arrangements applied in lines of business other than truck transport.

Viewed close up, men of quite well-known wealth publicized their capacities to oversee several small family business enterprises simultaneously, established their creditworthiness vis-à-vis other businessmen through their shrewd capacities to "turn capital," *zhouzhuan*, sought to create a reputation for capably managing their wives, sons, and daughters and "outsider" (*wairen*) employees working in their businesses, and for extracting advantages in their dealings with partners, suppliers, customers, and local bankers. These masculinist stylistics identified such men as having a classed-gendered identity of men with position and—for some of them—as celebrities.

It is worth viewing the situation at a different scale and through a different optic, from afar. What I witnessed in these performances by towkays vis-à-vis an aggressive predatory state were the traces, in one locale over a protracted period of time, of the combined processes of state formation and complementary class formation. These processes were ones in which these Chinese men became differentiated from a new bourgeoisie of Malay businessmen and women who were connected to the "business" of the state. This business centered on the enlargement of Malay "participation" (especially capital accumulation) "in the economy." The formation of a new class, the New Malays, Melayu Baru, was organically connected to the intense competition between a large number of marginal small-scale Chinese family enterprises, each vying with others like themselves to avoid state predation while competing with them for the patronage of the new large-scale corporations owned by state-associated managers and shareholders—the New Malays, and their partners, ultra-wealthy Chinese tycoons. For instance, in the case of the transport industry, truck towkays recounted to me instances when a large state-managed industrial enterprise like Mitsubishi Electronics or Malayan Sugar was able to play off one small-scale transport operator against others to obtain the lowest transport charges for carrying its freight. In aggregate, these small enterprises thus underwrote (in part) the profits of corporations that were state-owned or had wealthy Malay shareholders on their boards, and in this way were one source of the wealth that made the capital accumulation of the state-connected New Malay capitalist and managerial class possible.[9]

The Working Class and Its Spaces: Objects of Policing, Enclosing, "Improving"

I close on a note of caution. The focus throughout this chapter on the forma-tive aspects of state predation on identities among owners of petty property and those "doing business" implicitly risks replicating discursively the very real physi-cal violence and marginalization by the state of Chinese working-class men and women—and their neglect in the literature on overseas Chinese—which I cau-tioned against in the Introduction. Although working-class men were shaken down for "tea money" by police, army soldiers, and petty officials, it is in contrast difficult to describe their relationship to the personalized Malaysian state primarily as one of predation, since there was so little that could be squeezed from them on a sustained basis. Instead, state officials saw them as criminals and subversives, to be dealt with by violence, coercion, and insult. In 1978, government officials, most of them Malays, viewed New Village residents and kampung dwellers not only as ille-gitimately voting for the opposition party but also as dangerous, subversive, and criminal. As Mohamad bin Bakar put it, "Over there in Bukit Mertajam they do a lot of evil things. . . . You see, they are all grouped together, concentrated together in a very small area, some twenty to twenty-five thousand of them. Therefore, they let one another do all sorts of illegal things. . . . There are also Communists over there." Similar views among government officials were widely held.

It was no surprise, therefore, in areas where a majority of Chinese resided, as in Bukit Mertajam, a large majority voted in the 1978 national election for the candidates of the opposition party and against the ruling coalition of political parties dominated by UMNO. In Bukit Mertajam, this party was the Democratic Action Party (DAP), led by Mandarin-educated Chinese leaders. The "stronghold" of the DAP from the late 1960s through the 1970s were several thousand Chinese residing within the New Villages, and others living within the boundaries of the town itself in several densely populated squatting areas—called "villages" (kam-pung). These latter areas were occupied by poorer Chinese who had originally moved there and paid the landowners nominal rents, but later—even as down-town real estate values rose—resisted forced removal and insisted on remaining on as a customary right. Most New Village and kampung residents were workers, artisans, and petty traders, although over time some began to prosper by set-ting up small-scale manufacturing in their homes (including putting-out work in apparel), or working in the nearby export processing zones or for businesses servicing them, but remaining in their low-rent kampung homes. A minority of poor residents were members of "secret societies," engaged in illegal activities such as shakedowns of local merchants, samsu (liquor) distilling, and engaging in illegal lottery sales.

State-initiated class war between state officials, including police, and residents of the inner-city kampung and New Village areas took a variety of forms. First, throughout the 1970s, the government sought to extend its police powers throughout these urban kampung settlements, ostensibly against the Chinese secret societies who officials and police saw as the core criminal element there. Here is how the owner of a small restaurant located on the fringes of one of the town's kampungs described the actions of a particular police inspector who made continual incursions into these urban kampungs, viewed as the territories of specific secret societies:

> Inspector Kee has done a lot of good by threatening bad hats [criminals] with arrest and administrative detention on Pulau Jerejak. For instance, one bad hat named Henry is notorious on this street for his threatening behavior. He carries *parangs* (knives) and things like that. One time, I was disturbed by Henry and his gang who awakened me late at night and threatened me, and had his gang stand on my car. After a while, however, I saw no more of Henry. I found out later that Inspector Kee had sent him to Pulau Jerejak for at least a year. Inspector Kee can do this with the authorization of the magistrate, and no trial is needed. The bad hats respect Kee because he's aggressive and they know that since his youth he's been a good boxer.

The class character of state repression directed against the unruly youth of the kampungs associated with the Chinese urban working class is evident, as indeed is the intimidation of poorer Chinese, irrespective of their ties to secret societies, living in these areas.

Instead of seeing Chinese workers and petty commodity producers through a predatory optic, a state ethic of viewing them as "bare life" (Agamben 1998)—to be insulted, beaten, imprisoned, and otherwise treated as enemies of the Malay(-sian) nation—was more in evidence, judging from what I witnessed and heard. In return for the animosities toward them exhibited by state officials and police, they responded with anger, fear, a sense of being intimidated, and deep animosity toward Malays whom they identified with the state and its officials, police, and soldiers. Their animosity was a racial one, for despite the occasional presence of a Chinese official like Inspector Kee, the vast majority of these groups were, in fact, ethnic Malays.

Second, state-provided services were employed as a whip to enforce political discipline on a recalcitrant and dissatisfied Chinese population in these areas. This took the form of national and state government officials systematically penalizing the residents of the New Villages and town kampungs who had voted for the opposition by denying them postelectoral municipal services. Such services were provided to more politically loyal, wealthier Chinese constituencies residing in outlying areas, that is, the new suburbs where Chinese professionals and many business people had moved, and to the rural Malay-populated villages of the rest of the district. Here is how an informant who lived in one of the squatters' kampungs within the town described its situation to me in 1978:

> There are shortages in water and electricity that we residents experience there. Many residents, like my family, draw on wells for our water supply. This water and electricity shortage is due to the area I live in—Kampung Tanah Liat, which is like other kampungs in Bukit Mertajam. Unlike areas out of town where the wealthy live, electrical, water and road service is poor, in these areas. . . . Officials have never come to visit my neighborhood to inspect conditions there. This is due to two factors: our State Assemblyman is the DAP's man, and also our area is populated exclusively by Chinese.

Police raids, harassment, and imprisonment of kampung residents, combined with state denial of essential services were two means of establishing a state presence in and police controls over these spaces of opposition. Yet by the 1980s government practices led to an even more effective weapon being deployed against these spatially defined enemies of the developmental state: "improvement." This is intimated in a press release of 1979 by the local branch of the Gerakan Party, whose state president was also the chief minister of Penang and a strong ally of UMNO. It appeared in a regional Chinese-language newspaper under the innocuous-sounding title "Bukit Mertajam Gerakan Proposes Improved Traffic Measures":

> roads can be broadened, e.g., Jalan Aston can be widened and afterward converted into a two-way street; a new road can be opened to connect Tanah Liat intersection with a new Kampung Cross Street. When this road is finished, it will reduce the traffic on Jalan Tanah Liat. Vehicles coming and going between Kedah and Butterworth can use this new road, and at Kampung Wu-sha, another road should be opened up to connect Berapit and Kulim Road. This proposed road will directly reduce the town's traffic. (*Guanghua Ribao* 1979a)

These proposals for traffic "improvement"—which required extensive removal of thousands of squatters from several kampungs which happened to lay in the way of the proposed roads—were put into effect during the 1990s.

CLASS DISMISSED!

A Class Gone Missing—and Not Only in the Literature

The neglect of class, class conflict, and class practice among Chinese in South-east Asia by the sinological accounts of the overseas Chinese discussed in the Introduction is difficult to explain, for, at least for anyone who has spent much time with them, the presence of class-based interactions is difficult to ignore. Yet, it must be conceded, the presence of classes and class-based relations and animosities among Chinese in Malaysia and elsewhere in Southeast Asia take on an elusive quality. This chapter seeks to redress the reading out of existence by the scholarly literature of the Chinese working people in Southeast Asia and to sketch out an alternative perspective.

This is particularly true in those capitalist nation-states of Southeast Asia like Malaysia where, once having experienced the violent repressions associated with the Cold War, those who spoke of class or class conflict in public ventured into a risky politics that might itself invite further state violence. It is indeed notable that the last serious scholarly treatment of working-class Chinese in Southeast Asia, despite its serious flaws, was that of the Soviet N. A. Simoniya (Simoniya 1961). Yet this was at a time when the prominent sinological anthropologist Maurice Freedman (1979a [1960], 32) observed nervously that "during this century more than three quarters [of Malayan Chinese] have been 'working class'"—his unease about the very concept "working class" was symptomatic. In this respect, the tacit agreement over the last three decades between sinological scholars; the Western business press obsessing about Asian economies, "chopstick cultures," and "Bamboo Curtains"; and observers within contemporary Southeast Asia to ignore or neglect the existence of classes and class practices among Chinese in Southeast Asia has represented a formidable achievement in constituting a kind of truth through denial. Moreover, that the gendered nature of class practices have been so transparently overlooked speaks to the implicitly masculinist character of this truth—it was the Chinese business*man* who mattered.

Yet the existence of class, and of classed, gendered (and gendered-classed) practices and styles among Chinese in Malaysia will not simply go away through denial or conceptual conjuring acts. In this chapter, I examine the elusive presence of the performance of classed styles among Chinese men in urban Malaysia by arguing that persons, whatever their "consciousness" might be, engaged in practices in everyday life within a political-economic setting that made the articulation of a class identity, performed with a distinctive class-inflected cultural style, possible for men with wealth and power, but not—except under exceptional conditions like those described below—for the much larger group of men without property. As chapter 3 demonstrates, the modal identity arising from the dominant cultural style of "the typical Chinese" was that of men of property, and in contrast Bukit Mertajam towkays cast workers as a shadowy category of people defined by their deficiencies (crudity, lack of position, lack of business acumen), and thus on the margins of Chineseness. Within this bourgeois moral topography, working people were not allotted an identity defined by their subordinate place in society; they were simply cast as incapable of performing public identities within "Chinese society." The style and habitus of working-class men were not merely opposed to "being a typical Chinese" but were instead organized along entirely different, less overt and public dimensions.

Class Practice, Fugitive Cultural Stylistics, and Subjugated Standpoints

The identities that Bukit Mertajam people ascribed to Chinese merchants described in chapter 3 (those who do business, towkay, men of position) would not be unfamiliar to scholars who have studied the overseas Chinese or Western business pundits and journalists who prize their own expertise about Asian business. Merchants have been the focus of research by scholars who have studied urban Chinese in Malaysia, elsewhere in postwar Southeast Asia, and in China itself (Skinner 1958; Willmott 1960; Willmott 1967; Olsen 1972; Freedman 1979a, 1979b, 1979c, 1979e;

Wang 1981, 1991, 2000; Omohundro 1981; Lim and Gosling 1983; Yao 1987; Chan and Chiang 1994; Kuhn 1997; Ong and Nonini 1997; Ong 1999; but for exceptions that have examined laborers see Simoniya 1961; Siaw 1983; Loh 1988; and Pan 1994). Moreover, the widespread assumption by Western business journalists and pundits in the West was that Chinese "businessmen" described this way stand for all Chinese in Southeast Asia. To borrow a phrase from another context, for such commentators Chinese businessmen were "being all that Chinese (given Chinese culture) could be." Some scholars concede that given the rise to prominence of the "Newly Industrializing Economies" (NICs) of Southeast Asia, the older occupations of businessmen have during the last two generations been supplemented by those of Chinese professionals who have come into prominence with the rise of Asia's "new rich" (Pinches 1999; Robison and Goodman 1996).

But few scholars, and virtually no journalists, have given much attention to working-class Chinese citizens of Southeast Asian nation-states like Malaysia who, far from being celebrities or persons with position, are not even engaged in "doing business." Perhaps commentators believe that their lives are of little consequence for the weighty issues of "economy" and "economic development"? Chinese working people "do labor," *zuo gong*. They are collectively designated "workers," *gongren*, by employers and other outsiders, while among themselves, they refer to each other as *gongyou*, "working friends," or informally (among working men) as *dagongzai*, "working guys"—a gloss that seeks to capture this ironically affirmative self-referential term. In Bukit Mertajam, laboring men drove trucks, worked in foundries as welders, repaired car engines, engraved gravestones, cooked in restaurants, loaded freight, did carpentry work, and worked in the nearby assembly plants of the free trade zone of Prai and the industrial estates in Butterworth. Their wives, daughters, and mothers worked as seamstresses, laundresses, caterers, clerks, and accountants, and far more frequently than Chinese men, labored on the assembly lines of the nearby FTZ and industrial estates.[1]

The crucial point to be made is that in most public contexts being a "worker" or "doing labor" was not an identity that most such persons in Bukit Mertajam would proactively claim for themselves. While some business journalists and scholars might admit that such people have to exist in a statistical sense, they hardly ever write about them, and they are of little interest, best thought of if at all as businessmen manqué. If considered at all, they are viewed as a social and political control problem because of their supposed propensity toward crime and violence. In this chapter, I seek to refute this theoretical marginalization of Chinese working people in the mainstream literature as one effect of an uncritically celebratory capitalist discourse—one that itself more broadly perpetrates a kind of symbolic violence against a class dismissed.

To start with, working-class people are largely invisible to scholars because they are rendered mute by the silences of the elite informants who are explicitly or implicitly favored as "Chinese" subjects by most scholars.

A working-class identity among Chinese in Bukit Mertajam has been elusive for more than one reason, which has to do with the double-sided nature of classed practices: they confront material constraints *and* display competences related to classed styles and to social reproduction. On one side, there was the material aspect, that although Chinese working men were hospitable and shared resources like food with one another, they could not afford to engage in "entertainment," *yingchou*—the continuous rounds of dining, drinking at karaoke bars, and frequenting of prostitutes that were the required lubricants of sociable exchanges among towkays. Although they would try to display large public expenditures at times of life passage (e.g., the marriages of children), their attempts fell far short of those that characterized exchange relations among towkays—as when the few tables they paid for at wedding banquets were seen as laughably deficient compared to the scores that a wealthy man might pay for. Working men not only lacked the disposable income to spend on such pastimes, but also worked long hours at exhausting labor, often with irregular schedules imposed by employers, leaving them little time for socializing. Men of position who aspired to being celebrities also contributed money to the institutions of Chinese society, which set the bar even higher for working people who might be generous relative to their own incomes in support of such institutions, but whose small donations gained little public recognition.

Absent precisely the effects of institutions such as labor unions that affirmed more positive attributes of the stylistic practices of working-class people (e.g., solidarity, mutual assistance, generosity within means), working people were identified with an ascribed lack, deficit, and incapacity and represented at most a stigmatized position—an *identification*—not an affirmative *identity*. The moral topography of Chinese petty capitalists saw working men as impoverished, grasping, and dangerous and placed them on the edges of the moral and social order—as always already criminals seeking illicit income at least through petty theft, or on a grander scale "walking the dark road" through narcotics smuggling.

However, here I would like to emphasize a point that to my knowledge has not been made previously, that the class stylistics of laboring men and women could not readily be elaborated in a public identity because, in addition to the material constraints on their class positions, there was another side to working-class stylized practice that requires attention—the demonstration of certain competences took place beyond the frame of dominant stylistic practices that characterized men doing business, men of position, and celebrities. In the absence of an institutional structure of support for such working-class stylistic alternatives, working people were left with few publicly accessible symbolic resources for being positively recognized as such. In contrast, men of position were able to incorporate into the performance of their class identities authoritative *modes of representation* that appropriated (or co-opted) the criteria for public recognition of the ethnic identity of Chinese. These modes of representation were manifested in competences or "cultural capital" whose acquisition was closely connected, as a matter of empirical fact, to the ownership of economic capital (Bourdieu 1986). What counted was that a man's possession of these competences, whose acquisition and development was associated with wealth, signaled (if it did not ensure) that he had a proper Chinese identity.

What were the competences that implicated modes of representation whose deployment defined someone as truly "Chinese"—but which most working-class adults did not possess? One competence was the ability to speak Mandarin Chinese fluently, and to read and write the Chinese ideograms associated with it, most prevalent in the everyday form of Chinese-language newspapers. Being able to speak fluent Mandarin provided a man of position with the capacity to speak with other Chinese from beyond the Penang region (who might not speak the regional lingua franca, Hokkien) or even from beyond Malaysia, and to engage in oratory if asked to serve as a leader in an association of Chinese society, while an ability to read written Chinese characters in the Chinese-language press and literature allowed him the cachet of presenting himself as a man of learning. The ability to read and write Chinese fluently distinguished a man as having been instilled in the Chinese classics studied in the curricula of Chinese-language secondary schools. Learning the classics was, in itself, a mark of someone having absorbed, in the course of "reciting," (*du*) the classics, the discipline of the proper virtues associated with such schooling—deference to the authority of the teacher (and to political authority) and willingness to memorize, recite, and declare the wisdom of elders and Confucian scholars. Being fluent in the speaking, writing, and reading of Chinese, in short, marked a person as a potential elite and cosmopolitan.

A second related competence in the case of men of position was a form of learned male self-presentation and body *hexis* often translated as "having manners" or "being polite," *you limao,* associated with restraint and formality toward male peers in public interactions. You limao would more correctly be glossed as "being capable in etiquette," that is, displaying appropriate behavior toward others depending on their social status relative to oneself. Having manners was, in turn, acquired by having been properly inculcated in the Chinese classics, which allowed one to emulate the virtues of the *junzi,* or learned scholar, extolled in the classics. Having manners, in turn, signaled that a man might appropriately occupy the socially central spaces and built structures associated with Chinese society—downtown shop houses, association meeting halls, schools, and temples, especially on ritual occasions in the Daoist/Buddhist calendar of worship.

In contrast, working-class practice could rarely enunciate itself as such in public because the very channels of articulation it would have had to use to do so—speaking Mandarin, reading Chinese characters, and having manners—negated crucial features of working-class style. These included speaking Hokkien vernacular (called disparagingly a "dialect"), while failing to show fluency in Mandarin.[2] Beyond that, working-class practice showed a lack of manners and instead was "crude," *culu*: instead of restraint before social superiors, the worker were said to speak "wildly," irreverently, and out of turn. Connected with this unrefined talk (e.g., loudness, the use of curse words), the working-class body was one that did not utter a declarative language that used the "repeated speech" of the recited classics, but rather emanated a loud and boisterous physicality that lacked restraint toward the bodies of others and the spaces they occupied. It is quite evident that the distinction between "having manners" and "being crude" among Chinese reflected the hegemonic Malaysian cultural distinction between being "refined," *alus*, and being "coarse," *kasar* (Malay). These aspects of working-class style are the subject of the next chapter.

The reader may note the near impossibility of affirmatively performing working-class practice and the competences underlying it in these social conditions. The socially defined lack or deficit that characterized working-class people in Bukit Mertajam precisely indicated the double binds confronting working people who sought to assert a public identity. This putative deficit, derived from ethnographic investigation of the "experience" of elite informants, must not be replicated in our theorizations, which must be critical of such supposed revelations (Smith 1999, 8–12). Instead, we must examine the processes of domination that structure such broader public perceptions of deficits in working people, while they actually generate chaos and disorder in their daily lives (Sider 2005).[3] As I show in the next chapter, what was at stake with working-class crudeness were ways of learning and knowing central to the social reproduction of working people: a working-class embodied knowledge of "learning how"/"showing how" to do something, which combined the Hokkien vernacular with the acquisition or display of physical skills within the labor process, and beyond it in daily life.

These class competences were opposed to and set against towkay cultural styles associated with men of position based on displays of a moralizing knowledge most commonly coded in Mandarin and written Chinese characters, associated with a declarative "learning that"/"showing that" something or someone existed, articulated within a discourse grounded in etiquette, *li*, combined with a body hexis of restraint and a conspicuous lack of physical exertion.[4] Workers' inability to sponsor the rounds of business entertainment, much less the expenses associated with being a celebrity such as donating large amounts to Chinese society, their exclusive use of Hokkien combined with a (at times only assumed) lack of fluency in Mandarin, and crudeness in speech and action, meant that workers were excluded from, or at least marginalized from the socially and ritually central places of Chinese society, and relegated to peripheral or interstitial spaces. Workers might worship at major religious festivals, but as noted in the article on Yulanshenghui at the end of chapter 2, they were enjoined against too active participation—against "acting like a wild child" (being possessed) before the gods, while towkays were selected as the "incense urn masters" and "committee members" to lead such festivals, had their names celebrated, and collectively came together to occupy the spaces before the gods' altars on the climatic first and last days of festivals.

How could working-class praxis not be associated with avoidance, withdrawal, and a presumed reluctance to engage publicly in both religious ritual and ethnic politics, when to act otherwise required the use of material resources and stylized competences closely associated with the status of men of position and celebrities? For example, as described in chapter 2, why was it that the young seamstresses working for Tai Heng Garments were not seated next to their managers at the firm's Autumn Festival banquet, if not for their crudeness and use of dialect?

The possession of private wealth and its social deployment could—and often did—override any pedantic concerns with these stylistic competences that marked the presence of men of position. Where a man of position fell short in not having one of these competences—e.g., was not fluent in Mandarin—this would be noted, but having economic capital and showing hypercorrectness in one's performance in other ways functioned as compensation in its absence. For instance, in the case of the "older generation" of businessmen who could speak only "dialects" (like Hokkien or Teochew) and not Mandarin, but were celebrities due to their wealth and donations to Chinese society, other men of position deemed it acceptable for them to send proxy speakers to banquets when they were asked to deliver speeches before those assembled. In contrast, an adult working man's incapacity to speak Mandarin due to having grown up in a poor family and having been required to leave school at Standard 6 (after six years of primary schooling) to enter the labor force could never be redeemed in the elite opinions of who was acting appropriately "Chinese" and who was not—no matter how generous he might be in contributing part of his income to or seeking to be active in the associations of Chinese society. Rather than being regarded as a man of position, he would be an object of ridicule for his pretensions.

What I am calling working-class style was therefore based on an affirmative praxis of speaking the vernacular language, being crude, and avoiding socially and ritually central places, but these were characteristics that, when taken together, could rarely be articulated into a public identity as such. Under the conditions of the Emergency and the years that followed, which limited the possibility of the development of alternative institutions like labor unions among Chinese, which would have publicly affirmed and reinforced working-class styles, the fugitive competences and practices which made up working-class praxis arose instead from what the feminist theorist Donna Haraway (1991, 190–193) has called a "subjugated standpoint." The class-grounded "vantage points of the subjugated" Chinese working men I knew in Bukit Mertajam were simultaneously those from which these men contested the terms of their exploitation by men of position and from which they challenged the "god trick" (Haraway 1991, 189ff) of a purported omniscient vision by men of position who stipulated that there was only one way of "being Chinese"—*a way signified by the classed stylized performances of men of position.*

It is important to grasp the methodological implications for ethnography of this double-sided quality to working-class resistance to class oppression: both on the side of workers' struggle against material exploitation (e.g., over wages and working hours) and on the side of the ways (styles, modes) in which working men expressed their social status in opposition to dominant modes of representation. Such contestation by working men, and the antagonistic responses to them by men of position, formed the dialectics of class conflict and class struggle in Bukit Mertajam. Because the contestations by working men and women were most often expressed in language and behaviors that did not conform to the dominant modes of representation of Chinese ethnic identity, they were refractory to an ethnographic optic focused on the anthropologist's exchanges with prolix informants, articulated in the dominant commercial language of Mandarin, transacted in settings removed from the daily strife of the work milieu—often elite settings such as the air-conditioned offices of towkays' shop houses, at upscale seafood restaurants, at association banquets, or on similar ritual occasions. Yet such was my "default" approach that, for the most part, "worked" during my 1978–80 dissertation research when I sought to meet and interact with men of position. Indeed, what makes an elite perspective difficult to avoid is that this default approach has characterized most anthropological approaches to the economic activities of "overseas Chinese" in the literature.

Given the double-sided character of the stylized class practices of working men—material constraints on one side and stigmatized cultural styles on the other—two implications follow that dictate the strategy of my argument in the rest of this chapter. First, the occasions on which working-class resistance to oppressive conditions was expressed through dominant modes of representation (e.g., in Mandarin, publicly, in socially and ritually central places) were exceptional. When they did occur, they required not only clear ethnographic documentation but also historical context in terms of the extraordinary social and political conditions that made them possible. One such episode is described in the remainder of this chapter.

Second, these infrequent events do not adequately testify to the ongoing, everyday agonistics of class struggle, which simultaneously involved contention over both the "substance" and "style" and over the "content" and "form" of domination. Yet to investigate these two-sided agonistics, an ethnographic sensitivity to both aspects made the use of methods very different from the "default" approach imperative. This became clear, in retrospect, beginning with my fieldwork with truck drivers in 1985, five years after my dissertation ethnography with men of position, and largely inadvertently, became even clearer in my fieldwork in the 1990s with working men. Instead of seeking out verbose and articulate exchanges with men of position whom I tended to meet in elite spaces, with working men I discovered the need to share with them the experience of physical labor and the efficient use of aphoristic speech. Instead of formal interviews, I found it crucial to observe and (when I could) participate in the labor process and its classed and gendered aesthetics. Instead of looking for a declarative language of argument to "learn that" the labor process was exploitative, I came to realize the need to study an embodied pedagogy by working men to "learn how" the process occurred, and this is the subject of chapter 6.

Before proceeding, it is important to be clear about one issue. Class relations and class struggle in any complex society do not represent the only line of inequality and differential power that divides people from one another, and it is important from the outset not to be misunderstood about a crucial point regarding gender in particular. This chapter and the book of which is it part focuses on the class praxis of laboring men because work and social settings among working-class Chinese were largely segregated by gender, and because working men accepted my presence among them. Although I by no means uncritically accepted the views presented by working men about the women they knew and their own relationships to them, my ethnographic position as a man interacting largely with other men limits what I can say about the situation of working women.

An Exceptional Event: The Founding of a Working Men's Society

The ambiguities and contradictions that surrounded working-class male stylistic practices were particularly revealing on the rare occasions when laborers made themselves visibly known as such, as in their leaders' infrequent public speeches.

Consider the extraordinary speech made by the secretary of the North Malaysian Lorry Drivers Association in 1980 that recounted how the association came to be established two years earlier when drivers in Bukit Mertajam first organized the association to worship during Yulanshenghui, the seventh lunar-month Festival of the Hungry Ghosts. This was a speech delivered to refute the charge that drivers did so as a "secret society":

> At that time we were intimidated on all sides, with outsiders ridiculing [us], [saying], lorry drivers—how do they have the conditions and qualifications to establish an association? Because of this, it came about that many of our workers [*gongyou*] who are lorry drivers, had a hesitating attitude toward the association, and did not dare to come forward to participate in the association. Fortunately, our flock of old and crude lorry drivers [*women zhequn laocu de loli siji*] vowed with firm resolution that indeed we wanted the successful organization of the association, with the result that in an evil environment, our association finally came into being. (*Xingbin Ribao* 1980a)

Here, the "reported speech" (Bakhtin 1981) given in the regional newspaper *Xingbin Ribao* was a transformation that already compromised the semiotics of Chinese male working-class praxis, for the written language placed the narrative in the camp of representation monopolized by the dominant class and its spokesmen. Nonetheless, in political struggles, a group uses the weapons it has at hand—and one such was the oratorical competence of this secretary of the association. The words illuminated the malaise they diagnosed: "intimidation" on all sides led to a "hesitating attitude" by drivers, who at first "did not dare to come forward," yet "our flock of old and crude lorry drivers" finally did so despite being in "an evil environment." Avoidance and reluctance on the part of laboring men to engage with the dominant in its own terms were common practices. Some men with position saw such withdrawal in quite different terms as a reflex arising from "a feeling of inferiority," *zibeigan*. In my experience interacting with truck drivers at least, it was nothing of the kind.

This speech recounted an exceptional event, once placed into its historical context. To begin with, men who "did labor" rarely had an explicit collective presence in public life, hence their "hesitation" and lack of "daring to come forward" to organize the Lorry Drivers Association in late 1978 as a means to engage in public worship of the god Dashiye during the Chinese seventh lunar month. Second, evident in the secretary's speech, as also in one-on-one exchanges I had with some drivers, there was a strong critique of the symbolic violence directed against drivers by the truck owners, *chezhu*, who were their "bosses," when the latter accused them of being crude, by responding with an ironic affirmation of their own "crudeness" and ignorance that it was "our flock of old, crude lorry drivers" who had had the courage to establish the association in 1978.

The meaning of the phrase *women zhequn laocu de loli siji* beautifully captured the irony, particularly the numeral classifier *qun*, which I translate as "flock" because it is not usually used with human beings but with an aggregate of domestic animals, and placed before the noun phrase "old and crude lorry drivers," *laocu de loli siji*, thus having the force of modifying the noun phrase. There was the sense here of a collective natural force at work at odds with the carping voices of prolix "outsiders" who formed an "evil environment," and it was part of the sarcasm intended. Third, within its context it becomes clear that when the secretary alluded to a confrontation between "our flock" and "outsiders" who were part of an "evil environment," he was referring not only to the members of an opposed class of truck owners, but also to the representatives of an invasive and hostile state—to officials, for instance, like Mohamad bin Bakar, Road Transport Department official, who claimed that "drivers are gangsters."

Nonetheless, despite all obstacles, in late 1978, drivers, with the assistance of political allies, had "come out" to found the Lorry Drivers Association. Why was this so unusual, even exceptional? How was it even possible?

A Tumultuous History of Hidden (?) Working-Class Organization

"Aims and Objects" of the North Malaysia Lorry Drivers Association:

(a) to foster goodwill; to adjust [to] difficulties faced by members; to achieve unity and cooperation among lorry drivers of all races;

(b) to improve the welfare of lorry drivers of all races; to promote charity and philanthropic work; to encourage equality and mutual aid among lorry drivers of all races;

(c) to promote the driving skill and knowledge of members; to render loyal service to the people, the society and the Nation.

—File #4534, Pejabat Pendaftar Pertubuhan (Register of Societies Office), Pulau Pinang, October 14, 1978

In chapter 1, I argued that the three decades from the early 1950s onward through the 1970s were a period of Malaysian history marked by state suppression of a public language of class and of class struggle, and the achievement of an hegemonic set of countertruths about essential ethno-racial differences among Malaysians that dislodged and supplanted the discourse of class antagonisms that had prevailed among the population during the late colonial period. The displacement of specific class discourse did not eliminate class-based grievances, but instead led to their being channeled into the language of ethno-race, and ethno-racial differences. One of the fields into which this displacement had penetrated was organized labor and trade unions. For the postcolonial period taken as a whole, the situation can be summarized by stating that, as a consequence of the Malaysian government's continuous efforts against activist trade unions, union membership as a proportion of the country's waged/salaried labor force remained low, fluctuating around 20 percent between 1957 and 1980 (calculated from Jomo and Todd 1994, 8–9, 23, tables 1.1 and 2.1). From independence in 1957 through the late 1970s, the government spoke of trade unions as potential sources of subversion, and by the early 1970s it had supplemented this argument with the further claim that unions posed a threat to export-oriented industrial "development" as well, because labor activism and higher wages would discourage foreign investors. Government ministers thus cast trade unions as potential enemies of the nation.

Trade union organizing over this period varied in accordance with the history of the capitalist business cycle and the demand for labor, and with the force with which the state responded to such activity. For the decade following the peak in labor militancy in the early 1960s when there were a record number of labor strikes and workers out on strike, the government used the combined strategy of indefinitely detaining union leaders under the Internal Security Act, deregistering militant unions, and passing new draconian labor laws to limit the scope of union organizing, collective bargaining, and capacity to engage in strikes and other industrial actions (Jomo and Todd 1994, 106–145). The national emergency of 1969–70 declared after the riots of May 13, 1969, led to further laws restricting unions' rights to organize, bargain collectively, and participate in politics. Most trade unions had members with majorities consisting of only one ethno-racial group; of the thirty-one largest trade unions in 1983 representing 60 percent of all organized workers, twenty-seven had majorities belonging to one ethno-racial group, the average size of the majority was 69.4 percent, and its median size was 66 percent (calculated from Jomo and Todd 1994: 29, table 2.5). Despite the presence of a residue of language about "workers" and the like among trade union leaders, and despite some remarkably courageous leaders who persisted in forming cross-ethnic alliances while speaking about "workers' struggles," most trade union leaders and their members nonetheless organized their memberships' demands around ethno-racial-based discourses, practices, and patronage ties.

The organization of skilled Chinese workers around the workplace had long been shaped and constrained by the combination of hegemonic ethno-racialist discourse and state repression. There was a history to truck driving and its relationship to organized Chinese labor in the Penang region that lent force to the fears of both employers and government officials that truck drivers were particularly difficult to control and regulate, and this history ties the founding of the association closely to the repression of the Emergency. This history, or at least elaborated rumors of it, was familiar to employers, drivers, and government officials, and it is quite possible that some of the older truck owners and drivers were personal participants in it. According to Gamba (1962, 244), in the late 1940s

> in Penang ... the thousand strong Penang Motor Drivers' Association—the PMDA—prevented any Asian merchant, factory or company which owned lorries from competing with its members. The Chinese office bearers were all Hokkien, seventy per cent of whom were members of the *Aung Bin Hoay*, and belonging to all twenty-two "cells" or "rooms" of this society in Penang. Because the PMDA was under the influence of the *Hoay* the PMFTU [Pan Malayan Federation of Trade Unions] could not exert much influence over the Association. However, when the government forced the already illegal *Hoay* to disband [in 1948], the PMFTU tried to get the PMDA within its sphere of influence. The racket practiced by the PMDA was the intimidation of all Asian lorry owners who became afraid of operating their vehicles on the waterfront which was now controlled by the PMDA. Asian lorry owners who were not members of the PMDA dared not go to the waterfront without paying the necessary fee to the Association.

As discussed in chapter 1, the Aung Bin Hoay (i.e., the Ang Bin Hui) was one of the secret society groups operating in the Penang region suspected of Communist subversion, racketeering, and other criminal activity.[5] The PMDA certainly would have been active in organizing truck traffic ferried across from Georgetown (i.e., Penang) to the major transshipment point at Bukit Mertajam, some fifteen miles distant as the crow flies.

It was this history, or accounts of it, that in late 1978 induced one Bukit Mertajam truck owner, who was both an officer in the regional truck owners association, the North Malaysian Lorry Merchants Association, as well as an officer and stalwart in the MCA branch in Bukit Mertajam, to allege to the police inspector for secret societies in the district that the drivers who sought to register the Lorry Drivers Association as part of an ostensibly modest attempt to collectively worship Dashiye, were, in fact, hiding their true intentions: to establish a new secret society in order to gain control over the truck transport industry. Such reporting needs to be seen in the Cold War context of the alliance between Chinese capitalists and the Malaysian state. Nonetheless, I was told by one of the drivers who had worked to found the association in May 1978, that despite "much trouble this man caused" drivers by complaining to the police, the founding organizers were able to obtain the help of an independent state assemblyman for Penang Island who was able to use his influence to have the association registered as a society "within ninety days." His assistance came immediately after the 1978 national election that ejected several progovernment members of Parliament and state assemblymen from office in Penang state,[6] and the electoral victory of the DAP opposition in Penang provided him with the opening to successfully register the association. My informant noted that this success demonstrated how "efficacious" the god Dashiye was, as the drivers had devotedly worshipped it before and during the effort that led to the establishment of the association.

It is important to note that the Lorry Drivers Association was not registered as a trade union, but instead as a "society," which allowed it legally to be registered with and report to the Registrar of Societies. Had its founders attempted to register it as a trade union, they almost certainly would not have been allowed to. This was explicit: in Rule 10, "Prohibition," the drivers' charter specifically stated: "Neither the Association nor its members shall attempt to restrict or in any other manner interfere with the trade or prices or engage in any Trade Union activities as defined in the Trade Union Ordinance, 1959." As I discovered during my 1978–80 and 1985 fieldwork, the association functioned with many of the activities of a social club by providing a meeting hall where "long-haul" drivers could meet one another when not working, while away their leisure time playing *majiang* and other gambling games, and hold banquets for its celebration of Yulanshenghui, and on other occasions. Although the association was not a collective bargaining unit, its leaders all the same saw it as representing the "common and personal interests" of truck drivers, particularly long-haul drivers living throughout the northwestern region of Malaysia, and in 1979 it had more than two hundred members among the estimated one thousand truck drivers residing in or near Bukit Mertajam.

Given the circumstances under which it was founded—as a vehicle for the collective worship by (Chinese) drivers of Dashiye in the seventh lunar month, what then of the multiracial "Aims and Objects" of the North Malayan Lorry Drivers Association stipulated in its charter quoted above? A hegemonic discourse of ethno-racial difference is evident in the obsessive repetition of the phrase "lorry drivers of all races" within the "Aims and Objects" of the charter of the North Malaysian Lorry Drivers Association recorded in the Penang Registrar of Societies in late 1978. This phrase could not be stated often enough, when it came "to encourage unity and cooperation among . . . , to improve the welfare of . . ., to encourage equality and mutual aid among . . ." The charter of the Lorry Drivers

Association set it out as a reflection of the multiracial character of the Malaysian nation, which gave the charter a particular ideological force. Was this anything more than window-dressing for an ethnically controlled association to circumvent a hostile Malaysian state suspicious of organized Chinese political groups?

I would argue that the situation was actually more complicated—that a complex amalgam of classed and ethno-racial practices was evident in the labor politics of the association. The cross-racial composition of its membership—which in 1978–80 included not only Chinese (the great majority to be sure), but also Malays and Indians—was remarkable, as indicated in the language of solidarity that left its residue in the "Aims and Objects" sentences. Leaders of the association were quick to point out to me that the association provided assistance to members irrespective of their race, whether Chinese, Malay, or Indian, as when an injured Malay driver was awarded a stipend from the association to support his family while he was out of work and recovering from his injury. It is almost as if class became the unmarked signifier and unspoken principle of organization, despite the concession of racial diversity within the labor process itself.

Indeed, I wish to argue that in its brief heyday during the late 1970s into the 1980s, the Lorry Drivers Association operated in major respects as a class-based sodality—like a trade union—capable of organizing truck drivers toward common goals—but one "deformed by" or, better put, inclined in its political tactics through its de facto majority of Chinese men to engage with and appeal to a specific ethno-racial public.

A Paean to Truck-driving Labor

At the time I began fieldwork in 1978, I had no idea that my investigation of labor-management relations in the truck transport industry of Bukit Mertajam would provide me with an extraordinary "site"—one in constant, rolling motion—to study class relations among urban Chinese Malaysians. In the early months of my fieldwork, I decided to collect extensive data about the logistics of the town's truck transport industry in an inventory of trucks owned, routes traveled, freight carried, and the nature of consigners and consignees (see Nonini 1983b). Unlike sensitive economic information about cash flows, profits, and business partners about which truck transport towkays had little to say except that they barely "got by" with help from their "friends" in the industry while complaining about many sorts of hardship, the kind of dry logistic data I sought proved relatively easy to collect. Trucks could be counted, routes plotted on maps, freight tonnage added up, and the nature of freight inventoried—and the spatial organization of an industry that spanned cities and towns over hundreds of miles distance could be analyzed (Nonini 1983b). A dissertation could be written (Nonini 1983a). This was a positivist's dream, however intellectually uninspired.

What became increasingly clear as I collected such data from truck owners, transport company office managers, and clerks were my informants' claims about how "disputatious," unreliable, and dishonest truck drivers were. In contrast, in my few interviews with them, truck drivers and attendants graphically told me of the pressures placed on them by truck owners and the unrelenting nature and arduous labor involved in their work. I wondered at the time about the meaning of the discrepancy in claims made, and thus in 1985 I returned to Bukit Mertajam to study the working conditions of truck drivers and labor relations in the industry. While I turn to the results of that research in the next chapter, here I reflect on one aspect of the labor process in truck transport that made the conflict between truck owners and drivers I relate below such a serious threat to truck owners.

Above all, what made the labor process of truck transport extraordinary if not unique in the industrial history of Malaysia was the skilled nature of the labor required by the driver, and the extraordinary degree of control over the labor process this conferred on the driver. It was certainly not incidental that in 1948, the Penang Motor Drivers Association proved to be one of the labor organizations most refractory to pressures from capital and the colonial state alike: the nature of truck driving labor provides the driver with a very large degree of control over the labor process, unlike his employer, trade union leaders, or state officials. Fast forward to 1979 and on to 1985: long-distance truck driving remained highly skilled labor with substantial latitude for the driver to determine the conditions under which he labored.

Not only did truck driving demand someone with physical acuity, the stamina to deal with long hours, tropical heat, and polluted air,[7] and a degree of muscle strength to control long-haul trucks sometimes weighing thirty tons or more "on eighteen wheels" often driven hundreds of miles over poorly maintained paved roads. Driving also required highly developed and complex practico-intellectual skills. Drivers, particularly if they carried manufactured goods, had to know how to load their own trucks—thus know how to balance loads (to prevent their steering out of control when in motion) and what order to load goods in on the back (last on, first off). Furthermore they had to be familiar with not only major highways (like the north-south trunk road), but also the streets of major cities, large and small towns, suburbs, and in some areas, even rural kampongs; know how to navigate often dangerously crowded roads in bad weather (e.g., tropical downpours); know how to avoid roadblocks set by traffic police and Road Transport Department enforcement officers, to find consigners to pick up freight, and locate consignees to drop it off. They also had to be able to deal with consignees who make exacting demands about the freight delivered to them; be willing to argue, haggle with, and negotiate fines with police and officials if they were stopped; be able to make petty, and at times major, repairs on the trucks they drove, among many other skills grounded in deep experiential knowledge.

All these bodily capacities and intellectual skills, moreover, were harnessed to the task of meeting precise, even exacting schedules set by the truck owners who were their bosses, laoban. Truck owners expected drivers to adhere to these schedules, even when events occurred beyond the responsibility of drivers that led to delays (e.g., consigners suddenly unable to provide freight to carry, or a tire blowing out). These time pressures were enforced by a piecework wage rate set by truck owners of so many ringgit "per round trip," or *yi tang*, between two cities, and the wages of the driver thus depended on how many trips the driver could complete in one month.

As compensation for these hardships, the driver had very substantial control over the labor process. As complex as completing a trip was and dependent as it was on the driver's skills and abilities, how could the driver not have such control? While the driver might be "on the road" hundreds of miles away for sixty hours or longer in the course of a single round trip, the driver's boss, the truck towkay, sat in his office in Bukit Mertajam and had no means to monitor the minute-by-minute labor praxis of the drivers he hired. Truck owners told me that if they had to make trips to verify for themselves the claim by a driver of the need to pay a "compound" (fine) for an impounded truck, or for a truck's repair that stopped it en route, this took time they could ill afford. Drivers in their telephone calls to owners from outstation could easily fabricate a story that they required coffee money to pay police, or additional money for diesel fuel purchased en route. Many truck owners, and certainly those with the most successful and enduring businesses, had past experience as truck drivers before starting their own businesses, and they realized that they lacked knowledge of the specific and complex contingencies faced by drivers during a trip, and that they themselves were relatively powerless as a result. Not only were truck owners dependent on drivers to ensure the safety and security of their trucks and the freight they carried, but also drivers—especially experienced ones—were difficult to find due to the skills required for drivers under the conditions of a prevailing labor scarcity.

Truck driving under these circumstances conferred a high degree of control by individual drivers over the labor process, but it was entirely another question whether the individual differences in skills, wages paid, routes driven, and the like might be translated into a more collective and social objective of drivers' solidarity and common interest, or remain scattered and reinforce drivers' individualist habitus. Specific studies of labor relations have long demonstrated that labor recalcitrance and resistance to the demands made by capital are closely tied to the laborer's control over the labor process, but even more so to labor's *collective* autonomy with respect to that process (Edwards 1979; Peña 1997). The study of labor relations, however, has never been a purely academic pursuit, and the results of such study have, directly and indirectly, been incorporated into managerial theories *and* practices of labor control. Under the generally repressive conditions for labor set in the last years of the Cold War in Malaysia, nothing threatened the truck owners of Bukit Mertajam more than the idea of a truck drivers association—one in which drivers might be able to transform their individual control over the productive process into a form of collective power that could fundamentally restructure the relationships between truck towkays and the working men they employed as drivers.

Class Struggle in the Press and on the Roads: Who Was Responsible for Truck Overloads?

The North Malaysian Lorry Drivers Association brought into existence in 1978 provided the exceptional institutional locus that made possible the performance of an irruptive and episodic male working-class presence, at least among truck drivers, in Bukit Mertajam. Its existence allowed these men the voice and space—for a while—to present a united collective face and an opportunity to engage the sympathies of the Bukit Mertajam public.

The conflict I describe below represents a dispute between truck owners and truck drivers in Bukit Mertajam that lasted from early- to mid-1979, with its aftermath continuing for about a year thereafter. This dispute took the form of an argument between the leaders of their respective "occupational associations," *hangye gonghui*, regarding legal weight limits for cargo trucks carried and "the problem of overloading," in which they addressed their competing claims ostensibly to the Ministry of Transport. The dispute was thus a three-sided one that implicated not only the two associations but also the Malaysian state. The dispute played out on two fronts in the "war of position." One front was the public conflict set before an audience of Chinese-language newspaper readers—the "civilized" Chinese public. During this period of more than a year, with the exception of two face-to-face meetings, the dispute was fought through contested public statements—press releases, memoranda, and written responses—put out in Chinese by the two associations. Although the two associations did indeed send memoranda (in Bahasa Malaysia) to the Minister of Transport and his officials, the associations' proposals, counterclaims, and accusations published in the two regional Chinese-language newspapers that reported these transmittals were directed not at the government, but rather aimed at this Chinese public. The dispute, although at one level about overloading trucks and who bore responsibility for it, was at another level a conflict over the meaning of postcolonial development—and over who was to benefit from, and who to pay for, it. Above all, this was the discursive expression of ongoing class conflict.

This dispute also played out on the second front on the roads of Malaysia from 1978–79 in three-sided contests between absentee truck owners, truck drivers, and Road Transport Department enforcement officers, who forcibly stopped trucks en route (often carrying fresh fish, poultry and produce), inspected and weighed the trucks, issued compounds (fines) to truck owners if trucks were (or were claimed by officials to be) overweight, and suspended (or threatened to suspend) the licenses of truck drivers. Wages, profits, livelihoods, the futures of businesses, taxes, graft, reputations—all were at stake.

The Northern Malaysian Lorry Merchants Association located in Bukit Mertajam was founded in late 1976 by a planning committee composed of nine of the more wealthy and well-known truck owners with operations centered in the town. They were all towkays, and two were celebrities. All men, the members of this committee were not only the owners of the largest transport companies; several of them were also prominent contributors to the Malaysian Chinese Association, and others on the committee had served as officers of the local branch of the MCA in the past. Fast forward, then, to December 1978, when the dispute was about to begin, three members of this planning committee, closely affiliated with the MCA, were by then serving as chairman, secretary, and treasurer of this regional truck owners' association. As leaders and stalwarts of the local MCA branch, these men had but a few months earlier witnessed the overwhelming loss of the MCA candidate for Bukit Mertajam's parliamentary seat, a "Penang [island] man," to the candidate put up by the opposition party, the Democratic Action Party. They had, moreover, unsuccessfully opposed the founding of the North Malaysia Lorry Drivers Association. Perhaps it was time to jump scale in the political hierarchy (i.e., seek leverage against a less sympathetic state government by appealing to allies in the Barisan Nasional at the higher national level in Kuala Lumpur), and to show truck drivers and their newly registered association (really a "secret society"!) who was the "boss"?

In December 1978 the chairman of the association, Chua Tee Hwa, owner of one of the largest trucking companies in Bukit Mertajam, headed a delegation of the Pan-Malaysian Lorry Merchants Association, to which the North Malaysian association belonged, to visit the minister of transport in Kuala Lumpur. The delegation carried a petition. On his return to Bukit Mertajam, the regional truck owners' association rapidly endorsed this petition as its own in late December 1978 (*Xingbin Ribao* 1978). In the petition, truck owners called on the Ministry of Transport to approve a 30 percent increase in the allowable maximum tonnage that could be legally carried by a truck. This was to be an increase over the weight limits set by regulations passed by the ministry under the Transport Ordinance of 1958. This increase, the petition argued, was justified because of inflation in the cost of diesel fuel, spare engine parts, and tires, because of the extremely high degree of internal competition within the industry, and because of the new government-mandated ceiling on the transport charge per ton-mile throughout Malaysia, which held down the fees that truck owners could charge consigners (*Xingbin Ribao* 1978).

The petition went on to offer concessions, of sorts, if this increase was approved by the ministry. It proposed that after the increased weight limit was put into effect, whenever the Road Transport Department's enforcement officers discovered overloaded trucks, the truck's operating permit used by the truck owner should be rescinded; the license of the driver caught operating the overloaded truck be suspended; and all freight found in excess of the new weight limit be confiscated by the ministry (*Xingbin Ribao* 1978).[8]

These three concessions possessed an air of rhetorical virtuosity, for none of the three, if implemented, would have had much negative impact on truck owners. To take the most extreme proposal, the confiscation of the freight of a consigner who had no responsibility for overloading a truck would have been neither legal nor feasible. Nor would suspending the operating permit, far more often than not owned by a Malay Ali, have made much difference to the Chinese truck owner who played Baba in what was by then a very one-sided leaser's market. However, it was the second proposal—that the license of any driver operating an overloaded truck be suspended—that immediately drew fire from the Lorry Drivers Association in Bukit Mertajam.

Unlike the Lorry Merchants Association, the truck drivers association on the face of it had adopted a nonpartisan political position, signaled by the fact that it had as its official patrons leaders of all three political parties with Chinese members represented in Penang state—the MCA, the Gerakan, and the opposition Democratic Action Party. On January 9, 1979, a week after the Lorry Merchants Association publicly announced its petition to the Ministry of Transport, the Lorry Drivers Association released a press report that labeled the petition "stupid, unfair, and irrational." The proposal that drivers who operated overloaded trucks should have their licenses suspended led to the retort that

> we are dissatisfied and oppose resolutely the distortion of the facts by the truck owners association concerning the transport of overloads, and moreover the malicious, irresponsible and truculent shifting of blame onto our shoulders for it. We northern Malaysian truck drivers have for some time now followed the directions and orders of truck owners when we transport freight. We have never dared to defy or oppose them because of our rice bowls [jobs] and lives. . . . To take an example, according to government regulations a ten-wheeler truck can carry ten tons of freight, and fifty-five crates of fresh fish are equivalent to ten tons. The driver will always follow the instructions of the truck owner to load five

crates extra so as to deliver the fresh fish in time to its destination, and accept his opinion that there is no overloading. This kind of example occurs frequently. . . . The truth before our eyes is that truck owners who do not overload find it difficult to cope with the daily-increasing heavy expenses and responsibilities. If the drivers risk overloading, they must face the fact of having their licenses suspended; if they do not follow the directions of the owners, then they face the danger of being fired. (*Xingbin Ribao* 1979b)

On the front of public opinion, the petition of the Lorry Merchants Association and the sharp response to it by the Lorry Drivers Association were the opening salvos in the dispute between the two associations, a battle waged in a series of speeches and position papers issued by both sides, which appeared in the regional Chinese-language newspapers over the next several months.

The next step by the Lorry Merchants Association was to issue a report in early February 1979 that urged the authorities in the Transport Ministry to act quickly in approving the proposed 30 percent increase in allowable tonnage that the association had proposed, even as it urged owners not to overload (*Xingbin Ribao* 1979c). The report brought up what the association's leaders claimed was a recurrent problem—the price-shaving competition in which truck owners vied with one another to offer lower transport charges to factories and other businesses—and condemned the practice. As one member of the committee of the association issuing the report exhorted, "Members of the trade have to be strong and restrain their selfishness, and not continue to engage in practices that compete by shaving prices. In this way they can begin to hold fast to the future of our industry" (*Xingbin Ribao* 1979c). This in effect offered an explanation—and an admission of the motives owners might have—for overloading.

On the other front—on Malaysia's roads—what was evident from informants was that from January through July 1979, Road Transport Department enforcement officers and traffic police were stopping many trucks from Bukit Mertajam en route to cities outside the northwestern region for inspection and claiming that trucks were overloaded and exhibited other infractions. They assessed fines against the trucks' owners and suspended the licenses of the drivers for one, two, or several months, depending on whether the driver had been found previously to be driving an overloaded truck. Hence the warning against overloading given by the leaders of the Lorry Merchants Association—a warning to truck owners couched in such a way that these leaders could deny actually imputing the practice of overloading to truck owners.

Things were quite different for the Lorry Drivers Association. Its attack on the proposals of the Lorry Merchants Association came to have a double thrust in its published reports to the public and the Transport Ministry. One was that the responsibility for overloading *always* lay with truck owners, by virtue of the fact that they employed truck drivers and gave them directions. In its public report of March 13, it responded,

> Recently there have repeatedly been certain employers [*guzhu*] who continue to order their truck drivers to carry overloads. . . . The positions of the two parties are not the same. One is the truck merchant, who deals with business affairs within the company, and has to right to initiate [*zhudongquan*] and to decide [*juedingquan*], and who absolutely has rights and powers of management, and who has a broad economic base. One is the driving worker who does not have the right to decide or initiate, who moreover is in a position where he is managed and relies completely on his working wages for his livelihood. Therefore, given the organization of the entire company, and the positions of both parties, how can [the decision to] carry overloads be within the drivers' power? (*Xingbin Ribao* 1979d)

This was a forthright, if overly formal, statement of the differential class powers of the two sides.

The other argument made by the Lorry Drivers Association was that overloading trucks endangered the lives and safety of both drivers and other road users. Overloading ruined the roads by creating potholes and led to tire blowouts. Drivers would lose control over overloaded trucks when descending hills or at high speeds. Steering would be unstable and therefore dangerous (*Xingbin Ribao* 1979d).

Matters came to a head when the national deputy minister of transport, a Chinese leader of the Gerakan Party, was called on by local members of the party to mediate and proposed in early May 1979 that both sides sit down to exchange views and come to agreement. The "round-table discussion" in Bukit Mertajam that ensued, instead of resolving differences between the two organizations, exacerbated them. Over the next two months both sides put out press releases and newspaper reports that criticized the other side in harsh terms.

In an article appearing August 4, 1979, Chua Tee Hwa, president of the Lorry Merchants Association argued that many drivers deceitfully loaded on and carried (*touzai*) the freight of others to enrich themselves, and this led to overloading. If this was discovered by Road Transport Department officers during inspection, then it was only fitting that drivers should be punished by having their licenses canceled or suspended (*Guanghua Ribao* 1979b). Moreover, he went on, a major cause of accidents was not overloading but rather the fact that drivers were negligent in their driving and, in Chua's words, failed to display a "courteous attitude," *lirang de taidu*, by yielding to other road users, which led to accidents (*Guanghua Ribao* 1979b). His insinuation that drivers were "crude" cannot have gone unnoted by drivers.

A retort from the Lorry Drivers Association was not long in coming and provided insights into yet other aspects of the conflict—in the press and on the roads. On August 15, 1979, the association accused Chua of fabricating examples of dishonest drivers (who loaded on their own freight). In a breach of etiquette by addressing owners in person, it went on to make several other points which it had not previously raised. For one, the association alluded to truck owners' interests in Ali-Baba arrangements:

> You loudly complain that the "trucking industry will fall on hard times," unless the authorities allow an increase in freight carried by 30 percent. But at the same time, we want to ask the truck owners association why it is that some truck merchants who do not risk overloading, are not only surviving but growing? To put it another way, since the trucking industry has already fallen into a difficult situation, why do you still want to rent out Ali-Baba permits in order to do more trucking business? (*Xingbin Ribao* 1979e)

Moreover, the drivers association's press release claimed that truck owners forced drivers to drive rapidly, and it was this, and not the lack of a "courteous attitude," which caused drivers to have accidents:

> When you shirk responsibility for forcing drivers to carry overloads, you must confront two facts: first, trucks carry fresh cargo and this causes overloads, while at the same time drivers must hasten by driving at high speeds; second, a certain truck owner when he accepts applications for drivers' work has one precondition only—that the prospective driver dare to drive at a high speed and to "cut" other vehicles.[9] (*Xingbin Ribao* 1979e)

The telling aspect of this second accusation against a "certain truck owner" was that it was well understood by both sides—and by many among the reading public—that the "certain truck owner" referred to was Chua Tee Hwa himself, who was notorious among drivers for abusing his own drivers with physical threats and disrespectful speech.

On August 18, 1979, three days after the Lorry Drivers Association put out this press release, the Ministry of Transport formally approved the 30 percent increase in legal tonnage proposed by the truck owners, and this ended the public dispute (*Guanghua Ribao* 1979c). The state had intervened decisively on the side of capital.

Exceptional Times, Exceptional Circumstances

As I state above: wages, profits, livelihoods, the futures of businesses, taxes, graft, reputations—all were materially at stake in this conflict. But so too were classed stylistic practices and the possibility of enunciating a working-class identity. I want to conclude this chapter to reflect briefly on the conundrum of how it was that, despite the diverse obstacles against the public manifestation of a working-class identity for laboring men in Bukit Mertajam, truck drivers were able for a period of time to establish and maintain a worker's "society" that provided precisely the institutional setting within which such an identity could be publicly manifested. This allowed them a form of collective power through which they sought to challenge the demands of truck owners and other men of position—even if they were ultimately unsuccessful due to state intervention. There was an extraordinary confluence of conditions that made such an unusual manifestation not only of class power, but also of a class identity defined by class practice, possible. These conditions by the mid-1980s had started to come to an end, and with them, the possibilities for drivers to articulate a class-based identity.

Some of these conditions I refer to above. Truck drivers' very substantial control over the labor process of truck transport made them a "dangerous" class. Moreover, drivers' leverage over truck owners—and over Malaysian industrial corporations that depended on truck transport—rose to a peak in the late 1970s and early 1980s because of a very large "problem of labor scarcity," or *laogong quefa wenti*, as informants called it, associated with the rapid gearing up of the export-industrialization platform in Penang state, which was in turn connected to the implementation of the developmental objectives of the New Economic Policy. In 1978–80, truck owners told me that such labor scarcity made it very difficult for them to find, hire, and retain truck drivers, especially experienced ones. This labor scarcity passed: due to the worldwide recession then underway, by 1985 drivers had far less latitude in finding employment with truck owners, and truck owners had begun, in the interim, to turn to non-Chinese labor for drivers, to curb demands by Chinese drivers.

Drivers were able to organize their association as a registered "society" during a specific national political opening immediately in the wake of the 1978 national election that significantly diminished the political influence of the government's conservative allies in the MCA in Penang state and gave the association's founders an opportunity to form a coalition with an anti-MCA political leader who was able to have the association registered. This window in time was fortuitously short, for the ongoing 1979 labor dispute between the national airline, Malaysian Airlines Systems, and the Airlines Employees Union led to the adoption by 1980 of some of the most severe sanctions by the government against trade unions and labor organizing since the early 1960s (Jomo and Todd 1994, 142–143). Despite legal prohibitions against the association functioning as a trade union, the leaders of the association nonetheless were able to channel its "Aims and Objects" toward providing a collective voice for drivers' grievances around overloading and a public critique of the class practices of truck owners. Nevertheless the MCA-affiliated leaders of the truck owners association were able to successfully counterattack the driver's association through their capacity to jump scale to appeal to their allies at the national level of the MCA and Barisan Nasional, and to eventually force through the approval of increased tonnage in truck loads. This signaled a public defeat of the truck drivers' association as a collective voice for truck drivers.

What is most noteworthy was the presence of allies in the effort of truck drivers to register their association, then to wage the campaign in the Chinese press against overloads once they were put on the defensive by the petition of the truck owners' association. These included the state assemblyman who helped them register the association and the secretary of the association who had served as its articulate spokesman during the months of overt public conflict with the Lorry Merchants Association in 1979. Unfortunately, the participation by these allies is what I know least about. In 1985, when I asked leaders of the Lorry Drivers Association about the founding of the association and asked to interview the then-secretary of the association, they refused to introduce me to him. There had evidently been some falling out in the interim. Nonetheless, it can be inferred that this man, probably a client of the Penang Island state assemblyman, was able to use his considerable oratorical gifts in Mandarin, his written fluency in Chinese characters, and connections with Chinese language newspapers to provide the truck drivers with a collective voice.

However, the association secretary's speech was not in their *own* voice, for the vast majority would not have been able to fluently speak the dominant language of Mandarin, nor set out cogent arguments like those he gave in the Chinese press against overloads as prerogatives of capital that endangered the lives and livelihoods of drivers. This mode of representation was largely alien to their class praxis, which "spoke articulately" using other forms of cultural performance, as I will show in chapter 6. But the hybrid rhetoric that invoked "our flock of old and crude lorry drivers" and their capacity to act with "daring" in the presence of "outsiders" who made up an "evil environment" sufficed to carry through the public campaign in the press in 1979, which reflected the simultaneous struggles by drivers on the roads to protect their bodies, wages, and livelihoods, in other words, their drivers licenses, what they called their "rice bowls." This hybrid rhetoric was revelatory, for in its articulate irony, reflecting on a moment of danger yet opportunity for drivers, it demonstrated the limits on the public expression of working-class identity, given the constellation of class forces and the state arrayed against Chinese truck drivers and other workers.

PLATE 1 A past of counterinsurgency—district police headquarters and barracks, downtown Bukit Mertajam, 1979

PLATE 2   Street scene, Jalan Pasar, Bukit Mertajam 1979

PLATE 3   Fudezhengshen Temple, downtown Bukit Mertajam, 1979

PLATE 4   Towkay in his pork butcher's shop serving customer, downtown Bukit Mertajam, 1979

PLATE 5 Podogong (Dashiye), with money offerings piled up in lap, and worshippers, Yulanshenghui festival, Bukit Mertajam, 1979 (note Guanyin statue on center of headdress)

PLATE 6 Workers queuing for factory bus, downtown Bukit Mertajam, 1979

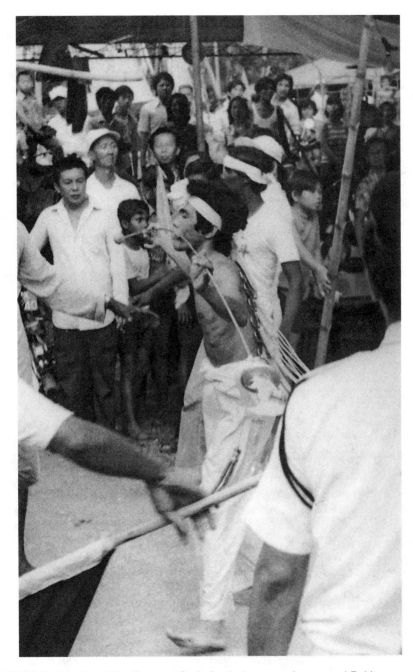

PLATE 7 Medium, Nine Emperor Gods festival, procession around Bukit Mertajam, 1979

PLATE 8 Funeral delegation of celebrities—the Jit Sin Independent High School Board of Trustees, 1979

PLATE 9 Truck drivers at Yulanshenghui worship pose for a photo, 1985

PLATE 10 Throwing divining blocks for next year's festival committee, Lorry Drivers' Association, Yulanshenghui, 1985

PLATE 11 Gods possessing mediums line up before procession, Shilinggong Temple, Sugar Cane Village, Bukit Mertajam, 1991

PLATE 12 Procession of gods possessing mediums, Shilinggong gods in palanquin, and festival incense master and committee, through Sugar Cane Village, 1991

PLATE 13 Men under the trees, Bukit Mertajam 1991

PLATE 14 Bandar Perda sign, western suburb of Bukit Mertajam, 1997

PLATE 15   Building hypermarket at Old Padang, downtown Bukit Mertajam, 1997

PLATE 16   New district office and road construction, Sugar Cane Village, 1997

PLATE 17 Downtown Bukit Mertajam 2007 (young man walking on Jalan Danby, Summit Hotel in distance)

PLATE 18 Fish market, Jalan Bunga Raya, Bukit Mertajam, 2007

PLATE 19 Farmers at sunset, vegetable fields, Kampung Caiyuan, near downtown Bukit Mertajam, 2007

MEN IN MOTION

The Dialectics of "Disputatiousness" and "Rice-Eating Money"

In a classic passage from "The Sale and Purchase of Labor Power," in *Capital*, Marx invites us to join the purchaser and seller of labor power in leaving the "market or the noisy sphere of circulation"—"a very Eden of the innate rights of man . . . the exclusive realm of Freedom, Equality, Property and Bentham"— and to "follow them into the hidden abode of production" (Marx 1976 [1867], 1:279–280). Once this abode is entered, where "the secret of profit-making must be laid bare," there "a certain change takes place . . . in the physiognomy of our *dramatis personae*. He who was previously the money-owner now strides out in front as a capitalist; the possessor of labor-power follows as his worker. The one smirks self-importantly and is intent on business; the other is timid and holds back, like someone who has brought his own hide to market and now has nothing to expect but—a hiding" (279–280). In like way, this chapter leaves the noisy sphere of public commerce and reputation in Bukit Mertajam, which celebrated the style of the "typical Chinese" as a bourgeois prototype, to examine the sphere of production in which class formation and class conflict among Bukit Mertajam's Chinese occurred. In this sphere, not only was new wealth for the capitalist created through "a hiding" of the worker but so too were the cultural styles of the towkay as "boss," laoban, and of his workers as "laborers," gongren, performed. However, going further, the hidden abode of production was where the social positions of men vis-à-vis the women they worked with were constituted.

In what follows, I investigate the labor process of one local industry crucial to the role of Bukit Mertajam in the regional economy of northern Malaysia—truck transport—to ascertain what this process tells us about these classed and gendered styles. Above all, given the focus of this book on Chinese citizenship in Malaysia, through distinct but complementary processes of oppression, these styles were constrained in ways that prevented the full citizenship of working-class men and of women. That is, a fuller account of citizenship among Chinese in Malaysia requires not only that the conventional distinction between "political" and "economic" rights be transcended in the case of class but also that the invidious inequalities of gender be confronted, to the extent this is possible—all within the asymmetries of power that have emerged around distinct ethnic positions of Chinese and Malays.

As I indicate in the Introduction, the conventional wisdom about overseas Chinese, or diaspora Chinese, among social scientists and business pundits has been that such people are all either capitalists, or that most are but all want to be, and thus those who are not are merely capitalists manqué, in which case they don't matter anyway in accounting for the adaptativeness or economic success of Chinese in Southeast Asia. Consequently, working-class Chinese are not supposed to exist. I have argued that among Bukit Mertajam Chinese the performance of the dominant class styles of doing business and of being a towkay reinforced and informed this scholarly and journalistic wisdom.

Given this assumption, I have my work cut out for me. I pointed out that in most public contexts being a worker and working at labor was not a social status that most such persons would proactively claim for themselves because towkays, men of position, and celebrities incorporated into their performance of classed and gendered styles the competencies and practices whose mastery signaled Chinese ethnicity as a valued social status. These included being able to speak Mandarin Chinese, or at least read and write the Chinese ideograms that connected those fluent not only with the Chinese language press but, more profoundly, with Chinese-language education. Also important were their presumed memorization of the Confucian classics and their inculcation in filial virtue that went with it. These involved competence in displaying a form of learned male self-presentation and body hexis called "having manners" or "being polite," you limao, associated with restraint and courtesy toward male peers in public interactions. They also implicated the unchallenged right of men of wealth to occupy socially central spaces and built structures—downtown shop houses, association meeting halls, schools, and temples, especially on certain ritual occasions.

To be working-class men in contrast meant to be illiterate, crude, physically dangerous, and—because they were out of the public eye—crafty, secretive, and criminal. The embodied practices surrounding the fugitive stylistics and subjugated knowledges through which working-class men dealt with these class stigmas—stigmas that disadvantaged the very ways in which they represented themselves—even as they found common ground with their bosses in their performances vis-à-vis subordinate women, is the subject of this chapter. In theoretical terms, a conceptualization of these embodied practices, I argue, poses a formidable challenge to postmodernist poststructuralist claims about the centrality of discourse—claims that I believe exemplify class privilege. Because of the significant implications of this question for anthropological research, I deal with this question in passing in this chapter, and I have dealt with it elsewhere (Nonini 1999).

Drivers as Tricksters: A Class-grounded Discourse on Disputatiousness and Cheating, 1979–80

When I interviewed Chinese truck owners and office clerks in 1979–80 about conditions in the local truck transport industry (Nonini 1983a; 1983b), truck owners and office clerks in transport companies very commonly claimed that their long-haul drivers, most of whom were Chinese, were difficult to manage.[1] Far from being deferential, drivers were *jijiao*, "disputatious," "cheeky," "argumentative." Drivers "cheated" owners in a variety of ways by "eating" their money and stealing the freight they carried. Drivers were disputatious when owners requested them to do some task. Drivers sought to argue the matter with them in minute detail, in order to gain advantage. Above all, drivers disputed their wages, making almost insatiable demands for wage increases. They still disputed with owners even when these demands were met, often threatened to leave for work in other companies, and then did so. Beyond this, drivers were disputatious in a variety of superficially unrelated settings. Drivers refused the owner's request to load or unload freight onto or from trucks when they went out to pick up or deliver freight at a customer's business. Drivers argued with owners about having to pick up freight from northern regional consigners before commencing trips to the south, or about delivering freight to consignees after returning from these trips, and at times refused to make these deliveries. In this situation, drivers not only were disputatious but even threatened to strike, *bagong*. Drivers disputed with owners when the latter requested that they work on holidays or on Sundays—the customary day off in the Malaysian work week.

According to truck owners and office clerks, drivers' cheating took a variety of forms—and in grudging praise they credited drivers with great inventiveness in finding ways to cheat them. There was often more irony than bitterness, more wink-and-a-nod than vituperation, expressed in these accusations—I observed

worked-up expressions of outrage, much shaking of heads with acerbic and articulate tributes to the trickery of drivers. Owners claimed that on almost every trip
their drivers made, they themselves lost considerable amounts of money from
drivers eating their money. An owner of a company with twelve trucks carrying foodstuffs and sundry goods between Bukit Mertajam and Singapore stated:
"I pay my drivers one hundred ringgit for every trip they make between Bukit
Mertajam and Singapore, but I expect that drivers will usually gain another fifty
ringgit at my expense by theft or cheating me every trip." Many owners asserted
that *all* long-haul drivers ate their money by cheating them.

One of the most common complaints by owners was that drivers exaggerated
the amount of money they spent en route on diesel fuel and—after being paid this
amount by the owner—divided the difference between themselves. The owner of
six trucks whose drivers delivered sundry freight (mostly manufactured goods) in
Kuala Lumpur told me, "I know that drivers use part of this [diesel] money to eat
rice. They put in less diesel than they claim and pocket the difference. This amount
comes to twenty to thirty ringgit every trip. This is 'rice-eating money' [*chifanqian*], and I know the drivers do it, and I pay no attention to it." Drivers, owners said, also demanded money before a trip, ostensibly to give as coffee money
to police stopping their trucks for inspection, but overstated the probable
amount of money, if any, they would have to spend. An owner of six trucks whose
drivers carried fresh fish on ice from southern Thailand to Bukit Mertajam and
from there to points south, stated, "Drivers often ask me to give them fifteen or
twenty ringgit. They say this is because the police will certainly cause them trouble
when they stop the truck and take it in to be weighed [for overloading]. They will
then give the police this as coffee money. I know this is probably false, but I have
no choice and I have to close one of my eyes, and give them the money."

Owners and clerks stated that drivers stole the freight of consigners from the
trucks they drove. They claimed that drivers who carried fish, poultry, produce
and other fresh foodstuffs to distant wholesale markets took one or two items
from each crate, box or sack, or took several boxes or sacks from the back of their
trucks for their own consumption, or to sell en route. As to the latter, one clerk
jocularly referred to such drivers as "doing roadside business," *zuo lupang shengyi*: drivers would stop somewhere along the way and proceed to sell off some of
the cargo being carried on their truck.[2] One owner even alleged that drivers had
engaged in a staged hijacking or robbery of his truck by colluding with outsiders,
and then received a share of the stolen freight. Covert major theft might also be
committed, informants said. One office clerk, clearly enjoying himself, recounted
to me an episode in which the driver of a tanker truck colluded with both the
storekeeper of a palm-oil factory and with outsiders to repeatedly drain off part

of the contents of a tanker trailer carrying raw palm oil, diluting the remainder with water so that when the truck was weighed the theft would not be missed, and to sell what he had siphoned off on the black market. One owner told me he knew that drivers might stop somewhere en route and call him in Bukit Merta-jam by telephone late at night, telling him that the truck had been stopped by the traffic police at an inspection roadblock, that police had taken freight, but then stole it themselves.

As in interviews where owners described their drivers' claims of needing cof-fee money for police as a pretext to eat their money, the reference to collusion between drivers and traffic police depended as a rhetorical strategy on convinc-ingly invoking the negative racial stereotype promoted by truck owners in my interviews about traffic police and road transport officials—almost all of whom were ethnic Malays—as "lazy" and "covetous." This in turn entered in another prevalent narrative theme: owners portrayed themselves as powerless victims of Malaysian state functionaries' capriciousness and petty tyranny, within a nation-state controlled politically by non-Chinese.

In one respect these claims made by truck owners were an element within a more inclusive moral vision that claimed it was the fault of drivers and state func-tionaries when owners failed to prosper, that the demands which owners made of drivers were thus right and proper, and that vigilance was called for to assure that these demands were met. Like petty property owners elsewhere (Bechhofer and Elliot 1981), owners portrayed themselves as victims of both labor and the state. In retrospect—from the 2010s looking back—the self-referential claims in interviews were ambiguous. On one hand, owners cast themselves as pas-sive victims—as petty businessmen under continuous and mortal siege from two sides; on the other, they attributed cleverness, resourcefulness, and agency to drivers who were Chinese men, like themselves. It was only many years after my 1978–80 interviews that I began to attend to the fact that owners' discourse about the disputatiousness of drivers (and the social relations that this discourse indexed) were distinctively gendered. Not only were almost all truck owners, drivers, and clerks in fact men.[3] This discourse and the practices it organized also characterized a response by my male informants to class differences that were best understood by way of contrast to a presupposed, unacknowledged *compliance* by women to men within the family and the workplace. The owners' rhetoric of victimization to which I was deeply sympathetic led me initially to assume such compliance; my optic was then focused on the travails of Chinese as an ethnically distinctive trading minority (Bonacich 1973), assailed by a hostile Malaysian state. It was only later, with subsequent research among drivers, how-ever, that I was prompted to reinterpret this discourse in broader terms.

"The Boss Sucks Our Blood" and "Rice-Eating Money": Learning through Labor, 1985

> **Many non-class discourses are influential, but work is a dominant if not absolutely determinant fact of working-class life. This fact may be difficult to grasp for those whose occupations allow some control over their own schedule.**
>
> —Thomas W. Dunk, *It's a Working Man's Town*

My early interviews of 1979–80 were almost all with truck owners and office clerks, and not with drivers. These interviews represented the "hidden transcript" of owners—narratives told in the absence of drivers, as distinct from either the hidden transcripts of drivers, or the "public transcript" of both sides interacting—neither of which I then had much access to (Scott 1990).[4] In contrast, as I developed an interest in the relationship between class and ethnic formation within Chinese workers' experience, in 1985 and later I began to gain access both to drivers' offstage talk and to observe their public interactions with owners. In this talk, drivers detailed what they saw as the oppressive practices of owners. In direct interviews, and while driving or at roadside coffee shops, drivers gossiped about their working conditions and their employers, about—as one driver irreverently put it—"whether the boss pisses or not." Such talk performed a variety of tasks for drivers.

First, it allowed drivers to exact revenge by engaging in character assassination against owners whom they saw as having acted badly toward them by making excessive demands, accusing them unfairly of theft or fraud, "cursing" or otherwise insulting them to their faces, or being stingy or late in their payment of wages, diesel money, or coffee money for police. The driver who complained about the pressures placed on him and other drivers by his boss to drive their trucks overloaded with fresh fish between Bukit Mertajam and Malacca, the dangers this posed, and the numerous accidents and deaths this caused (see chapter 2), provides one such example. He went on to say, "My boss stands to earn a lot of money if one of his drivers is killed because he has insured our lives with a private insurer. What happens when a driver dies is that the insurance money passes to my boss, who hands only part of it over to the family of the deceased, and pockets the remainder. This is one reason why our boss presses us to drive so fast, since this leads to accidents."

Second, in addition to damaging the reputation of truck owners, gossip among drivers disseminated information about hiring opportunities, wages, and working conditions in different companies, police or Road Transport Department roadblocks on specific routes, road detours, traffic delays and driving conditions, and other knowledge crucial to drivers' everyday labor. Third, it allowed drivers to articulate a class-specific moral vision and history to themselves and to sympathetic outsiders. For instance, in 1985, one driver recounted the history of a conflict whose origins predated my fieldwork:

> We only drive the truck back to the Bukit Mertajam office: these goods are unloaded by general laborers into the warehouse, and delivered later by them.... Before 1975, the boss insisted that we long-distance drivers deliver freight carried back from Kuala Lumpur—despite our already having worked so long, and despite *what this meant for us having little or no time for our families.*[5] We would be pressed to no sooner deliver freight to consignees than have to pick up freight again and start a new trip on the same day. However in 1975 we drivers refused to do this any longer and demanded instead that we be given the time off, rather than have to deliver freight in northern Malaysia on our return [emphasis added].

Critiques of a Language of Domination

Stories such as these were embedded in drivers' critiques of a language of domination used by employers, and they served as an element within a pedagogy—a classed style—enacted as much physically as it was articulated in language. When drivers spoke at length, they did so on the discursive ground set by the linguistic capital (Bourdieu 1991) of owners, but they at times showed a critical reflexivity with respect to it. In my later interviews and conversations, drivers took the opportunity to comment critically not only on the putative theft and cheating that so exercised truck owners but also on owners' discourse as such. Drivers told me that much of what owners viewed as theft and cheating by drivers should be seen instead as creating "rice-eating money," *chifanqian* (Mandarin), or *ciaq-pui-lui* (Penang Hokkien). As one driver put it to me when we were alone,

> When you interview truck owners *they only tell you* the good things they do and not the bad, and they *speak of the bad things* that drivers do. They *never speak* of the bad things they do. They *accuse* drivers of stealing freight. So what if a driver "takes" one or two fish *to feed his family,* not to sell?[6] If a driver takes a few fish and has them cooked for him to eat, then he will not have to pay for his food on the road, and wages are low enough as it is. This should *not even be called stealing,* but instead rice-eating money. [emphasis added][7]

This reflexivity by drivers marked their awareness that the struggles they experienced with owners were not only over material issues (i.e., wages, informal income and working hours) but also over authoritative discourse—how these struggles were to be defined and understood by themselves and others.

Embodied Working-Class Pedagogical Styles

Reflexive critiques like this one of a language of domination were connected to a drivers' pedagogy that I call "learning *through* labor" (cf. Willis 1981)—one that implicated an embodied semiotics grounded in a shared experience of male labor and was articulated in speech by episodic synoptic comments or aphorisms. It represented a form of class-specific pedagogy far more prevalent than many anthropologists schooled in postmodern approaches are willing to concede. It reflected a widespread set of antagonistic working-class practices vis-à-vis language, at least toward locally defined elite forms of speech expression, in favor of signification through embodied practices. Such a pedagogy taught others through their constrained imitation of the habits and styles of work and ways of embedded speech practiced by those who participated in processes of physical labor. These attributes serve as more generic signifiers of a shared class condition.

Embodied pedagogies as performed classed styles have been evident in other cultural settings, but they hardly ever merit serious attention from social scientists. It may be that they threaten the epistemological privilege of many social scientists by calling into question the legitimacy of their linguistic competence—their linguistic capital (Bourdieu 1986) and its connection to their own social class. This may be particularly true for postmodern and poststructuralist anthropologists as I suggest below. Nonetheless, embodied pedagogies as one form of articulated bodily experience are frequent, if not frequently noted.

For instance, in the working-class milieu of the industrial working-class "lads" of Midlands England, Willis (1981) observed a "deflection from the dominant mode of signification—language—into antagonistic behavioral, visual and stylistic forms of expression" (124). In quite a different setting, Bourdieu (1984, 208–225) noted an association between working-class sports such as rugby that involve physical contact and even violence and participants "little inclined to verbalize and theorize," in contrast to sports such as golf or tennis practiced by French middle-class participants who disdained body contact and engaged in polite verbal exchanges. Dunk (1991, 148–149) wrote of Canadian working-class men that "the dichotomy between words and things is also expressed in the opposition of talkers and doers. In this form, it is inscribed as a dominant theme in the personal style of the Boys. . . . linguistic practices which are cultural capital within the dominant culture are seen as empty signifiers by the Boys. One's competence and worthiness is the product of one's action, not one's verbal sophistication." There was a similar animus toward "empty talk" among the largely working-class, inner-city audiences at live professional wrestling cards in the United States (Nonini and Teraoka 1992).

An *embodied* class-based pedagogy was indeed evident among drivers I spent time with, in both work and leisure settings. In the beginning of the Introduction to this book, I recounted the truck trip from Bukit Mertajam to Kuala Lumpur in 1985 during which I accompanied the two drivers, Ah-Bah and Kou-Kian, and here I return to it. The difficulties and challenges of this trip in carrying high-value and fragile miscellaneous cargo over a long distance, navigating crowded streets to deliver it to shopkeepers while avoiding the traffic police were not unique; other trips I went on and driver's stories provided very similar descriptions. I remember keenly how little I felt I could do to help Ah-Bah and Kou-Kian—although I did not unload parcels or carry them into the shops of consignees, I served some small function by opening and closing the back and side gates of the truck and by watching for traffic—and for traffic police. Even so, as the day drew on, I grew increasingly exhausted, while the men worked mostly in silence.

In the Introduction, I note the physicality of Kou-Kian's response to my remark on the small amounts charged by the boss for each parcel they delivered: he thumbed through the thick stack of freight invoices attached to the dashboard, and stated that although the boss received a small amount for each delivery, he was not bothered by this, although for Kou-Kian and Ah-Bah, its repetition through the scores of deliveries consumed a whole day's labor. It was at this point that Kou-Kian reminded me of my responsibility in writing this book to inform readers that the "boss sucks our blood" like a vampire. But there was more.

That day both men showed visible exasperation and anger when, at one shop, they were asked to wait while a clerk counted each small piece of crockery in a consignment they delivered, and when later at a factory warehouse, where they had driven to pick up freight for the return trip to Bukit Mertajam, when they were pressed to wait more than an hour before a manager had employees select the freight that the two drivers were to load and carry back. Later, on our way north out of Kuala Lumpur, Ah-Bah driving, said: "We've been working constantly since five the previous evening, and we're still working. You can see how hard things are for us [*ni kan, zheyang xinku*]. As my friend Kou-Kian said to you earlier as a joke, the boss is a bloodsucker." Such aphoristic speech would have made no sense if they had been divorced from the shared experiences and context of physical labor, ennui, and fatigue that connected Ah-Bah, Kou-Kian, and me: a "showing how" on the way to a "showing that."

Showing How Leading to a Showing That: A Note on Theory

Taking off from the philosopher Gilbert Ryle's (1949) distinction between "knowing how" and "knowing that," I hold that much Chinese working-class pedagogy in urban Malaysia took the form of "showing how" leading to a "showing that"—a lived demonstration that I was allowed to witness only when I accompanied the drivers on this exhausting trip, a learning-through-labor of how drivers articulated and lived through their own exploitation. As an exemplar of such practices, "showing how leading to showing that" poses a major challenge to the postmodernist focus on ethnographic writing and to poststructuralist theories of discursive (read *linguistic*) determinism (Laclau and Mouffe 1985). If anthropology is to be scientific and ethically accountable, it cannot accept the postmodernist fetishization of ethnographic writing, its tropes, and genres (Clifford and Marcus 1986; Marcus and Fischer 1986; Clifford 1988)—which as Fox (1991) points out already risks compromise with an "industrial" logic of professionalism—and turns decisively away from the ethnographic encounter between the anthropologist and those she/he does research on and with (Page 1988; Nonini 2013).

Fabian has observed in *Time and the Other* (1983, 156–164) that anthropology has long been prone to denying the coevalness of the peoples it studies—that is, it has used various conceptions of time (e.g., evolutionary time) to position them as living outside the same history as the West and anthropology itself, as living in "another time," and thus denying them a shared humanity. Postmodern fixations on ethnographic writing do not escape this trap. Fabian (156–164) argues that the denial of coevalness can be avoided only by examining the lived reality of the encounter between anthropologist and his or her subjects, and specifically the language that Fabian sees, following Marx and Engels's *German Ideology* (1970, 50–51), as a form of "practical consciousness" embodied in that encounter—a consciousness moreover deeply implicated in the labor processes that produce and reproduce social life. The encounter that I had with Kou-Kian and Ah-Bah in 1985 was one in which the material bonds of shared labor, copresence, and language formed within that encounter were sufficient to engage their embodied pedagogy about class struggle—providing a lesson not available either through the words of my elite informants, or the mainstream literature on the overseas Chinese.

Put more bluntly: the denial of coevalness is the chronic disease of a detached liberal, elite, and avowedly literary anthropology—one that not only focuses overmuch on the stylistics of writing, but also one whose "discursive turn" obsesses about what is said and written, instead of looking to broader patterns of embodied semiotic practice, and thus endows glib and voluble informants—whose class backgrounds are similar to most anthropologists—with epistemological privilege. Taken to extreme form, this perpetrates symbolic violence against working and other subaltern people.

The Dialectics of Disputatiousness: The "Trip" as Terrain of Cultural/Class Struggle

My interviews with and observations of truck owners, office clerks, and drivers alike point to the wage-labor contract between truck owner and driver as representing a terrain of struggle. It was a continuously changing, dialectically charged relation between the members of two simultaneously antagonistic yet cooperating classes: they contested not only over surplus value as one form taken by economic capital but also over specific resources of symbolic, social, and linguistic capital—including authoritative definitions of what was at stake in the struggle itself (Bourdieu 1977, 1986). Long-distance truck drivers worked for the truck owner on the basis of a piecework wage agreement, in which an owner promised to pay a driver a set wage in return for the driver's completing "one trip," *yi tang*. A driver's wage for a trip was based on the figure offered by an owner for a round trip at a rate prevailing at the time in the local industry. What was being contested was not the going wage for a trip. No driver questioned that the proper work of the driver for one trip was to haul freight on the truck to its destination and to carry another load of freight back—all at a wage rate that the truck owner had the right to set in advance. The everyday struggle between drivers and owners—manifested in the disputatiousness and cheating of drivers in 1979 and 1980—lay instead in contestations over the specific tasks demanded of drivers by owners at the margins of a trip.[8]

What were these crucial demands? Owners called on drivers to go out to specific consigners' sites within the northern region to pick up freight and even asked them to reload it into trucks back at the company's depot.[9] Having their long-haul drivers rather than local delivery drivers and general laborers go out saved owners money and expedited freight movement, thus pleasing their customers. Owners also demanded that drivers carrying "miscellaneous" parcel freight, most of it valuable manufactured cargo, load it themselves, and refused to ask general laborers to do this task. Owners gave the rationale that drivers should be able to quickly locate one or several pieces of freight in the back of the truck for a specific consignee.

Shifts in this demand revealed a past history of partially successful struggle by drivers over time and industrial discipline (Thompson 1967). Prior to 1979, I was told, owners previously requested that *both* long-haul drivers in a team of drivers be present in depots to load freight for the trip south. But in 1979, drivers throughout the local industry refused, claiming that at least one of them needed to rest for the long trip ahead. As one owner later rationalized the fait accompli, "I have general laborers do the loading to prevent the drivers from becoming tired and then falling asleep while driving, which would cause an accident."

Even more contentious was the demand by owners that long-distance drivers deliver freight after they returned with full loads to Bukit Mertajam. Drivers by this time had hauled, delivered, loaded, and unloaded freight episodically for at least thirty hours and on longer trips for forty hours or more, with little sleep or rest. Drivers were by then exhausted—by a deep tiredness that my own learning through labor during three such long-distance trips emphatically attested to. Drivers argued that, exhausted, they should not have to deliver the freight brought back. The issue had long been acrimonious. Owners stated that drivers threatened to strike, bagong, and even went on strike when owners insisted that they make such deliveries. As a result, some truck owners no longer expected long-haul drivers to deliver such freight. In others, owners successfully insisted that one of the two drivers accompany a general laborer in making deliveries in the northern regional area; drivers grudgingly accommodated to this by taking turns doing so.

There were other tasks that owners insisted were merely ordinary and intrinsic parts of a trip, but which arose from what were for drivers unpredictable events, such as encounters with police or government Road Transport officers. Both sides saw these police and functionaries as antagonistic toward drivers *and* owners, because *both* of the latter were Chinese—thus allowing them to share a common ethnic narrative, while arguing over the details. One principal example elaborated on in the previous chapter: owners whose trucks carried bulk freight routinely overloaded their trucks and insisted that drivers carry as much as twice or more freight tonnage than allowable by law. Both owners and drivers knew this was done. This was not only physically dangerous to drivers and others—given high speeds, narrow and crowded roads, and changeable weather conditions—but also made every driver carrying such overloads the potential target en route for harassment by police or Road Transport officers. If they were stopped carrying illegal overloads several times and cited for it, drivers might have their licenses suspended for as long as three months to a year. Their standard tactic if stopped was to try to avoid having their overloaded trucks weighed and impounded by paying coffee money to the police or Road Transport officers. However, as I have described above, it was precisely in this area that owners were most sure that drivers cheated them, by falsely reporting that they had been stopped by police.

There were also time uncertainties arising from owners' insistence that drivers "provide service" to consigners and consignees which placed burdens on drivers. As a favor to the consigner, owners expected drivers to wait for an hour or more at a consigner's factory or warehouse if freight was not ready to load; and they demanded that drivers making deliveries to consignees wait, if asked, while the clerks or laborers of a consignee meticulously checked the condition of freight received. In both situations, prolonged delays would lead to arguments between drivers and those causing the delays. Despite such delays, owners expected drivers to adhere to precisely set schedules of departure from and return to Bukit Mertajam.[10] Owners thus pressed drivers to intensify their labor, while insisting that drivers bear the monetary and physical costs of overloads and delays.

A review of the history of the local truck transport industry recounted to me from the early 1970s through the 1990s strongly points to the existence of a period of worsening profits and recurrent profit crises from the early to mid-1970s onward (Nonini 1983a, 352–362). Under these conditions, truck owners struck bargains (Edwards and Scullion 1982) with long-distance drivers by contracting with them to complete "a trip" at the going rate. Yet, driven by worsening profit margins, truck owners themselves violated these agreements by adding to the tasks of drivers they wanted included in one trip—by chipping away, as it were, at the ambiguous edges of the piecework contract and pushing drivers to intensify their labor at no cost to themselves. Drivers resisted these pressures or compensated for them by being disputatious with truck owners, articulating offstage discourses critical of truck owners, and attempting to cheat owners and create rice-eating money.

Toward an Alternative Heuristic: The "Affectively Necessary Labor" that Forms a Classed and Gendered Style

My experiences with drivers in 1985—their enacted pedagogy of learning through labor, and my interviews with them at work and beyond the workplace—taught me a deeper understanding of drivers' work and of the two-sided active constitution of class conflict. Yet the shift in my perspective provoked me further than I expected. What did it mean, for example, that this struggle reflected not only the everyday interdependencies of capitalists and workers in the labor process, but also that these interdependencies were between *men* who were almost all, moreover, *Chinese*?

I read, not long after it was published, Gayatri Spivak's essay "Scattered Speculations on the Question of Value," in which she argues that labor can provide its
own satisfactions to those who labor—that the labor process is not all suffering
and unrequited effort, "since one case of use-value can be that of the worker
wishing to consume the (affect of the) work itself. . . . The question of *affectively*
necessary labor brings in the attendant question of desire" (Spivak 1987, 162). It
also, I would add, brings in the question of the connection between work, pleasure, and cultural styles. An example she gives of "affectively necessary labor" is
the creative labor conveying the "use-value of manual composition" predating
the integration of the word-processor into the work habits of academic professionals, just as, at present, "the word-processor might itself generate affective
use-value" (162). Spivak's question, as unsettling as it is, perhaps evoked more
rigorously something that my own experiences as a rider on several truck trips
had pointed to. What was the culturally defined use-value of the affectively
necessary labor that harbored and expressed desire and pleasure within the labor
process of the truck transport industry considered here?

How did truck drivers—and owners—seek to consume "the affect of the work
itself"? Of course, this depends on how the "work itself"—the capitalist labor
process—was defined. Ethnographic research by Weston (1990) in auto mechanics' shops in the United States demonstrates that notions about both productivity
and the nature of the labor process itself are deeply gendered—that hegemonic
definitions prescribe the nature of "men's work" and "women's work," extending from the ways in which tasks are to be accomplished in terms of quality of
labor they require ("heavy" versus "light" work, among other things) to detailed
matters of work style, minor work habits, and body habitus. "What Marx does
not explore," Weston (1990, 141) writes, "is the possibility that labor power, in
the sense of capacity and capability, is not a neutral term. Our society describes
people in general and job applicants in particular as possessors of inherent 'traits'
of character and competence—traits that incorporate cultural notions of gender,
race, class, age, and what it means to be 'able-bodied.'" At the same time, Weston
points to the class differences between men working in auto mechanics shops as
they position themselves in "work" and at "the job":

> Extremely significant in this context are nascent class differences that
> divide men from one another. To "work smart," to pause for a moment
> to don safety equipment, to think through a problem before running
> to the parts shelf or tool chest, all represent work styles that implicitly
> reconstitute a mental/manual division of labor. In my experience, these
> styles are more likely to be promoted by supervisors than male workers,
> suggesting that resistance of male workers to women in the trades may
> be different in kind than that of their male employers. (147)

The interplay of gender and class in the labor process was amply evident in the Chinese truck transport industry of Bukit Mertajam once I began to look for it. I thought of the sites of drivers' labors, and the borders between them and other, nearby spaces. Working spaces in truck transport depots and the labor practices enacted within them were both gender-specific. One principal spatial boundary lay between the "inside" and "outside" of the shop houses in which small Chinese businesses, including local truck transport companies, located themselves. An air-conditioned office with a large plate glass window faced and allowed observation of the exclusively male "outside"—the open-air truck depot (made up of a freight storage area and a loading zone for trucks)—and marked at its other end the beginning of "inside"—the domestic spaces of the family of the proprietor (cf. Bourdieu 1977, 90–92). In branch offices in other towns, a dormitory room for drivers encroached further on inside space. The office was a liminal area where the boss and his managers (in smaller companies, either his brothers or sons), had their desks, along with that of one or more account clerks, *shuji*—almost always women, who sat at desks furthest from the office door. Truck drivers did not enter the office unless they had specific business to transact with the boss before they departed on a trip. They did not remain there beyond the minimal time they had to. I never saw a truck driver directly address a clerk, or a clerk on her side initiate a conversation with a driver.

The outside of the truck depot was an almost exclusively male domain: it was in this area in which truck drivers and casual manual laborers, all men, worked loading and unloading freight into and out of the company's trucks. Bodily displays of male power and strength (leaps into the backs of trucks, lifting and throwing heavy packages) and agonistic play, accompanied by banter among drivers, and between drivers and general laborers, demarcated this area as male space. Men on the ground or in the trucks joked with or cursed one other, and engaged in mock displays of shoving or slapping each other. Consider men unloading a truck in a company depot in Bukit Mertajam, 1985: "The men one by one queued up at the edge of the truck, took a piece of cargo, and carried it into the depot. . . . Thus: lots of talking, usually—so far as I could tell—in good humor—and occasional jostling where (if a man was not handling cargo), one man would come up and pinch him on the shoulder, rear end or thigh, or slap him on the shoulder, go briefly into a boxing pose before him (and pretend to take a punch at him) and make some comment to him." In contrast, the boss who emerged from the office to supervise the loading of freight stood stiffly separate, and spoke in a voice of command, "Kuala Lumpur—Ban Heng!" naming both destination and consignee, and so signaled a truck for the package to be loaded on. Then bantering and rowdy play among the men ceased.

On several truck trips, I observed a related pattern of separated gendered spaces and practices both en route and in companies' branch offices in Kuala Lumpur. On arrival at the branch office in Kuala Lumpur on the trip described above,

> I went into the drivers' dormitory room where Kou-Kian was sitting on one of the bunk beds. There were men coming in and out of the room continually, some to talk to others there for a few minutes, some to undress and go bathe. There was a good deal of animated talk, and much friendly "horsing around"—Kou-Kian pinched the legs or thighs of one of the men trying to get some of his articles out of the wardrobe; at one point, Ah-Bah and Kou-Kian began to play-wrestle, and Ah-Bah appearing to tickle Kou-Kian's groin and genitals, saying, "here is your *laksa* [spicy Malaysian dish of noodles, hot peppers and fish]." . . . There was a lot of such kidding and teasing between men.

Such "wild" (*luan*) speech in Hokkien and Teochew accompanied by bodily interactions such as those just described, marked a distinctively male Chinese working-class style: that of being "crude," *culu*. Truck drivers were crude in the sense of acting both ill-mannered toward middle-class authority and vulgar in their speech—particularly about sex and women.[11] In contrast, bosses "showed manners" (you limao) rather than crudeness as in the example just described by employing a voice of dignified command combined with bodily self-restraint, while women working as clerks in inside offices were expected to avoid contact with drivers and casual laborers altogether by withdrawing from interaction or calling on the boss to intercede, and by being spatially segregated away from outside. In the one exception I encountered where a young woman who called herself a clerk had been given the duties of a manager by her absent boss, it was, she said, precisely her ability to speak directly and forcefully to drivers who cursed her to her face (and over the telephone) that allowed her to do her job—that is, to speak to them with authority, but not crudely. That is, she acted like a boss—a man owning property.[12]

As such, crudeness as in the example just given, represented not only an embodied performance of Rabelaisian inversion (Bakhtin 1965) of the proper forms of Chinese middle-class manners, limao, but also marked off an urban topos—the working-class Chinese male space of production, and more broadly, spaces in which men who worked together interacted. This topos included not only the outside, but en route, where truck drivers encountered other men—drivers of other vehicles, the bosses, managers, clerks, forklift operators, storekeepers, and manual laborers who worked for consigners and consignees, petrol station attendants, and representatives of the state—traffic police, RIMV enforcement officers, truck inspectors. It also encompassed the roadside restaurants and coffee shops where drivers stopped for meals en route, and the spaces where they congregated in their leisure hours—dormitory rooms, gambling halls, and the like—and it extended to quests for prostitutes when drivers stayed overnight on the road.

Reflecting back on drivers' critique of the language of domination, I noted a clear element of symbolic violence (Bourdieu 1977) directed against drivers when class superiors labeled them crude—an overt reflexive criticism of their cultural style. When I once told two drivers that others spoke of drivers in general as crude, they reacted in heated anger. In other contexts, however, drivers occasionally referred to themselves as crude in an ironic inversion of the hegemonic term: drivers said they became crude toward others when someone arbitrarily made their work harder, for instance, by requiring them to wait before loading freight. Under these circumstances, "being crude" was an affirmative and ironic self-ascription that alluded to what happened when one was pushed beyond an acceptable level of effort and patience: one acted like a man through crude speech, cursing, *ma*, those in authority. Such affirmation can mark out a new site for the making of positive working-class forms of collective practice.

It was for this reason that when bosses, who faced no such pressures but rather imposed them, themselves acted crudely, they were harshly judged by drivers, as in the case of one notorious and very wealthy proprietor condemned in drivers' gossip for having routinely cursed his drivers and threatening more than one with a gun, among other abuses. Characterizing the behaviors of certain bosses as crude extended to their relations with women, as in the following revealing criticism leveled by one driver at a well-known truck owner who had recently been conferred "titles" by the Malaysian government for his public-spiritedness: "His name [with its titles] sounds very pretty, doesn't it? But he is very cheap—he seeks out ten-ringgit prostitutes, even though he has a lot of money. So he competes with poor men for the services of inexpensive prostitutes. Shouldn't such a man seek out prostitutes that charge a thousand ringgits instead of ten?"

To bring the discussion full circle: the style in which truck drivers are seen as disputatious with truck owners lay in their being crude. Crudeness was a male Chinese working-class style that conspicuously consumed "the (affect of the) work itself" and defined the "affectively necessary labor" of driving as male Chinese working-class work. In contrast, the ideal boss displayed manners—he was restrained but authoritative in speech, controlled in body, showing a sparse economy of gestures. Drivers' crudeness, and the cheating of which it was a sign, marked a gender-specific mode of contesting the appropriation of surplus value (Marx 1976 [1867]) by truck owners: how a trip undertaken by a man was to be defined. In this context, the authoritative speech of the boss to do this or that incited either the driver's silence and deference on one hand, or his crudeness and disputatiousness on the other, depending on mutual perceptions of the balance of economic power, including drivers' capacity to move to other jobs within the national labor market. In the midst of the worldwide recession of the mid-1980s drivers were far less disputatious with owners than they had been five years previously, and they told me of the reasons for it.

In either instance, the male sphere of production and work was discursively reproduced not only through language but also through gendered bodily practices. "Crudeness" and "manners" formed a contrast set demarcating class distance while affirming the shared condition of a common gender. The manners of truck owners were defined by courteous but commanding speech and a body habitus of reserve and public self-control, associated with being Chinese men possessing social capital: having manners thus made truck owners eligible to tell authoritative narratives to others about drivers' disputatiousness and cheating in which they depicted themselves as those abused by drivers and hostile state functionaries. In contrast, drivers did not contest these narratives directly, but countered with specific crude acts of disputatiousness and cheating, by ongoing critical commentary against owners' use of language to justify their ratcheting up the effort required for a trip ("this should not even be called 'stealing'. . . ") and by an undervoiced pedagogy of learning through labor, reflecting simultaneously their active male powers and their lack of position, *diwei*—that is, of social capital—in Chinese society.

As I mentioned above, the early (1979–80) accounts given by truck owners of driver's disputatiousness were often couched as grudging admiration or respect. These gestures in the direction of pleasure reflected distinctively male experiences that owners and drivers shared—at work (many owners having previously been drivers before acquiring their own trucks) and outside it, in urban places defined as ideal venues of male display—the public work sites of businesses, coffee shops, restaurants and banquets (with competitive drinking and toasting), nightclubs, gambling halls, and karaoke bars. These places were where women appeared only if they were laborers with even less position than drivers (e.g., as "hostesses"), or if escorted by their husbands, fathers, or brothers. And whether they were crude drivers who "took" a few fish or other pieces of cargo or transport company proprietors who "overcame bitterness and labored patiently," *kekunailao*, in their businesses, the men said, when I pressed them, that they did so "for our families."

Women were in everyday practice largely excluded from the public or outside spaces of the Chinese-owned truck transport industry. With a very few exceptions, they owned no trucks nor managed their operation, and never drove trucks, loaded them with freight, or engaged in similar tasks.[13] As noted above, a few women worked as account clerks in the offices of truck depots. Such women tended to be younger and were usually either unmarried daughters of older proprietors, wives of their sons, or of more remote relatives. They were expected to defer to the older males in authority over them—their fathers or fathers-in-law—and avoid contact with males who were relative strangers to them. Not only were they expected to be deferential to the men to whom they are related by birth or marriage, but my attempts to interview them also led to a polite refusal or deflection ("I don't know about any of this, please talk to my boss"), withdrawal, or embarrassed silence.

My findings are therefore similar to those of Oxfeld (1993), who studied Hakka leather tanners in Dhapa, Calcutta. She writes: "Business activities that are generally more 'public'—or, to be more specific, involve a high degree of sustained interaction with unrelated males—are usually undertaken by men. . . . A separation exists between a totally male sphere, which deals with the external world of the rawhide market and the leather buyer, and an internal sphere of factory production, in which both male and female family members participate" (145–148).

If there is little in the way of women's voices reflected in my account, then, it is not for want of my listening for them. Women were excluded from or, when they were present, largely silent within the outside spaces of the Chinese truck transport industry. In these spaces filled with male meanings, men spoke of women as an essential absent presence, as in the phrase "for my family" spoken frequently to me, or as objects of sexual predation. One principal task of ethnography in these circumstances may not be to try to hear the voices of all those who are excluded when this is not possible but to examine the operations of regimes of power that allow such gender exclusion and its associated symbolic violence to occur, by elucidating how power is inscribed in the performance of gendered and classed styles.

Such an exploration suggests that the affectively necessary labor of Chinese male truck drivers—their "excess" labor displayed in class/gender-specific form—became aspects of classed and gendered style ratified by the capitalist workplace but extending beyond it—a style whose agonistic and exclusionary stratagems and positions affirmed the pleasures of domination they experienced as men vis-à-vis the women and children they are related to. In chapter 10, I show the ways in which the globalization of the Malaysian labor market allowed Chinese laboring men to be physically mobile over transnational spaces, thus conferring on them a gendered privilege to elude control not only by employers, by the Malaysian state and its hostile non-Chinese functionaries, *but also* by the women to whom these laboring men were related.

Epilogue, 1990–92: Men in Motion and Gendered Styles

By 1990 I discovered that one assumption that I had previously made—that there was a Chinese truck transport industry—no longer made sense in that there was increasing evidence that very large numbers of Chinese men employed as drivers had left or were leaving driving for other kinds of work, and that in their place truck owners had hired ethnic Indian and Malay men as drivers. The pattern admittedly varied in terms of a major division within the local industry—between companies specializing in "bulk goods" transport (iron rods, flour, cement, etc.) and those carrying heterogeneous and more valuable "piece goods" (televisions, appliances, crockery, canned foodstuffs, etc.) (Nonini 1983b). Within the former, there had been a marked transition to a majority of Indian and Malay drivers, while companies specializing in "piece goods" transport had retained most of their Chinese drivers. The former were said to require less in the way of driver's Chinese language skills, and the drivers were on average younger and less well paid, whereas I was told the latter hired older Chinese drivers who were "more reliable" and "recognize Chinese characters" (i.e., Chinese-owned consignee's names written on invoices, freight packages, and shop signs), and generally were higher paid. What had appeared earlier to me to be a clear case of ethnic preference—Chinese owners for Chinese drivers—had by 1990 itself become problematic. As I reconsidered the dialectics of disputatiousness between owners and drivers, I could directly point to owners' seeking out non-Chinese drivers who were willing to work for lower wages as a means to undercut Chinese drivers' demands by playing the race, *zhongzu*, card. This partly explained this change.

Nonetheless what is one to make of the following? When I asked one owner whose trucks transported bulk goods about this in 1991, he brought me up short with the reply: "Only stupid drivers will remain in the employment of a truck owner for a long time," and pointed to the many opportunities available to ambitious Chinese men to find other, better-paying work—not only in Malaysia, but in Japan, Taiwan, and Singapore. My time spent from 1990–92 with Chinese working men in Bukit Mertajam during their leisure hours, described in chapter 8, confirmed the relevance of his remark. The cultural styles of Chinese working men were linked to gendered imaginaries of idealized male mobility, physical power, and social/economic self-uplift. For long-haul drivers, their physical mobility and even their crudeness were aspects of the classed and gendered style through which they sought to perform these imaginaries. This working-class cultural style of these men was gendered as distinctively male, for its performance presupposed the relative immobility of the women to whom they were related—their wives, mothers, and sisters.

CHINESE SOCIETY AS "A SHEET OF LOOSE SAND"

Elite Arguments and Class Discipline in a Postcolonial Era

A Story of Origins

According to the official narrative for the founding of the Fudezhengshen Temple in the downtown business district of Bukit Mertajam,

> More than a century ago, Huizhou Hakkas planted nutmeg, cloves, and other fruits to grow on the northern side of the mountain of Bukit Mertajam, and carried their produce down from the mountain top to set it out to sell at the location of what is now the Fudezhengshen Temple. At that time, the place contained a deep pool, and so it was not convenient for the work of setting out and selling produce, and [its depth] even endangered the lives of the people there. Since they set out each day from the mountain top to carry down, slung across their shoulders, a pole with a bamboo chest containing nutmeg, they each also began to carry [on the other end] a basket of stones to fill in this deep pool. After several long and tiring years and months of uninterrupted hard work, they persevered in filling up the deep pool. As a result, there was an empty piece of land filled in, which was beneficial for setting out and selling fruit and other produce. About the eighth year of Guangxu [1885], it came about that it was proposed that a temple be built on this land. The needed expenses were derived from [taxing] each load of nutmeg, and added to this the gift of land by the landowner, the materials were brought together to accomplish the construction of the temple. "Bukit Mertajam Fudezhengshen Temple 100th Anniversary: Building Report." (Wu 1985)

The Fudezhengshen Temple was the most popular Chinese temple in Bukit Mertajam in 1978–80, when I first did fieldwork there. It symbolized much that most local Chinese saw as true and good about Chinese society vis-à-vis the hostile Malay world that encompassed it. Built in 1885 by Chinese immigrants and located in 1979 in the center of the town's business district, cheek-by-jowl with the pork vendors' shops whose goods were forbidden to Malays who were Muslims, the temple was the temporal home for four Chinese gods—the best-known being Duabogong (H)—the colloquial name of Fudezhengshen. These gods, when one petitioned before and bargained with them, could grant fortunes to the poor and heal the sick. As a nonprofit society registered with the state since the colonial period, the temple owned valuable income-generating property, including several rows of shop houses along the principal commercial street of the town, a Chinese cemetery outside the town—out of which plots are sold to families—and nearby rubber plantations. The Managing Committee, *lishihui*, of the temple administered its property and disposed of its income. The Managing Committee was responsible for the expenditure of temple income on worship of the temple's gods, on charity, and on the subsidy of local Chinese-language schools, the most important being Jit Sin Independent High School, the town's only Chinese-language high school, and located in its central downtown district. Thus in a six-month period between November 1979 and May 1980 the Managing Committee allocated MR$ 100,000 to the building fund of this high school, provided one Chinese-language primary school with MR$ 20,000 for construction, and was in the process of purchasing the land on which another primary school was sited. To local residents, the Managing Committee was the trustee of resources required for the cultural reproduction of a diasporic habitus—Chinese language-schools, temples for the gods of the syncretic Daoist/Buddhist pantheon, and a graveyard whose graves, precisely positioned in accordance with *fengshui* geomantic principles, assured the prosperity or decline of the descendants of the deceased interred there.

The narrative of the temple's founding told above was not, of course, an innocent one bereft of a history. Although it circulated in various printed forms previously, its appearance in the Chinese-language paper *Xingbin Ribao* in 1985 as well as its publication in the official Commemorative Volume on the occasion of the one hundredth anniversary of the temple's building (Hock Teik Cheng Sin Temple 1986), installed it as *the* authoritative version of the temple's founding—and of the founding of Bukit Mertajam as a Chinese topos in a coastal British colony in the Nanyang, the "south seas" of Southeast Asia, far from the Guangxu emperor in Beijing. This was a story moreover of the naming of contributions made by people from China not to the building of China, but to that British colony far from the homeland.

"In Unity There Is Strength"
(*Tuanjie jiu shi liliang*)

By the late 1970s, when I began my fieldwork in Bukit Mertajam, the implications of the postcolonial state's initiatives for "development," as the state contrastively defined development for "rural" Bumiputras and for the "urban sector" of Malaysian Chinese, were becoming increasingly evident. In the opinion of Chinese in Bukit Mertajam, neither formal representation through the Malaysian Chinese Association (MCA) or Gerakan Party within the National Front, nor through opposition in Parliament by the Democratic Action Party (DAP), had proven effective in resisting state policies and practices that Chinese saw as creating their status as second-class citizens, dierdeng gongming. Such was their status, they felt, since *Wuyisan*, "May 13," the trauma of May 13, 1969, in which hundreds of Chinese were slaughtered in the streets of Kuala Lumpur by Malay mobs outraged by electoral victories by Chinese-led opposition parties in Selangor and elsewhere. This event led to the imposition of martial law and the forced implementation of the New Economic Policy on Chinese a year later. Nor were street protests, political party assemblies, or even criticisms by the opposition in Parliament available as means of political expression or pressure, due to government bans on political party marches and rallies, the imposition of the Sedition Act of 1971 that prohibited public discussion of "sensitive issues" related to the constitutional rights of Bumiputras,[1] and the occasional use of the Internal Security Act to detain political dissidents without trial. Chinese felt under assault in the spheres of private business ownership, Chinese-language education, the new government examinations that stressed fluency in Bahasa Malaysia instead of English, and the new quotas for admission to Malaysian universities that limited Chinese to 30 percent of the freshman intake. There was a sense of foreboding about just how far the government might go in these and other areas in ways that diminished the rights of Chinese. The people I met during my first several months in Bukit Mertajam were deeply angry, and once identified as a sympathetic listener I soon became accustomed to hearing an enumeration of complaints and criticisms about the Malaysian government and its policies that favored Bumiputras and discriminated against Chinese. It was, people said, "their government"—referring to what they saw as a government of, by, and for Malays. In November 1978, three months after I arrived in Bukit Mertajam, Chinese voters in its electoral district overwhelmingly voted for the candidate for member of Parliament fielded by the opposition DAP, defeating by a wide margin a "Penang man" selected by the MCA to replace the outgoing MP Tan Cheng Bee, an "old guard" MCA leader who had fallen out of favor, and elected the same DAP candidate as their state assemblyman as well.

In this chapter, I narrate a public dispute in Bukit Mertajam that took place during the eighteen months that followed the election from early 1979 through mid-1980. I do this to sketch out the shifting landscape of Chinese political identities and subject positions vis-à-vis the Malaysian state during the period of Malaysia's postcolonial development. In this dispute, the Chinese-language press, in particular two regional newspapers, *Guanghua Ribao* and *Xingbin Ribao*, played a major role not only in providing fora for antagonists to articulate their arguments vis-à-vis each other, but also and more crucially, for discursively constituting "Chinese society," *huaren shehui*.

Chinese society in Bukit Mertajam was not, as sinological anthropologists who focused in the 1960s on "overseas Chinese segmentary structure" (Crissman 1967; see also Skinner 1968; Freedman 1957, 92–98) would have had us believe, primarily the preexisting social organization within which these disputes were situated but was instead very much the discursive construct created by these disputes. This is not to deny that material and symbolic resources were being allocated, arranged for, or contested within the organizational structure of temples, associations, and schools serving Chinese in Bukit Mertajam, much less that there was no institutional reality or history to Chinese society. Of course, there were material resources at stake, and temples, associations, and schools were corporate institutions with specific logics of governance and control. Yet, I shall argue, for most Bukit Mertajam people, Chinese society served as a rhetorical construct central to their conception of their power (or lack of power) as citizens, and not as a functioning power structure with access to resources they needed in everyday life. By describing and interpreting this dispute, I seek to examine features of the complex relationship between inequality, representation, and power among urban Chinese Malaysians.[2]

In late July 1979 Tang Wee Tiong, the wealthy owner of a Chinese medicinal hall and chairman of the Hakka Association, held a banquet to ostensibly thank thirty-eight local Chinese associations for their financial support in a fund drive for which he was chairman. In the course of his speech to these associations' representatives, Tang recounted a past history of local Chinese disunity, and called for a new beginning. "Chinese society,"[3] he said,

> has in the past fallen into the predicament of being a sheet of loose sand, with each group looking after only its own affairs. But the period marked by a lack of mutuality has already passed. Today we have already arrived at the point that if we do not unite then we will degenerate, even to a time when we have lost all our rights. . . . I want to take this opportunity to call on the leaders of this area's society to identify clearly what our goals are, to all take the people's welfare as central . . . to eliminate

selfish bad habits, and to expand our powers of judgment and look even further, to really unite as one in word and action. Unity is strength. (*Guanghua Ribao* 1979d)

Tang's reproachful speech must have occasioned sarcastic comment among many of those attending, for most knew of his longstanding local reputation as a leader who promoted rancor and fission among local Chinese associations. Moreover, most persons who heard or read the speech in the newspaper reports printed in the two regional Chinese-language newspapers, *Guanghua Ribao* and *Xingbin Ribao*, knew that his metaphor that "Chinese society" was "a sheet of loose sand" was by no means original but had been one of the most memorable figures of speech used by China's "national father," *guofu*, Sun Yat-sen, in a famous passage in the nationalist classic *San Min Chu I* (Sun 1953 [1927]).

This was a prelude to a dispute among the "leaders," *lingdao*, and "celebrities," *wenren*, of Chinese society in Bukit Mertajam that continued for several months and produced rare public manifestations of strong animosity within the mercantile elite of the area. In what follows, I narrate the collective performance of the dispute between the leaders of the Hakka Association and the Fudezhengshen Temple Managing Committee that occurred over several months in 1979–80 and was initiated by Tang's reported diagnosis of its ills in July 1979. I propose that the representations of Chinese society and of the causes for its "lack of unity" revealed in this dispute point to a residual diasporic subject-position, but as such, one certain to fail in articulating Chinese subjects to the *Malaysian* as distinct from the China state. This dispute articulated and performed by antagonists and promulgated by Chinese-language newspapers inscribed a reality about Chinese society that naturalized the political weakness of the Chinese population vis-à-vis the Malaysian state, defined the incapacity of its leaders to do anything about it, and enjoined Chinese residents to reconcile themselves to self-inflicted political impotence.

Through its installation as a regime of truth, this narrative disciplined working-class Chinese to accept the limits of the "practical" within a post-colonial developmentalist state. Even if its aura of naturalness and inevitability was tarnished as I show below by its own internal contradictions, this mediated narrative about Chinese society preempted a public space, and by displacing alternative and more critical visions of class and racial domination also extant in Malaysian politics, worked to create a certain hegemonic common sense. It operated to create its effects above all through its circulation and deployment as a language of representation in the Chinese-language print media: indeed, Chinese society, in one sense, was an imaginative construct defined by no more, but certainly no less, than the readership enclosed within the circulation hinterlands of the two largest Chinese-language newspapers distributed throughout northern Malaysia.[4] Leaders and celebrities—their spokespersons and speech writers, and the journalists who reported their words and acts—actively performed these representations of Chinese society, while the mass of Chinese-language readers were the audience at whom these representations were directed.

"Why Is It So Difficult for Chinese Society to Really Unify?"

> Here [Bukit Mertajam] even though it is not a metropolis with roads leading everywhere, all the same there is every kind of organization. . . . There are people who say: the organizations are many, [speech group] factions are certainly many, and in taking care of affairs there can be no unanimity. But this saying does not exhaust the matter: here one finds everyone being able to sincerely cooperate for the public welfare, and indeed not distinguishing one from the other. This is indeed a very fine phenomenon.
>
> —Xu Wurong, *Malaiya Chaoqiao Yinxiangji* (Notes on Impressions of Teochews in Malaya) (1951)

In 1979, there were a multiplicity of Chinese community associations, *gonghui*, and groups, *shetuan*, whose meeting halls occupied two-story shop houses whose distinctive architecture have defined mid-twentieth-century Malaysian urbanism, and bore their association names (the Chinese ideographs and, by law, the Bahasa Malaysia equivalent) above their doorways. In the district as a whole, there were approximately one hundred associations and groups, and of these about forty were located within the town's downtown business district and its surrounding suburbs. These organizations included five native-place or speech-group associations; occupational and trade organizations; surname associations; school unions or old boys' clubs; "moral uplifting societies";[5] religious organizations such as the Confucianist society; youth and sports groups; temple managing committees; school boards, school-building committees, and parent-teacher associations.[6]

The segmentary imaginary promoted in the Chinese schools from Sun Yat-sen's *San Min Chu I* predicated that Chinese society consisted of those belonging to China's "nationalities," *minzu*, made up of progressively larger kinship units oriented around native place—district, prefecture, and province—and the surnames which mapped on to them. Within this imaginary the paramount local

Chinese organizations of the town—those deemed most important in terms of the numbers of their members, their geographic inclusiveness, and the wealth of their officers were, with one exception, the China prefecture-based native-place associations: the Hokkien, Teochew, Cantonese, Hainanese, and Hakka associations.[7] The single exception was the Fudezhengshen Temple Managing Committee which (as a protagonist to the dispute put it) "belonged to the mass of Bukit Mertajam's Chinese and had a long history of achievement."

The temple's Managing Committee was composed of twelve representatives from *four* of the five native-place associations mentioned above—the Hokkien, Teochew, Cantonese, and Hainanese Associations—but *not* from the Hakka Association.[8] These men, consistent with the segmentary imaginary, also held the highest offices in the four native-place associations and included among them the most wealthy Chinese merchants of the town—two partners in a large supermarket chain, the owner of a large truck transport company, and several real estate developers and rubber estate owners. They were all, it should be added,

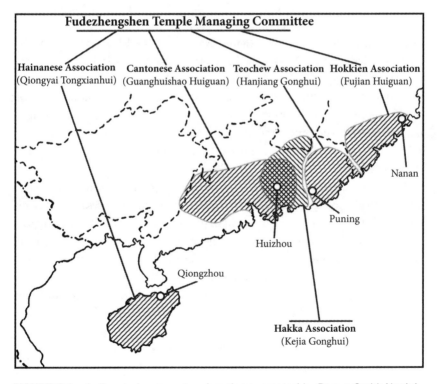

FIGURE 7.1 A disputed segmentary imaginary, created by Roque Smith-Nonini

prominent contributors to the Malaysian Chinese Association—one of the two Chinese political parties in Penang state supporting the Malaysian government's National Front.

I have heard only one version of the exclusion of the Hakka Association from representation on the Managing Committee, and it is inevitably a partial account. A supporter of the Managing Committee in its dispute with the Hakka Association pointed to a long and involved history of conflict. He said that unlike the other four associations that were established either before World War II or immediately thereafter, the Hakka Association was formed only in the mid-1960s, and its ambitious and greedy leaders (especially its chairman Tang Wee Tiong) then attempted immediately to gain representation on the Managing Committee. However, he observed, the committee at that time refused to admit Hakka representatives *as such*, for it held that the Hakka Association, unlike the other four associations, did not truly represent Chinese from a specific regional native place in China. To members of the Managing Committee, although the Hakka Association claimed to represent *all* Hakkas in Bukit Mertajam irrespective of their China place of origin, in actuality Hakkas were *already* represented by the delegates from the Hokkien, Cantonese, or Teochew associations on the committee if their ancestors came from the regions of southern China covered by one of these associations (see figure 7.1).[9] By the late 1960s, the ongoing disagreement led to severe bad feeling between Tang and the members of the committee. And in fact, my informant said, in 1979 there were now two prominent Hakkas on the committee—men whose ancestors came from Huizhoufu—among the five representatives from the Cantonese Association—precisely, he claimed, because they were descendants of the valiant and sacrificing Huizhou Hakka nutmeg farmers invoked in the authorized history, given above, of the building of the temple in 1885.

In late August 1979, a month after the newspaper report on the speech of Tang Wee Tiong described above, I attended the fifteenth anniversary celebratory banquet of the Hakka Association held in the gymnasium of a Chinese-language primary school located downtown (*Guanghua Ribao* 1979e). As succeeding courses of the banquet went out to the several hundred people gathered at banquet tables, prominent representatives from outside organizations spoke from the dais. One such speaker was an officer of the Malaysian Federation of Hakka Associations, a nationally known young Hakka leader, from the national capital, Kuala Lumpur. As he began to speak, people stopped talking to each other across the tables and listened in rapt attention. In a fiery speech of alarm mixed with regret, he spoke of the deteriorating position of Chinese businesses and the decline of Chinese-language education because of pressures from the national government over the last several years. He also recounted the efforts of Chinese associations throughout Malaysia to campaign for the establishment of Merdeka University by seeking to convene in late 1978 in the national capital, Kuala Lumpur, and the government's prohibition of the meeting on grounds that it would raise "sensitive" constitutional issues forbidden for public debate under the Sedition Act (*Guanghua Ribao* 1979e).[10] He concluded his speech by claiming that this and similar incidents demonstrated the weakness of Malaysian Chinese and attested to the need to unify across the divisions between major speech groups such as Hokkien and Hakka. His speech was received with a standing ovation by the several hundred people attending the banquet.

He was followed to the dais by the spokesperson for Tang Wee Tiong.[11] This man repeated the previous speaker's point about the need for Chinese unity, and then went on to say on Tang's behalf that the Hakka Association was itself fortunate to have an excellent corps of youthful leaders to carry on the unfinished work of others. This brief statement by Tang's representative proved to be the lead-in for the next speaker.

This was Soo Meng Lai, the assistant secretary of the Hakka Association. A wealthy man of about thirty years of age—quite young for his position—an articulate and passionate speaker, Soo appeared to be on his way up in local Chinese leadership circles. The gist of his speech, delivered with alternating alarm and enthusiasm, was that the members of the Fudezhengshen Temple Managing Committee should take up the "holy mission" of uniting all the town's registered Chinese associations under its aegis, in order to overcome the "factional consciousness," *bangpai sixiang*, internally dividing the local Chinese community, and thus work together for the welfare of all Chinese in Bukit Mertajam. He put the matter as follows:

> Under the slogan of "move from small unity to great unity" . . . the more Chinese society has come together the more it has scattered, the more it has been tied together the more it has unraveled, and become a sheet of loose sand. This point about the decline and deterioration of the present situation of Chinese can be seen by everyone. Why is it so difficult for Chinese society to really unify? Because among the reasons there is still prevalent in Chinese associations a narrow sectarian perspective and factional consciousness. (*Guanghua Ribao* 1979e)

The solution was for an organization that "belongs to the mass of Bukit Mertajam's Chinese and with a long history of achievement" to call together the more than forty registered Chinese associations within the town. This organization could only be the Fudezhengshen Temple Managing Committee. The Managing Committee, of course, would have to be reorganized to reflect the composition of all registered associations within local Chinese society (*Guanghua Ribao* 1979e).

His unstated implication was that representatives from the Hakka Association would have to be appointed members of the committee. Those attending gave resounding applause for his speech, and the two regional Chinese-language newspapers read throughout the larger Penang region gave it prominent coverage.

What Soo invoked, as had Tang a month before, was not a sociological analysis of the political position of Chinese in Malaysia, but instead the famous diagnosis of the failure of China to unite as a nation—one whose locus classicus was Dr. Sun Yat-sen's *San Min Chu I*. This was evident in the central trope of both Tang and Soo's speeches: that Chinese were a "sheet of loose sand." Compare, for instance, its appearance in their speeches with its use in the following passages from *San Min Chu I* in 1927: "Foreign observers say that the Chinese are like a sheet of loose sand. Why? Simply because our people have shown loyalty to family and clan but not to the nation—there has been no nationalism" (Sun 1953 [1927], 2). And "the Chinese people have only family and clan groups; there is no national spirit. Consequently, in spite of four hundred million people gathered together in one China, we are in fact but a sheet of loose sand. We are the poorest and weakest state in the world, occupying the lowest position in international affairs; the rest of mankind is the carving knife and the serving dish, while we are the fish and the meat" (5).

Similarly, when Soo recited the slogan "move from little unity to great unity," this was a calling up of Sun's argument in *San Min Chu I* that "an easy and successful way to bring about the unity of a large group is to build upon the foundation of small united groups, and the small units we can build upon in China are the clan groups and also the family groups. The 'native place' sentiment of the Chinese is very deep-rooted, too; it is especially easy to unite those who are from the same province, prefecture, or village" (31).

Over the next week of early September, among friends and acquaintances in the stores of merchants' shop houses and at the tables of the open-air coffee shops in the downtown business district, I found Soo's proposal to be the subject of much animated discussion. Business people, journalists, and others concluded that there was much public support for it. Yet, my informants concluded, despite the widespread enthusiasm for it, there were only a select number of people who mattered in the forthcoming debate—the small number of prominent businessmen who were the delegates from the four native-place associations represented on the temple Managing Committee, and whose cooperation was needed if the committee was to assume its "holy mission." What took place in the weeks that followed was an extended battle of words played out before a reading public through reports made in the Chinese-language press consisting of rhetorical ploys and ripostes fashioned from "reported speech" (Bakhtin 1981) by speakers at association banquets as well as by more direct asides in anonymous letters to the editors—all directed to persuade the leaders of the Hokkien, Teochew, Cantonese, and Hainanese associations to either accept or reject Soo's proposal, and all that it implied.

The day after Soo's speech the headmaster of an primary school located in one of the New Villages outside town voiced his support for Soo during a banquet given as part of the school's musical evening (*Guanghua Ribao* 1979f). He served on the Executive Committee of the Hokkien Association. On the evening of September 10, at the anniversary banquet for the district's Hawkers Association, its chairman, Teh Swee Nai, a Teochew textile merchant who was also a member of the Executive Committee of the Teochew Association, added his support by proposing that the Fudezhengshen Managing Committee call together local Chinese organizations to discuss their common problems (*Guanghua Ribao* 1979h).

In the days that followed the Hakka Association's banquet, Soo Meng Lai began to lobby for his proposal, making reported appearances and speaking at banquets held by several local Chinese associations—as a featured speaker. On September 7 he appeared before a banquet I attended held in a local restaurant by the regional Lorry Merchants Association to commemorate its anniversary (*Guanghua Ribao* 1979g). The chairman of this recently established association, Chua Tee Hwa, was vice chairman of the Hokkien Association and one of its two delegates on the Fudezhengshen Temple Managing Committee. When Soo spoke, he reiterated his proposal and larded it with fulsome praise for Chua. Much as Chua had recognized the importance of uniting local merchants in his past leadership in associations, he himself was trying to do the same when he proposed that the Managing Committee "take on the burden of uniting all the registered Chinese organizations" of the district. The premises of both men were the same, he insisted, and he hoped that Chua would "give attention to this problem of uniting Bukit Mertajam's fellow-countrymen of Chinese descent" (*Guanghua Ribao* 1979g).

Chua's reply—not published in the Chinese-language newspapers but disseminated widely by word of mouth—"satirized" (*fengce*) Soo, as one informant put it, by stating that Soo was "like a Bumiputra," that is, like a Malay. Here, this analogy represented what in rhetoric is called an *enthymeme*: a compressed syllogism, often reduced to a single word, in this case, Bumiputra. Unpacking this utterance: a Bumiputra, a Malay, was someone who wanted however improperly to assume control of a source of wealth whenever he saw it in order to obtain a share of its profits, unlike a proper Chinese. Soo, being like a Bumiputra, was thus not acting in a proper Chinese way. As an officer of the excluded Hakka Association, he was improperly seeking to gain control over the resources of the Fudezhengshen Managing Committee. Therefore Soo was not acting like a

Chinese but like a Bumiputra. Chua's racialist comment was not only a criticism of Soo, but also a reminder to his audience of a sensitive matter—the government's Industrial Coordination Act of 1975 that required Chinese and other non-Malay businesses to sell 30 percent of their equity to either Bumiputra partners or their trustee—usually a government agency. Chua's witty comment at the banquet occasioned some laughter at Soo's expense, which no doubt was its aim—since oratorical wit was highly prized, and this was eminently repeatable as gossip to others later. Through invoking a racial imaginary that recast the dispute among Chinese leaders as a conflict between Malays and Chinese by claiming that Soo (and by implication, his supporters) were "like a Bumiputra," Chua, a member of the temple Managing Committee, signaled his rejection of Soo's proposal.

A few days later on September 10, the regional Hawkers Association held its fourteenth anniversary banquet (*Guanghua Ribao* 1979h). One of the first speakers was Teh Swee Nai, its president, and he spoke in favor of Soo's proposal. He was followed to the dais by Ng Heng Kee, another member of the Managing Committee and its formal representative to the banquet, who also responded to Soo's proposal. In fact, this was surely his major purpose in attending (*Guanghua Ribao* 1979i). Ng was a prominent Teochew merchant who held the office of secretary in the Teochew Association. Ng in his speech immediately focused on Soo's proposal but addressed its implications for relations with the Malaysian government. He argued that if the Managing Committee were to be reorganized to include delegates from local organizations other than the four native-place associations already represented, this would threaten the tax-exempt status of the Managing Committee. Under its bylaws, the Managing Committee had the sole aims of worshiping the gods, carrying out benevolent works and supporting local Chinese-language education. The committee could not "involve its bylaws in outside affairs"—that is, seek to unify local Chinese—without the national government canceling its tax-exempt status (*Guanghua Ribao* 1979i). Furthermore, he stated, any proposal to amend the Managing Committee's bylaws would lead to consternation and misunderstanding among the elders of the four native-place associations currently represented on the Managing Committee. This was because, as things stood, the two organizations to which the majority of Bukit Mertajam's Chinese were eligible to belong—the Teochew and Hokkien associations—each had fewer delegates on the committee than did the Cantonese Association, which represented the much smaller Cantonese population. In agreeing in the past to this concession, these two associations had subordinated their interests to that of Chinese society. The three native-place associations had previously arrived at a modus vivendi, and the present arrangement should not be disturbed. Ng alluded to Soo as a youthful leader and as an outsider not born in Bukit Mertajam who misunderstood the purposes of the committee. He also intimated that Soo's proposal was merely a fresh ploy in the Hakka Association's long-standing efforts to gain representation on the Managing Committee, from which it had been excluded several years before (*Guanghua Ribao* 1979i).

Within the segmentary imaginary of Chinese society, the contrary opinions voiced by Teh and Ng had different weights. Ng was secretary, a chaired officer position, of the Teochew Association, which had immediate standing as a represented association on the Managing Committee, whereas Teh was only a member of its executive board, a less prestigious position.[12] Ng's rejection of Soo's proposal, within the game of status being played within Chinese society, trumped Teh's support.

On September 17, another member of the Managing Committee addressed Soo's proposal, and his response was prominently reported in the regional newspapers (*Guanghua Ribao* 1979j). Booi Ah Keik, one of the delegates from the Cantonese Association on the Managing Committee and also the secretary of the association, spoke at the banquet held at its meeting hall celebrating its autumn worship. He emphasized the benefits of the current income accruing to the Managing Committee, which was used to subsidize local Chinese-language schools. He went on to say that a representative of the Managing Committee had approached both the office of the Registrar of Societies, a department in the national government, and its own accountant, to ask what would happen if organizations other than the four native-place associations already involved were represented on the Managing Committee. The upshot of these inquiries, he said, was that it was impossible to change its bylaws, which limited representation to the four native-place associations, without first consulting the members of each association. Moreover, the tax-exempt status of the Managing Committee would be at risk because if its bylaws were changed to include communication among organizations as one of its aims, "the government would not permit it, since if there were any communication taking place, [its income] could be used for some other expenses" than the approved ones of worshiping the gods, performing benevolent works, and supporting local Chinese education (*Guanghua Ribao* 1979j).

By this time three prominent leaders who were delegates from three of the four native-place associations represented on the Managing Committee had come out publicly against Soo's proposal—Chua Tee Hwa, Ng Heng Kee, and Booi Ah Keik. Undeterred, Soo pressed on, and with great temerity directly criticized Ng's reply in an essay published in each of the two regional Chinese-language newspapers (Guanghua Ribao 1979k). He said that the committee members were being arbitrary and authoritarian in their response to his proposal. He demanded that "in order to demonstrate to the mass of the Chinese in this area that it is abiding by its rules in the discharge of its official duties," the committee now call a meeting since its bylaws stipulated that it hold a meeting of all Chinese in the town, every year or more often, whenever fifty or more Chinese brought up some matter of importance for discussion (*Guanghua Ribao* 1979k). He concluded by stating that his own inquiries with government departments and with friends who were lawyers and accountants had convinced him that committee members had been negligent in investigating the question of its tax-exempt status, and he called on each registered association in the town to publicly express its own opinion about the committee and to work for the unity of all Chinese (*Guanghua Ribao* 1979k).

A week later, in the third week of September, the Managing Committee provided its collective reply to Soo's proposal in an essay that appeared in both regional Chinese-language newspapers (*Guanghua Ribao* 1979l). In a highly sarcastic reply, larded with "four character phrases," *sizici*, and particles of classical Chinese, the Managing Committee accused Soo of actually seeking to divide local Chinese society instead of trying to unite it. The committee stated that Soo's proposal

> has come to be distorted and pretentious, as Soo lifts high the banner of all Bukit Mertajam's Chinese and of their registered associations, and provides himself with an excuse for being famous and prominent. . . . The behavior of Soo is all-encompassing: beginning with uniting all of Bukit Mertajam's registered Chinese associations, he ends up wanting to change the organization of the Fudezhengshen Managing Committee. (*Guanghua Ribao* 1979l)

The committee's statement went on to characterize its own history since its reconstitution at the end of the Japanese occupation in 1945. This history was one in which the majority of Bukit Mertajam Chinese were represented by the four native-place associations, during a period in which the members of the Managing Committee, with the extraordinary assistance of these associations, had selflessly navigated through dire financial straits over several years to finally emerge solvent and very active in worship of the gods, in good works for the Chinese community, and in their support of Chinese-language schools (*Guanghua Ribao* 1979l). The reply of the committee concluded by contrasting, on one hand, the actions of "all the members of the Managing Committee, absolutely honest and with integrity, and modestly vowing to the gods and to the area's public not to act proudly or arrogantly," with, on the other, Soo's behavior in reviving speech-group antagonisms with the old demand by the Hakka Association for representation on the Managing Committee, albeit in a new guise. The committee went on to state, "this animosity [between speech groups] has a deep root. Now Soo, with his slogan of using all registered Chinese associations, is feigning action in one place in order to make the real move in another, and isn't that remarkable?" (*Guanghua Ribao* 1979l).

This collective public retort by the Managing Committee was the turning point in the dispute, for within the segmentary imaginary that ordered Chinese society in Bukit Mertajam its members had publicly signaled the existence of their power and its bases. The public commitment by members of the committee to exercise overwhelming influence against Soo's proposal through their extended ties to many local Chinese associations made sense to readers because of their shared understanding of what constituted Chinese society. Within this semiotics, members of the Managing Committee stated: count up our positions, not only as officers of our own native-place associations, but also of twenty other local associations (surname halls, old boy's clubs, school board of trustees, and other organizations), and think too of how the leaders of these associations whom we influence know and influence other leaders. . . and you will see, Soo, that you are decisively outmatched. In fact, members of the committee held positions as officers in associations, and shared officer's positions with other leaders who also were officers in yet other associations, within thirty-three of the forty Chinese associations located within the town and its suburbs. In contrast, Tang Wee Tiong and his protégé Soo Meng Lai could point to connections by virtue of their officeholding to only ten associations other than the Hakka Association.

Although clearly outnumbered, Soo and his supporters in the Hakka Association persisted for several months in raising the issue at association meetings and banquets and in the press, without measurably gaining support from other leaders. The dispute concluded abruptly in January 1980 when Sim Chew Yen, the headmaster of Jit Sin National Type High School, interceded as mediator (*Guanghua Ribao* 1980). Headmaster Sim was a member of the executive board of the Hokkien Association, had been headmaster of Jit Sin for many years, was a valued supporter of the MCA from the Emergency period onward, and was indebted to the Managing Committee for its fund-raising on behalf of Jit Sin. Above all, Sim's reputation as a disinterested and somewhat monastic leader, unlike the businessmen on both sides of the dispute, was most important—with this reputation, he possessed an undisputed claim to being selflessly devoted to Chinese education and, by extension, Chinese society. In an essay published in two Chinese-language newspapers after his meeting with representatives of the Hakka Association and the Managing Committee, Sim stated that he had scrutinized this "serious misunderstanding," concluded that it "would probably lead to a bad influence on educational matters," and demanded that both parties set the dispute aside and work together for the interests of local Chinese society (*Guanghua Ribao* 1980).[13] Immediately after he made this request, he wrote, "the misunderstanding disappeared without a trace" (*Guanghua Ribao* 1980), and in fact nothing further about it appeared subsequently in the Chinese-language press.

A Diasporic Segmentary Imaginary, Nostalgia for Patriarchal Elite Practices

What was this dispute about? Spokesmen for both sides despite their differences emphasized the value of unity among Chinese, and they portrayed Bukit Mertajam Chinese as a metonym for *all* Chinese in Malaysia. Their evocation of "Chinese unity" was also a reference to the unsuccessful "Chinese Unity Movement" sponsored by the national MCA leadership under Tun Tan Siew Sin in the early 1970s as part of its "reforms from the top," the foundering of the Perak Task Force of the mid-1970s (Loh 1982, 17), and the failure of the movement sponsored by the MCA to establish Merdeka University. What resonated strongly with those present at the Hakka Association banquet, and those who later read the newspaper accounts of the speeches delivered there, was that all disputants pointed to a need for unity among Chinese in Bukit Mertajam in light of the "degeneration" and "deterioration" of the position of Chinese *everywhere* in Malaysia. For this broad audience, decline was symbolized by government pressures against Chinese businesses, the substitution of Malay language for Mandarin in Chinese school classrooms, ethnic quotas disadvantaging Chinese in the universities, and most recently the defeat of Chinese associations seeking to meet to protest the government's decision against Merdeka University.

What then was the meaning of "Chinese unity"—what Loh called an "otherwise abstract symbol"—or put another way, of a lack of unity? (Loh 1982, 43) *Both* sides to the dispute invoked the diagnosis by the famous physician nationalist Dr. Sun Yat-sen of China as the "sick man of Asia," *Yazhoubingfu*—the weakness of China confronted by invading foreign enemies. The speakers' implicit references to Sun's diagnosis of the sources of disunity in China were rhetorically effective because they invoked the school-boy experiences of learning, that is, recitation from memory *dushu*, passages from *San Min Chu I* in Chinese secondary schools from the 1930s through the 1960s shared by these now (mostly) middle-aged and older leaders. What was recalled was the imagined community of the nation of China itself threatened by foreign invaders, while riven by family, surname, and speech-group divisions, now being recapitulated as Chinese society threatened by the Malaysian state. Despite the indirection of the rhetoric, the elite disputants declared a certain moral equivalence of conditions— Chinese nation/race : oppression by foreign imperialism :: Chinese nation/race in

Malaysia : oppression by the Malaysian state.[14] Chinese in Malaysia, like the residents of China, were after all "a sheet of loose sand."

In conceiving of the causes of Chinese disunity, the parties to the dispute alluded to, if they did not explicitly use, Sun Yat-sen's concept of China's "nationality," minzu (implicitly the Han nationality) and extended its meaning from their shared imaginary of China's crisis, derived from his *San Min Chu I*, to Chinese society in Malaysia. To use publicly the concept of minzu would have been indelicate and impolitic, and they instead used the euphonious neologism, "Malaysian fellow countrymen of Chinese descent," *Malaixiya huayi tongbao*.[15]

The segmentary imaginary that all parties to the dispute shared was one which was embodied in Soo's moral injunction to "move from small unity to greater unity," following from Sun's argument that "an easy and successful way to bring about the unity of a large group is to build upon the foundation of small united groups, and the small units we can build upon in China are the clan groups and also the family groups" (Sun 1953 [1927], 31). This was however no more than, in Bourdieu's (1977) words, a "rule," and it was the envisioned set of past practices to which it alluded that were crucial, practices that validated and supported the "position," *diwei*, of Chinese "community leaders" like the disputants from the early twentieth century onward in colonial Malaya. "Celebrities," wenren, who were (always) men of wealth, high status and propriety, heads of their families, *jiazhang*, owners of businesses, or towkays, acting in accordance with principles of *li*, or etiquette, cooperated to achieve worthy goals within a segmentary hierarchy made up of organizations whose membership was progressively more inclusive in spatial terms. These included families and patrilines, then clans, or districts, prefectures, then provinces, to encompass at their highest level the entire minzu or nationality—Han China, on one hand, or Chinese society in Bukit Mertajam and Malaysia, on the other.

Those men, most wealthy and most worthy, envisioned themselves as those whose moral worth was measured by their selection as officers and representatives of the progressively more inclusive organizations—such as the prefecture-level native-place organizations of Bukit Mertajam (Hokkien, Teochew, and others) represented on the Fudezhengshen Temple Managing Committee. Here, the patriarchal practices that justified and reinforced the privileges of being male, wealthy, aged, controlling the property and people of a patriline, owning and managing a business, were themselves being justified. What more, for example, could be asked of the worthy elite gentlemen who led the Cantonese, Teochew, Hokkien, and Hainanese associations than when they had created a modus vivendi in the years after the Japanese occupation to work together to support Chinese-language education? What more could be asked, for another example, of the celebrities who now served on the Fudezhengshen Temple Managing

Committee, which, in Soo's words, "belongs to the mass of Bukit Mertajam's Chinese and with a long history of achievement," than that they serve as an instrument to unify Chinese against the alien threat of the Malaysian state? Disputes like the one described here thus reaffirmed the segmentary spatial imaginary and celebrated the patriarchal practices it encapsulated, which prevailed in 1979–80 among the local mercantile elite. These practices systematically disadvantaged women, the young, those without property or position such as Chinese laborers, and those who even if they owned property acted without propriety, as well as those beyond the minzu—whether called Bumiputra, Malays, or more derogatorily, Huānà.

Sinological anthropologists who studied overseas Chinese from the 1950s to the 1970s saw this segmentary imaginary not as the cultural artifact it was, but rather as an analytical concept that pointed to the objective reality of the "social structure" of Chinese "communities," not only in cities and towns in colonial and postcolonial Southeast Asia, but indeed in early modern China itself. According to these scholars such a social structure of segmentary organizations functioned as a mechanism of internal governance as well as a means for providing essential welfare services (lodging for a traveler, burial expenses for a deceased migrant from a shared native place in China, and other services) and as a source of sociality among otherwise isolated Chinese sojourners in China cities, in Singapore, Bangkok, Batavia, and elsewhere in the Nanyang (Crissman 1967; Skinner 1957, 1958, 1968; Kuhn 1997). But note the slippage of tense in Crissman, "The urban Chinese abroad *are* nearly autonomous and self-governing and their system of government *is* uniquely Chinese" (1967, 200; emphasis added), and urban overseas Chinese *show* a "surprisingly structural uniformity" in their social organization (202). This, a mere decade prior to the fieldwork carried out for this chapter.

Without entering into the interesting historical question as to whether such functionalist characterizations by sinological anthropologists were *ever* valid across the broad range of populations, cities, and periods they claimed to cover, I would simply like to point out that as a supposed portmanteau template for a social organization this segmentary imaginary in Bukit Mertajam in 1979–80 was neither the frame of a "social structure" that actually existed, nor a pure construct of "Chinese culture," but rather a discursive residue of early twentieth-century diasporic nationalism now framed by a servile relationship on the part of mercantile elites to racialized colonial and later postcolonial states.[16]

The genealogy of this segmentary imaginary that caged itself within a racialized modern state emerged from the rhetoric of the dispute. The allegiance by Soo and by his opponents to the state as the proper arbiter of who could legitimately participate in Chinese society and under what conditions was both extreme and exacting. On one side, Soo repeatedly argued that those organizations which the Managing Committee should convene to commence the movement toward unity were not merely *any* group of Chinese who were inclined to participate, but instead all "registered" associations—registered, that is, with the Registrar of Societies under the Societies Act. These associations having undergone the bureaucratic niceties of "registration"—requiring an annual report of their officers by name, a notarized balance sheet of funds held, an official organization address, and their activities—had been brought within the surveillance penumbra of the state, becoming thereby adjuncts to it.[17] Members of the Managing Committee, on the other side, while agreeing that only "registered" associations should be included, countered Soo's proposal on the grounds of pragmatism, that if the Managing Committee were to undertake the task demanded of it by Soo, the government would not permit it.

Postcolonial Governmentality and the Diasporic Imaginary: Whose Nation, Whose State?

Restated in more general theoretical terms, there existed a form of Malaysian postcolonial state governmentality (Foucault 1978)—a set of ruling rationalities that channeled the Chinese population in certain directions with respect to market forces and "society." The rationalities that altered the biopolitics of Chinese status vis-à-vis the state drew on mechanisms of predation, surveillance, normalization through registration, and financial cooptation. The stance toward the state and its powers taken by those elites participating in the dispute were thus not incidental, but rather represented the subject positions that that governmentality called into existence. These generated a broad set of elite practices.

The leaders on both sides of the dispute made accommodations with the Malaysian state which benefited them in ways not possible for other Chinese, despite the antagonisms that set them off from the state. After all, the state was the ultimate guarantor of their rights to private property and to continued exploitation of their employees. For this elite, bribes to state officials and employees for permits and licenses were but normal overhead expenses for their very profitable businesses, and making friends with influential Malays lubricated by money brought them lucrative contracts and concessions. Both sets of practices were aspects of the predatory logic of the postcolonial state. Moreover, local elites' connections to leaders in the MCA and the Gerakan Party built by their generous financial contributions gave them access to insider information and government contracts, and made them eligible for the feudalist titles conferred by national and state governments, which were a mark of high prestige.[18] The compromised quality of this elite segmentary imaginary accounts in large measure for the odd juxtaposition of publicly clamorous rhetoric heard in the speeches of both sides about the "weakness" and "disunity" of Chinese, with the submissive, almost devotional, attention the disputants paid to the pronouncements of state officials they consulted or claimed to consult in marshaling evidence against the arguments of the other side.

This compromise was evident in the ways in which the activities of the temple Managing Committee, which became a focus of the dispute, reflected on Sun's problematic about the future of the minzu and on the theme of its lack of unity, on one hand, but was also co-opted by the Malaysian state, on the other. At a time when educational policies set by the Ministry of Education restricted access by Chinese to universities and required the use of Bahasa Malaysia rather than English or Mandarin as languages of instruction, and when UMNO leaders made public utterances calling for the abolition of Chinese-language primary schools in the name of national unity, was not the future of the minzu in Malaysia at stake? As Bergère and Lloyd note, minzu for Sun was defined in part by "blood," in part by patriliny, but also by "style of life, language, religion and customs" (Bergère and Lloyd 1998, 357). Following Sun, the local elite held that Chinese-language education, grounded in the study of morality through the Chinese classics and *San Min Chu I*, was the core of the cultivation required for the advancement of the minzu. Was not the control by local celebrities of finances supporting Chinese education, epitomized in the subsidies provided by the temple Managing Committee, central to such a future? In actuality, however, this control was hedged all about by the powers of the Malaysian state—power well known not only to the elite but also to the broader Chinese public.

The executive committees of the boards of trustees of the two Chinese high schools in the district, Jit Sin National Type High School and Jit Sin Independent High School, consisted of wealthy Chinese celebrities—in fact, several school executive committee members were also members of the temple Managing Committee.[19] Yet, in the case of Jit Sin National Type High School, there was a division of powers in governance between its Board of Trustees and the Malaysian state—the Ministry of Education decisively set the school's curriculum and paid its headmaster's and teachers' salaries, while its board only owned and subsidized the school's grounds and its buildings. In contrast, the Board of Trustees for Jit Sin Independent High School had more power, for it hired the personnel, owned the grounds and building of the school, and was able to set a higher proportion of instructional hours in Mandarin, although it still had to adhere broadly to a national school curriculum.

However, as partisans for Chinese independent schools conceded in frustration, curricular standards at the national type high schools were more demanding and their students more academically qualified for university study than in the independent high schools, for teachers' salaries in the former were far higher and their training more rigorous, and their facilities and texts were better than in the latter. Parents in Bukit Mertajam therefore were far more inclined to send their children to Jit Sin National Type High School, if they could get them in, despite the school's reliance on and guidance by the Ministry of Education, while Jit Sin Independent High School had by 1979 acquired a reputation for accepting mediocre students—such as the children of the local elite who were unqualified for either Jit Sin National Type High School or (what was at the time) the English-language high school, Bukit Mertajam High School.

Therefore, despite the fact that the prominent men sitting on the executive committees on the two Jit Sin High Schools' Boards of Trustees participated in setting policy for Chinese-language schooling for local students, they were required by law to share influence with the Ministry of Education. Notwithstanding their financial power, they had to accommodate to the ministry's requirements when it came to policies that set the language of instruction (in 1979, either Chinese or English, but mandated to soon become Bahasa Malaysia), determined the content of the curriculum (which valorized the history and indigenous or Malay origins of the Malaysian nation and had little place for celebrating the accomplishments of the Chinese minzu), while ministry officials administered, set the content of, and graded the post-Form 6 national examinations that determined university entry, and much more.

Nor were Chinese temples or worship of gods of the Daoist/Buddhist pantheon completely independent of state control—as Ng Heng Kee had argued when alluding to registration of the temple Managing Committee as a "society" with the government's Registrar of Societies. Not only were the temples' bylaws subject to registration, but the finances and officers of the temples' managing committees were also monitored through the annual reporting required of them as societies. The worship practices that temples sponsored, such as the annual festivals celebrating the gods' birthdays and processions of gods (in the form of possessed spirit mediums) through the streets, required police permits in order to be held. (Although, as I argue in chapter 9, these festivals and processions promoted an alternative cosmopolitical sovereignty to that of the Malaysian state, it was a sovereignty that also escaped control by the local elite.) Moreover, the national government, on grounds of promoting religious freedom, provided subsidies for the construction and repair of temples, churches, mosques, and other houses of worship—and this constituted a further form of state financial control over Chinese religious activity.

Contrary to the idealized depictions of the segmentary "social organiza-tion" of urban overseas Chinese by sinological anthropologists of the 1950s and 1960s, the elite of Bukit Mertajam in the 1970s and 1980s and the asso-ciations it controlled had virtually no powers of "self-governance," performed minimal welfare functions,[20] and found itself co-opted by the state in the realms of education and worship. Instead, postcolonial state surveillance and regulation—the set of rationalities deployed by the state toward Chinese as a docile urban population—hemmed it in on all sides.

Chinese society and the elite segmentary imaginary that produced it were dis-cursive devices that disciplined the Chinese population—particularly its nonelite and working-class segments—to submit to the classed and patriarchal practices of the elite that were ultimately harnessed to the rationalities of state governmen-tality. Women, the poor, the working class, youths, and those without "position" were inscribed as docile and passive bodies to be mobilized in a hierarchy by wealthy, male, older, propertied celebrities in the direction of Chinese "unity," along, however, only those lines the government allowed.

Nonetheless, disputes like the one described here have a way of escaping the discursive frames that initially give them meaning. Celebrities on each side of the dispute sought to occupy the moral high ground by portraying their own views as disinterested, while they cast their opposition as selfish and debased. However, the result of proclaiming one's motives pure while accusing the other side of acts of knavery reinforced a general devaluation of the reputations for disinterestedness and benevolence held by celebrities.[21] When antagonists on both sides publicly invoked the state in different ways to support their arguments, they nonetheless did so uneasily and with some ambivalence, for they knew that most of their non-elite audience in Chinese society had reason to be less enchanted with the niceties of registration and the preemptive rights of the state than were they themselves.

It was for this reason that the dispute threatened to escape the frame placed around it by the antagonists' allegiances to the state. Soo's innovation—ascribed by his opponents to his impulsive and hotheaded youthfulness—was to brashly transgress the boundaries of loyalty to the state normally demanded of aspir-ing Chinese leaders by invoking on at least two occasions a more populist con-ception of participation in Chinese society. One was at the anniversary banquet of the Hakka Association where he first put forth his proposal. There he spoke of the Fudezhengshen Managing Committee as a group "belonging to the mass of Bukit Mertajam's Chinese," thus rendering transparent the contrast between the small local elite's control of the committee and its ostensible accountability to all Chinese in the area (*Guanghua Ribao* 1979f). The other occasion was his pub-lished criticism of Ng Heng Kee's reply, when he demanded that the committee act in accordance with its bylaws to hold a yearly meeting of all Chinese in the town whenever fifty or more Chinese brought up some matter of importance to discuss (*Xingbin Ribao/Guanghua Ribao*, September 18, 1979). This demand, if implemented, could have led to a democratic mobilization of grievances among local Chinese—one escalating beyond the capacity of the small local elite to contain. It was for this reason that it was rumored that the Malaysian Special Branch—the secret police charged with monitoring political "subversion" and threats to public order—had taken special note of what Soo had said. Whether or not the rumor was true was hardly as important as that it was thought to be so, for the emergence of rumors like this one demarcated the perceived limits of the challenge to authoritative discourse allowable by the Malaysian state—beyond which lay its threatened recourse to violence.

I found it difficult to assess the distribution of reactions by nonelite readers of the Chinese-language press covering the dispute, even those living in Bukit Mertajam who may have personally known the participants. Overall, however, nonelite people I knew said it had little if any relevance to their own lives. To my initial surprise, of the people I asked, few displayed any personal engagement as if the outcome mattered to them or voiced strong opinions about the question of how Bukit Mertajam Chinese should unify or whether Soo's solution, or that of the Managing Committee, was more appropriate. Instead, their comments were directed not to the issues involved in the dispute, but to the status of the people involved in it—the celebrities. They were not themselves celebrities, and it was best therefore that they were not involved, nor was there therefore a need for them to form opinions about it.

The responses by nonelites toward the politics of celebrities and "social associations," shetuan, shifted between the three poles exemplified by the following responses. My landlord, Mr. Tan, a foreman at a rubber estate in Kulim: "It's best not to get involved with these celebrities and their association matters. They have nothing to do with us." Chuah Eng Huat, my field assistant: "My grandfather still sends these people [in the Teochew Association] money, and acts as if he's a big shot knowing this and that celebrity! They pay him no attention except when they ask for money. What a waste of his money!" Mr. Chao, secretary of the Liu-Kuan-Chang-Chao Surname Association: "I've tried to bring people into our association, but many have a feeling of self-inferiority, *zibeigan*, and for this reason don't want to join even if they are eligible. This is particularly so when they aren't wealthy and don't have much money to give." From disengagement and avoidance, to cynicism and a sense that Grandfather shouldn't put on airs, to an imputed sentiment of feeling embarrassed and inferior when one cannot contribute money freely to social associations, those who did not participate in Chinese society acted as if they were powerless to act with respect to it, given the overweening powers of the Malaysian state over their lives.

Why the Local Mattered: Topos and the Imagined Territorialization of Chinese Society

One might argue that the segmentary imaginary I have described of a mobilized Chinese nation confronting a menacing Malaysian state was such an extravagant fiction even by 1979 that it would have had little purchase on the thinking of most Bukit Mertajam residents to begin with. But to say as I have above that most working-class or nonelite residents felt they had little or no role within the leadership dispute did not mean that most felt that the conditions it ostensibly addressed mattered little to them. On the contrary, they *did* feel threatened by the Malaysian state, and they believed this threat existed because they were Chinese. One of the most effective devices that created this perceived reality was the territorialization of the local that spatially anchored Chinese society.

Here I point to what Henri Lefebvre (1974) referred to as two aspects of the analytics of space in everyday life—"representations of space," and "representational space," or cathected emotive space connoting certain events of birth, marriage, and other moments in the life passage—such as churches or cemeteries or hospitals. Representations of space are most often official devices such as maps or diagrams representing the built environment that allow state or capitalist agents (e.g., urban planners) to envision and deploy their powers over space vis-à-vis subject populations (Lefebvre 1974), or to confer legibility on them (Scott 1998). However, those who either resist or at least seek to deflect the truth-defining nature of official spatial representations also create and consume alternative representations of space. Moreover, those envisioning alternatives may represent "representational spaces" in discourses that deploy the emotive loads these spaces invoke and reinforce as part of their rhetorical tactics. In the case of the dispute, such alternatives were conceptual and perceptual frames for visualizing a figured world lying outside the territorial claims of the state.

The dispute over representation on the temple Managing Committee was almost at no point conducted in face-to-face confrontations between sides. Instead, it consisted of speeches delivered at successive banquets held in association meeting halls and at two well-known restaurants in town, of off-record commentary by participants, and of gossip in coffee shops and other public places. Most residents, whether or not they were leaders or active members of the native-place associations involved, were unable to attend these banquets. What transformed this series of speeches into a *dispute* was their conspicuous serial coverage by both Chinese-language newspapers over a period of several months. Newspaper articles recording celebrities' speeches and critical letters to these newspapers' editors published under noms de plume reported the praise or criticism directed at one or other party to the dispute, incited and provoked the disputants (who themselves were avid readers), and provided the defining frame for the dispute. Only when the Chinese-language press disseminated such coverage over the course of several weeks to readers did local gossip about the dispute, the motivations of parties, and the like circulate through coffee shop circles like those I discuss below.

The dispute as it transpired was therefore articulated through several connected referential levels of space of public concern. Taken together, these levels formed a complex representation of space that framed materialization of the segmentary imaginary of the moral community of Chinese society. The Chinese society invoked by leaders during the dispute made little sense outside the process of people acting within, envisioning, representing, and expressing their opinions about people in certain places within local space. To start with, the dispute itself could be viewed as a struggle for control over authoritative local representational spaces—the Fudezhengshen Temple, its Chinese-language schools, its cemeteries—which were focal to the cultural reproduction of Chinese residents of Bukit Mertajam. Second, the reporting of the dispute, as was true for coverage of other less rancorous association affairs, required the representations of space that validated the sites of specific association banquets as nodes of social power—those where local celebrities and leaders met—such as this association hall or that restaurant. (These spaces of cultural reproduction and power were precisely those where Chinese workers were not allowed to express their solidarities.)

Third, the coverage of the dispute in articles reported in two Chinese-language newspapers in their "local news" or "North Malaysian edition" inserts placed the town's Chinese society within a larger *regional* setting—Chinese society in northern Malaysia—delineated by the circulation of these two newspapers.[22] The tens of thousands of readers of these newspapers residing over a large area that extended from northern Kedah and Perlis states to central Perak state were a vast envisioned audience for the local drama about Chinese society in Bukit Mertajam. As to the imagined local stage for this drama, the delimitation of Chinese society to include only those associations *in and near the town* "registered" by the government was a construct that both Soo and his opponents agreed on.[23]

This multireferential complex of representations of Chinese space in Bukit Mertajam and beyond, with its rooted connotations of knowable and experienced places—homes, temples, graveyards, schools, association meeting halls, and the restaurants of elite sociality—provided the figurative scaffolding called Chinese society. It was this envisioned world that animated the local elite's segmentary imaginary of an aroused Chinese nationality which, forming initially out of a "sheet of loose sand," would congeal into a united nation standing against a formidable enemy.

The End of the Chinese Diaspora?

Yet I am led to wonder at the costs for the majority of Chinese Malaysians of anachronisms like this one, when their elites, to borrow Marx's (1963 [1852], 15) luminous description of Bonapartism, sought to "anxiously conjure up the spirits of the past to their service and borrow from them names, battle cries and costumes in order to present the new scene of world history in this time-honored disguise and this borrowed language"—however much the caricature arising from a supposed repeated history served as the instrument of class domination. The discourse that framed the dispute on all sides was contradictory and unstable in its effects. Hybrid and anachronistic in its construction—containing elements from both early twentieth-century China nationalism, and from more recent rhetoric derived from the field of political recognition of ethnic groups before the postcolonial Malaysian state—it intimated alternative constructions of politics. Consider, as a specimen for scrutiny, Tang's claim that "if we do not unite then we will degenerate, even to a time when we have lost all our rights." In it there was an invocation of the segmentary imaginary of Sun Yat-sen in which people oriented by native-place ties in China sought to mobilize into progressively inclusive segments or failed to ("if we do not unite then we will degenerate") *and* a reference to group "rights" before the state ("even to a time when we have lost all our rights")—a distinctive concept within postcolonial Malaysian politics. Thus were the (ethnic-bound) aspirations for political participation by Malaysian citizens of Chinese descent being imaginatively constructed out of the detritus of an earlier—and by 1979 quite moribund—diasporic (China) nationalism. Diasporas, like the Chinese diaspora in Malaysia, can and do come to an end.

Part II

GLOBALIZATION (1985–97)

GOING GLOBAL

Globalization and State Formation, 1985–97

In Malaysia, by the mid-1980s the government-owned public enterprises that dominated the most dynamic sectors of the economy had suffered major losses not only due to the countrywide recession of 1981–85 brought on by declines in Malaysian export markets, but also because of their poor and inefficient management. The approaches to business taken by these public enterprises were driven far more by their managements' interests in cultivating their UMNO patronage ties, and for some managers by their own self-aggrandizement, than by careful considerations of profitability (Gomez and Jomo 1997). A lack of accountability by managers to branches of government other than their UMNO patrons in the executive, a commitment to ethnic redistribution instead of efficient business methods, and inexperience and lack of training appear to have been common (75–76). As a consequence by 1987, the debt held by public enterprises (among those whose books could be audited) amounted to more than 30 percent of all government debt servicing (78).

As a result in part of this financial crisis compounded by the global recession of the mid-1980s, and in part due to pressures toward economic liberalization coming from the World Bank, other international financial institutions, and the U.S. government, the Mahathir administration embarked on a new campaign of privatizing the public enterprises, first transforming their organization into public and private limited companies, and then selling their assets to preselected or favored bidders. This was a sign not of the advent of neoliberalism or of a process of cultural neoliberalization imposed by the West, but of a shift in the state formation process and the class formation processes connected to it. Privatization occurred through sale of assets and equity, leasing out of assets, management contracts, and the "build-operate-transfer" process in the case of new projects, such as the North-South Expressway. Although privatization was a radical measure that reduced the size of the public sector and public enterprises as instruments for the NEP, UMNO leaders chose their current clients, previously the managers, individual owners, and Malay-equity trustees of public enterprises, as those to sell the newly privatized corporations to. The process of managing the economy through political patronage via the state-corporate nexus continued in altered form. There is evidence that publicly owned assets were divested at prices far below their market value to Bumiputra managers with political connections to UMNO (Gomez and Jomo 1997, 81–83). In the course of this process, the notion that a very few politically connected Bumiputra rentiers and entrepreneurs were merely serving as "trustees" of property they held on behalf of the larger Bumiputra population, and would eventually turn such property over to them, became increasingly untenable.

By the mid- to late-1990s, through this process those very few who were the New Malays, Melayu Baru, condensed into a new upper-class faction separated by vast differences in wealth, power, and social status not only from other Bumiputras but also from all other Malaysians except for their UMNO patrons and a very few extremely wealthy Chinese tycoons. By the inception of the successor to the NEP, the National Development Policy (1990–2000), these changes were well underway.

There were institutionalized efforts by Chinese to challenge the rapid concentration of capital by the numerically small class of New Malays and its translation into political power. The most important response was that of the MCA, which launched a holding company, Multi-Purpose Holdings Berhad (MPHB) in 1975, in order to concentrate Chinese share capital by calling on smaller Chinese capitalists to pool their investment capital. By the late 1980s, under the leadership of the MCA President Tan Koon Swan, MPHB had become one of the largest corporations listed on the KL Stock Exchange (Gomez 2008, 97–98; Heng 1999, 518). However, mismanagement of MPHB and its deposit-taking cooperatives (DTCs) by Tan and his MCA followers led to a major scandal when the Malaysian Central Bank, Bank Negara, froze the assets of thirty-five DTCs for a loss of 3.6 billion ringgit; 500,000 depositors failed to recover more than one-third of their deposits (Wong 2009); and Tan was tried, convicted, and imprisoned in Singapore for criminal breach of trust in 1986. MPHB was thereafter restructured by the tycoon Robert Kuok and sold off in 1989 to the Kamunting Group owned by another Chinese tycoon—thus ending the collective effort among Chinese to mobilize small capital as an institutionalized counterpower to the new rising Malay economic upper class (Gomez 2008, 97–98; Heng 1999, 518).

In part due to the failure of MPHB to mobilize small-scale Chinese capital, the financial influence of the MCA, the political party of Chinese capital associated with the ruling Barisan Nasional, waned considerably vis-à-vis UMNO leaders. Also the latter increasingly drew on the greatly increased wealth of their clients among New Malays in return for favors (Gomez and Jomo 1997, 44). As a result, by the mid-1990s leaders of the MCA (and the Gerakan Party in Penang and Perak states) had become increasingly ineffectual in representing Chinese economic and cultural interests at the highest levels of UMNO and the national government, even as "the trends toward 'Bumiputerization' ... continued unabated, in education, in scholarships, in employment, in privileges for housing, loans, and so on" (Munro-Kua 1996, 151).

Years of Prosperity—But at Whose Expense?

The global recession of 1985–86 lowered economic growth and called UMNO's legitimacy with its Malay clientele into question, as it failed to deliver to them jobs and other patronage goods. As a result of the ensuing splits within UMNO (the emergence of Semangat 46 and other groups), UMNO and the Mahathir administration turned toward Chinese for electoral support in the 1990 and 1995 elections by policies of cultural and educational liberalization (Jesudason 1999, 165–166). This was followed by a decade of rapid economic growth (with real GDP growing 9.3 percent from 1990 to 1995) (Ramasamy and Rowley 2008, 122) under the export-oriented industrialization policies of the Mahathir government until the Asian financial crisis of 1997–98.

Jesudason poses the most relevant question given the theme of this book: what made such rapid growth possible? He argues that one major reason was the weakness of labor due to the prior counterinsurgency suppression of the anticolonial movement of militant trade unions and the Malayan Communist Party: this was "a mortal blow to the labor movement" up through the 1990s. This allowed for a smooth transition by the Malaysian economy from import-substitution to export-oriented industrialization from the 1970s to the 1990s, which was consistent with the logic of Western and Asian corporate globalization—the logic of capital mobility to seek out new domains for the exploitation of labor through lowered wages and workers benefits (Jesudason 1999, 146–147).

Yet, in this respect, the Mahathir administration did not rest on the accomplishments of its colonial predecessors but continued to disenfranchise Malaysian laborers of all ethnic groups—preventing the formation of trade unions, dividing them by ethnicities when it could not prevent them from forming, requiring them to be "house" unions, making it difficult for unions to gain the recognition of employers, limiting their rights to strike, and importing foreign labor (Ramasamy and Rowley 2008, 133–134; Miles and Croucher 2013, 417–418; Jomo and Todd 1994, 128–167). Moreover, Mahathir's "Look East" policy denied that labor had rights such as collective bargaining on the grounds that these rights were an artifact of decadent and self-centered Western liberalism and had to be rejected in Asia in favor of "Asian values" of paternalism, social order, austerity for labor, and political stability (Miles and Croucher 2013, 414). As a result of these policies aimed at working people, wages and working benefits have been far lower than they would have been otherwise, while increasing wealth has accrued to the relative few, with increasing degrees of economic and social inequality.

Thus the general prosperity identified with two decades of the NEP and NDP was one built on the exploitation of Malaysia's working people, including its Chinese workers. This book therefore adopts a different perspective on the meaning of bourgeois prosperity and political stability than most observers, when I discuss such questions as "Chinese support" for the economically conservative policies of constituent parties of the Barisan Nasional—UMNO, the MCA, and Gerakan, as well as the failure of the latter two parties to challenge UMNO's policies of ethnic discrimination. For example, the thesis of the "politics of developmentalism" proposed by Loh (2001), in which Chinese were seen as supporting these policies during the 1990s, can be critiqued by its failure to distinguish between the class dynamics around wealth, interests, and inequalities prevailing among Chinese as these factors affected support, or not, of Barisan Nasional economic, cultural, and educational policies.

Malaysian Class Formation, 1980s–97

It is important to consider the changed status of the Chinese national economic elite, given the long-standing prior status of the most wealthy Chinese Malaysian businessmen as the leaders and celebrities of Chinese society. According to the ideology of Chinese society, these men were the leaders whose power protected Chinese interests, while their philanthropy subsidized the associations that reproduced the cultural capital of Chinese ethnicity—chambers of commerce, native-place associations, clan halls, school board, Buddhist temples, Confucian study societies, Christian churches, among others.

In actuality, from the beginning of the NEP onward, those belonging to the wealthiest business families in Malaysia—bankers, real estate developers and resort owners, manufacturers, monopoly wholesale distributors—hedged their bets in response to government pressures on Chinese-owned businesses by developing new patronage ties with UMNO leaders in joint ventures with these leaders' relatives and friends and New Malays (Gomez 2008), and by moving part of their capital overseas (Gomez and Jomo 1997, 48–49). During the same period from the 1980s to 1997, they grew increasingly wealthy from the profits from these joint ventures.

As a consequence, those belonging to the most wealthy Chinese fraction of capital shifted from support of collective Chinese economic and cultural interests identified as Chinese society to developing specific ties with UMNO patrons on one hand, while going global through capital flight and corporate relocation overseas on the other, although this trend had never been absent since independence. There is evidence that huge amounts of Chinese capital fled Malaysia to overseas locations. According to a Morgan Guaranty estimate, US$ 12 billion was repatriated overseas from Malaysia from 1976 to 1985 (Gomez and Jomo 1997, 44). The families of wealthy tycoons accounted for most of this capital flight. This trend continued through the 1990s and 2000s.

Local Chinese business elites, like the three hundred or so towkays who were substantial capitalists and employers of labor in Bukit Mertajam, faced different prospects. Consigned spatially to develop their business capital within the Malaysian political setting, most experienced the upper limits on capital accumulation set by the Industrial Coordination Act and other ethnically discriminatory laws and policies of the NEP and the NDP. At the same time, the rapidly expanding economy led to very good business and high levels of profit. Some were able to forge partnerships with the newly privatized Bumiputra-owned corporations but were also the targets for takeover of 30 percent or more of their equity by Bumiputra partners. More often, their own relatively small businesses provided services, for instance, truck transport, wholesaling, and retailing for these corporations at adverse terms of trade because of the large scale and overriding market share of the latter. Still a new government initiative to support Malay entrepreneurs in their line of business might force them out of business or limit their capacity for capital accumulation and technological innovation. These local elites also received favors (for example, advance notice of project location so as to be able to buy up land speculatively) from the MCA and Gerakan officials who knew of development plans, in return for their support during the elections. At the same time, some sought during these years and into the 2000s to move their business capital and family members to other nation-states, particularly in the Anglophone Pacific Rim that were more politically congenial to "economic migrants" (as I will discuss in chapter 10).

The owners of petty business property and professionals (like those in Bukit Mertajam who owned more than six hundred businesses operated solely by family members) fared well during these years; they benefited from the increased incomes that the population as a whole had to dispose of due to steady employment and rapid economic growth. Moreover, some of their grown sons and daughters were able to enter Malaysian national universities despite discrimination against them as Chinese, others entered the new private institutes, colleges and "twinning" programs set up in the 1990s as a result of liberalized education policies, while still others went overseas to enter foreign universities as part of transnational traversals. The petty capitalist class formed the core of the Chinese supporters for the politics of developmentalism.

The Chinese working class, at least insofar as my own ethnography illuminates the more general situation, could "get by" in this period of full employment and rapid economic growth. For approximately a decade during this period, Chinese working men and women were able to live a better material life—with somewhat higher levels of consumption—and entertained the prospect of medium-term financial security through steady employment and house ownership. It is questionable however just how much they shared in the prosperity enjoyed by those who owned productive wealth. Certainly, there is little evidence that Chinese working youths were able during these years to take advantage of such prosperity to move out of the working class through education or upward mobility in the workplace.

The Asian Financial Crisis and After—Into the 2000s

As during the recession of 1985–86, UMNO's legitimacy and capacity as a patronage machine to provide jobs, contracts, and material awards for the vast majority of Malays who supported it were tested by the economic strains of the 1997–98 Asian financial crisis. Unlike the 1985–86 recession, however, UMNO leaders were not only split by personality differences and rivalries over position but also by serious philosophical differences about how the crisis—one of capital flight and the radical devaluation of national assets within the global economy—should be resolved. Whereas Deputy Prime Minister Anwar Ibrahim argued for "the embrace of austerity and tight money" in line with the strictures of the IMF, Mahathir himself argued that the economy was robust and did not require restructuring, but instead insulation from the "contagion effect" of capital flight occurring in Thailand and Indonesia (Bowie 2004, 196). The upshot was Mahathir's decision to impose controls on capital circulation, including a moratorium on the withdrawal of capital by foreign investors from Malaysia (197).

This was followed by the firing of his deputy prime minister, followed by Anwar's trial and conviction on trumped up sodomy charges, the establishment of Parti KeAdilan in his support, the emergence of the Barisan Alternatif, new "civil society" opposition and online political media, and the advent of a whole new era of Malaysian politics (Loh and Saravanamuttu 2003; Loh and Khoo 2002; Bowie 2004; Collins 2006; Pepinsky 2009; Weiss 2013).

How the national political and economic changes associated with the privatization of governance, globalization, and processes of class formation from 1985 to 1997 affected the Chinese of Bukit Mertajam, and how they responded to these changes, are the subjects of part 2, which follows. The epilogue considers the situation of the people of Bukit Mertajam in 2007, ten years after the financial crisis.

8

SUBSUMPTION AND ENCOMPASSMENT

Class, State Formation, and the
Production of Urban Space, 1980–97

In this chapter and the next, I discuss the politics of Chinese citizenship in Malaysia from the 1980s until the 2000s by means of an analysis of how state and class power has produced and ordered urban space. In this chapter, I consider the ways in which Bukit Mertajam residents of different classes experienced state reform and economic globalization under the Bumiputra ascendancy of the New Economic Policy and National Development Policy, and examine the spatial dimensions of Malaysian state formation as these came to affect the daily lives of Chinese in Bukit Mertajam. I demonstrate that the contested politics of Chinese citizenship in Malaysia during the years 1980–97 can best be understood by the ways in which different classes of Bukit Mertajam Chinese and the Malaysian state that increasingly sought to encompass them, each respectively produced urban spaces, that is, sought to control, regulate, and appropriate such spaces and the activities occurring within them.

Production of space is one aspect of all power relationships, and the organization of such spaces is an effect of power. Returning to Lefebvre's views on space referred to in the previous chapter (Lefebvre 1974), I argue that the state, classes, and ethnic groups in Malaysia have produced urban space through three distinctive aspects or moments whose interplay must be understood in any deeper analytics of space in everyday life—"spatial practices," "representations of space," and "representational space" (Lefebvre 1974). By spatial practices Lefebvre means the embodied habitus and routines persons engage in as they move through and appropriate space as users; representations of space are conceptions of spaces within systems of verbal and visual signs such as maps—this aspect of space is derived by "scientists, planners, urbanists, technocratic subdividers, and social engineers"; and representational space is space as affectively marked in perceptions, memories, and cathexes (38–42). All three aspects are dimensions of the politics by which people appropriate urban space, its resources, and its connotations.

By 1992, the city of Bukit Mertajam and its surrounding district had grown to more than 100,000 people, with the city's population more than 80 percent ethnic Chinese, but surrounded by rapidly growing majority-Malay townships and neighborhoods. Until the 1995 election, the local Chinese population's articulate opposition to Bumiputra political domination reaffirmed the area's reputation as a "stronghold" of the Democratic Action Party (DAP)—the largest Chinese-controlled party in Parliament opposed to UMNO and its coalition, the Barisan Nasional (BN) composed of governing parties, including the MCA and Gerakan, which had formed the Malaysian national government since the inception of the New Economic Policy (NEP) in 1971. As I noted in chapter 4, Bukit Mertajam people felt that their reputation as an opposition stronghold meant that they suffered more than Chinese elsewhere from ethnic stigmatization in being bypassed in government development expenditures—that they were not provided amenities such as new roads or new schools, nor favored with the facilities needed for export-oriented industrial growth. This lasted until 1995, when the MCA candidate for Parliament won the election.

Towkays of the Petty Capitalist Class: Being Small but More than "Getting By"

During the 1990s, more than twenty years of life under the NEP and its successor the National Development Policy (NDP) instituted by UMNO had still not inured Bukit Mertajam towkays, men of position who were the proprietors of family-owned businesses, to what they considered the many insults and injuries inflicted on them by the government, although most conceded that whatever else the NEP/NDP had done, the policies had brought political stability and, moreover, they were able to "get by." Local business people viewed Malay exercise of their special rights in gaining corporate equity through the Industrial Coordination Act (ICA) as the manifestation of a unfair racialist politics in which the leaders of UMNO passed out access to equity shares as spoils to new "rich Malays" who were their supporters—even though their own business operations were far too small to be affected by ICA provisions.[1] Still, the ICA posed a perceived upward limit to their aspirations to increased capital accumulation. Many complained that wealthy "New Malays" (see Kahn 2006) had come into existence in large numbers through UMNO and state interventions at Chinese expense. More than one Bukit Mertajam businessmen stated ruefully but with some admiration, "Although we Chinese are good businessmen, the Malays have been even more clever than us" through their use of politics to gain their business fortunes.

Despite their bitterness, during the years following the 1985 recession until the onset of the Asian financial crisis in 1997, globalization was kind economically to the towkays of Bukit Mertajam. Many I talked to did not deny the existence of new conditions of accelerated economic growth and high employment brought on by export-oriented industrialization, although some neglected to credit the policies of the Malaysian and Penang governments for these changes, while most felt that prosperity had not been equally shared by different ethnic groups. These policies encouraged the location of new factories by foreign investors such as Taiwanese manufacturers in the export-processing zones and industrial estates of Seberang Perai, including several near Bukit Mertajam. The appearance of these factories stimulated the labor market for jobs for which their university-educated grown sons and daughters were eligible—for engineers, managers, technicians, accountants, and other educated employees. Young Chinese fortunate enough to acquire university degrees in engineering and other in-demand professions benefited, even as rapid expansion and the underproduction of educated Malay workers in these areas allowed Chinese to find jobs in the factories that otherwise would have gone vacant, at least until the 1997–98 financial crisis and the reduction in foreign investment.

A widespread complaint among petty employers during these years was about the "labor shortage problem," *laogong quefa wenti*, for the same dynamics of export-oriented growth increased demand for factory workers (most of whom were increasingly Malay women) and for workers employed by towkays who were local wholesalers, transporters, suppliers, and owners of businesses such as the blue factory buses, *bas kilang* (M). While this labor shortage raised wages and improved working conditions for working-class people by increasing their opportunities for finding jobs and for doing business as petty entrepreneurs, for those towkays who hired "outsiders," this precisely was the "problem."

Over the same years, government policies that liberalized education allowed the emergence of a private higher education sector consisting of colleges (e.g., new branches of Tunku Abdul Rahman College) and technical institutes that accepted privately subsidized students for technical and managerial training (Toh 2003, 152). Most such students were Chinese. Moreover, people knew that these policies allowed foreign (e.g., Australian) universities to establish twinning programs with Malaysian colleges, so that students spent the first three years of their university studies at these colleges, and went overseas in their final year to graduate from a university abroad. Thus although middle-aged parents complained that their highly qualified children were denied entry to government-run universities and to employment in Malaysian corporations and government, the barb of discrimination had less sting to it than in previous years (152). Nonetheless, many towkays and professionals still sought to send their grown sons and daughters to foreign Anglophone universities, feeling they had been prevented by discriminatory policies from entering the best Malaysian universities, and thus attempted broader strategies of mobility and class reproduction associated with middling modern transnationalism under the conditions of globalization (see chapter 10). That said, small-scale business proprietors, like truck transport towkays, were situated within the wider metropolitan area of the island of Penang and the port of Butterworth, with nearby free trade zones and industrial estates that were the center of export-oriented industrial growth in northern Malaysia. Thus they were geographically well situated to take advantage of the many urban commercial and professional opportunities associated with rapid export industrialization, while their grown children gained access to university and college educations and skilled professional employment.

Moreover, the Gerakan Party, a constituent party of the Barisan Nasional, controlled the government of Penang state during the entire period from the 1970s through the 1990s (under two Chinese chief ministers, first Lim Chong Eu, then Koh Tsu Koon). While the influence of these Gerakan leaders and their supporters in the government (e.g., in the Penang State Assembly) was limited by their UMNO overseers (i.e., the national government and the UMNO-appointed deputy chief minister), local businessmen were well aware they benefited from the industrial development policies of the Penang state government—as long as rapid economic growth continued.

Loh (2001) has argued that during the 1990s a widespread "politics of developmentalism" emerged among Chinese and other non-Malay citizens, which replaced the previous politics of protest connected to a sense of ethnic injustice and associated with the opposition parties, especially the Democratic Action Party. Made possible above all by rapid economic growth and new economic, cultural, and economic liberalization policies of the late 1980s–1990s, and reinforced moreover by Vision 2020—Dr. Mahathir's vision of a fully developed Malaysian society in 2020 no longer divided by ethnic inequalities—Chinese began to accept and to support the policies of the BN parties during this period. As Loh (2001, 186) put it, "This discourse valorizes sustained economic growth that facilitates improvement in one's material standard of living, including a measure of consumerism. The corollary to this is an emphasis on political stability." Part of this new politics of political stability was an emphasis by MCA and Gerakan members of Parliament and state assemblymen on service: opening and operating "service centers" that provided constituents with brokering services in mediating between their needs for official assistance and national- and state-level bureaucracies; constituents resorted to these services, which no doubt attracted them personally to these politicians (Loh 2001; Toh 2003).

There is evidence that supports the appearance of a politics of developmentalism among the petty property owners and professionals of Bukit Mertajam, who came to reconcile themselves under the conditions of rapid economic growth to rule by UMNO, Gerakan, and MCA parties. Indeed, particularly for this class of local petty property owners, life was good: "getting by" and more. Small business fortunes were being made, business continued to grow, children were educated in universities and colleges through diverse means, and a consumerist ethic—one that challenged the virtues of public thrift, stinginess, and industry that had been practiced by the older generation of towkays—was evident in the new houses people occupied, the new cars they bought, and their increasing levels of personal consumption. Even among business families of small means, the consumption of meat, poultry, and fish, for example, was a daily occurrence.

In 1995, the district's Chinese majority voted in large numbers for a parliamentary candidate from the MCA, for by then, informants stated, people had become collectively fed up with the vain protests and melodramatic ineffectiveness of the two previous DAP MPs who had failed to bring in government development funds to the area. Many, no doubt, were attracted to vote for the MCA and Gerakan candidates, given the new prosperity these parties appear to have delivered in Penang state. Moreover, by the early 1990s Chinese in Bukit Mertajam became alarmed by the claims of MCA and Gerakan leaders that "Malay extremist elements" within the opposition Islamicist party, PAS, had demanded that *sharia* (M), or Islamic, law be implemented nationally and applied to non-Muslims as well as Muslims. As a result, local Chinese voted in large numbers for the candidates of the Barisan Nasional as the coalition of parties that provided political stability while "delivering the goods" of rapid industrial growth. As a result of this long-deferred victory for the MCA, whose last member of Parliament from Bukit Mertajam had held office in 1978—in 1995 special discretionary development funds disbursed by the new MP, the district officer, and government ministries were being targeted to building new roads, improving sewage and water treatment facilities in the city's neighborhoods, and constructing a new park for recreation at a nearby dam site, among other amenities, for the first time in fifteen years.

In retrospect, Loh's thesis of a new politics of developmentalism requires reconsideration as it applies to Bukit Mertajam. First, the positive Chinese response to BN rule during the 1990s–2000s was always partial (involving commitments by Chinese of petty property and Chinese capitalists, not the working class), nor was this politics only a matter of the "economy," as if Chinese were essentially pragmatic economizers living outside culture. It is true that the rapid period of economic growth during the 1990s until the Asian financial crisis of 1997–98 was the heyday of such a developmentalist politics. Despite the low-ered growth rate during the years following the crisis, Chinese of property con-tinued to support the BN, in part because the effects of the crisis were short in duration, but also because the internal divisions within UMNO brought about by the split between Mahathir and Anwar Ibrahim after 1997 meant that local Chinese with petty property continued to benefit from relatively liberal eco-nomic and cultural policies put forward by Mahathir and a weakened UMNO. These policies, as much as rapid economic growth, mattered for Chinese support.

However, the fact that the DAP candidate for Parliament in the 1999 elections won in Bukit Mertajam suggests that the developmentalist thesis needs additional modification. Not for the first time, Bukit Mertajam voters split their affiliations, electing the opposition DAP candidate to their parliamentary seat, but voting to elect Gerakan candidates in their Penang State Assembly constituencies. While their parliamentary member expressed Chinese discontents about discrimina-tion, their Gerakan state assemblymen provided crucial brokering between them and government officials through weekly meetings at their service centers. This suggests that local voters adopted a mercenary perspective toward the BN parties: get what you can when you can from them but maintain a broader commitment to those who speak out on behalf of your rights, when the BN candidates dare not to (Chin 2006, 72).

The politics of developmentalism went in eclipse in Bukit Mertajam with the worsening economic conditions from 2007 and 2008—the rising costs of food-stuffs, drastically increased oil prices, the rising cost of living, and the percep-tion among Chinese that during these hardships they still suffered from ethnic discrimination in employment and education (Ho 2012). This was compounded by the 2008 global financial crisis that originated in the United States and sent its shocks in the forms of capital outflows, devaluations, and strikes by capital to peripheral capitalist economies like Malaysia. These changes led to the end of developmentalism and to the decisive victories of the Barisan Alternatif opposi-tion parties in five Malaysian states, including that of the DAP, which formed the new state government in Penang.

"Enough to Get by On"

> You can get by here in Malaysia. If you are willing to work, you can make money here.
> —Ah-Huat, stonemason, July 1993

During the years from 1985 to 1997, Chinese working men and women in Bukit Mertajam sought out wage work in the local petty capitalist sector and found new ways of earning income as petty entrepreneurs (e.g., in hawking, Amway sales, or illegal informal activity such as gambling). A relative few also labored in factories of the export processing zones—a far third choice for most men, and to a lesser extent, women. Working-class youths experienced a continued lack of educational opportunities and the possibilities of upward mobility into small business or the professions, with the majority joining the active labor force by leaving secondary school after the end of Form 3 examinations. The new private technical institutes and universities established during the early 1990s were not for most of them—these their families could not afford to pay for, much less spare their labor. Nor was the Malaysian university system—driven by preference for students with either ethnic privilege (for Malays) or class privilege (for better-off non-Malays) structured into its mechanisms of entrance—for them either.

During this period, the vast majority of Chinese workers in Bukit Mertajam, who were not organized into trade unions, found themselves subject to the contradictory pressures arising from the vagaries of the export-oriented industrializing economy: while there was downward pressure on their wages due to the absence of effective trade unions and employers' increasing use over time of immigrant workers, there was upward pressure on wages due to labor scarcity arising from increased industrial and commercial employment associated with rapid economic growth.

During what might be called the post–Cold War "golden decade for (unorganized) Malaysian labor" from approximately 1988 to 1997, workers had steady work and incomes, and many were able to purchase their own houses, for the first time, in the low-cost housing estates that proliferated in the outlying areas of Bukit Mertajam and nearby. However, with the advent of the Asian financial crisis in 1997 and strikes by foreign investment capital against Malaysia for several years thereafter (foreign direct investment decreased from 18.4 billion ringgit in 1996 to 2.7 billion ringgit in 2005) (Ramasamy and Rowley 2008, 134), harder times returned.

My ethnography among male laborers in Bukit Mertajam during the early 1990s captures certain aspects of their lives during this golden decade, but therefore itself must be historicized as witnessing their lives during a transitory period marked by a degree of working-class arrival at full employment, relatively high wages, the initiation among many workers of petty property ownership of housing, and the rise of what could be called a microconsumerist ethic.

Fugitive Spaces of the Working Class

As part of my ongoing effort to learn more about the perspectives of Chinese workers on the labor process and Chinese society, I spent further time from 1990 to 1993 with several long-distance drivers and other skilled manual laborers who made up a variable group of ten to fifteen men meeting on an almost daily basis during their leisure hours at a site they referred to simply as "under the tree," *shuxia*. I had informal conversations with these men as they sat around a table in a shaded area at an intersection of a cross street to one of the main thoroughfares leading out of the city. I also went on several excursions with these men at times outside of Bukit Mertajam when they were not working. I supplemented participant observation with seven life-histories gathered from them in 1991.

By the early 1990s, the North Malaysian Lorry Drivers Association had fallen on distinctly hard times, with its membership declining from more than two hundred drivers in the early 1980s to only "several tens" of members in 1991. No longer did it even attempt to engage in informal negotiation with truck owners, in contrast to the conflict between drivers and employers over overloads in 1979 that I described in chapter 5. According to one of its ex-presidents, Yeoh Beng Keow, one of the major causes of its decline was the purchase of a new association meeting hall in 1985, made possible by a major fund-raising campaign by the association, which failed due to the bankruptcy of the building developer as a result of the economic recession in 1986 and deprived the association of its fund. Because even truck towkays and retailers had contributed to this fund-raising campaign, the loss was particularly disastrous to the standing of the association:

> YEOH: The developer cheated the association [by going bankrupt] after having received all MR$ 58,000 of the money we raised.
> DMN: Didn't the association at least gain ownership over the unfinished building and land?
> YEOH: No, this land was pledged as security by the developer for its loans in the bank, and when it went bankrupt, the land was reclaimed by the bank. Because of this, members of the association really lost hope. Drivers said, "What do I need an association for? The association does nothing for me."

Now (1991) the old meeting hall, still rented out, only served as a meeting place for members to gamble when not working or spending time with their families. Members of the association still came together to collectively worship Dashiye during the seventh lunar month.

It is perhaps symptomatic in this "golden decade" of unorganized labor that the associational and social connections of truck drivers, and therefore their bargaining power with respect to their employers, should decline, even as their personal economic fortunes improved. Facing the decline of the association, an institution based on a "strategy"—"the calculation (or manipulation) of power relationships that become possible as soon as a subject with will and power (a business, an Army, a city, a scientific institution) can be isolated" (Certeau 1984, 35–36)—drivers reorganized themselves with other workers into the fugitive space of "under the tree." This latter effort was based on a "tactic" ("a calculated action determined by the absence of a proper locus. . . . The space of a tactic is a space of the other . . . it must play on and with a terrain imposed on it and organized by the law of a foreign power") (36–37). In the case of Chinese workers, this foreign power was capital. This fugitive space under the tree was not the only one that came into existence—I heard of others—but it was the one I came to know best.

This shift occurred under the conditions of dispossession of large numbers of working-class squatters, which occurred during these years. This was a process in which hundreds of working-class households occupying land under usufruct in kampungs close in to the center of the city—Kampung Cross Street, Kampung Fish Pond, Kampung Kovil, Sugar Cane Village, and others—were cajoled, paid off, or failing the efficacy of these first two measures, evicted and forced to leave these areas, so that development could take place (see last section of this chapter). Thus the very existence of spaces where working-class people could meet was threatened by these developments.

The space "under the tree" was in no way institutionalized or permanent. Instead, it was a space of leisure that truck drivers and other workingmen were able to claim temporarily as their own—a fugitive space. It was located in the parking lot in front of a coffee shop which also served as a seafood restaurant in the evening. The grove of bamboo shoots that constituted the space under the tree was their space of occupation. It was delineated by two or three collapsible metal tables and several plastic chairs, as needed, around which five to ten men sat every day from midafternoon to late evening, talking, drinking tea from a thermos, and occasionally bringing in fresh fruit for the group to consume.

Although this group of working men, most of them physically strong and imposing, may have secured the permission from the coffee shop owner to occupy this space, I was never able to find out about that, but I was able to determine that they were viewed as having rights of occupation that were based not on legal right so much as their capacity to threaten and possibly do harm to the owner and his property. For instance, during the annual Saint Ann's Festival held nearby, several members offered car owners, looking for a place to park, the "protection" of watching over their parked vehicles, once the owner paid them a small fee to make sure that nothing went wrong in the owner's absence. In short, the men took tactical advantage of an image widely held about them, that they were gangsters, to gain control over this small space.

In addition to five to eight drivers, other "members" of the group meeting under the tree included stonemasons, hawkers, other skilled laborers, a retired ex-policeman, and a schoolteacher. All were Chinese men between thirty and seventy years of age; all but one were married. They spoke to one another in Hokkien or Teochew, occasionally changing to Mandarin when talking to me. "Member" (in English) was their own term to describe someone who joined this group, which nonetheless changed in composition on a daily basis, with a core of three to five men who were to be seen there most afternoons, and observable to people passing by on the major thoroughfare.

It was in this setting under the tree that I began to spend considerable periods of time during the afternoons and evenings of three or four days per week with the men. I wanted to find out how, despite the fact that the truck drivers among them no longer had much contact with the association, they spent their leisure time, and what they had to say about the condition of their lives and work in this period of capitalist prosperity. One driver, Tang Ah-Meng, himself in his early sixties and still driving long distance, pointed to the changes since the mid-1980s when I had last been there saying, "There is now difficult competition from other races, who wish to become drivers, and so the older [Chinese] ones are retiring, the younger ones are leaving for other work, while others have bought their own trucks."

One of the principal themes that came up as I listened to their conversations and asked them about their work was that "we can get by." This response always came with qualifiers, however. As Ah-Huat the stonemason cited above put it, "If you are willing to work, you can make money." Another older driver, who transported sundry goods from Bukit Mertajam to cities to the south, put it slightly differently: "I make enough to use, *gouyong*, and I can get by, but in fact I spend all I make and have little to show for my efforts after all these years of work." He then pointed to a car parked in the distance and said, "This is my old crate, *laoyeche*, it's all I can afford." Yeoh Beng Keow, the ex-president of the association, by then in his mid-fifties, who rarely joined the group, took me to visit the house he had just purchased but even at that point observed: "One can only get by—that's all. You can get by day by day, that's all [*yitian guo yitian baliao*]."

The men I talked to often put their sense of getting by in Malaysia within an international perspective, based on new ideas gained from their transnational travels as labor migrants, or the stories of the travels of others (see chapters 9 and 10). The men made new moral comparisons between different national spaces and the labor markets they represented. One driver said to me in 1991, "In Singapore things are too expensive. You can't buy a house, and food there is very expensive. The place is very small. Also the government is very strict, and regulates its citizens closely. But in Malaysia you can afford to buy a house, there is more room, food and other things are cheaper, and there is more freedom." Another driver stated that in comparison to Thailand, "Malaysia is a good place to live. Compared to Thailand and other countries, no one here starves to death."

During these years, focused on their leisure space, I had little direct opportunity to learn much about the conditions of labor under which they worked, but it was evident that not only were jobs easy to find, but also that men could and did strategize to move from one job to another with higher wages. In one episode, one driver mentioned to another that he was going to leave his employer for another transport company: "I'm going to move because the wages are too low. Fundamentally, I can't get by on them. When I worked for this towkay, the wages were low, but at least I had other outside income [*waikuai*]." He went on to mention that as a driver who transported fish from Thailand through Bukit Mertajam to a city to the south, he had been able to smuggle through a bag or two of Thai glutinous white rice, *baimi*, in the fish crates, for sale on the side. "However, I was caught by Customs in [southern city], because of people who complained [to Customs], and this is serious. So I can't do this anymore, and I'm going to an interview with another transport company for a new position. Would you [asking another driver] like me to set up an interview for you there?"

A second theme that emerged as I talked with the men under the tree was the extensive time and attention they devoted to leisure activities, to thinking about and planning them. A new ethic of microconsumerism had emerged in this period of relative prosperity: "micro" because the consumption involved was episodic, part-time, and not all that expensive for the men involved. Still, a new attention to leisure and working-class male cultivation was evident. As one driver put it, "If you have money, you should spend it. Otherwise you really don't have any money. People should spend money on what they enjoy. When it comes to hobbies, different people have different hobbies. Some like to go fish, although I don't. Someone like my friend Ah-Teong here likes to drink. He likes to drink a lot of alcohol every night. I myself like to go play, to visit places I haven't been to before like overseas, like Taiwan." Bus touring and fishing expeditions for a day or two were common themes of conversation. One driver, Mr. Xu, invited me to go fishing with him in a forest reserve in Perak that had previously been a "black area" frequented by Communist guerrillas but was now opened up to fishing; on another occasion, he also took me to visit a friend of his who operated a coffee shop but whose dedicated hobby was to make customized fishing lures.

One noteworthy feature of the time spent in leisure among the men under the tree was that for most of them, this leisure time was spent with other working-class men, and not with their families or children. The timing was highly scripted. After three to five men met there between about 3:00 p.m. and 6:00 p.m., there would be a period of one to two hours in which they would disperse to their families for dinner. Then by 8:00 to 9:00 p.m., unless they had to set off on a truck trip that evening, they reconvened with other men who had not been there in the afternoon in the space under the tree, which by then they had moved away from the dining area for the seafood restaurant whose proprietor owned the space on which they met. This points to the gendered nature of this space. Another topic of conversation were women that the men had met in their travels, seducing or being seduced by them, and prostitutes they visited while they were out of town, and the rare woman who walked past the men under the tree during the day.

This topic however marked the boundary between acceptable and unacceptable leisure—at least within the boundaries of the hometown. One evening I asked Mr. Khaw, the driver who loved to fish, if he was married. My initial assumption was that he was not, and therefore would be more likely to go fishing as an amusement if he were not married. This proved to be untrue. He said he was married and already had a daughter several years old. I asked, "Doesn't your wife curse you if you go fishing every week?" He replied, "Not at all. If I go fishing or am out gambling, there is no problem; it's only if I were going out with women that she would curse me." A few weeks later, when I returned to the topic upon seeing him, I asked him how his wife reacted when he went on the road? Khaw said that when he is on the road, his wife "does not worry." When he is in Thailand, sometimes he has sex with Thai women, but, "I don't bring it home; I keep it outside; my own affairs, I keep it outside" his family and home in the city.

A final theme that emerges in my interactions with several of the men under the trees was their purchase of new houses that they owned, or putting it more precisely, which they intended to own over time, because banks were now willing to provide them credit in the form of mortgage loans, to purchase one of the new low-cost houses being built in suburbs to the east and west of the city. Thus, for example, I accompanied Ng Ah-Huat, one of the men who became one of my major informants and a good friend, as we attended the housewarming of a driver who was his "partner" (co-driver). We found ourselves in a new, single-story house, whose front room, which is all I saw of the house, had an inlaid shiny stonework floor, but was itself quite small. There was the family altar, and the television set, which was on all the time I was there, with children and a few adults sitting on the couch and on stools and chairs. Ng averred, "The whole row of houses in this project [where his partner's house was] has truck drivers and their families. The area is convenient for truck drivers." On another occasion, I visited a driver who showed obvious house pride as we sat in the front room the house, positioned to admire the lustrous marble floor tiles. He described the improvements he had made on the basic design to his newly purchased house—in addition to finishing the marble floor, he had his front eave extended to provide shade, added on a back room which had become the kitchen, and had installed iron grill work on his front door. The house had cost him only MR$ 25,000, he had added MR$ 23,000 worth of improvements, and the purchase had been financed by the OCBC Bank. He paid only MR$ 350 per month for the loan and would own the house in ten years.

During this golden decade, the working-class men of Bukit Mertajam, largely secure in their employment, able to shift to other jobs when they felt the need, devoting much of their nonwork time to socializing with other men, taking advantage of the women to whom they were related (wives, mothers, sisters) to look after their personal reproduction (e.g., preparing meals) and social reproduction (e.g., child care), and engaged in self-making of subjectivities connected to microconsumption and petty property ownership, hardly provide the material for an heroic narrative of working-class resistance against capitalist exploitation. However, who is to begrudge them these small satisfactions earned from a life of hard labor, labor which most of their growing or grown children were relegated to repeating because of the absence of possibilities for them of upward movement out of the working class? However shiny their new marble floors, and however gendered their forms of privilege, these men led insecure and difficult lives, while the men felt their labors to be essential to "supporting" their wives and children.

Moreover these working men lived in fear of the Malaysian state and its violences. More than one told me that when discussing politics or criticizing their bosses, they felt fear and the need to be cautious, for otherwise, the Malaysian Special Branch might "invite them to drink tea," in other words, detain them. There were certain topics, they knew, that they should not raise in public. Moreover, they recounted stories of arrogant state officials and police who threatened them with violence and offended their dignity. One driver spoke of the haughty traffic police who commanded him to stop while driving and show his license, using peremptory commanding language and beckoning toward the driver with his hand, palm up, fingers together motioning flickering toward himself. "Because of this, we get into fights with the police. We are always fighting with them." While during these years I was usually in no position to see such encounters personally, I was witness to one such interaction in 1985. I was riding with three Chinese friends, all skilled laborers, one day as we drove up in a battered old car to the tollbooth for the new Penang Bridge across the mainland from Bukit Mertajam to the island of Penang. My friend, who was driving and seated next to me, and the toll taker exchanged cross words, which I did not catch. Just as we were leaving after having paid the toll, the toll taker yelled out after us the insult "Chinese pig," *babi cina* (M)! Ethnic animosities have exacerbated class antagonisms and shadowed the lives of these working men and their children.

By the late 1990s and into the early 2000s, the golden decade for Chinese laborers came to an end. Jobs were far less easily found and kept, and new forms of state repression of labor unions, new and disadvantageous labor rules, and the movement of Indonesian and other immigrant labor into the lower levels of manufacturing, construction, and domestic work (Ramasamy and Rowley 2008; Miles and Croucher 2013) were under way and made the bases for their class reproduction more tenuous and their lives less free.

Chinese Society—A Still Lumbering Old Machine, Operating toward What Ends?

The previous chapter demonstrates that during the period of the New Economic Policy the "celebrities" among the mercantile elite of Bukit Mertajam dominated the institutional complex of Chinese society. This elite was positioned by their financial support of and control over the institutions of Chinese-language schools, temples, and native-place, clan, and other associations—the organizations, *she-tuan*, which made up Chinese society. I have shown that the apex and most prominent institution of Chinese society in Bukit Mertajam was the Fudezhengshen Temple Managing Committee. In the years from 1980 to 1997, this committee continued to draw for its members leaders from the four native-place associations in the district, which were envisioned in the segmentary spatial imaginary discussed in the last chapter to be the totality of territorial spaces of southern China from which Bukit Mertajam's Chinese had come.[2]

Even as committee members during these years fought among themselves to decide who should be members of these schools' boards of trustees (especially their chairmen), the committee consistently provided funds to Chinese-language primary and secondary schools, allocated scholarships to students, cemetery plots to those who died, and funds for medical care and welfare to a select few of the district's poorer Chinese, and maintained the temple and its properties.[3] Their capacity to cooperate as a small clique to exert influence and a degree of control over the lives of Chinese affected by these institutions—primary and secondary students and their families, worshippers, pensioners (who received *angpao*, "red packets," of money distributed by the committee on Chinese New Years), and those who were sick and in need of medical care—marked off these men (and a very few women, usually widows of previous members) as persons of power and influence.

From 1980 to 1997, the worthy activities of support of Chinese society by this mercantile elite of men who served on the Fudezhengshen Temple Managing Committee expanded into other areas. The committee managed to raise funds from its members and from other people of position (officers and stalwarts of other associations) to purchase additional pieces of land and finance construction for the new Hall of the Committee (adjacent to the campus of Jit Sin Independent High School (JSIHS) downtown), for a new office building downtown, and for a new crematorium and mausoleum at its Berapit Cemetery site (Property Report in Fudezhengshen Temple Committee 2007, 117–118). One of its major projects was its donation from 1988 to 1991 of MR$ 500,000 to subsidize the cost of buildings construction on a new campus of Jit Sin National Type High School (JSNTHS) in a southwestern suburb of the city, while its members successfully raised additional funds from their native-place associations and other organizations. This allowed JSNTHS to move its facilities in late 1992 to the new site, and separate from the JSIHS, which remained on the old campus abutting Jalan Aston downtown (Treasurer's Report, op cit. 2007). On the whole, the record of accomplishment by the Managing Committee during this period was one, as Chinese-language newspaper articles put it, "worthy of praise."

Subsumption of Chinese Society and Attenuation of Powers of the Mercantile Elite

Yet all was not well with Chinese society in Bukit Mertajam. Let us consider the four resource bases that members of the Managing Committee brought together—enhanced capital accumulation; political party influence; the Chinese language press; and the moral stature of supporting Chinese-language schooling, scholarships, charity for the poor and sick, and worship of the gods.

As to the potentials for accelerated capitalist accumulation under the conditions of export-oriented industrial growth, state strategies of predation vis-à-vis Chinese enterprises meant that, increasingly, the capacity of Chinese entrepreneurs to concentrate capital unfettered by the government's claim to equity and managerial control (its "30 percent" under the ICA) grew increasingly slim; instead, the Chinese counterstrategy was to stay small and proliferate. In the case of the city's mercantile elite of several hundred wealthy men and a few women, the limitations on Chinese capital accumulation imposed by UMNO elite aggrandizement through the ICA were compounded by two other shifts. Concentrations of capital by local Chinese capitalists depended on licenses and contracts with foreign corporations, which they held from the colonial period and which gave them oligopoly control over certain commodity markets—in rice, oil, alcohol, manufactured foodstuffs, among others. Yet these inherited licenses became early targets of government initiatives of nationalization, takeover, and redistribution to Bumiputras under NEP policies. For instance, the management of Petronas, the national oil company, came to favor Bumiputra distributors with licenses over Chinese, even when the latter had been in business since the colonial period, and Petronas reduced the number of Chinese-owned distributorships and franchises (e.g., petrol stations) nationally over these years.

In general, the need to appear small and evade Bumiputra ownership left Chinese capitalists taking up the runt end of industrial development. Under the NEP and NDP during these years, the national and state governments expanded their export-oriented industrialization platforms by giving out contracts to construct major infrastructure projects in and near Bukit Mertajam—building new townships with their housing tracts, schools, government office buildings, commercial centers, sports stadia, and hospitals—to the newly privatized Bumiputra-controlled national corporations. The huge profits to be made from the construction and sale of such infrastructure went to these corporations and their UMNO-connected managers, the New Malays. In contrast, Chinese developers were left with the "scraps," smaller, less-highly capitalized housing projects, and even then possible only when Bumiputra partners fronted for them, which grew less frequent over time.

Another economic handicap for Chinese capitalists was that initiating technological changes to remain competitive in their industries became increasingly difficult, unless they acquired partners that were Bumiputra-owned corporations, which were of such large size that an Ali-Baba relationship was impossible. For example, truck transport towkays informed me that due to administrative prohibitions they were unable to acquire permits for either refrigerated or containerized cargo trucks, because these new technologies were restricted by the government to the largest Bumiputra-owned trucking companies. Containerization, for example, allowed transport companies to connect their operations to that of the increasingly globalized shipping industry. These were all impossible for Chinese-owned firms to adopt.

The most profitable among those smaller projects to which Chinese capitalists gained access were based on insider information about the location of future roads and development projects available to a select few merchants with friends among Gerakan Party and MCA leaders with ties to UMNO and related Bumiputra leaders and to the national and state development agencies and corporations they headed. These merchants then were able to engage in politically informed speculation in land and housing projects. But most Bukit Mertajam merchants, outside the charmed circle of the few wealthiest celebrities with political connections, were excluded. Another source of profit were the new factories producing electronics, appliance, food, medical goods, and apparel, yet only a very few of Bukit Mertajam's wealthiest towkays were at first able to capitalize and set these up, for they competed with larger-scale foreign investors (especially Taiwanese firms) with larger amounts of capital and more attractive wages and working conditions for the young Malay women who made up the vast majority of factory operatives in a period marked by a labor scarcity problem. If local towkays, as many told me, were "just getting by," one could understand what they meant, once they explained these new constraints on their capacities to build and keep wealth.

Nor were Gerakan Party or MCA influence in Bukit Mertajam politics what they had been during the late 1970s. MCA and Gerakan leverage over UMNO's policy directions weakened during the 1980s and into the 1990s, as UMNO leaders came to increasingly depend on New Malays and the privatized national corporations they controlled for the wealth that went into their campaign funds, their favorite projects, the local and state UMNO political machines they ran, and into their personal pockets. MCA and Gerakan leaders often were constrained in this way to endorse or make only nominal objections to laws and regulations that favored Malays over Chinese in the economy and education, and as a result (and this was evident in Bukit Mertajam) were seen as weak and ineffective among their Chinese constituents. This was the case although, as mentioned above, Chinese voters were susceptible to the politics of developmentalism and were thus supporters of BN candidates from the MCA and Gerakan as long as rapid economic growth made jobs for some, and profits for others, continually possible.

Under these circumstances, MCA and Gerakan leaders, although they were able to provide development funds and continue their personalistic services to Bukit Mertajam residents as long as they were in office, still became progressively less influential in the setting of national policies that affected Chinese as citizens, *and* less well-regarded personally among local residents. In short, Chinese voters simultaneously took advantage of the services provided them by MCA and Gerakan politicians, while looking down on them for their weakness and being subject to control by the UMNO elite. The politics of developmentalism implied a mercenary, instrumental attitude by voters toward their elected politicians—their support depended on their sense that the whole package brought to them by BN policies would continue to provide them with jobs, profits, and other benefits. Local men of wealth such as those on the Managing Committee or leading other community organizations found that other than giving them leads on government development plans and nominating them for the feudal titles ("Datuk," etc.) they prized, Gerakan and MCA leaders in Bukit Mertajam did little to assist the flourishing of Chinese society.

Similarly, the local Chinese language press hardly prospered during this period. As younger Chinese spent less time on Chinese language and literature in schools compared to other subjects, while beginning to identify strongly with a world of Chinese glamour in Hong Kong and Taiwan which they discovered on TV and video, increasingly fewer read the Chinese-language newspapers which carried the events of local Chinese society. One of the newspapers, *Xingbin Ribao*, had gone out of business. One informant joked that many people called the two regional newspapers *Guanghua Ribao* and *Guangming Ribao* "newspapers about dying" because they carried so much news about funerals, and by implication were themselves "dying" except among a dwindling older generation interested in local events such as deaths, marriages, and the awarding of feudal titles to local towkays by the government. Most young people had little connection to local Chinese associations, other than their participation in the "cultural evenings" required by celebrity leaders and school principals at school fund-raising banquets. In short, few young Chinese of high school or university age knew much about or cared about the goings-on of Chinese associations in Bukit Mertajam reported in the Chinese language press. When in 1990 I asked one of the current members of the Temple Managing Committee what he thought was the future of native-place associations in Bukit Mertajam, he replied, "I'm not optimistic. Many younger people don't know where their "home," *jia*, is. They don't know what place their ancestors came from in China. Besides, people from different groups intermarry—Teochews with Hokkiens, etc."

Nor did the fee-based Jit Sin Independent High School, the Chinese-language high school directly under the administrative control of the Temple Managing Committee, particularly distinguish itself during these years in the eyes of Bukit Mertajam people. Preferences among Bukit Mertajam parents to send their children to the government-funded Jit Sin National Type High School with its higher academic standing and free education pointed to a disquieting broader shift in attitudes toward Chinese-language education during these years. As much as the parents of students at both high schools esteemed Chinese-language schooling for at least some of their children,[4] students at both schools were far more inclined to take electives in mathematics, sciences, or business, than they were in Chinese language and literature. High examination scores in math and the physical sciences were essential to a successful application to a university in Singapore or in Australia. When it came to language, if a student had to focus on one language only, it was Bahasa Malaysia, for the key to entry into Malaysian universities was a students' successful "pass" in the language section of the Form 5 examination—not Mandarin. If a student had time to study another language, the preference for most students and their parents was English—the language needed for entry to Australian, British, New Zealand, and Singaporean universities—not Mandarin. Irrespective of many middle-aged parents' preference that their children receive the Confucian moral inculcation they associated with the study of Mandarin and the written classics through recitation, *dushu*, most viewed the pragmatics of their children taking more courses in science, business, Bahasa Malaysia, or English as overriding. As a result, many middle-aged Chinese-educated informants deplored the low standing of Chinese language among the youths of the city.

If Chinese society functioned under new constraints arising from the state formation process and the rise of a New Malay wealthy class aligned with UMNO and the state, this is not to say that it failed to function as it had before—although its quotidian aspirations had long fallen short of the segmentary imaginary that still animated its elderly leaders. Nonetheless, during the 1980s and 1990s, the efforts of the leaders of Chinese society in Bukit Mertajam to protect and sustain the representational spaces of temples, Chinese language primary and secondary schools, cemeteries, native-place, clan, and other association halls in the face of these constraints was an admirable one, much deserving of praise.

What I *am* asserting is that although Chinese society continued to function in the 1980s and 1990s, its institutions did so in ways that were increasingly disarticulated and irrelevant to the everyday lives of most Chinese residents. By the mid-1990s when local leaders spoke on issues of concern to Chinese, few Chinese listened, or—unless they were part of "the older generation," *lao yibei*—even read their speeches in the Chinese-language newspapers. Leaders still strutted their stuff at association banquets and gave trenchant speeches; newspaper reporters still routinely reported their doings to readers in the region at large; the Fudezhengshen Temple still owned schoolyards, graveyards, and valuable rental properties. But local Chinese society from the 1990s onward represented little of concern to most Bukit Mertajam Chinese. Although its elements still functioned mechanically, they no longer came together into a spatiosocial order that could sustain an imagined ethnic community that had even the pretense of empowerment through segmentary mobilization.

I find it symptomatic that "due to increases in the population, people gradually came to accept cremation" instead of far more expensive burial at the Temple Committee's Berapit cemetery, and in 1988 the cemetery constructed a crematorium and mausoleum ("Building Report" in Fudezhengshen Temple Managing Committee 2007, 104–105). Cremations began, and rapidly came to surpass burials in number, so that by 1997 there were three times as many cremations as burials, and thereafter as burial plots became increasingly scarce and expensive, the number of burials continued to decline in number (104–105). It was a sign that even the *fengshui* attuned to the prosperity of one's descendants—which depended on the proper siting of the coffin in one's burial plot—was a disappearing technique in Bukit Mertajam's Chinese society.

However, I propose that urban growth was by no means merely a natural demographic or economic process but also an explicitly political one of inscribing expansive state and class power on urban spaces in the local landscape, and thereby invading and reducing spaces that Chinese had previously considered their own.

Official Public Space: Maps, Development, Police Powers

In chapters 1 and 4, I describe the effects on the landscape and Chinese residents of Bukit Mertajam of the counterinsurgent logic of selective point-to-point deployment of police and military force still evident by 1978 when I arrived to undertake dissertation fieldwork. During the years from 1980 to 1997 there was a shift from this counterinsurgent logic to a spatially more inclusive logic of administrative encompassment and management of the population—both outside of Chinese dissident areas, and within them. The police raids, violent harassments, detentions, and imprisonment of kampung residents in the 1960s and 1970s had been the means of establishing a selective penetration by state police and military into these spaces of opposition defined by subordinate class and ethno-racial position.

By the mid-1980s, however, these efforts had given way to far more effective technologies for the containment of these spatially defined enemies of the state: "development" and "improvement"—intimated in the Gerakan Party press release on the city's "improved traffic measures" cited at the end of chapter 4 (*Guanghua Ribao* 1979a). These proposals for traffic improvement—which required extensive removal of hundreds of squatter households living in several kampungs in the downtown area who happened to lie in the way of the proposed roads—were put into effect during the 1990s.

Even in 1978–80 Chinese residents had expressed fears that the rhetoric of improvement presaged the coming of grander measures of state and Malay encompassment of Chinese space. For example in 1979, after I noticed that an open area of ground abutting the city's municipal square, *padang*, was being used on a daily basis by vegetable dealers as a depot for sorting vegetables brought in from outstation, I asked a vegetable wholesaler about it. He replied, "We won't be here much longer, because the Malays are going to move us out in order to construct an Islamic courthouse for themselves." For years there persisted an endemic conflict in which Chinese vegetable merchants protested through the Vegetable Wholesalers' Association to the government about their forced relocation, while carefully couched but nonetheless critical articles appeared against the displacement in Chinese-language newspapers, and DAP leaders visited the site and declaimed against the government in press conferences. All to no avail. By the mid-1980s, a gleaming white new sharia courthouse had been built, while the vegetable wholesalers had been forced to move to the west of the city and abdicate their informal claim over municipal space to the new authority—one they saw as alien, threatening to expand Islamic law to encompass them as non-Muslims. The courthouse, they said, was a structure that belonged to "them, the Malays." The padang itself still remained—a large sward of grass where students had for years played soccer, music bands performed, and police paraded on public holidays—that is, however, only until the early 1990s.

By the early 1990s, however, state formation was much more evident on a quotidian basis in and near Bukit Mertajam in the form of a constant, busy,

SUBSUMPTION AND ENCOMPASSMENT

mobile power—a combined official and (privatized) national corporate impetus to plan and build new infrastructure projects—new townships, housing tracts, commercial areas, hospitals, schools, and government offices—combined with incursions and surveillance on the lived spaces of city residents.

Squatters' Displacement and Concrete Monumentalities of the Ethnic State

By the late 1990s, working people, professionals, and petty family business own-ers were confronted by the massive material presence of Bumiputra-owned privatized national corporations connected to UMNO and the Malaysian gov-ernment, whose new constructions encompassed the urban landscape. These took the form of huge, state-subsidized built structures—government office buildings and complexes, and huge multi-story "hypermarkets"—supermarkets of mall size.

For instance, returning to the status of the city's padang, by 1997 not only had the Sharia courthouse long since supplanted the Chinese vegetable wholesalers' depot on the edge of the municipal square, but

> now occupying what used to be the municipal square is a large, even monumental, commercial building under construction and financed by a Malay-owned corporation connected to the national government. It is 8–10 stories high and occupies the entire space that used to be the padang. Across from this complex is a recently built building, about 3 stories high, which I was told was the headquarters for the Depart-ment of Inland Revenue. If so, how fitting: located in the center of this tax-evading town! (Nonini, fieldnotes 1997) (plate 15)

Technologies of Working-Class Containment and Dispersion

Such massive state-sponsored projects of commercial and residential construc-tion and the new roads built to provide access to them had razed much of the area of the squatters' kampungs that had been the sites of determined political support to the DAP opposition two decades previously. A largely unannounced struggle between hundreds of Chinese and Indian squatter families, who previ-ously had usufruct rights over the land their homes and businesses occupied, and landowners and developers near the city center took place during the 1990s but went publicly unrecorded. According to informants, conditions for families living in squatting areas like Fishpond, Kampung Kovil, and Sugar Cane Village near downtown Bukit Mertajam became worse after an amendment to the Land Acquisition Act in 1991 that made it possible for landowners to devalue the prior use rights of plots by squatters, who had often held such land for decades in their families, and evict them at a much lower compensation rate than before,[5] with the result that many squatting households near the downtown area were evicted to make way for development during the mid- to late 1990s. Working-class Chinese removal had been widely, if not completely, accomplished. It should be noted, however, that many Chinese workers were able to move into new housing in the housing projects then being constructed, and often at very affordable terms. Hence displacement of working people, preventing their previous concentration in the kampungs areas of much of the city's underdeveloped spaces, was by no means always dispossession.

Several other state-sponsored hypermarkets and large office buildings had by 1997 not only been constructed on the edge but indeed extended (via eminent domain) into poorer neighborhoods in suburban areas as well. This included a new District and Land Office, Magistrate's Court, and office complex for Municipal Council services, which had expanded onto land that previously formed part of one of the city's oldest Chinese kampungs, Sugar Cane Village (see next chapter) and was connected by a new road that extended into the poor area of Kampung Bharu to the southeast—another Chinese squatter area (plate 16).

Pressure on Chinese commercial and residential spaces by Bumiputra-owned corporations occurred on an even grander scale nearby. Approximately two miles to the west of downtown, on what had previously been uncultivated padi lands abutting on the western edge of the Chinese squatter neighborhood of Permatang Batu, a new city, Bandar Perda, was being constructed when I visited Bukit Mertajam in 1997. Bandar Perda, according to the sign displayed at its entrance, was being built by Bumiputra-owned Aseania Company and was a project of the Penang Regional Development Authority, or PERDA (plate 14). Since 1997, a new district police headquarters and fire station, both relocated from downtown Bukit Mertajam, as well as the local offices for the agencies of the Municipal Council of Seberang Prai, have been moved to Bandar Perda.

The association between state-sponsored infrastructure projects like the new District Office complex and Bandar Perda, new Bumiputra wealth and power, and the occupation of space that has not just expanded to the edges of but indeed displaced previously built Chinese kampung areas where hundreds of working-class families had lived, was evident by the end of this period. The fact that for some working people there were opportunities to become owners of small houses in suburban housing projects nearby was however no compensation for the destruction of their concentrated communities.

9

COVERT GLOBAL
Exit, Alternative Sovereignties, and Being Stuck

In this chapter, I discuss the ways that, in response to globalization, people from Bukit Mertajam came to express an antistatist politics that defined, represented, and appropriated urban spaces in and beyond Malaysia during the 1980s and 1990s. On one hand, globalization has led to an increased velocity of human movement and interaction over and across nation-state spaces; on the other, as Harvey (1989) and others have noted, globalization has also generated as part of its dialectics new territorializations and defensive attachments to specific urban spaces by publics who are ambivalently linked to the narratives of global modernization. Bukit Mertajam residents manifested both transnational mobility and defended local ethnic space. During the years of prosperity from the early 1990s to the early 2000s, they learned of, imagined, and at times lived in places beyond Malaysia; and during the years of recession and extreme state ethnic chauvinism before and after saw themselves as under assault by the Malaysian state and felt eager to leave to explore other possibilities. In what follows, I examine the ways in which both the claims of the Malaysian state and of Chinese society during this period were contested, resisted, or fled from through a tense set of practices that simultaneously spoke of exit from Malaysia via transnational travel, and yet embodied alternative claims to sovereignty by local groups and persons engaged in cultural struggles (Ong 1991) with the state to define the meaning of Chinese citizenship in Malaysia.

At the same time, set against and disrupting the exercise of power through the production of space by the state and by Chinese society were three forces.

One consisted of the powers generated in the consumption-focused spaces of open-air coffee shops where patrons simultaneously explored and rehearsed the transnational exit option from Malaysia while manifesting an everyday physical massing of the ethnic body that interrupted the naturalized sovereignty of the Malay-controlled ethnic state. There, in these spaces of coffee shops, people declared both their fascination with the imagined, expanding transnational public spaces of work and consumption defined by emigration from and travel out of Malaysia, while showing their physical recalcitrance toward Malay governance within. Yet another form of power were the collective performances of transgressive embodiment by working-class and other residents in "popular" religious processions and public worship that pointed to an alternative, cosmological sovereignty by the Daoist/Buddhist gods over specific places as challenges to the sovereignty of the secular state. A third form of power producing new spaces was that created by the imaginative displacement of Chinese youths from Malaysia through their identification with the glamour and mass-media pop imagery connected to the centers of transnational Chinese cosmopolitanism, which during the 1990s were Hong Kong and Taiwan.

Malaysian Coffee Shops: Public Consumption and Discursive Juxtapositions

I propose that a good point of departure for an ethnographic investigation into Chinese transnationalist practices in Malaysia were the omnipresent open-air roadside coffee shops still found in most Malaysian cities and towns in the late 1980s and 1990s. These coffee shops provided one important venue for performances in the local ethnically marked public sphere. Open-air coffee shops provided a visible venue in which the heterogeneous itineraries of Bukit Mertajam people crossed and intersected. Most coffee shops were sited along the major thoroughfares that entered and passed through the "business district," *shiqu*, of the city. Such coffee shops were often located at the corners of intersections of these roads, situated on the bottom floors of two-story shop houses, and open to the outside on one or two sides. They were unpretentious settings with plain metal folding tables and plastic chairs, dirty floors, dusty overhead fans, and poster ads on the walls, which associated modernity with attractive young women and specific brands of beer or cigarettes. They had a transitory air fitting to both those who patronized and worked within them, and those engaged in many forms of transit. In these very public and visible settings, persons of different classes and genders ate, drank, and talked together—towkays with their customers and employees, or on Sundays with their families; high school students on their way home; travelling salesmen, retired schoolteachers, quarry laborers on break; or truck drivers passing through, with occasional non-Chinese, such as an anthropologist or Indian schoolteacher, also in evidence.

In the ubiquitous roadside coffee shops that were distinctive to urban Malaysian life, petty property class and working-class residents constructed narratives of their transnational experiences that implicated new representations of national spaces and juxtaposed these stories to their daily preoccupations of work and life in the city and elsewhere in Malaysia.[1] These narratives carried, particularly for petty property class residents, implicit challenges to the legitimacy and sovereignty of the Malaysian state. At the same time, through their spatial massing together, people sitting in these coffee shops constructed a realm of visible public space that signified to the Malaysian state and its functionaries the very massed powers of bodies that the latters' language about the dangers of public assemblies deemed threatening. Taken together, the effect of multiple modes of spatiality gave an unpredictable and unsettling quality to coffee shop encounters, despite their manifestly quotidian backdrop.

One principal feature of roadside coffee shops that conferred publicness on them was their structured visibility. The coffee shop as such almost always occupied the open, unwalled bottom floor of an urban two-story or three-story shop house. The design was such that there was a permeable boundary between inside and outside: tables and people occupying the sides and interiors of open-air coffee shops were at once open to the outside while closed in part from it, access to them impeded by the motorcycles, cars, bicycles, pushcarts, and vendors' stalls clustered around their edges, occupying and extending beyond the "five foot way" between the coffee shop and the public roads. During the evenings when it began to cool, or under shade during daylight hours, this boundary extended out beyond the shelter of the coffee shop.

Nonetheless at any one time this boundary was a definite one. The effects of permeable boundaries and a flexible proliferation of liminal spaces between street and built structures (Holston 1989) was enhanced both by the visibility for passersby of the inside from outside, and for customers already seated at tables, of the outside from inside. This allowed for continual interaction between outside and inside, between people who were seated and those in motion. Malaysian roadside coffee shops were quintessential structures within which to see and be seen by others. They were also, therefore, built structures accommodating the operation of networks of power associated with seeing and visibility—a quality which, until the early 1990s, made them unacceptable sites for young women, especially alone, to visit or eat in. These public spaces therefore are not to be idealized, for they acted as venues for exercising powers of the male gaze (Mulvey 1994) over women who entered them, or even passed by.

Coffee shops in urban Malaysia sorted out by ethnicity—almost all were mono-ethnic in terms of their ownership, customers served, and food prepared and eaten in them. Ethnically specific food preferences combined with legal prohibitions for Muslims against consumption of pork, alcohol, and other foods defined as *haram* ("impure," and prohibited), could explain to some degree the patterns of ethnic patronage, but there was an independent effect of self-segregation by ethnic group. The coffee shops I knew best served almost exclusively Chinese clientele.

Coffee shops were also differentiated by class. Class differences were displayed through a spatial hierarchy within which coffee shops serving primarily the mercantile elite were situated downtown, (i.e., in the "market district," *shiqu*), while those serving more broad-based clienteles were further out from downtown, sited in large number along the major thoroughfares that carried travelers into and out of the city. This was a matter of degree; although members of the mercantile elite did take care of much business in air-conditioned downtown restaurants (often the upstairs areas of coffee shops) closed off from and set back from public view, they also patronized the open-air coffee shops I discuss here.

Imagining the Transnational: An Amble Down Kulim Road

Roadside coffee shops in Bukit Mertajam were spaces of public consumption and the sites of embodied spatial practices; at the same time, the juxtaposition of bodily occupation of public space with coffee-shop talk also mattered greatly. I would like to describe my visits to three such coffee shops, all within a few minutes' walking distance along Jalan Kulim, the road leading east from Bukit Mertajam to the city of Kulim in southern Kedah state. The first such coffee shop was the Lam Hong. Among residents, the Lam Hong had a reputation for its Cantonese *dim sum*—which, along with copious amounts of bitter tea, were leisurely consumed in the morning by its clientele of towkays, their wives, and children, while they conversed and read Chinese-language newspapers. I had eaten at the Lam Hong for ten years prior, but it was only in 1991 that it began offering morning dim sum.

One morning in 1991, sitting across from a towkay I knew in the Lam Hong, I asked him about the change. He observed that the coffee shop's owner, a Cantonese speaker born in Bukit Mertajam, had traveled to Hong Kong, met and married a woman there—and here she was, over there, he nodded in the direction of a middle-aged woman standing nearby. She was Cantonese, had previously overseen the preparation of dim sum in Hong Kong, and had now with her husband's help begun to manage the production of dim sum at the Lam Hong. I urged my friend to tell me more about the Lam Hong. He referred to three young women who periodically came by the tables with trays laid out with fresh dim sum, and carried tea kettles with boiling water to refill teapots, when summoned by customers to do so. These women were Indonesian labor migrants, he said, who worked and slept at the Lam Hong. Why, I asked, were local residents not employed in these jobs? My friend replied that no local person wanted such work, for they could find far better-paying jobs in their own family businesses, or in the nearby factories of the export processing zones. There was, he said, using an expression I had heard many times before, "a labor shortage problem," *laogong quefa wenti.*

A second coffee shop, the On Yuen, was located further down along the same road, about one hundred yards further out of the city. The On Yuen was operated by two sisters and their children, and unlike the Lam Hong, was only a coffee shop; that is, its proprietors sold only beverages, while the food for meals was prepared by independent hawkers who operated stalls surrounding the open-air premises. Its clientele tended to be more mixed in terms of class than the Lam Hong's, although virtually all its customers, with rare exceptions such as an anthropologist and an infrequent Indian businessman, were Chinese. Here, in 1991, I sat early one afternoon having lunch and talking with Beh Kou-Kian, a veteran truck driver I had known for six years, when I was hailed from a nearby table by a towkay, Mr. Tan, whom I had met during my dissertation fieldwork more than ten years previously. In 1980, Tan owned and managed a truck transport company whose trucks hauled freight throughout northern and central peninsular Malaysia. Coming over to our table and sitting down, Tan loudly reintroduced himself and interjected his speech over Beh's words to tell me of his current worries. He said that he was now retired from truck transport, although still "doing business" in another line. He needed to know: should his son continue for his master's degree in computer engineering at the University of Utah? If so, how was he himself to find the money? Could his son work part time? Beh, piqued at Tan's interruption, commented caustically to Tan, that there was no problem because "you have money."

Directly across from the On Yuen on the other side of the cross street intersecting with Jalan Kulim was yet another coffee shop, the Ping Mooi Kee. The Ping Mooi Kee was open from late morning until late at night. It had a clientele as diverse as that of the On Yuen, yet catered to a more permanent, less transient clientele. During the afternoon, retirees gathered there to drink tea and chat, while in the evening it was the meeting place for towkays, skilled laborers, school teachers, government workers, and their families—who stopped in for a meal or drink after shopping at the evening market, *pasar malam* (M), immediately adjacent. Again, as was true for the other two coffee shops, almost all customers were Chinese. One evening in 1992 I came into the Ping Mooi Kee, and recognizing two acquaintances at a table, sat down to join them. Altogether five men were seated there. Four I knew from elsewhere were then working as truck drivers or stone-masons. I discovered after some inquiry that I had come in during one man's telling of his experiences laboring as an operative in a factory outside Tokyo, Japan. I did not recognize him. He said that he recently returned from Japan, where he had "jumped airplane," *tiaofeiji*, for about two years—that is, had stayed in Japan illegally to work as a casual laborer. He was recounting the experience of another man, also from Malaysia, who was seriously injured in the factory. The details of the accident were unclear to me, so I asked, hoping for elaboration: what sort of treatment for his injury did he receive? He replied concisely, "My friend received no treatment at all" and refused to elaborate.

A Profusion of Places and Confusion of Prepositions

These three mundane exchanges and the narratives embedded in them showed a curious quality in that they juxtaposed the local and everyday with the transnational and the extraordinary. The exchanges were set in three local sites and were exemplary of the experiences of many Chinese men and women who lived in and near the city in which my ethnographic research has been carried out intermittently during the last twenty-five years. The narratives I heard and have described from encounters in these three settings were not, however, only about life in or about this city as such—including its public life—but rather were frequently marked by the spatial and temporal disjunctures arising from the experiences of travel and sojourning elsewhere, many other "wheres" in relation to this city situated in a highly urbanized region of northwestern Malaysia. In the encounters described in these three coffee shops, these other places included, to name those I know with certainty, Hong Kong; Indonesia (probably Sumatra); Kuala Lumpur and other cities in central and southern Malaysia; Salt Lake City, Utah; the west coast of the United States; New York City; and Tokyo, Japan. These narratives defined the distinctive experiences of Bukit Mertajam people engaged in movements along transnational routes of migration, paths of capital flow, and the movement of ideas, within a more inclusive cosmopolitanization of that city. In contrast to these articulate and often moving narratives of travel, *the places where these tales were told*—three roadside coffee shops in a Malaysian city—took on an elusive and almost unreal mediating quality. Nor were these narratives from a distant past long since gone but related an immediately recent time—or even simultaneous time—as in the case of Mr. Tan's son then in the United States, or other people whom my informants spoke of as their kinfolk or friends working at that time as illegal "airplane jumpers" in Japan. Sociality in these coffee shop settings was suffused with multiple awarenesses of present absences like these, expressed in stories that embodied aspirations, fears, longings, fantasies, cynicism, and pathos.

However, the settings of these three coffee shops were far more than the bus or taxi stations or hotel lobbies within which James Clifford (1992) would have us do our ethnographies, although Clifford's call is an important one. Many men and increasingly some women frequented these and other roadside coffee shops in the daily course of highly localized—indeed local—work within and near the city I stayed in. What I want to point to was the *juxtaposition* of stories about the local—gossip about which towkay was opening up a new business in the city, ideas of what new job prospects were available nearby, speculation about who the new representative from a native-place association to the city's independent high school board of trustees might be—with stories about the extralocal—from sojourns in southern Malaysia, Singapore, Thailand, or Japan. This heady pastiche of differentiated spatial representations characterized the public conversations that people in Bukit Mertajam joined and overheard in roadside coffee shop settings.

But not for all residents in the same way. By the early 1990s, among petty property owners engaged in transnational ventures, a new world of imagined possibilities had come into existence: should Mr. Tan's son continue to study at the University of Utah—or should more Cantonese dim sum coffee shops in the city be opened by people from Hong Kong? It was among these informants that the legitimacy and hence sovereignty of the Malaysian state was being debated, if not usually in so many words. Given the constrained options of "exit," "voice," and "loyalty" (Hirschman 1970) that Chinese could adopt toward the Malaysian state, transnational narratives by petty property owners in coffee shop talk explored the exit option. Their narratives also served as one index of the unraveling of the segmentary imaginary of local Chinese society—after all, Bukit Mertajam people might become citizens of distant nation-states; find their children educated in schools and universities in North America, Australia, or Europe; be buried in faraway graveyards overseas; worship in foreign temples or churches; or join Chinese associations in other countries in the Asia Pacific.

In contrast, working-class men who labored overseas narrated stories of hardship ("my friend received no treatment at all"), danger, and sacrifice, but always ended these stories with the coda of return to Malaysia, either in triumph with money saved, or in failure. But things could have been worse: after all, these men felt that "in the old home town," they could take advantage of the "labor shortage problem" prevailing in one of Malaysia's prime industrial regions during the 1990s to find work at a low but livable wage. The economic possibility of "getting by" reconciled them to life in Malaysia, but not to the legitimacy of the Malaysian state, for they and their families continued to be the most frequent targets of various forms of state-induced violence, and they resented this violence deeply and lived in fear of it. They and their family members were also those most active in the forms of religious worship of embodiment that questioned state legitimacy, which I discuss below. As to their relationships with local Chinese society, these laborers and their families, as one man told me, "had no position"; its subsequent unraveling was of little relevance to their lives or of interest to them.

Yet another form of inequality—the national—was associated ironically with transnational travel evident in the new, deferential, and generally silent presence of Indonesian women in the coffee shops of Bukit Mertajam in the 1990s. The scene in the Lam Hong pointed to the large-scale influx of Indonesians from Sumatra and elsewhere in the archipelago to the highly urbanized states of Malaysia, like Penang, where they worked in large numbers as casual and temporary laborers in housing construction, and for small businesses and families. Taken together, the complex overlayerings of travel and spatial practices—movements by Indonesians to urban Malaysia, by Bukit Mertajam people to Japan and by others to the United States—indexed the tiers of national difference associated with mobile capital and mobile people within the new international division of labor. In any one site, like a coffee shop in Bukit Mertajam, they also pointed to ever more heteroglossic combinations of voluble discourse about transnational travels among some of those present (e.g., Malaysian men), which was juxtaposed to silences among others present about their transnational travels (Indonesian migrant women)—a juxtaposition connected to these tiers of difference and the symbolic violences that conditions of inequal power made possible. Moreover, the manifestly gendered character of these coffeehouse narratives was a crucial issue, which I turn to in the next chapter.

A Massed Ethnic Body Politic

At the same time, Malaysian coffee shop sociality displayed another dimension of power. The physical occupation by large numbers of Chinese residents of approximately one hundred open-air road-side coffee shops in and near the city—sitting, eating pork, and drinking alcohol forbidden to Muslims, at times raucously talking, beckoning to passersby, coming in or leaving on motorcycles or bicycles, in cars, or trucks—was an imposing presence that no one, whatever their ethnicity, could ignore. It displayed the power of massed bodies, a demographic and electoral force to be reckoned with in a Chinese-majority state (i.e., Penang) and the city itself. Their occupation of not only coffee shop spaces but also of the public roads through which they passed to and from these spaces, conveyed a sense of entitlement—a de facto claim to citizenship made material by visible occupation. The presence of massed ethnic bodies threatened to encroach on the roadways or their shoulders, for instance when tables were set out—creating a liminal zone whose usage was ambiguous (is this state space—or ethnic space?), but one on which an implicit political claim was being made.[2]

The quotidian and widespread visible display of an embodied ethnic mass of people occupying urban space resonated with speculations by informants that proposals by UMNO leaders which supported large Malay family size and in-migration from more rural states to Seberang Prai were designed to increase local Malay electoral strength at the expense of Chinese. The physical massing and display of Chinese bodies in local coffee shops must be seen within this broader zero-sum ethnic biopolitics—in either case, strategies of swarming to overwhelm one's opponents by numbers within contested spaces were invoked, in two different registers.

At the same time, one must keep in mind that there were also present those who were less visible—Indonesian and other foreign workers who were out of public view but labored in the construction sites, laundries, and small shop houses of the city's businesses.

Worshipping the Gods: Transgressive Embodiment and Cosmopolitical Powers

The Malaysian Constitution, in addition to provisions assuring legal privileges to Malays and other Bumiputra, also provided guarantees to non-Muslims of their freedom to worship. Bukit Mertajam people took full advantage of the rights thus guaranteed to appropriate and redefine public space in the name of religious freedom. There were two such modes of appropriation among worshippers of the Daoist/Buddhist pantheon: *influx*—participating in festivals on the birthdays of the gods by traveling to and massing at their temples to worship; and *circumambulation*—joining in processions of the gods and their worshippers in a tour of their domain—a neighborhood, a municipality—during one day of a festival honoring the gods. A similar appropriation of space occurred among Chinese worshippers during the Catholic St. Anne's festival.[3]

In the first, worshippers moved inward, to the center—the temple—to worship the gods; in the second the gods moved outward in a circumambulation to "inspect" those who worshipped them. In both situations, appropriations of urban space by worshippers challenged the territorial claims of the Malaysian state by imaginatively dislodging it through the presence of an enacted transcendent sovereignty over space. Such an alternative sovereignty was spoken of as a god being *ling*, "efficacious," having the capacity to transform the everyday world and the lives of the people who inhabit it. The "efficacy" of gods was effected *over space* through the bodies and associated materialities of worshippers and was contrasted to the "strength," *liliang,* of the Malaysian state. The gods' presence did not specify or point to power; it *was* power over humans, enacted through their bodies.

Unlike the authoritative ethnic space underlying Chinese society, the appropriations of public space associated with temple festivals were truly popular, being associated with territorially specific allegiances to city and neighborhood that transcended classes and genders. Temples, after all, were the homes of the gods. It was true that the small committees managing festivals, each with their head, the incense urn master, *luzhu,* and committee members, *xieli,* usually consisted of wealthy neighborhood men who made large donations and played a prominent ritual role in the festivals. Nonetheless, the vast majority of worshippers were far less wealthy and lower in status. They participated in a variety of ways in worship—young working-class men acted as spirit mediums, older women came to the temple to make offerings and pray on behalf of families, and so on.

Influx. In situations of influx, worshippers of gods in a temple moved toward it from throughout its hinterland—the urban and suburban spaces over which the temple's gods had efficacy—toward the temple itself, to make offerings and pray to the gods during the several days that celebrated their "thousand autumns of precious birth," *baodanqianqiu.* A conspicuous example was the climax to the annual ritual calendar of worship in Bukit Mertajam, the Festival of the Hungry Ghosts, Yulanshenghui, held for twenty-three days during the seventh month of the lunar calendar, and described at the end of chapter 2. This festival centered on the oldest and best-known temple in the city, the Fudezhengshen Temple and on an adjacent open space across an alleyway from it. This festival honored the return of ghosts, *gui,* to the overworld of the living from the underworld for one month; during this month, they were visitors. Ghosts did not simply disperse throughout the overworld, but rather were overseen collectively and controlled by a god addressed as *Dalaoye* or *Dashiye,* referred to less formally as the "king of the ghosts" (*guiwang,* in Mandarin), or most intimately by his Hokkien name Podogong. For worshippers, Podogong was a ravenous, gluttonous, greedy, and unpredictable god—the godfather of an unruly pack of ghosts who during their visit to the overworld could bring human beings much "trouble"—make them sick or cause them accidents. They corresponded in supernatural form to the gangs of secret societies, *sihuidang,* who were said to control squatter neighborhoods on the edge of the downtown area.

During Yulanshenghui, the altar of Podogong was erected in an open-air pavilion sited a few feet across an alleyway from the Fudezhengshen Temple.

Within the pavilion, the red-and-black effigy of Podogong towered nineteen feet high, his fierce visage peering from on high down on the worshippers. Worshippers piled high stacks of Hell Bank notes, ("spirit money") in the lap of Podogong as offerings (plate 5). Facing his altar was an area thirty feet wide by fifty feet long, occupied by tables overflowing with goods offered by worshippers. Offerings were stacked high on the tables, one case of liquor piled on another, or slaughtered pig carcasses each laid over the next, like cards fanned out on a table. Surrounding the tables were baskets of slaughtered chickens and ducks. Beyond the altar and in the adjacent temple courtyard giant joss sticks burned—as many as one hundred or more. In one sense, these visibly abundant offerings were put out to attract and please Podogong and his followers, the gui; in another, they conveyed the wealth and prosperity of the groups that sponsored each day's worship,[4] and it also marked them as distinctively Chinese, that is, as not Islamic—instantiated in the hog carcasses, the crates of liquor and beer, the bodies of fowls slaughtered in ways that were haram or forbidden to Muslims. The conspicuous excess of the forbidden offerings, then, was an implicit affront to the modern Malaysian state and its ethnic supporters. As one pork vendor whose family had rented a shop house abutting the Fudezhengshen Temple since the 1940s bragged, "Municipal Council enforcement and sanitation officers have never come here to interfere with or make trouble for our pork selling business" (Fudezhengshen Temple Managing Committee 2007, 94)—perhaps no surprise, since most such officers were Malays, who were Muslims (plate 4).

What I want to specifically emphasize about the festivals associated with offerings to Podogong were their visibility, their physicality, and their centrality. These characteristics generated a performance of excess power that enacted a cosmopolitical sovereignty over the public space of the city and manifested an alternative sovereignty to that of the Malaysian state. This enactment of power and sovereignty was first of all visible from the street, which was a principal thoroughfare through the downtown area: visible to passersby on foot, on motorcycles, in cars and trucks, and to vendors and customers in the city's public market across the street. Other senses were also implicated: the loud sounds of the Teochew opera—songs sung in high-pitched archaic Teochew with cymbals clashing—in the temple courtyard, and the profuse smoke rising from the joss sticks—smoke which was so dense that if one came close enough and tried to remain, made one dizzy and disoriented.

The overloaded offering tables stacked high with offerings for Podogong, the back side of the opera stage, the size and smoke from the joss sticks, and the high nasal singing of the opera, all taken together encroached on the roadway itself, and threatened to overrun the boundaries between temple and thorough-fare. Over several years, there was an ongoing dispute between worshippers who erected gigantic joss sticks—as much as a foot in diameter and eight feet high—before the altar of Podogong, and police who sought to limit their size on the grounds that they posed a fire hazard. Eventually, through the interces-sion of an MCA leader, the police and the incense urn master of the festival agreed on the maximum height and width of these joss sticks. It was in just such microdisputes that the boundary between secular state sovereignty and that of the Chinese gods was contested and negotiated.

Such excess extended to the worshippers affiliated with the group sponsoring the day's festivities—who at times came together to overflow exuberantly into the roadway itself—as did other, "public," *dazhong*, worshippers who came and went continually. Such a material occupation of space indexed a culturally specific conception of sovereignty over a domain of cosmopolitical space: the god's effi-cacy extended concentrically outward in all directions from its altar to affect any persons who were their devotees. Podogong was most "powerful," ling, to people close to his altar: I was told of a child who once misbehaved while at an offering table before Podogong and later became mad as a result. But even further away, one might still be affected by a god's power: during one day of the festival, one of my friends warned me, "If you speak ill of him, Dalaoye may kick your car and cause an accident!"

State functionaries—most of whom were Muslims and Malays—misrecognized or denied the existence of such power: to the district officer or OCPD (officer in charge of a police district), this material occupation of municipal space by wor-shippers was a mere nuisance. The overriding ontology of official state space, described above, was one in which this alternate power simply did not exist, and so made such misrecognition well-nigh certain. Yet these officials knew that this would not quite do, for, after all, Chinese leaders repeatedly sought them out and applied for the permits required to hold this and other festivals—all in the name of religious freedom. At the same time, a discreet class disciplining of worshippers by the local elite also occurred. A sign in Chinese was posted to one side of the altar of Podogong, and stated: "No disorderly behavior through spirit possession is allowed.—Public incense master and festival committee." Young working-class men, those most frequently possessed by gods, were not to serve as embodiments of this ruling and unruly god: who knew what the god might do when possessing *them*?

The cosmopolitical power and controlled violence associated with the worship of Podogong was best illustrated on the evening of the last day of Yulansheng-hui, which marks the return of Podogong and his gang of ghosts to the under-world. In late August 1979, at the altar of Podogong, glowering policemen from the Anti-Secret Society Unit of the police confronted eager young working-class men, said to be members of local secret societies. After the closing incantation by a Daoist monk, the public incense urn master, a wealthy truck transport towkay, went up on a ladder to retrieve the small figure of the goddess Guanyin, mounted over the fierce visage of Podogong, which was said to control him while he visited the overworld, but after his visit became a talisman of good fortune for the public incense urn master (see plate 5). After the figure was retrieved, the young men surged up onto the altar of Podogong, and pulled down the god's wooden and paper figure piece by piece, which they then carried out to a nearby road intersection and set afire. Since 1979, this ritual destruction and burning of the figure of Podogong has continued.

Circumambulation. A second form of cosmopolitical appropriation of public space by Chinese vis-à-vis the Malaysian state was circumambulation. This occurred in the case of certain gods residing in temples who "went out to tour," *chuyou*, of their domain, and in the case of gods coming from afar to "patrol" or "inspect" their "boundary circuit." It was only the gods from specific temples who "went out to tour"; for instance, the gods of the Fudezhengshen Temple did not. Temples associated with certain neighborhoods near downtown, especially squatter areas, were those whose gods "toured" the "boundaries" in a move of encirclement demarcating the cosmospace of the neighborhood. One such tour I observed took place on the first day of the sixth lunar month of 1991, to close the five-day annual festival that honored the collective birthday of the god Lushanshigong (known also as Zhegong) and the other nine gods of Shilinggong Temple, and located in the squatter kampung of Sugar Cane. Sugar Cane was an older kampung situated in what had been a coconut orchard at one time but had partly reverted to secondary forest, dotted with single-story wooden houses with zinc or even thatched roofs, each house with its red-and-black sign mounted over its doorway with the characters for the China original native place of the clan of the owner and connected one to the other by unpaved paths: clearly a working-class neighborhood with a majority of DAP supporters, not favored with pavement paid for by Barisan Nasional development funds. On the last day of the festival, it climaxed with a tour by the gods who resided in Shilinggong Temple.

On that afternoon, worshippers crowded within and outside the temple to pray to Lushanshigong and its other gods. The incense urn master and members of the committee who sponsored the festival each in turn carried out the figure of one of the temple's gods from its altar to place it in the "gods' sedan chair," *shennian*, standing outside the temple at the entrance to the unpaved lanes leading through Sugar Cane. Over the course of the next hour, accompanied by raucous beating of drums in a rhythm that invited the gods to enter ("dum-da-dum-da, dum-dum-dum-da") the temple gods took possession of fourteen young men as the latter were surrounded by fellow worshippers before the temple—several bodies having long barbs pierce their cheeks without signs of pain. The entry and possession of a body by a god was complete when, in turn, the god-body manifested the movements, gaits, and gestures that identified a specific possessing god, such as Sumugong, "the monkey god," Santaizi, "the three princes," Jigong, and others. The possessing gods (as they had by then become) were then one by one led gently by members of the festival committee outside the temple—although each threatened to go its own way—but were persuaded to sit waiting while other gods took possession of the mediums' bodies (plate 11). Finally, the possessing god Lushanshigong (having entered the body of the chief medium), came outside, went out to the open platform directly opposite the temple on which he called to Yuhuangshangdi, "the Emperor God of Heaven," and having received permission from the god for the tour, started the procession.

Lushanshigong and the other possessing gods led the tour, followed by the sedan chair with the figures of the temple gods, carried on the shoulders of the members of the festival committee—with the main body of worshippers and a North American anthropologist in train (plate 12). We proceeded down the paths of Sugar Cane. At the places where the paths from perhaps three out of every four houses intersected with the lane, families had erected offering tables on which residents set out bottled beer, incense, fruit, and nuts. Possessing gods took offerings from this or that table as we moved along. At each offering table, the possessing god Lushanshigong stopped and drew a paper talisman, *futou*, with the Chinese characters naming the god on it, and left it with household members to protect them. The tour proceeded in this way for more than two hours along a route of lanes and paths within Sugar Cane and paved roadways on its edge, in ritual that inscribed both the Chinese families who were the subjects of the gods and the community's socially and cosmically recognized boundaries.

A tour by the gods of the same temple, but a decade earlier in 1980, was described in the following words in an article announcing the festival published in a regional Chinese-language newspaper: "The god's sedan chair will go out on tour, and at the appointed time all devotees along the way should burn incense, kneel and worship together, in order to pray for peace in the area [*hejing*], good weather, and prosperity and peace for the nation's people [*guotai minan*]" (*Xingbin Ribao* 1980b). Claims over cosmopolitical space that impinged on and indeed denied the sovereignty of the Malaysian state were not so much described or prescribed in the written language as they were matters of neighborhood knowledge, widely shared, and bodily enacted through the tour itself.

In one other important religious festival in the city, that of the "Nine Emperor Gods," or *Jiuhuangye* (see Cheu 1988), held during the tenth lunar month, these gods arrived from afar via water—from the ocean via the Prai River—to "inspect," *xun*, the "boundaries" of the domain of those who worshipped them. As in the case of the festival of Shilinggong, the Nine Emperor Gods took possession of human bodies, and in this embodied form encircled the domain of worshippers within the city (plate 7). A Chinese newspaper article from October 10, 1978, wrote of their visit that: "the gods rode on inspection in a circuit of downtown (*jiaxun huanyou shiqu*), with prayers for peace in the area and good weather" (*Guanghua Ribao* 1978). The language, particularly the predicate *jiaxun*, for knowledgeable worshippers alluded precisely to the inspection tours of emperors and their entourages of officials in imperial China, the material presence of sovereign power in its circuit. The very language of circumambulation in the case of the Nine Emperor Gods, like that for the gods of Shilinggong Temple, pointed to a region of cosmopolitical sovereignty associated with Chinese powers over and against those of the secular, Malaysian, state (figure 9.1).

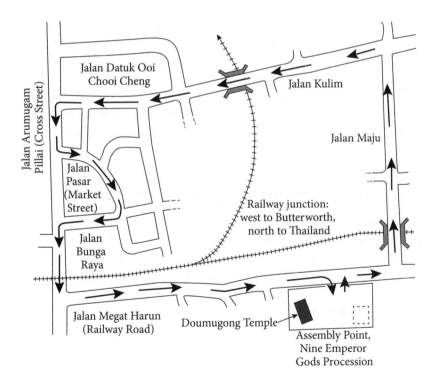

FIGURE 9.1   Circumambulation of downtown Bukit Mertajam, Nine Emperor Gods festival, 1979

It should be noted that the detailed newspaper accounts of circumambulation quoted above were from the late 1970s or early 1980s; indeed, I was unable
to find similar newspaper accounts for the early 1990s.[5] In the 1990s, circumambulating processions like the one I observed for Shilinggong still took place,
and their semiotics were clearly real to worshippers, but I suspect that the overt
invocation within the Chinese-language press in the 1970s and 1980s of a transcendent cosmological sovereignty was no longer favored in the declining and
more politically constricted press of the 1990s. I am suggesting, therefore, that a
lay or working-class semiotics of sovereignty existed that was increasingly out of
kilter with elite accounts.

The challenges to state sovereignty posed by the appropriation of urban
space in the course of influx and encirclement were temporary and in accordance with the lack of political "strength," liliang, on the part of Chinese nationally, always contingent on the concessions made by the state. Nonetheless, these
religious processions by worshippers invoked an alternative cosmo-power—one
inscribed through embodiment, the body's disciplines, and the discourses these
harnessed—that perennially called into question the bases of legitimacy of
the Malaysian state. This power cemented solidarities that were distinctively
local—our family, our kampung, our temple, our gods—with respect to which
the incursions of official state space associated with the projects of Malaysian
state formation were deemed, in the deepest sense, to be radically illegitimate. For
people at home, the effects were to redefine the "public" aspect of Malaysian public space associated with the welfare of populations. Governmentality was a game
that gods as well as humans played: worship did not only honor the gods but also
pleaded with them, after all, for "prosperity and peace for the nation's people."

Transnational Yearnings and "Being Stuck"

As I indicated in the previous chapter, among both younger adults and the
middle-aged generation of the urban Chinese petty-propertied class, who still
formed the postwar readership of the Chinese-language press, neither the local
mercantile elite, nor the spaces they controlled and organized, were as crucially
relevant as they once had been to their cultural and economic reproduction. The
globalization of the Malaysian economy since the 1980s opened up new capital
accumulation strategies for the city's petty-propertied class, particularly if they
were men, that allowed them to bypass or forego altogether access to local public
resources and spaces and to the patronage of the local elite for jobs and commercial connections. Many property-owning families of university-educated "youths"
who were not recruited directly into the technocratic and managerial elites of

corporations in Kuala Lumpur or Singapore engaged in transnational strategies of "traversal"—a phased exiting from Malaysia of family members (particularly their young adults) and of family wealth overseas to the Anglophone regions of the Asia Pacific.

In contrast, local Chinese society long held little attraction to the working people of Bukit Mertajam, who knew the grinding and bitter exertions that towkays demanded of them, like those imposed on truck drivers. The tedious work in the factories in the export processing zones of Penang, which combined hyperexploitation with the indignities inflicted under the surveillance of non-Chinese corporate overseers, was even less attractive. When, as during the prosperous years of the 1990s and early 2000s, working people sought to "get by," they actually got by by doing business as hawkers, truck and bus drivers, stone masons, insurance agents, and the like. However, at other times, such as the recession years of the mid-late 1980s to early 1990s, many working-class men attempted to play off the Malaysian labor market—with all its state-imposed discrimination against them—against other markets in the Asia Pacific by opting for extended labor sojourns in Japan and Taiwan. These sojourns were illegal according to the migration laws of these countries, and working men came to engage in transnational strategies of "reversal" in which they sought to avoid deportation by planning to return to Malaysia. It was precisely these traversals and reversals that were alluded to in the dissonant conversations "in" but not "of" this city, overheard in its coffee shops.

From the mid-1980s onward, the effects of projects of state formation and globalization were reinforced by those of a third process, the production of new transnational imaginaries through the dissemination of the electronic media imageries of "Chinese youth" culture within Asia Pacific at large. This led to deracinated virtual cosmopolitan subjectivities among younger men and women interested in the music of Canto-Pop and pop music in Taiwan and the films of Jackie Chan and Bruce Lee. But this process of self-making did not occur by means of an unmediated connection through which local youths somehow absorbed the Chinese "essence" via videocassettes of Hong Kong gungfu films or music tapes of Canto-Pop stars. Instead there was an enhanced valorization of a new form of mediated quasi-interaction (Thompson 1995) between the media of the Malaysian state and Chinese youths, which displaced the older ethnic form of mediated quasi-interaction—Chinese society—articulated through the Chinese-language press read by older middle-class readers in Bukit Mertajam. Instead, the government's monopoly over television and radio meant that this was the first field of engagement for youths, as they became more affected not only by American cop films and Hollywood dramas but also by the Malay-language media in which so many of the Malaysian programs were cast. This cultural and linguistic influence occurred when students had to master the Bahasa Malaysia crucial to their passing the Form 5 national exams required for university entry.

While most were antagonistic toward the Malaysian state, they were receptive to the congeries of messages its agencies promulgated, directly and indirectly, through the electronic media—modernity, modernization, and development—but indexed not by the opening of government dams or clinics, but by transnational travels, sojourning, and consumption-driven forms of identity. There was "Chinese youth," its styles of dress and music displayed in the Cantonese sitcoms broadcast on late-afternoon TV4, the then-new privatized television network. These messages were then reinforced by access to Mandarin-, Taiwanese-, and Cantonese-language videos from Taiwan and Hong Kong that constituted a new transnational public of Greater China among younger adults. I seriously doubt that there was a single Chinese household in Bukit Mertajam whose television set was not accompanied by a VCR to play videos from Hong Kong, Taiwan, and China as part of its strategy of dissociating and decoupling their own visions of Chinese or Asian modernity from the Malaysian state.

One outcome was that although Chinese society was dislodged as a central trope of Chinese ethnicity, it was not replaced by an identification by most Chinese youths with the projects of the Malaysian state. For most Bukit Mertajam people, to be "modern" was not encompassed by their connections to the Malaysian state, which defined them as second-grade citizens. Instead, to be modern was to belong to a world that included Malaysia, but extended far beyond it to Greater China and the utmost reaches of the Chinese cultural ecumenium throughout the Asia Pacific. This was a world grounded in imagined affinities, not in everyday social connections.

Coffee shop talk clearly entered into this process of being modern and going global. Discursive juxtapositions of the local, the extralocal, and the transnational in coffee shop talk provided one important context for articulating issues that residents of Bukit Mertajam saw as shared among them, and in that sense, as public. Over the previous two decades, these juxtapositions were elaborated and made habitual, meshing with the cosmopolitan imaginaries that television, film, and popular music promoted. A new propertied-class structure of sentiment arose through a complex mixture of face-to-face interactions and mediated quasi-interactions, tying the public discourses of coffee shop talk to television watching as an active rehearsal for cosmopolitanization, one that rejected an alien Malaysian nationalism, largely ignored Chinese society, but favored virtual identifications with the realms of commodities (e.g., pop music, Bruce Lee and Jackie Chan gungfu films, and "world class" luxury goods), people, and places deemed to be Chinese, prosperous, and modern beyond Malaysia.

In contrast, the massing of Chinese bodies in open-air coffee shops and the periodic possession by gods of the bodies of men to create alternative cosmopolitical spaces through influx and encircling were challenges to state legitimacy and sovereignty *within* the local spaces of the national territory. Both strategies were based on subterfuges—if indeed they were strategies. As to the former, the power of exhibiting a massed presence made the best of an ambiguous situation: it was a second-order effect of sociality—after all, no one individual was responsible. It also happened to display a potentially unruly crowd of Chinese bodies not subject to state disciplining, particularly in its association with substances (i.e. pork and alcohol) forbidden by an official Islam.

The latter, worship of the gods, was for poorer Chinese men a way of dealing with "being stuck"—I allude to the statement by Rodney King after the L.A. uprising that "we're all stuck here for a while" (Gooding-Williams 1993). For working-class residents of Bukit Mertajam, the "exit" option was at best only temporary—for without capital one could work overseas but not remain there—while the "voice" option of protest was politically dangerous, and the "loyalty" option distasteful. "Being stuck," Gooding-Williams writes, "is a matter of being inexorably caught up in a network of political, economic, and cultural legacies that escape the aura of the extraordinary" (3). Being stuck for working men and women in Bukit Mertajam could be traced to the violence of state repression, intimidation, and marginalization that their parents and grandparents experienced during the Emergency period—and whose effects and legacies worked on them still in the 1990s.

When working-class men and women formed defensive attachments to spaces of family home, neighborhood, and locale they were taking the only course possible for those who were stuck with no position of wealth or standing in Chinese society, while also being discriminated against and stigmatized not only as nonindigenous and non-Muslim but also as crude and poor by the Malaysian state. One had nowhere else to go—so even the bitter coffee shop transnational narratives of working-class labor sojourns seemed to say. One was stuck "in one's place." Under the circumstances, the cosmopolitical challenge to state legitimacy constructed by working-class men and women from the physical presence of possessing gods and those who worshiped them offered a temporary transcendence of the condition of being stuck, a form of power that recaptured "the aura of the extraordinary."

"WALKING ON TWO ROADS" AND "JUMPING AIRPLANES"

The Classed Stylistics of Exit and Return

More than three decades of "Malay supremacy" as the governing discourse of the regime of the Malaysian state has left its mark on the subjectivities of citizenship of the Chinese population of Bukit Mertajam. This chapter describes the ways in which Bukit Mertajam people sought to avoid the suffering imposed on them by Malay supremacy in its various forms by exploring differing strategies and imaginaries of transnational exit.

As should be evident, however, class divisions and gender distinctions among Bukit Mertajam people make it impossible to speak of only one such strategy and imaginary of exit. The proprietors and family members of small-scale, family-based business enterprises sought to emulate the performances that signified the towkay cultural style (if they were men) or otherwise came to terms with its demands (if they were women or youths in such families) in their imagining and strategizing of transnational exit. In contrast, among working-class Bukit Mertajam people, the class-specific practices of identity construction—marginalized from the public sphere of reputation and thus rendered invisible—were spatially localized, embodied in daily labor of "showing how," not "showing that," and gender-based, and this constrained the possibilities for working persons' transnational movement. For men, these were improvisations based on a male imaginary of travel, adventure, and the accumulation of petty capital through labor sojourns overseas, and I discuss them below. In contrast, working-class women of child-bearing age were largely constrained to remain in and near Bukit Mertajam—their recognized contributions limited to wage work in the factories of the nearby export processing zones (in Prai and Bayan Lepas), in the piecework regimes of local small-scale factories, at home in putting-out systems, and in doing business as street hawkers and vendors—but this did not speak to their unpaid labor in maintaining households, preparing meals, rearing children, and caring for the aged and sick in working-class households.[1]

It is therefore necessary to take into account the major class divide between people in Bukit Mertajam if one is to make sense of their transnational practices. In political terms, this divide has important consequences. The profound antagonism felt by people who saw themselves as middle-class professionals and owners of small-scale businesses toward state indigenist discourses and practices surrounding education, language, and culture has become one side of a schismogenic complex, whose counterparts were the state racialist policies of Malay domination that have lasted more than four decades since May 13, 1969. These state policies have promoted transnational exit among this group and have provided them with further reasons to disaffiliate from the Malaysian nation. The tense and contradictory interplay between the adverse identifications of "Chinese" and "urban" within the official indigenism, and the attempts undertaken at many levels by middle-class Chinese to nullify or transcend these identifications, has constituted a new "Malaysian Chinese" identity, *Malaixiya huaren*. Some people from this group have permanently left Malaysia for work and life in other nation-states of the Asia Pacific region, never to return; others have returned, but not because of state policies so much as despite them, as I suggest below. In either case, referring to them as living in a diaspora, or as being diasporic is particularly problematic, as I argue at the end of this chapter.

Working-class men have had no such options—excluded as they have been for more than five decades from the public sphere of politics and subject to the repressive conditions of labor and life in their encounters with Malaysian state police and functionaries. They cannot leave Malaysia for overseas permanently because they lack the resources that, for instance, families owning small businesses, have for doing so. Seeking access to better-paying and even perhaps more dignified labor overseas as a means of gaining leverage vis-à-vis discriminatory and punitive labor markets in Malaysia, they have instead turned to temporary labor sojourns, despite the many risks and dangers of illegal and illicit transnational travel and work. However, return for them to a reckoning in Malaysia has been for them not an option but a necessity—a return to being people with no position.

Mobilities, Imaginaries, People In/Out of Place

From the late 1980s until the Asian financial crisis of 1997–98, the high romances of transnational Chinese capitalism—the triumphant narratives of the founding and growth of family business empires throughout the Asia Pacific—were compelling for many reasons, not least of which is that they registered major shifts in economic dominance between regions of the global economy toward an emerging Asia-Pacific node of capital accumulation, as the preexisting industrial centers of North America and Europe have entered into a protracted period of hegemonic decline and stagnation in the contemporary period of globalization (Friedman and Friedman 2008; Harvey 1989). Stories of the dynastic histories of Liem Sioe Liong, Li Ka Shing, Li Kung Pao, and other Asia-Pacific entrepreneurs have become emblematic of "overseas Chinese" economic success and its prominence in the new global order (Weidenbaum and Hughes 1996; Hiscock 2000). These narratives herald in congratulatory prose the arrival of a small elite of extraordinarily wealthy Chinese transnational business figures as the new entrepreneurial heroes on the deterritorialized stage of late capitalism. In their telling, these romances celebrate putatively primal features of "Chinese culture"—thrift, family, commercial acumen, networks, *guanxi* connections, Confucian hierarchy, and above all extraordinary capital accumulation. Such narratives also index new cultural shifts and the emergence of alternative modernities, as Aihwa Ong and I (Nonini and Ong 1997) have argued elsewhere.

In this chapter, I argue that this discourse of economic success obscures the quotidian, contingent, and uncertain conditions under which most Chinese who moved transnationally in/from/out of Bukit Mertajam to other countries in the Asia-Pacific lived and acted. Parallel to the earlier local hegemonic view of the "typical Chinese" consisting of the "old generation" of Chinese merchants in Bukit Mertajam, but now amplified through media imagery via film and the Internet, the revived (post-1997) transnational romance of the Chinese business empires of the Asia Pacific region provide a dominant narrative of how overseas Chinese in the age of globalization are supposed to live, make money, and thrive. A collective obsession with the new forms of flexible capitalism associated with global supply chains, subcontracting and sub-subcontracting, and spatial arbitrage between labor markets, in which ethnic Chinese elites in the region are implicated, however, hides as much as it illuminates.

While this dominant narrative for the most part thrives on the public fascination in both the West and in Asia with stories of the comings and goings, family feuds, and conquests of a very small extraordinarily wealthy elite and registers their success, this narrative preempts and displaces the experience of the vast majority of Chinese who travel transnationally. A less fulsome and adoring analysis, but one more sensitive to the vulnerabilities of the Chinese of Bukit Mertajam as they engaged in transnational practices over the last thirty years will serve, I hope, as a salutary corrective to this dominant narrative that celebrates a supposedly Asian liberal capitalism at "the end of history," in Fukuyama's words. To not engage in such a corrective would be to allow the obliteration (or negation) from awareness of the everyday contingencies in the lives of nonelite Chinese, and would represent but the latest infliction in a multilayered cascade of class-based symbolic violence (Bourdieu 1977) in which they are implicated—always as objects of such violence, at times its perpetrators.[2]

Under these conditions, we must guard simultaneously against the reification of transnational overseas Chinese capitalism and the essentialization of people called Chinese by making a double theoretical move. On one hand, there is the need to examine the interplay among practices that articulate the provincial with the cosmopolitan and the national with the transnational in the construction of identities. On the other, we must consider the constitution of such practices out of those interconnected class, race, and gender divisions in which people identified as Chinese are variously implicated. A starting point should be that for nonelite Chinese from Bukit Mertajam, their mobility across national boundaries represented a repertoire of strategies for exerting power vis-à-vis the regime of the modern Malaysian nation-state; however, the forms these strategies took depended on the class and gendered cultural styles they manifested in navigating lives of great uncertainty and complexity.

These strategic practices were informed by *imaginaries* of power and desire. Here I follow Castoriadis and Curtis's (1997; also see Elliot 2002) focus on the role of the imaginary, and Deleuze and Guattari's (1983) emphasis on desire to posit the existence of imaginaries, or utopian, cathecting fantasy scripts for enactable practices—products of the imagination that transcend the limited spaces and powers of the Malaysian nation-state. Imaginaries are thus generative schemas for new habituses (Bourdieu 1977) of power.

In what follows, I first show how older Chinese men who owned small-scale business enterprises in Bukit Mertajam over the last two to three decades sought to act out the transnational imaginaries of towkays, or men of position, by emulating the envisioned cultural styles of transnational business tycoons in attempting to place family members overseas, but were unable to escape the vulnerabilities of their class and ethnic statuses. Second I examine the ways in which working-class Chinese men imagined transnational ventures of labor migration to Japan in order to bypass regimes of control directed at them by state functionaries and employers in Malaysia, yet depended on the labor of the wives, sisters, and children placed within working-class domestic spaces in Malaysia, who waited for their return.

Middling Transnational Traversals: "Walking on Two Roads, Not One"

Among those who owned petty capitalist enterprises or were professionals in Bukit Mertajam, state discursive control and disciplining of young Chinese above all called forth elusive practices of transnational escape, for these practices were elements of a larger strategic game of class and gender reproduction situated within a politics of antagonistic ethnic groups.

For almost four decades since 1970, the basic contours of Malay domination, ketuanan Melayu, favoring "special rights" for Bumiputras have remained in effect. From the early years of the Emergency, the convergence of state biopower (Foucault 1978, 140–144) and Malay indigenist supremacist discourses acted to discipline, register, and locate Chinese as questionable and problematic citizens. While residing in Malaysia, they were positioned *within* Malaysian space yet are not identified as being *of* Malaysian society or history. The photograph and name of the citizen on the "I.C."—"Identity Card"—marked the race of its holder.[3]

In this racialist context, protestations by Chinese over state-set ethnic quotas and what they regarded as underhanded means of restricting the university admissions of Chinese youths have been particularly bitter—and have persisted with a remarkable consistency over the last three decades (1978–2007). In 2002, on a brief visit to Bukit Mertajam, I renewed my acquaintance with Mr. Lee, then in his forties, the proprietor of a photographic studio and supply shop. I had first met him in 1978 as a youth angry at having failed a national qualifying examination which graded Chinese unfairly, and thus agonized by his failure to get into a Malaysian university. When I asked him in 2002 about how the economy of the town was doing, he replied that the economy was stagnant, and Chinese were having a hard time of it. Then in an exasperated tone of ennui from having to repeat an old tale too many times told, "You should know from before, from studying Chinese here for all these years, how things are." He then went on:

> The government still favors Malays, gives them special rights, *tequan*. The New Economic Policy was supposed to end in 1995, but the same policies continue after it. Chinese are limited in the number of universities they can enter in Malaysia. And even then there aren't the same admissions standards for both. Let's say you need 66 points out of 100 on

the exams in order to enter the university. But there are two streams by which persons can be admitted to a Malaysia university. One is through the regular Form 6 examinations—the old Cambridge examinations that came out of the British colonial period—this is what the Chinese go through; the other stream is the "Matric" [Matriculation] that only Malays go through, and it has its own examination. Even though the 66 points may be required of each, who knows how different the grading is of the examinations students in each stream take, or how easy the second [matric] is compared to the first?

He was no doubt thinking of his eldest daughter, who was enrolled in Jit Sin Independent High School and would soon herself be undergoing the rigors (and discrimination) of the national qualifying exam.

Bukit Mertajam people were aggrieved by discriminatory state admissions quotas for Malaysian universities that excluded Chinese young men and women from entry because this impeded their acquisition of the "degree," *wenping*, which was the essential "qualification," *zige*, for well-paid and secure jobs not only within the rapidly expanding high-tech sector of the Malaysian economy, but also beyond Malaysia in the corporate sectors of the Asia Pacific. Moreover, they saw government quotas favoring the hiring of Bumiputras over Chinese within the corporate sector in Malaysia and hiring within government service as having similar injurious effects on the employment prospects for Chinese youths. As one informant put it, referring to a saying in circulation in 1991, when it came to hiring "it is *kulit-fications*, not *qualifications* that matter"— *kulit* being the Malay word for "skin," with the English word appended in contrast.

It is therefore not surprising that the history of the tertiary education of the Chinese populations of Malaysia over the last thirty years has shown a consistent effort by many petty capitalists to send their grown sons and daughters to "study overseas," *liuxue*, that is, to pay for their children to enroll in and take degrees from universities outside Malaysia, particularly in the Anglophone Asia-Pacific of Australia, Canada, New Zealand, and the United States, but also in Taiwan. Many felt that their children had nowhere else to go to receive a university education qualifying them to participate in globalization—although this presupposed that they already possessed or could acquire wealth to spend on overseas travel and university costs.[4]

Moreover, a man who sent a grown son or daughter to study overseas saw this as a possible initial move in the relocation overseas of other family members, including the men and their wives, and the expatriation of the family's business capital. Nonetheless, the class positions of these men and their families made this far from assured, as I show below. I have called such envisioned transnational relocations "traversals" (Nonini 1997) to point to the lateral nature of such movements.

The Social Imaginary of Sending a Child to "Study Overseas"

In what follows, I reconstruct the narratives of older, petty-property-owning Chinese men who were my informants. They were towkays, men of position who controlled small-scale capitalist enterprises that depended on family labor and employed between five to ten workers. Since my research in 1978–80 focused on the trucking industry, most but not all were owners of trucking businesses, and I was able to follow them for many years thereafter. They were not, however, among the celebrities (or related to the celebrities) of Bukit Mertajam who formed the small elite of men owning the largest enterprises of the area that employed more than ten employees, often far more. They were even far more removed in economic degree and social connection from the national elite of Chinese tycoons in Malaysia, and further still from the very small and select stratum who formed the wealthiest Chinese business people of Southeast Asia and were the stuff of legend fashioned by business-school pundits and the global business media of CNN International and the *Wall Street Journal Asia*.

These distinctions—ones that my informants had no difficulty in making themselves—mattered greatly, for I argue that despite seeking to conform to the cultural styles of "Chinese-educated," or less often "English-educated" men of position, which required their unquestioned patriarchal authority over family members, when it came to transnational practice, they were out of their league. Once displaced from their local sources of power and influence, unlike the famous transnational tycoons, they simply had insufficient command over fungible capital and other mobile resources to carry out the patriarchal injunctions toward control over female and junior family members that characterized the lives of the celebrated Chinese rich and famous, whom they sought to emulate. For these men, transnational movement was by no means easy or straightforward, nor was it undertaken lightly; it had a high "coefficient of friction." Petty capitalist families had fixed investments in their business inventories, facilities, real estate, customers, suppliers, and credit, the latter acquired over long periods of steady repayment of funds or goods lent. Liquidating these assets so that capital could be invested elsewhere was by no means an easy matter, yet once underway was not easily reversible.

That said, however, in structural terms these men faced a "petty accumulation trap" (Nonini 2003) regarding social reproduction that confronted them with difficult choices in addition to these constraints on transnational movement. On one hand, the successful performance of towkay cultural style required a man to manifest his command not only over the family business in all other aspects of its operation, but also over the women and younger family members who were part of it, which implied that he sustained and supported them. This style demanded for its successful performance that a man provide equal shares to his grown children of an inheritance—a normative equipartibility. On the other hand, in the case of the proprietor of a small business enterprise, unlike the owner of a larger capitalist firm, a man saw his business fortune as quickly dissipated through the practice of equipartible inheritance of business assets. Men expected to have to leave such a small family enterprise to the eldest son or if he was not capable or interested, to another son, or if there were no sons, to a daughter married to a capable son-in-law. But what then to do about—and for—a man's other children when it came to their shares of the inheritance? Nor was it a matter of a man looking only after his sons. Men told me they expected to follow the norm of "not favoring the male over the female" (*buzhong nan qingnu*), by providing their daughters with comparable endowments to what their sons received.

As part of being modern, towkays owning petty property interpreted the demands of equipartibility to require them to provide their other children with the economic resources to acquire the university degrees, which were the qualifications for becoming a professional, preferably in a high-paying job and hirable by a corporation. Computer engineering, accountancy, or medical degrees were favored for sons; business, teaching, and nursing degrees for daughters. A towkay to be accounted successful, therefore, in managing not only his business but also his family had to be able to demonstrate that he had provided for the future of his other children in this way. This dominant interpretation among towkays of how to manage equipartibility represented a reputationally acceptable means through which a man *might* surrender patriarchal control of those of his children who no longer worked in the family business and were thus no longer subject to his surveillance, but now subject to other forms of control—disciplinary (e.g., in medicine, academia), corporate, or and in the case of his daughters, surveillance by other men—husbands and fathers-in-law.

I only note in passing that I focus on the performance of cultural styles among older men who owned petty property because they made up most of my informants, not because their points of view were somehow to be privileged as "true." The familistic regime that bolstered the cultural style of the towkay allowed older male claims to have hegemonic status. Yet this is not to deny that the perspectives of women, children, younger grown sons and daughters were equally valid and insightful. Although these were usually not accessible to me, I provide them when they were, and otherwise try to suggest what they might be.

The petty accumulation trap of social reproduction that confronted thousands of men and their family members who owned petty enterprise went far to explain both the deep rage that Bukit Mertajam people felt toward the national government's entry quotas that prevented many Chinese youths from enrolling in Malaysian universities, and the willingness of older men, their wives, and grown sons and daughter to engage in transnational moves—despite the risks and uncertainties these entailed.

The men I interviewed described to me the broader changes in their lives that they associated with sending a son or daughter to study overseas, which might include a more comprehensive relocation of the family as a whole and its fortune. To begin with, men often tried to send more than one son or daughter to the same overseas country for university degrees, an attempt to reconstitute the family, at least younger members of it, outside of Malaysia but within the same overseas country—whether Australia, New Zealand, or elsewhere.

They saw such study overseas as providing one or more of their grown children with the opportunities to qualify as professionals not only in the countries they studied in, but also in Malaysia if they chose to return. At the same time, they acknowledged that the latter option was hedged with the contingency that their childrens' overseas degrees be recognized by the Malaysian government, thus qualifying them for corporate employment in Malaysia, and since it frequently occurred that the government refused to recognize a university degree from a specific overseas university, this was an ongoing sore point.

Still, for their sons living overseas with an undergraduate or graduate degree in hand from a local university in one of the highly valued majors such as medicine or computer engineering, this made them potentially hirable by corporations in the country in question and thus desirable immigrants, and men saw their children securing such degrees as the first step to acquiring permanent residency. Despite their explicit claims that they were modern by not favoring sons over daughters, the less desirable degrees they urged their daughters to seek placed the latter at a competitive disadvantage compared to their brothers, in this global competition.

Men told me that during the period their grown children studied overseas and then, having acquired degrees, found employment, and applied for permanent residence, they (and their wives) were able to visit not only their children (and grandchildren, since this was a time their children married—usually a local woman or man—and had children) but also to learn about the business and living conditions of the country. Such repeated visits allowed them to envision what living there in retirement with one or more of their grown children—or doing business there—might be like. Their descriptions of their visits revealed their wonder at the "clean streets" or anti-Chinese attitudes of residents of Melbourne, or the long distances between towns and the depressed real estate market of New Zealand. However, on the whole, they did not find business opportunities for investment in these overseas countries.

The imaginaries that come out of these experiences form the basis of what I call "middling" transnationalism among these men. Based on the towkay cultural style for managing the family regime, middling transnationalism also reflects the limits of this regime posed by petty property.

In 1991, I met Mr. Ang, the ex-owner of a truck transport company in Penang state:

> Ang drove us (his wife, Xiujin, and I) to Kulim. He said his reason for doing this was that it was his old home, where he had grown up. The family had included 13 children, had been very poor, and his father had died when he was about 8 years old—whereupon he began working. . . .
>
> Ang said that he now lived with his family on the outskirts of Auckland, New Zealand—the capital—about 30 km. from the city itself. Says New Zealand consists of one little town after another. Of his three children, all three are in New Zealand, and two are presently studying at a university there. He is presently not engaged in any business—I asked whether he was planning to open a business in New Zealand and he said no, not at present, since the economy there is currently not doing well. Says the New Zealand economy is largely agricultural, and depends little on industry. On the other hand, he said that he was presently in Malaysia—most of that time in K.L.—until the end of August, looking after some property he owns there.
>
> He has Permanent Residency in New Zealand, but has not given up his Malaysian citizenship. He and his family only moved to New Zealand last year—late in 1990. When I asked him later about this, he said, Why should a person who can walk on either of two roads cut himself off from one—and leave only one? What if that single one were cut off as well?
>
> I asked him why, if the N.Z. economy was so bad, had he emigrated? He replied that he did this in order to give his children the opportunity to study in New Zealand universities, where they would learn English. He said he hoped to later send his eldest child, a son, who has been studying computer science in New Zealand, to America for graduate study in computer science, where it was most advanced [*xianjin*]. His second child, a daughter, also studied at the university in commercial studies. It was to give them an opportunity that he had not had himself, to help them make a life for themselves. He said he had told all his

children that they would not inherit any property from him—that their educations represented his "capital" [*benqian*], given to them. He did this, he told me, in order to avoid the common situation where the children of a Chinese man with money would spend it freely, thoughtlessly, not realizing how hard it had been to earn. "I earned my money a penny and a penny at a time." But they would not be able to understand how hard the money had come—even though he told them this repeatedly.

In 1991, I visited Mr. Lim, in Seberang Perai. He was the owner of a small transport company whose trucks carried freight from northern and central urban areas to the east coast states of Pahang and Trengganu:

> Lim looks much the same as six years ago, except for being a bit frail, though not much. He still is thin, wiry and muscular. When I asked him today he said his age is 67. Until he was 65, he said, he would lift and carry freight to his lorries all day. Now, however, he says he can only lift several pieces of freight before he is out of breath, and then has to stop. . . .
>
> He said that he now has three sons who work in Australia. Two are medical doctors with their own clinics. The other, the youngest, is a computer specialist with an American company that transmits financial transactions overnight from Australia to the U.S. His oldest son is the only one of his four sons here in Malaysia, and works with him in operating the trucking company. One of his sons (a doctor) has become an Australian citizen, while his youngest son has received permanent residency in Australia but—although he could do so—has not applied for citizenship because he is not sure whether he wishes to stay in Australia.
>
> All three of his sons there are married, two to women who are Malaysian Chinese and have worked as accountants. The other wife is also Chinese. One of his sons, a doctor, has two children, and his youngest son has a child, so he is a grandfather. . . . His wife has gone to visit his sons in Australia only last year, but he has not been to visit them since 1987. Next year, for Chinese New Year, all his three sons in Australia are going to come back to visit him and his wife.

The narratives by Messrs. Ang and Lim illustrated particularly well two features of middling, as distinct from elite, transnationalism. One was that the determinate Malaysian space from which they came—an area near the border between the states of Penang and Kedah—was still for both men their "old native place," *laoguxiang*: the space to which they affectively belonged was not indeterminate, flexible, or global, but quite fixed in memory and association. On balance, it was, in the terms of the philosopher Henri Lefebvre, affective representational space in a way that New Zealand or Australia were not. In the subjectivities of older men like Ang and Lim, then, there was a painful tension between this affinity for specific Malaysian places and the space-independent sensibilities required for what could be called full-bore transnationalism, as observed, for example, among the wealthy male Hong Kong entrepreneurs discussed by Ong (1999).

Second and related, Mr. Lim's narrative reinforced a point repeatedly made clear to me: the *contingency* and *difficulty* of transnational traversal. For petty property owners such as Mr. Lim, unlike what is depicted in the romances of the trans-Asia tycoons, most of the material resources they held were not liquid economic assets easily shifted overseas, but were instead invested in the persons working in and enterprises situated in specific Malaysian sites—in the goodwill of Lim's local customers who required the services his piece cargo trucking business provided, in his relationships with foremen in truck repair shops, and with the local police, among many others; or in Ang's nonliquidated real estate in Kuala Lumpur. On one hand, the mobile business practices that Mr. Lim and those like him in other commercial businesses (wholesaling, distributing, and other services) engaged in did overcome space,[5] and so predisposed them to transnational moves. On the other hand, profitable business practices required them to make time-consuming and vexatious visits outside their hometown to provide service for and entertain customers and suppliers dispersed regionally. In this respect, petty capitalist businessmen were confined by space in ways that wealthier entrepreneurs, with greater liquid capital, were not.

These tensions exacted a toll on bodies and subjectivities, and could push such Chinese men into becoming middling transnationalists. For example, it is worth noting in passing that Mr. Ang decided in 1989 to retire from the truck transport business and move to New Zealand because, he said,

> the work of a truck owner has gotten harder and harder. I would be called up any time of the day or night, with news that a truck had stopped running, or been hijacked—this happened to my own trucks twice—or were in an accident. Thus the work was "nerve-wracking" [*jinzhang*]. It was as because of this that I suffered a heart attack two years ago. Now I am different from the way I had been previously, all my life. From early on I had always had a plan about the future—of things that would need to happen in the future, and of how to go about achieving them. Now I live from day to day, without a plan. A person has only one life.

For Mr. Ang, a life-threatening conversion experience nudged him into a transnational move—one that, as his narrative makes clear, was reconciled with the demands of managing a family in accordance with towkay cultural style, while allowing his family to "walk on two roads." Nonetheless, despite the contingent character of their transnationalism, Messrs. Ang and Lim, their family members, and petty property owners like them were actively engaged in transnational traversals over space that connected vastly distant places.

In late May 2007, I visited Yap Beng Seng, by then in his seventies, whom I had interviewed during my 1978–80 fieldwork in what were among the most illuminating exchanges I had with any truck transport towkay at the time. I appreciated his articulateness and fine sense of irony as he recounted the vicissitudes of being the proprietor of a truck transport firm. Although we had cursory contact during the interim years, my 2007 return to his shophouse in Taman Sri Rambai was my first opportunity to speak with him at length about his life since 1979.

> We arrived at his shophouse and found his two sons at work in the air-conditioned office of the company. Yap himself came from the upstairs where he was staying and joined us. After we exchanged pleasantries, he talked for a bit about his family. His eldest son works in the family business [in Bukit Mertajam] as does his youngest one. Two other sons live in Australia where one works as a computer engineer and the other is in some other skilled profession. He says he has visited them in Australia. At present he is retired from truck transport, a business which his two sons manage. Now however his enterprise is involved in wholesale trade in rice, and is about to engage in import of rice from overseas. . . .
>
> A few minutes later, almost as an afterthought, he mentioned that his youngest son has gone for university study in Melbourne where he studied at the Royal Melbourne Institute of Technology. A friendship his son formed with another Malaysian studying there provided him with connections that have proven valuable for his business in Malaysia [the details of which he proceeded to relate to me].

In a second interview two weeks later, Mr. Yap commented on the three sons he had sent for university degrees to Australia: "Between the three of them, I have spent about 500,000 ringgit on their educations, because this is fundamental. All three of them had been sent to Australia for education, two of them to Monash University,[6] and one to Sydney. . . . The most impressive [*lihai*] of the three is a middle son who trained in engineering and now has a great job at a factory" in Australia. Yet in a third exchange two days later, Mr. Yap informed me that he had also sent his oldest son to Taiwan for education, his son had married a Taiwanese woman, and indicated that his son's Taiwanese connections had proven valuable because a Taiwanese factory operating near Bukit Mertajam had hired their transport services due to this.

I suggest that Yap's talk about his sons and their overseas educations, and how this talk was prioritized and segmented, displayed a fine sense of how the towkay cultural style was to be performed. At our first meeting in 2007, while in the presence of his oldest son and youngest son, both of whom had inherited and operated the family trucking business, he first mentioned his two *other* sons, who were sent to Australia for university education, and there, successfully attained their degrees, found highly skilled employment in Melbourne and Sydney, and acquired permanent residence. His statement declared that his responsibilities as a patriarch toward the grown children not inheriting the family business had been discharged. Yet parenthetically he later returned to the benefits arising from his having sent both his eldest and youngest sons overseas for education—but in the context of the advantages this then conferred on the truck transport business they have inherited from him and currently operated.

Yet, when I spoke separately with Yap's eldest son and youngest sons, I discovered from their perspectives the disadvantages of the patriarchal dispensation they had received. The eldest son: "I was educated in Taiwan and my wife is Taiwanese. I would like to move to Taiwan and do other business there because it is so vexatious to engage in truck transport here" in Malaysia. The youngest son was even more unhappy, yet resigned to having been summoned by his father from his studies in Melbourne to return to work in the family's trucking business: "While I was at the Royal Melbourne Institute of Technology, I studied information science, and would like to have continued in graduate work in this subject, but I was called back to help in the family business." In a later exchange with the youngest son, I asked him about Australia: did he miss being there? He said he missed it greatly, especially in the first couple of years after he returned to Malaysia. After all, he had lived in Melbourne for about ten years and had become very accustomed to it. Would he go back? I asked. He said he hoped to go back when he was retired, and when he had children who needed secondary schooling.

The narratives of transnational traversals by small-scale businessmen—Messrs. Ang, Lim, and Yap—discussed here point to the inextricably connected aspects of class and gender that are deeply implicated in the new globalized lives of Chinese Malaysians, in the symbolic violence and euphemization central to these lives, and in the unstated losses as well as celebrated gains of Bukit Mertajam towkays in motion. Indeed, the narratives as such manifest a gendered imaginary of male mobility and achieved desire, an idealization of what Chinese men who own and dispose of property, place family members where they wish, and move across national spaces and international boundaries as they are inclined, can and seek to do.

Yet these narratives also point to surprising vulnerabilities among the men whose stories were being told and whose imaginaries were being revealed. These stories point to the men's attachments not to global travel or to the lifestyles of the "new rich in Asia" (Robison and Goodman 1996; Pinches 1999) but instead to specific Malaysian places and local Chinese society; not to the ability or inclination to shift one's capital and one's business at a whim in an electronic instance to another social setting in another nation-state but instead to nurturing one's grounded, face-to-face friendships and business relationships in Malaysia. Furthermore, they speak not to the capacity to tightly organize and control the lives of one's grown children but instead to the willingness to subject one's relationships to them to the risks of distant and possibly permanent separation from them, and of exposing them to culturally alien moralities and lifeways one may not accept, as well as to the modern technologies that would make their professions possible.

Finally, what my interviews with these men demonstrate is that the period of neoliberal globalization in the Asia Pacific has not, despite some theoretical claims to the contrary, necessarily called forth the flexible, labile, rationally calculating subjects that neoliberalism supposedly requires—and gets (see, e.g., Ong 1999). That is, one could point to the fact that from the 1980s through the 2000s, neoliberalization of the economies of Anglophone countries of the Asia-Pacific—Australia, the United States, Canada, New Zealand—has led to the emergence of the category of "economic migrant" associated with the global competition for scarce technological skills and mobile capital. While it is evident from the interviews discussed in this chapter that petty businessmen and their family members sought to take advantage of these changes, they also demonstrate the ways in which these changes constrained and restricted them, as much as they opened them up to opportunities. The limitations of their class positions, in particular, led them to improvisations on the towkay cultural style in aspiring to performances they could not fully meet. In contrast, the romances of Chinese tycoons such as the "astronauts" and other jetsetters of the "transpacific shuttle" (Nonini and Ong 1997, 167–169) and others celebrated in the business press point to a much more elite Chinese subjectivity—one whose propensities shape, as much they have been shaped by, these changes.

"Airplane Jumping" and Gendered Imaginaries

In quite a different way, the interconnected aspects of class and gender were also evident in transnational reversals—movements associated with the sojourns of labor migrants from Bukit Mertajam in Japan and Taiwan.[7] We gain much theoretically if we view such movements as culturally creative reversals—transnational endeavors achieved through return—rather than as mechanical responses to the operation of international labor markets (Cohen 1987), for it allows us to situate the practices of highly mobile working-class Chinese within the field of transnational practices.[8]

In this section, I draw on interviews of the self-declared members of the informal peer group of more than fifteen working-class men, all but one married, with whom I spent time episodically from 1990 to 1993, whom I followed up with in a brief visit in 1997, and whose situation I described in chapter 8. In 1991, approximately one-third had either sojourned as laborers in Japan or intended to do so. Other members of the group were off sojourning in Japan during my fieldwork in Malaysia. When members convened after working hours in their meeting place under the tree to talk, eat snacks, and drink tea, one of the most frequently discussed topics was their sojourning experiences in Japan, recalled vividly, and often with nostalgia (plate 13).

In the case of working-class transnational strategies, transnational reversals were gendered, for by and large they are undertaken by men, and when labor migration was undertaken, men and women traveled, worked, and lived separately.[9] Among people from Bukit Mertajam, labor sojourning in Japan and Taiwan was almost exclusively the practice of young working-class men, who thereby reinforced the privileges of male mobility vis-à-vis working-class women in general, and the women they knew and had domestic relationships with, whose movements were far more constrained. In contrast, among the working-class people I knew, the familistic regime dictated that laboring women were to be restricted to local spaces—to the residences of parents, brothers, and husbands, while they either engaged in various forms of "homework" (e.g., sewing garments through piecework contractors) or labored in the nearby factories of local small-scale businesses or of the export processing zones. Thus their surveillance by older family members, if not continuous, took place daily; this was true even when women moved to other cities and towns for employment, for most lived with older relatives already residing there (see Strauch 1984, 70). Younger working-class women who were not so limited by the surveillance of family men or older women, I was told, were "bad" women and would be expected to leave (or be ejected from) their parents' households and move to locales elsewhere. In contrast, some older women from Bukit Mertajam, no longer nubile and usually separated from husbands or widowed, undertook labor sojourns as domestics in Australia, but in very small numbers.

Those who organized international labor markets such as overseas employers and labor brokers saw certain kinds of labor as essentially gendered—e.g., construction work was male, while certain kinds of factory work were female and other kinds male—and thus colluded with state functionaries and older male family members to reinforce the gender hierarchy associated with the familistic regime. It was within such a setting that male labor sojourning as a transnational practice took place. During the 1980s through the mid-1990s, male Malaysians traveled in very large numbers on tourist or social visas and "overstayed" their visas in order to work as undocumented laborers in Japan and Taiwan: in 1992, Malaysians formed the largest contingent of estimated illegal workers in Japan—fourteen thousand, with the vast majority (79 percent) being male (Shimada 1994, 28, table 2.9); in Taiwan, in 1992, there were about four thousand Malaysians working illegally, although the figure had been as high as sixteen thousand in 1990 (*Star* 1992; see also *Xingzhou Ribao* 1992). The numbers of men engaged in such work varied from year to year, depending on labor market conditions in Japan and Taiwan, and the stringency of enforcement of immigration laws by Japanese and Taiwanese governments. According to my informants, men who overstayed tended to concentrate in construction, certain labor-intensive factory labor, and in restaurant work; in the case of Japan, official estimates provided of all illegal male laborers (irrespective of their nationality) in these categories of labor suggest the same pattern (Shimada 1994, 31, table 2.10). Large numbers of male Malaysians in Japan, with whom I am concerned here—along with other illegal labor migrants from the Philippines, South Korea, Thailand, China, Pakistan, and Bangladesh—came to constitute the public "'problem' of foreign workers in contemporary Japan" during these years, in that they challenged Japan's hegemonic myth of racial homogeneity (Lie 1994).

Transnational reversals by working-class men were called "airplane jumping," *tiao feiji.* Recruited by Malaysian labor contractors working on behalf of Japanese and Taiwanese firms, flown to Japan and Taiwan where they entered on tourist visas and then overstayed, these men set out to spend from one to three years working to earn the very high wages, by Malaysian standards, paid by these firms. They lived in dormitories or houses with other men from Malaysia, at times cheek-by-jowl with labor sojourners from other countries in Asia.

The men I interviewed told me that in this way if they labored continually, lived frugally, avoided the financial perils in situ of excessive gambling, visiting prostitutes, and sightseeing, and so saved their wages or remitted them back to their families in Malaysia, they could earn sufficient savings for a down payment on a house or to start their own small businesses. This discourse of transnational reversal constructed a modal Chinese male imaginary—a fantasized life trajectory of upward mobility grounded in the privileges of male movement, a path marked also by formidable challenges to be heroically overcome by labor.

In 1991, I interviewed Mr. Teoh, married and in his early thirties, then working as a stonemason near the town of Pekan Tebu:

> TEOH: One of my younger brothers went to Japan to do physical labor.
>
> DMN: Haven't you thought of going yourself?
>
> TEOH: I went, but they did not allow me to enter [at Narita Airport]. I couldn't pass through.
>
> DMN: If in the future you have an opportunity to go to Japan or Taiwan to earn money and return, what would you do with it?
>
> TEOH: I haven't thought about what I would do with it. It's just that I'd heard that it was very well-paying there. We want to go look around. My younger brother went, and has just returned. He went there to work for more than two years.
>
> DMN: Did he save money or not, was he able to save money?
>
> TEOH: He was able to! He saved money, and he just returned.
>
> DMN: What did he think of the life there?
>
> TEOH: Life in Japan is like this: you have to be frugal and thrifty [*shengchijianyong*]! You can still save money this way, but if you are going there to spend money, you don't have enough to spend.
>
> DMN: In order to save, therefore, you have to spend a period of time there before returning?
>
> TEOH: Yes, when he went to Japan, he did two kinds of labor, and worked until eleven o'clock before stopping.
>
> DMN: Eleven at night?
>
> TEOH: Yes! He began in the morning and went to a little after 6 p.m. He worked from 8 a.m. like this until 6 p.m. From 7 p.m. he worked until 11 p.m. before stopping. By the next day at 8 in the morning, he was working again.

In 1991, I spoke with Tan Ah Soon, at that time a truck driver living near Bukit Mertajam about his recent sojourn in Japan:

> TAN: I sold away my car and used the money to go to Japan to work. This was my capital [*benqian*]. I was in Japan for five months; at that time, my child had just been born.
>
> DMN: Didn't you find this difficult, what with your child being born, to go overseas?
>
> TAN: I didn't have any choice. For the sake of my future, for my life, I had to run off to Japan.
>
> DMN: What kind of work did you do in Japan?

TAN: Refurbishing, I worked in construction. In a single day, I could make MR$ 200,[10] but the work was very filthy. . . . When I went to Japan, my assumption was that I would return only after a year in Japan. But I hadn't thought about the fact that in my dormitory there, everyone was gambling. So every day there I gambled. [He would gamble all night long, and then be exhausted while he worked during the day. As a result one day he had an accident and fell down a story of the building. Fortunately he was not badly injured.] After that, I saw no meaning in the work, and came back.

DMN: At that time, were your family members here in Penang?—your two small children, wife, parents, older brother, older sisters?

TAN: Yes.

DMN: Didn't you think of your family in Malaysia, and feel lonely?

TAN: The first month I was in Japan, it was fairly difficult, but after that I became used to it. Still I thought of them a lot and often called home on the telephone, and also sent them money.

DMN: So all this time, before your return, you were in Tokyo?

TAN: Yes. Especially, if I had time, I would go out and play, walk around.

DMN: So after five months you returned to Malaysia?

TAN: Yes. But I hadn't earned much money—it had been spent away. My capital in order to go there about 7–8 thousand ringgit.

DMN: From selling your car?

TAN: Yes, I made MR$ 8,000 from the sale of my car. In going to Japan, I thought of changing my life, but I was not able to change.

In 1997, I interviewed Mr. Seow, who was then a thirty-four-year-old unmarried man working as a scaffolder near Bukit Mertajam, about his sojourn in Japan during 1992–94. During most of that time he worked as a day laborer in construction and factory operative in Tokyo, but for several months when he could not find work he left to work in housing construction in a remote area near the mountains.

In Tokyo, he lived with five to ten other men from Malaysia and rented a room with them and cooked his own food.

DMN: What did you do when you had free time?

SEOW: I and my roommates would spend time talking, and this way we got to know one another, and became friends. Sometimes we'd all go out together and sightsee. I've gone all over the Tokyo area this way. On Sundays, we would go down Halajuku Road, where the nightclubs and bars were open, and foreign workers and Japanese went to enjoy themselves, to dance, and drink.

Nonetheless, life as an airplane jumper in Tokyo was strenuous and anxious. His dormitory was far from his worksite and this required a long commute; labor recruiters defrauded workers by promising them long-term work in return for a fee and then absconded ("They cheated all the time!"); people had accidents in construction and came down with illnesses: "You remember Ah-Huat [another "member"], who died just before you came to visit in 1993? He came down with liver disease while working in Japan." Work as a day laborer was seasonal and insecure:

> DMN: What was the most serious problem you faced in Tokyo?
> SEOW: There were three months when I could not find work. Many days I'd go out to the worksite, but wouldn't get hired, and then I'd return to the dormitory to sleep all day or watch videos. This was a really difficult time and I became sad and depressed.

It was after that that he left Tokyo for the remote area near the mountains, where he stayed for six months; "The people there were like gangsters and were not very polite; it was a difficult time for me."

Despite these hardships, when I asked whether he would want to return to Japan if he could, he replied, "Yes, definitely. In Japan I can earn so much more money than in Malaysia—four or five times more! If I were working there, I could save up several tens of thousands of ringgit to spend when I came back." Unmarried, he still called his parents once or twice a week while in Japan. He recalled the importance of (male) friendship as a sojourner: "In Japan, if you are going to do well, the scope of your friendships must be wide," for friends could put in a word to a labor broker to hire you for the day.

In the narratives of Teoh, Tan, and Seow, male imaginaries of male freedom and mobility, overseas economic opportunity, the pleasures of male company, waning and waxing attachments to family and Malaysian place, and the need for self-mastery to overcome obstacles all converged in their stories of transnational reversal. This, despite the fact that in Tan's case, sojourning was largely a failed strategy of mobility, of "changing my life," and none of the three reported being able to save much from their work in Japan. The modal male imaginary required the possibility of failure to reinforce its hegemonic claim to fact: one did what one could, and as Seow said, if one could have the chance to go again, one would do so. Such narratives formed the substrate of experience shared among working-class men returned from sojourning in Japan and Taiwan.

The gendered solidarity of the members of the peer group I spent time with in 1991–93 reflected that of other male groups to which they were connected by virtue of their transnational sojourns—Malaysian men boarding together in the illegal laborers' dormitories of Japan and Taiwan. As Mr. Tan observed, "Everyone with me there were Malaysians. They were from Penang state, Kulim, Ipoh, Johore—many places. We rented a space together—each of us paying five hundred ringgit per month. It was very convenient, with many facilities."

The imaginary of self-uplift through labor sojourning took a transnational form, yet it was but one of a class of such imaginaries narrated by working-class men, a utopic fantasy that valorized male mobility and labor power, cleverness and tricksterism, and heterosexuality, male bodies and bodiliness, and that conformed to a broader Malaysian narrativized practice of *merantau*, or "wandering" by unattached men to work sites throughout and beyond Malaysia. At the same time, when enacted this imaginary perpetrated a kind of symbolic violence against working-class women, by bracketing out the fact that its realization was dependent on the latter's reproductive labor (e.g., child and elder care) and consequent confinement to domestic and adjacent spaces—in short, to their placement.

In (In-) Conclusion I: A Cascade of Symbolic Violence

The triumphalist narratives of legendary Chinese tycoons and their family enterprises spanning the Asia-Pacific nation-states should certainly continue to be grist for our theoretical mill in seeking to understand the transnationalization of overseas Chinese capitalism. Yet capitalism cannot be identified solely with a form of economic organization, nor Asian capitalism with a family form of organization—but must also be considered within the frame of associated modernities that encompass and position specific bodies, identities, and spaces within the Asia Pacific, particularly as these modernities are imposed by the interface between state powers and civil society. Nor should Chinese throughout the Asia Pacific be reduced to being represented metonymically by a very few, most spectacularly successful capitalist exemplars, however much rightful ethnic or racial pride might seem to call for it in the current "Chinese Century."

These two related caveats suggest the virtue of investigating the full range of transnational practices available to ethnic Chinese throughout the Asia Pacific and beyond it. In this chapter, I have merely begun to point to the extent of this range—not to delimit it—through the concepts of traversal and reversal. What this suggests, immediately, is the necessity for rethinking the tropes of Chinese subjectivities and identities inscribed *implicitly* in these narratives of triumph. The themes of the incessant deterritorialized search for profits, the improvisational genius of founding fathers of business dynasties, the flexibilities in operation allowed to family firms, the "bridgings" engaged in by Chinese capitalists as cultural brokers, and the instrumental deployments of guanxi personalism—these are all standard features of the essentializing narratives of triumph. These themes need to be rethought and certainly require reframing in terms of broader considerations of the working of fields of class, gender, ethnic/racial, and national relations and identities.

When examined within the field of transnational discourses and practices among Chinese in/from and of Malaysia, the strategies of both elites and nonelites are grounded in imaginaries of desire in tension with cascades of symbolic violence. Symbolic domination works through the operation of nation-state, workplace, and familistic regimes of truth and power that constitute this person as a "citizen," "woman," "worker," or "Chinese," that person as "citizen," "male," official, and "Bumiputra," and the like. Aihwa Ong and I (Nonini and Ong 1997) and Ong (1999) point to the symbolic violence behind the elite discourse of guanxi—one euphemizing unequal interdependencies and interpersonal domination in terms of human "relationship." Similarly, the elision of nonelites from the narratives of triumph centered on the wealthiest Chinese transnational capitalists represents the bracketing of shadowed, subordinate others who were treated as the audiences and objects of such narratives, never their subjects—a subtle intimidation and putting-into-their-place of those left out.

Such narratives index a cascade of intimidation that "goes all the way down"—distributing both agents and victims in its operation, and moreover, with perhaps the exception of those who are most dominant and those most dominated, makes certain persons perpetrators in some relationships, the acted-upon victims in others. Furthermore, in connection to Chinese transnationalism, the cascade of symbolic violence operated most effectively through probabilities bearing on populations in which each person sought the discursive and embodied placement in space of other subjects—putting people in their proper places within ordered national, workplace, and domestic spaces—while attempting to elude being so placed oneself. Older Chinese male owners of petty property making transnational traversals to escape Malaysian state cultural indigenism aspired to do this to their grown children; Chinese working-class men engaged in transnational reversals to elude capitalist and state disciplining in Malaysia tried to do this to their wives and daughters. Transnational mobility as a feature of the current epoch is thereby inextricably interlinked with forms of power, but these forms are in turn the circumscribed effects of class and gender constraints.

In (In-) Conclusion II: What about "Diaspora"?

What then to make of the idea of the "Chinese diaspora" as it applies to the people of/from/in Bukit Mertajam? In chapter 7, I set out what I hope is the compelling argument that by the late 1970s, it made absolutely no sense to speak of a "Chinese diaspora" in the sense of a "scattering" of people from China with a primary or even residual allegiance to it. The celebrities and men of position who rhetorically dressed themselves in the nationalist discourse of Sun Yat-sen to invoke Chinese unity were, we saw, largely going through the motions, while engaged in demonstrable servility toward the Malaysian state and its repressive ethnic and class policies.

But are the men and women discussed in this chapter part of a new Chinese diaspora—one in which the imagined homeland is Malaysia itself—not China? This is neither a simple nor straightforward question to answer, and I am not sure it either can be answered, or *even* should be answered. Should it even be answered when the recent romance about "diasporas," "deterritorialization," and "globalization" within cultural studies and postmodern anthropology in effect collude with indigenist xenophobia by imagining that Chinese in Southeast Asia are always already disloyal, discontented but wealthy transients celebrating globalization and its cosmopolitan gratifications?

Putting aside these reservations, a point to start with would be to take seriously Clifford's (1995) caveat that no diaspora exists without its problematic class and gender dimensions. Viewed in this light, the working men whose experiences of reversal I have described here are not diasporic because not only do they have no intention of staying abroad permanently, they have little capacity—little economic or educational capital—that might allow them to do so. This is even more the case for the relatively few working women who have sought employment overseas. Working women and men engage in reversals because they have to "return home." Put contrastively, to be diasporic is, after all, to be marked by certain kinds of material and symbolic privilege.

What about those who are the middling transnationalists interviewed for this chapter who engage in traversals, or aspire to—petty capitalist and professional men and their family members? A quantitative case can and has been made that a brain drain of highly educated Malaysians—most of whom are Chinese—who have left Malaysia and relocated to other countries in the Asia Pacific region and elsewhere has emerged since the 1980s (Azizan 2011). According to Azizan there has been a steady increase in university-educated Malaysian citizens living abroad over this period, with about 80 percent of those who have left moving to Singapore, Australia, and the United States (173–175). Azizan cites World Bank figures that show an increase from 184,014 such people in 2000 to 276,555 in 2010, living in twenty-five different countries, and refers to estimates of 785,000 skilled Malaysian workers working abroad in 2006, and of 304,000 who left Malaysia from March 2008 to August 2009 (173–175). The statistical caveats of course apply: how one is to distinguish between those who have left permanently and those working and studying temporarily overseas who will return to Malaysia; how many people are returning annually to offset those who leave; among other things. Nonetheless, the range of estimates in the several hundred thousands is significant for a country with a total population of 29 million in 2010. However, there is little general understanding of the subjectivities of those who have emigrated from Malaysia, and my own limited number of informants whose experiences are described in this chapter would be difficult to generalize from. Are most expatriates committed to returning to Malaysia, do they identify with their native place, do they feel a deep and lasting affinity with not only family members and kin remaining in Malaysia, but more broadly with Malaysia, and the "customs and habits," *fengsu xiguan*, of other Malaysians? Are they Malaysian nationalists—and in what ways? We are in a realm of great uncertainty.

What is however, quite clear from the broader argument of this book is that the workers, small business people, professionals, and other residents of Bukit Mertajam whose lives I have sought to understand, and by extension other Chinese Malaysians, have over the last two generations since independence earned the right to be treated as Malaysian citizens who have repeatedly shown and performed their loyalty and attachments in their everyday lives toward the Malaysian nation and state, even as they have been treated as second-class citizens who have endured decades of legal and political discrimination and prejudice. Perhaps given this past, it is just for them to intend to "walk on two roads" if they are able to, crossing and negotiating with the citizenship regimes of the capitalist states of the Asia Pacific. Perhaps not.

Under these circumstances, whether a diaspora emerges of Chinese Malaysians living abroad who become new ardent "long distance nationalists" (Anderson 1994), or who seek to return to rejoin Malaysian society "at home," or to the contrary have finally turned away from the Malaysian national project, should be thought of as a politically open question. The resolution of this question depends on the courage of others needed to at last bring to an end the perfect ethnic dictatorship of Malay domination that has lasted for more than four decades, and is embedded in the institutions, practices, and policies of the Malaysian state.

Epilogue

1997–2007

> The Bukit Mertajam area is unique. Two of the state's top high schools, first Bukit Mertajam High School and now Jit Sin National Type High School, are located there, showing how much people there really prize education. There are also very many wealthy businessmen in Bukit Mertajam, but there is also the reputation that some of them have for having made their money in some very shady ways, like drug smuggling.
>
> —Penang state assemblyman, 2007

Transformed Landscapes of Globalization

Some features of the social landscape show continuity, as seen in the observations of the state assemblyman given in the epigraph above, which, with quantitative differences, might have been stated twenty years previously. But there have also been major transformations in the city and the lives of its residents.

After very brief visits in 2002 and 2004, I returned to spend several weeks in Bukit Mertajam in 2007. The ambitious representations of state-corporate spaces on maps that I observed in the early 1990s I could no longer consider fantasies, because since then, these representations had become material fact—built structures that colonized the space of the city and its environs. During my visits in 2002, 2004, and again in 2007 I saw as I passed through the town the material effects of the huge projects drawn on state maps years earlier, which had been undertaken by Bumiputra-owned national corporations. For example, a new District Office and courthouse, *maklamah*, and Municipal Council (Majlis Perbandaran) office complex had been built in Bukit Kechil on the western edges of downtown and a new road opened to them. This project had displaced the homes of scores of Chinese living in the urban kampong whose residents were the worshippers of Shilinggong Temple, whose circumambulating gods had declared an alternative cosmological sovereignty vis-à-vis the secular state.

By 2007, after the construction of new drainage controls over the Sungai Juru/ Rambai River, much new space had opened in what had previously been the river's (often flooded) flood plain to the south and west of the city for development, and the Penang Development Corporation (owned by the Penang state government) had as part of its strategy for Penang's globalization completed facilities for two new industrial estates in the Bukit Tengah and Bukit Minyak areas, and these were partially occupied by new factories operated by Japanese, Taiwanese, U.S., European, and Malaysian manufacturers.

But the scale of state-induced development extended far beyond the immediate suburbs of the city. Megaprojects of new townships like Bandar Perda, of hypermarkets, shopping centers, and housing estates undertaken by national Bumiputra-owned corporations reached far beyond the city itself to the south, west, and east—extending from the coastal towns of Seberang Prai Tengah district in the west in a continuous strip of metropolitan in-filled construction and dense new settlements that extended eastward from the port of Butterworth though Bukit Mertajam to the town of Kulim in southern Kedah thirty miles to the east. Construction of a second and new Penang Bridge connecting the island of Penang to the mainland at the town of Batu Kawan was just getting underway when I arrived in 2007.

During the previous decade, local Chinese developers with connections to UMNO, MCA, or Gerakan leaders also prospered by acting as subcontractors to the national corporations and by constructing smaller housing projects and commercial properties (e.g., Auto City in Juru), and a few had become enormously wealthy. The material transformations of the local landscape made clear to residents who was in charge: as Bukit Mertajam Chinese put it, it was "their [Bumiputras'] government" and "their corporations" that were initiating these changes. Strictly speaking, one could argue with this claim, since in 2007 the Barisan Nasional in the form of the Chinese-controlled Gerakan Party still held the Penang state government, although only with the effective co-governance of UMNO. Bukit Mertajam's Chinese residents in 2004 had played a role in this by electing two Barisan state assemblymen and one assemblywoman, although for Parliament they had turned out the MCA, and elected a DAP woman as their parliament member to protest what they viewed as the Barisan's discriminatory policies against Chinese. One Bukit Mertajam journalist noted to me that although the city's residents found much to complain about with their treatment at the national level, they were far more congenial toward the Barisan's and Penang state government's projects of building for export-oriented growth and industrial employment within Seberang Prai. The advantages of being co-opted at one level, while dissenting at another, were not to be denied.

Even in 2002, I observed that some of the patronage-driven projects undertaken by national and local business elites had led to speculative overreach, for some projects had failed, with partially finished and unoccupied housing in evidence—in part due to the Asian financial crisis of 1997–98. By 2007, the residue of failure was still in evidence. For instance, one hypermarket out of the three I saw operating in 1997, located near the overpass over the railway called locally "clothes-washing bridge," *xiyiqiao*, in Kampung Baru, had gone bankrupt for lack of customers, and its huge vacant structure remained. In 2007, many partially and newly constructed residences, shophouses, and factories were still vacant, while developers hoped for the overflow of people and enterprises from a crowded and congested Penang Island that would seek cheaper housing and business spaces in the area of Bukit Mertajam on the mainland. During my 2007 visit, I also discovered that despite the construction of the Municipal Council office complex in Bukit Kechil a few years previously, the administrative offices involved were being relocated yet again to the only partly occupied Bandar Perda township. Two Bukit Mertajam towkays darkly stated to me that this was an attempt to "bypass" the city and its Chinese population by relocating these offices to the township to the west of the city itself.

During the decade from 1997–2007 these construction projects pointed to new processes of class and ethnic formation then underway. While some poorer Chinese had been displaced by these state projects, others had obtained the new skilled labor jobs in local businesses (transport, logistics, construction, and others) that served the influx of new residents and the populations working in the factories of the industrial estates and export processing zones in the district. Chinese workers were able to buy houses in the new low-cost housing projects located in the southern and eastern suburbs of the city. While they might have a life of hard physical labor at the workplace, given the high levels of employment and a regional labor scarcity they were able in the early 2000s to obtain wages sufficient for the new consumer-driven, if low-end, lifestyle they adopted outside of work. Compared to a decade earlier, their material standard of living had improved, and they eagerly sought the consumers' commodities associated with modernity. However, these came at a cost: by 2007 neither Chinese, Malay, nor Indian laborers were any longer the major fractions of the working class, which had in fact become stratified by nationality as well as ethno-race, with Malaysian workers having access to wages and working conditions superior to those of hyperexploited immigrant workers.[1]

From the early 1990s, Indonesian migrant workers, who even earlier played a major role in Malaysia's rural plantation sector, had moved in even greater numbers into urban housing construction. In 1997, I noted the following: "Having passed through the main entrance to the Bandar Perda project, after about a quarter of a mile, I saw on the left side the company offices of the project. Behind these offices, were much more modest lines of white houses, which [my friend] indicated were the dormitories of the Indonesian laborers who were working on construction there."

What became evident during the Asian financial crisis of 1997–98, when huge numbers of Indonesian and other immigrant laborers were subject to police roundup, harassment, torture, and deportation, while hundreds of thousands of illegal migrant workers returned in panicked flight from Malaysia to Indonesia (*Far Eastern Economic Review* 1998), was the emergence of new forms of capitalist labor discipline enforced by the state in the name of the Malaysian nation. On the one hand, this new regime indexed the new division of labor within ASEAN countries and more broadly the Asian region regarding national "comparative advantage" in labor specializations. By 2007, not only had hundreds of thousands of laborers returned from Indonesia, but also a large proportion of them had been hired into full-time factory work in the country's industrial estates and export processing zones, thus displacing the more costly rights-bearing Malay industrial proletariat. Indonesian migrants, in turn, had been succeeded by Pakistani and Afghani migrant laborers, who moved into the onerous labor of road and public works construction. Over the same period, Indonesian and more recently Philippine women moved into domestic work and into general laboring jobs in the petty capitalist sector. Changes toward this regime have occurred in the factories, road construction projects, residences, and small business shops of Bukit Mertajam and its district, as elsewhere. This new regime conveyed a clear message of intimidation to Chinese, Indian, and Bumiputra workers that they were indeed replaceable. It reminded them of what could happen to them if the militancy or solidarity of Malaysian workers increased, or if less flourishing economic conditions dictated a more coercive response by the state to the unruliness of labor.

A Far-Too-Short Visit

My visit in 2007 lasted only six weeks—the longest period of time I spent in Bukit Mertajam since 1997. Although these six weeks were ethnographically rewarding in terms of the people I met and events I observed, it would be arrogant to think of its findings as sufficient to sketch out an update, much less a restudy. I decided that in a brief period of time I could at least investigate the then-current state of the local truck transport industry and focused—when I had the choice—most of my efforts on this.

My ethnographic research in 2007 was also circumscribed by the imperative of revisiting my old friends and informants—some of whom I had known and worked with closely as a dissertation student in 1978–80. Once they knew I had returned to the city, my old friends would have it no other way, and I felt both desire and an ethical obligation to spend time and accord respect to those from whom I had learned so much for more than three decades—a large proportion of whom, moreover, I very much wanted to spend time with because of the plea-sures of past companionship. However, with old friends came perhaps old and too familiar ethnographic concerns, as my informants resumed telling me their stories—and occasionally disrupted or rewrote these stories—of their lives as narrated to me during the previous two to three decades. With most of my infor-mants by 2007 in middle age or old age, it is undeniable that the persons I spent time with during my 2007 visit were a highly selective lot, which implied that there were many others not within their circle whom I did not meet, and I thus missed much I might have learned otherwise of the changes then taking place among Bukit Mertajam residents. But how could it be otherwise?

With this caveat, in what follows, I revisit several of the themes brought up in the analyses of the previous chapters by taking up an account of the stories of old friends I had known for many years and encountered again during my 2007 visit.

Working Men Aging and the Body's Response to a Life of Hard Labor

Chinese workers whom I knew as young men from the late 1970s to the 1990s and who had recounted their experiences to me while working in Bukit Merta-jam or as airplane jumpers in Japan, by 2007 had labored for many years under exhausting, dangerous, toxic, and stressful conditions, and were in their fifties, sixties, and even seventies. They continued to work if they were physically able, often because they had no choice. Pensions and Employee Provident Fund retire-ment payments from the government were small and insufficient. Some men I had known since the 1980s and 1990s were still working as truck drivers, scaf-folders, and restaurant cooks. Beh Kou-Kian, who had taught me so much about learning through labor, the ironic and ludic side to drivers' crudity, and the experience of class exploitation and privilege, still drove as a long-haul truck driver. One day in late May 2007, I waited for him to return, sitting with his wife and two small daughters watching CCTV4 in their comfortable semidetached house in a middle-income neighborhood off Kulim Road:

> More than half an hour later at very least, Beh and a companion, a very overweight young man of perhaps 30 years of age, arrived. He had been on the road all day coming back from Singapore, which also involved delivering freight from Singapore or at least other points south of here in this area in Penang state. He had been gone since Sunday, making for a five-day trip altogether from Bukit Mertajam to Singapore and back. . . . He told me he earned about 350 ringgit for the entire trip. . . . There was

some discussion of cigarettes which he had brought back from Singapore where he had bought them at a lower price, which could be sold for much more in Penang.

I went on to write in my fieldnotes:

> It appeared to me that he was fairly exhausted from the trip. So we didn't stay much longer. A note about him . . . visibly aged since I saw him last, which probably was sometime in the mid-1990s. . . . He has lost all his teeth, a point that his wife made to me as he was about to enter the house when he first arrived. Of course she said I knew him from a time when he had his teeth. In addition, he has visibly aged in terms of lighter hair, a slumped posture, and a potbelly. I don't doubt that a physical toll is taken of most men who do such hard physical work for so long. . . . [At one point] I asked him why he continued to work when he could retire? He said, "Well if a person retires he just comes up with malfunctions [*maobing*], and then he dies." I couldn't argue with that.

Another friend from the 1980s and 1990s, Tang Ah-Meng, also still worked as a truck driver. Despite his lack of formal schooling he had taught me to appreciate the critique drivers had of truck owners' discourse of drivers' being "crude," pointing out that owners "only tell you the good things they do, and not the bad, and they speak of the bad things that drivers do." Tang had also served as a leader in the 1990s of the North Malaysian Lorry Drivers Association whose founding I recounted in chapter 5, and he had generously hosted me numerous times at his home over many years. In 2007, he appeared indefatigable still:

> Since his "retirement" about eight years ago, Tang has gone in to see the XX company physician every year and passed his physical examination, and gone on to work as a driver on a regular basis. Although he is now 68 years old, he drives constantly for the company, still delivering [freight] throughout southern and central Malaysia. Last week he went to Johor. Again this week after first making two trips in the northern region on Monday, he will undertake another trip to Johor Baru this week. He said at one point . . . this afternoon that he had been driving trucks for more than sixty years.

Other informants who had been vigorous and active in the 1980s and early 1990s when I interviewed them were in 2007 ill or dying from diseases and injuries, no doubt caused or exacerbated by the conditions under which they had worked. When I arrived in Bukit Mertajam in 2007, I sought out Tan Ah Soon, a truck driver who had previously gone to Japan as an airplane jumper and had sensitively recounted his difficult experiences there; in 1991 he had taught me the meaning of "rice-eating money" for truck drivers, despite my clear initial obtuseness about the subject and my poor Hokkien. He was then only in his early thirties. After making inquiries, I found out from Tang Ah-Meng that Tan had developed serious kidney disease three years ago and did not wish to see me because he was too sick. He was taking Chinese medicine but hasn't yet started to undergo dialysis—the implication being that it was too expensive for him any-way at a thousand ringgit per month. He had to quit his job as a driver because he was becoming dizzy while driving. I hope as I write that Ah-Soon is still alive and doing better.

The caring work of the kinswomen of Chinese laborers like Tan Ah Soon have become no easier over the last two decades. Most injured and sick working men depend on their wives, sisters, and daughters for their daily care, and do not ben-efit much if at all from Malaysia's modern biomedical establishment. A worker with kidney or heart disease will occasionally be featured in the local media as the publicized poster person to advertise a charitable fund-raising drive to build a kidney dialysis center or new wing of a hospital for heart patients, organized by the richest merchants in Bukit Mertajam in acts of kindly condescension.

If the grown sons and daughters of these men can now "get by" as small ven-dors or hawkers, or as skilled laborers employed by local towkays, these men count their children fortunate. Few men have been able to keep their children in school past Form 3, or afford the school fees allowing their children to graduate from high school, much less enter a Malaysian university or privately operated academy, and thus become professionals or small business people. Unlike the situation for poor Bumiputras, government scholarships have not been targeted for them.

As I asserted in the Introduction, classed performances always take place under situations of duress within a matrix of the inextricably connected mate-rial and symbolic dimensions of unequal power. For working-class people, these situations of duress are not only the conditions of structural violence under which they live but ultimately the effects of such violence—not only exhaustion and mortality but also hope foregone.

Towkay Classed Performances: A Brief Recap

In what follows I briefly describe two encounters with businessmen I had met previously and, in the case of one, had worked with extensively in my previous ethnographic research in the city. Their recounting suggests several of the main points of this book—appearances often deceive, moral ambiguity lies deeply at the core of doing business, and ultimately Chinese businessmen and women are constrained not only by their performances but also by the "language games" and "forms of life" their classed performances entail.

How Towkay Style Is Made

Over the course of almost thirty years of intermittent ethnographic research in Bukit Mertajam, I have had the good fortune of working with six field assistants, all of whom have contributed greatly to my research. Of them all, Chuah Eng Huat, my assistant for eleven months during my dissertation research from 1978 to 1979, only then in his mid-twenties, showed the greatest anthropological imagination. He was intellectually gifted, having graduated from Jit Sin National Type High School, completed Form 5 and received several high passes in the national examinations. Nonetheless, his poverty (coming from a family in a New Village with little property, with his mother supporting his family and separated from an absent father) and a lack of government scholarships for outstanding Chinese graduates threw him squarely into the labor market in the mid-1970s, and he found work for two years as the outstation office manager of a (relatively) large truck transport company in Bukit Mertajam. He quit work for the company several months before I hired him in late 1978.

Chuah was as it turned out perfectly placed as a consultant for my ethnography of the transport industry for the dissertation. His reflections on his practical experiences as an office manager who was neither a driver nor a relative of the owner, yet having had to work with both, were invaluable, and they are reflected throughout chapter 6. He had a keen ironic sense of distinguishing between what people said they did and what they actually did, and clearly articulated his recognition of the performative dimensions of class among the men he'd worked with; he was the first to bring rice-eating money and the tricksterish quality of drivers' crudity to my attention. Moreover, his interest in my project and his social imagination extended far beyond the industry. He assisted me in interviewing his grandfather about life in a New Village in the early 1950s and pointed me repeatedly toward insights into the subjectivities of small-scale capitalists and their classed and stylized performances under the conditions of intense commercial competition they experienced in the late 1970s.

After he left working with me in late 1979, Chuah went on briefly into work in sales in truck lubricants, followed by a shift by the time I met him again in 1985 into starting his own restaurant supply wholesaling business. He operated the business out of his house, but it led him to go out on a monthly circuit to sell to and entertain his customers throughout central and southern West Malaysia. During my fieldwork visits in the 1990s, we came together over dinner or tea whenever I returned to the field; he married, he and his wife had three children, and he continued to do business in wholesaling. His tours to visit his customers out of town made him an absentee father during much of each month.

In May 2007, I was eager to see him again and to find out how his life had changed. I did not have an up-to-date telephone number, but fortunately on a day in late May my field assistant and I were able to find his family still living at his address from years previous in an older suburban housing estate to the east of Bukit Mertajam. Chuah was away; his eldest daughter called him on a cell phone at his factory located in a town a few miles to the south.

> About 15 minutes later, Chuah arrived. He looked somewhat older, certainly middle-aged, with his hair thinning but still black, slightly pudgy but basically still quite muscular. He was quite friendly. He said I hadn't aged very much since we last seen one another, and I said the same thing about him. (Were we lying to each other to be polite?) It was clear that he had come from an industrial setting—he wore shorts, a singlet, and sandals—looking like a "typical Chinese." He was also covered with wood dust. After a few minutes exchanging pleasantries, he invited us to go with him to his factory, saying that he had a certain problem he had to deal with there.

During the previous decade, Chuah had moved up the value chain to manufacture, as well as wholesale, the goods he sold. This had been a difficult transition for him. At first he employed twelve workers, but then only four, since he eventually bought machinery that allowed him to be more productive than with twelve workers. Now, he said, his factory produced wood bar stools, cutting boards, wooden utensils, and other wood items; he no longer sold restaurant supplies since these became unprofitable because of the recession in Malaysia in 2001–2.

Chuah gave us a tour of the factory: the three CAD machines that made the molds, did the shaping of the wooden pieces, and sanded them; the raw wood pieces, the stacks of finished and semifinished pieces, the packaged goods, the fork lift, and the Indonesian worker who was rapidly sanding some pieces. The machine that made the molds cost him MR\$ 400,000, and was manufactured in Japan, with proprietary software that cost MR\$ 30,000. He described how, in order to save money and not pay for software or expensive technicians to fix a problem, he himself studied how a problem was to be solved and found a less expensive go-around. He learned how to program the software that required more than fifty parameters needed as input into the mold-making machine, and he discovered tricks that could be done to keep the machine up and running. At one point, he pointed to the notes written in Chinese in dark ink on the back of the machine that described the shortcuts or measures that needed to be taken to fix a problem when it arose. He machined his own replacement parts for the machine instead of buying the manufacturer's new and far more expensive ones.

Chuah recounted the trials of the transition:

> For a period of 12 years I and my wife worked from early in the morning until midnight or even 1:00 a.m. or 2:00 a.m. in the factory overseeing production. . . . When I went out to sell my goods, this was on a circuit which extended all the way to the south to Singapore, Johor, Kuala Lumpur, and Ipoh, and elsewhere, and my wife worked in the factory overseeing the workers in my absence. This went on for years when I was unable to see my children very much—nor when I was gone would my wife who was their mother. It was just last year that I asked my wife to start leaving the factory at 6:00 p.m. to go home and prepare dinner and be with our children.

At one point as we were in the stairwell going up to the second level where his office is, he stopped in front of the altar to a Buddha which was set in the wall before us. He said that he had made the altar, including engraved Buddhist sayings on its rear wall, arduously in his spare time over more than a year, during a very difficult period in his life when he was facing serious financial difficulties. I got the sense that this altar simultaneously represented his plea and his thanks to the Buddha whom he had called on for help at that dire time, and received it.

When I asked him how his business was going, he said that it was now "stable": "It's not a matter of making money now so much as saving money, continually trying to save money."

By 2007, Chuah had remade himself in the mold of a towkay, much as he had machined parts of wooden bar stools or cutting boards. Showing the dress style of the older generation of typical Chinese, having shifted much of his everyday speech away from Mandarin (in 1978–79) toward Hokkien, he told a story of persistence, grit, hard work, thrift, embodied learning, and long hours of sacrifice away from his children. Now he said his eldest son worked in the factory with him; his two daughters attended Jit Sin Independent High School. Moreover, like his clothes that day, his house displayed a perhaps misleading modesty; it was a single-story house he purchased in 1982 and could hardly be considered an equal in price or value to the ones constructed more recently with two stories nearby. Yet, that said, he was "getting by," and besides, "you can't tell from external appearances."

When I later asked my assistant what he thought of Chuah, he said Chuah was selfish, fearful that others might steal his commercial secrets, and guarded his techniques from being used by others. But also: "He would be a very difficult person to cheat." As Chuah had mentioned to me in late 1978, "You can't intend

to harm someone, but you can't do without seeking to protect yourself from him"
(*hairen zhi xin bu keyou, fangren zhi xin bu kewu*).

The Stylistics of Public Benevolence

One morning in mid-June 2007, when visiting the Meeting Hall of the Fudezhengshen Temple Managing Committee, I came across the supermarket magnate, Ooi
Swee Huat. I had previously been introduced to Ooi during my very brief visit to
the city in 2002 by Dr. Oon, an old friend of mine who was a prominent educator and highly placed member of one of the Barisan Nasional party branches in
Bukit Mertajam. Then in his late forties, with his stylish clothes and Mercedes
sedan and Chinese-language education, Ooi positioned himself within "our generation" of men of position. At the time, I was intrigued by Ooi's business card.
On one side he gave his commercial business identities as supermarket owner
and investor, and on the obverse he listed his title as *zongfuzeren*, "the person who
takes general responsibility" in front of the names of several groups engaged in
charitable fund-raising for local institutions, including Jit Sin Independent High
School and the Doumugong Temple (which sponsored the Jiuhuangye festival).

That day in 2007 Ooi invited my assistant and me to join him for lunch in an
air-conditioned coffee shop across the street. As soon as we had placed our orders,
he took out his cell phone and called my friend Dr. Oon, who had retired from
politics and lived in Bukit Mertajam but was in Kuala Lumpur that day engaged
in a new business venture. Talking to my friend, Ooi indicated that he had just
run into me and hoped I would be able to speak before the liaison committee
he chaired of assembled representatives from sixteen charitable organizations
that was holding a banquet later that month as one of their periodic meetings
to decide how to spend charitable funding in and around Bukit Mertajam. He
said he hoped to invite reporters from the major Chinese-language press. Ooi
then passed his phone to me, and Dr. Oon began speaking. He said, "You know,
you've been talking to the greatest philanthropist in Bukit Mertajam. He belongs
to many organizations, has contributed lots of money and is a good friend of
mine." These are circumstances under which Malaysian friendship artfully pulls
one into work deemed socially essential.

After the phone call, Ooi explained that the sixteen organizations included
groups that raised funds for renal dialysis patients; provided grants to people
who were poor, sick, and needed assistance; loaned money to students who didn't
have sufficient funds for their school costs; donated money to the volunteer fire
brigade; and engaged in giving of related charitable aid. Thus I found myself
enlisted willy-nilly into Chairman Ooi's fund-raising activities only two weeks
before being scheduled to leave Bukit Mertajam to return to the United States.

Four days after encountering Ooi, he asked me to join a delegation of the committee he was leading to travel to a regional hospital on Penang Island to present
it with a MR$ 5,000 donation to pay for indigent patients' care. After we arrived
at the hospital, before the hospital's welcoming officials, he gave

> a prolix speech stating that he was very glad to hear of all the good
> work the hospital has done, and the delegation today hopes to contrib-
> ute just a little bit to that broader effort. He then went on to describe
> how the sixteen organizations operated. Each organization pledges its
> members to contribute a small amount of money per month to helping
> the poor Chinese in the Province Wellesley region pay for medical care
> they need. . . . He said he'd gotten this idea from his experience in the
> supermarket business when charities asked for a few left-over pennies
> of change that customers got back after paying at the counter. Even if
> only one person put in a cent or two, over time a huge amount of money
> would be built up by each person giving just a little bit of money to the
> fund. . . . With the thousands of members of these organizations, the
> MR$ 5,000 the delegation was contributing today to the hospital repre-
> sented only a month's effort.

A week later, I found myself posing with Ooi and representatives from the
liaison committee he chaired for press photos as they received a MR$ 2,900 check
from one of the groups described in a local newspaper article as having as its purpose to provide help to "poor but clean and virtuous friends," *qinghan xianyou*.
Quoted in the same article, Ooi stated that the liaison committee had been registered with the government to "gather together the charitable strength," *jihe sishan
liliang*, of Chinese organizations (*Xingzhou Ribao* 2007).

Two days before leaving for the United States, I also spoke before the banquet of the liaison committee. Having been impressed by the recent increased
incidence of chronic diseases of affluence (kidney disease, stroke, heart disease,
etc.) among the population, I took the liberty of invoking Confucius's golden
mean to suggest that moderation in what local people ate and drank, and an
increase in their exercise, might actually be a cost-effective form of preventive
medicine, but I think this made little impression on those attending as they proceeded to consume the banquet dishes at their tables, although my comments
were picked up by the Chinese-language press.

Towkay Ooi manifested the consistent class style of celebrities I identify in
chapter 3 for "our generation" of men of position: showing their wealth in personal goods publicly displayed (expensive clothes, luxury car) but referencing
their wealth through their financial contributions to Chinese society, to seek
their fame as leaders through publicity provided by the Chinese-language press.

In addition to his generosity, his self-important presentation, prolixity, bodily formality, and command of Mandarin oratory, and condescension toward the poor also conformed to the prevailing style for a celebrity. It is interesting that Ooi, however, sought to create a niche for himself as a generalized philanthropist to support a variety of local institutions. This makes sense given that after the leadership dispute in 1979–80 analyzed in chapter 7, a more or less stable succession to leadership on the Fudezhengshen Temple Managing Committee (and on the boards of trustees of schools connected to it) had set in, which excluded a younger leader like Ooi from consideration. The conundrum of bringing about the "unity" of associations within Chinese society (and all its compromises) still remained in Ooi's talk of "gathering together the charitable strength" of organizations—as allowed, of course, by the government's registration system.

Transnational Shifts Present to Future I: The Rewarmed China Connection and the Globalized Supply Chain

Capitalists in Bukit Mertajam, as elsewhere in Southeast Asia over the decade of the 2000s have invested in industrial operations in China, which has followed on previous instances of capital inflows from Hong Kong and Taiwan in China that began in the 1980s (Smart and Smart 1999; Hsing 1997).

But this is stating the situation too temperately. Among the city's towkays, there has been a China-investment "fever." According to one politician I interviewed in 2007,

> Many merchants here in Bukit Mertajam have become very wealthy because of their trade with China—there's a lot more wealth here than people could possibly know about due to such trade and investment in China. Many Malaysian Chinese have invested in factories in China. This is really booming. Much of this wealth of course is being kept from the Malaysian government's knowledge. Wherever there are clothes, fabric, all sorts of items of everyday use, these come now from China. This has all happened in the last ten years or so. This is so much the case that when I go to China to visit, far away from Hong Kong and Guangzhou, people in China have heard of Bukit Mertajam, because of all the people from this area who have gone there to do business and invest. When I went to Guangzhou, I found more people doing business there from Bukit Mertajam than from any other city in Malaysia, including

Kuala Lumpur, and Penang. It shows that Bukit Mertajam people are in the vanguard of trade with and investment in China.

Let me briefly discuss one example of a capitalist in motion between Bukit Mertajam and China from my fieldwork observations in 2007.

Jason Tan was one of the most wealthy young businessmen among the local mercantile elite; in 2007 he was then only in his early thirties, and the son of a prominent local merchant. Jason was the proprietor of a clothing wholesale enterprise that sold apparel manufactured in China to supermarket chains throughout Malaysia. He was thus an importer but like other merchants had moved up the value chain into the production side of the inter-Asian supply chain that designs, commissions, and manufactures apparel. Jason solicited orders for specific lines of apparel from supermarket managers in Malaysia, then commissioned the orders based on these designs with factories in China. These factories manufactured these garments to-order on a just-in-time basis. He then imported these garments, brought them through Bukit Mertajam, and distributed them to supermarkets throughout Malaysia. He said the total whole time elapsed between the placement of an order by a supermarket manager and its delivery was about one month.

Jason often commuted to China, at least once per month, where he visited the factories with whose managements he had a relationship, in order to oversee the quality of their production. Currently (2007), however, he said he was dissatisfied because the cost of production was still too high in the areas of China he had access to. One day, I asked him about his travels to China.

> JT: It is really difficult to make money in Malaysia as a Chinese businessman. What I really hope to do is to invest in a factory in China.
> DMN: Where would you invest—would it be around Guangzhou for example?
> JT: No, I am planning on investing in a factory in Anhui Province. . . in the city of Hefei.
> DMN: Why are you going to invest in such an out-of-the-way place?
> JT: The labor costs are so much lower in an internal province like Anhui compared to Guangzhou or nearby, as in Shenzhen. In Shenzhen, the wages for factory labor could be as high as MR$ 200 per month [about US$ 100], whereas in Hefei wages were as low as MR$ 50 to MR$ 70 per month. Besides, in Anhui they are eager for investors to come in.

Jason's residence where he, his wife, and their two young children lived, and the headquarters of his enterprise were in Malaysia. But note that he identifies himself as a "Chinese businessman." His fluency in Mandarin Chinese and competence in deploying a discourse of guanxi personalism and other ascribed items of "Chinese culture" (cuisine, Daoist/Buddhist beliefs, among other things) are elements in a shared habitus he has mastered as have his arriviste capitalist counterparts in China, which smoothed the way for a mutually beneficial capital accumulation strategy. For example, he shared with his China partners in China the aesthetics of preparing and drinking the famous Pu-er brand of tea from Yunnan, and in collecting and speculating in disks, *pian*, of the tea on the international market.

Yet despite his aspiration to open a factory to manufacture apparel in inland China, his long-term plans were quite different. Stating that Malaysian government officials and agencies mistreat Chinese, and that the government is "incompetent," he told me he sought to make his fortune in manufacturing in China, but then to retire to Australia, and once he has moved there to engage in day-trading in stocks as a way of making his income. "First my children will go to Australia for education, and later I will join them."

Theoretical Interlude: Chinese Business in a "Global Era" and What This Book Is About (and Not About)

Much has been written about Chinese entrepreneurship in the period of globalization from the late 1970s to the present. Themes in the literature include business success; family structures, Confucianism, and familist ideologies; strategies of accumulation; networking and guanxi ties; enterprise organization and dispersed transnational operations (e.g., through global supply chains); adaptations to multicultural political settings; and hybrid enterprise structures—neither distinctively familistic nor bureaucratic but innovative combinations (Redding 1990; Whitley 1992; Lever-Tracy et al. 1996; Orrú et al. 1997; Gomez 1999; Yeung and Olds 2000; Yeung 2004; Gomez and Hsiao 2004; Wong 2008). Indeed, in earlier work with Aihwa Ong (Ong and Nonini 1997; Nonini and Ong 1997), I began to set out what we then saw as some of the new characteristics of modern Chinese transnationalism—which included but was not limited to capitalist practices. We thus discussed such concepts as "flexible accumulation," "third cultures," diasporas and the "diacritics of difference," the violence of guanxi and familistic discourses, postmodern imaginaries, and much more (Nonini and Ong 1997; see also Ong 1999). Although I am pleased that more recent literature such as that cited above has innovatively employed, critiqued, and developed further the concepts we presented (e.g., in Yeung and Olds 2000; Yeung 2004; Gomez and

Hsiao 2004; Wong 2008), this book is emphatically *not* about transnational Chinese business practices nor the elements of Chinese "business success," although if I wished to make greater sense of Jason Tan's 2007 practices and strategies, it would be to this important literature that I would first turn.

Unlike this literature, I have been interested in this book not only in Chinese capital and capitalists, but also in people who have lived in a specific place during a specific period of Malaysia's history, and are not capitalists but are workers, students, teachers, accountants, owners of petty enterprises who are not capitalists *sensu stricto* because they do not hire outside labor but depend solely upon family labor, and thus on women, youths, and many others. I believe that people of Chinese descent, people who identify themselves as Chinese and are so identified by others (some quite hostile to them) as Chinese, deserve such human and intellectual respect. They deserve to be free of the suffocating requirement that their lives, their practices, and their cultural productions all be measured against whether they are "successful" capitalists or only capitalists-manqué.

Equally to the point, I am appalled by a post–Cold War history that has had the effect of reading out these alternative identities other than the "Chinese businessman" from not only the historical record of accomplishments, heroisms, and foolishness of those who happen to be Chinese in Malaysia—and thus the tragedies of Chinese citizenship in the country—but also from the intellectual agendas of so many scholars over the last five decades. This intellectual marginalization has been particularly the case for the Chinese working class, which fifty years of capitalist celebrationism and triumphalism, and the literature which has been spawned by it, have largely ignored.

Transnational Shifts Present to Future II: "Where Have Your Children Gone?"

The desires of younger better-off Bukit Mertajam residents (like Jason Tan) to send their children overseas for education have not abated in the decade from 1997–2007. Among an even younger cohort, many adult children of small-scale business people and professionals, even if they have been educated in Malaysia, continue to explore the exit option, and others have already left. This was also evident when I spoke to my middle-aged and elderly friends whom I visited in 2007. One opening pleasantry with them was always "How are your children doing, and where are they now?" The attitude of Mr. Lee, a self-employed insurance agent, is not atypical of parents whose grown children have received university education and certification in specializations deemed in demand in the global economy: "Each of my children hopes to go overseas to find work there. My daughter who is a financial officer for a corporation in Kuala Lumpur, is hoping to find work in Australia. My oldest son already works in Bahrain as a risk management officer and has applied for permanent resident status in the United States. My other two children [with university degrees] have plans to seek work overseas." In the case of Dr. Oon, the educator, his son was already working in computer engineering in the western United States, and his daughter had just left for a graduate degree in business in Australia. Neither intended to return.

Nonetheless there are many—a majority of the university-educated children of the city's residents with advanced professional degrees and certification—who have sought the rewards of upward mobility that exist for those who are well-placed, educationally and socially, to take advantage of the still-booming Malaysian economy. Those who are able to enter Malaysian universities do so with alacrity; after graduating, they tend to stay in Malaysia and find work in business or the professions. The children of the Lims, my host family from 1978 to 1980 and again in 1985 illustrate this: two of the three sons of the family have degrees from Malaysian universities. One after graduating in computer engineering from Universiti Malaya began working for a computer firm in Kuala Lumpur in the 1990s, now owns his own thriving company, and has become quite wealthy; his younger brother graduated in medicine from university and has set up a private practice in Penang state.

There has been a resolute passion that parents in Bukit Mertajam have shown throughout the last thirty years of my fieldwork to seek formal advanced education for their children. This can be said to be well-nigh universal in the city. However, aspiration—and efforts behind it—are a luxury that is not available to all, for neither the opportunities for education nor the resources that make it possible are evenly distributed in the population. Class privilege does, ultimately, reassert itself. The many children of Bukit Mertajam workers and others lacking such privilege should never be forgotten.

A PROFILE OF ECONOMIC "DOMINATION"?

In this appendix, I discuss my findings summarized in chapter 2 about the distribution of wealth among Chinese in Bukit Mertajam during 1978–80, particularly as this bears on the claims by NEP advocates, both scholars and politicians, that Chinese in Malaysia were wealthy, economically dominant, and "clannish."[1] My data point to two relevant key findings.

My first key finding is that the majority of Chinese adults residing in Bukit Mertajam worked for wages and salaries, and did not primarily depend on profits from businesses, because either they did not own businesses, or if they did, derived only small incomes from them. The numbers are at one level straightforward even if "only" estimates: according to my 1979 commercial census of Bukit Mertajam, only 2,531 Chinese were either proprietors or family members of proprietors of businesses the census found within the town limits, while 4,051 were employees of locally owned businesses (Nonini 1983a, 132–133, 135, tables 23–25). The Malaysian Population Census enumeration for Bukit Mertajam for 1980 recorded a total population of 28,675 persons in residence, of whom 73.3 percent, or 21,026, were Chinese (Khoo 1986, 169, table 7.1). If we apply the percentage of the population aged ten and above active in the labor force given for all ethnic groups in Bukit Mertajam from the Malaysian Population Census of 45.9 percent (Khoo 1986, 181, table 7.4) to the enumerated Chinese population, then there were an estimated population of 9,651 employed/employable Chinese adults and youths living within the town limits.[2]

Yet according to my 1979 census, only 2,531 Chinese residents among this population were owners of businesses or their family members (26.2 percent), while 4,051 Chinese employees of local businesses worked as shop clerks and overseers, accounting clerks, truck drivers, garment factory workers, hired opticians, stonemasons, and other positions (42.0 percent of this population). What did the other estimated 3,069 Chinese youths and adults who lived in Bukit Mertajam and were active in the labor force (31.8 percent) do for a living?

I would argue that they fell into two categories—either employees (and a very few employers) working outside of Bukit Mertajam, or those who were self-employed. In the first category were those who worked outside of Bukit Mertajam as hired waged or salaried employees, most at large institutional corporate and government employers—as production workers (particularly if they were young women), managers, and engineers for foreign-owned factories in Prai and

Butterworth industrial estates; as managers of nearby rubber estates; as teachers in primary and secondary schools in town or nearby; as technicians, clerks, cooks, and accountants in Georgetown (Penang); as inspectors or technicians for the Municipal Council in Butterworth; as shop clerks or laborers in nearby towns in Seberang Prai and southern Kedah—to name a few examples of people whose commuting patterns I knew of.

In the second category were those self-employed Bukit Mertajam residents engaged in "doing business," zuo shengyi. People personally owned and operated enterprises that were too small in scale for inclusion in the 1979 census (because they did not advertise or operate out of permanent business sites), but had temporary sites (e.g., hawkers) or worked out of their homes (e.g., insurance agents, land brokers). Thus I surmise that they would have fallen into the occupational categories of "sales workers" (N = 2,192), of "those with activities unclearly described" (N = 395), or of "those with activities unknown" (N = 393) listed among the total labor force of 9,820 people (including all ethnic groups) enumerated by the 1980 Malaysian Population Census (Khoo 1986, 181, table 7.4). It was the constant activities and presence of such a large number of individuals "doing business"—a flexible category if there ever was one—that may have conveyed the impression to observers that urban Chinese "dominated" the economy, but this would be a simplistic and fallacious conclusion. What is far more clear is that only one-fourth of Bukit Mertajam Chinese in the labor force were owners (or their family members) of businesses located in permanent business sites, while three-fourths were employed by others or were self-employed.

My second key finding is that the vast majority of local businesses surveyed in the 1979 census were small enterprises. They were owned by single families, with ownership and control vested in an older Chinese male, and for labor most depended either on their own family members or on a very few hired employees. With the exception of a small minority of businesses I deal with below, when my census team and I asked who the owners were, we received the name of one older male. My ethnographic inquiries with business people I met combined with my census findings showed that the majority of businesses depended heavily, indeed entirely, on the labor of family members, and not on the labor of hired "outsiders." To be specific, the average number of family members (including the owner) working for a business was 2.25 for the total 1,242 businesses (out of a total 1,271) for which I had workforce data, and ranged between two and three persons irrespective of the nature of business done (retailing, wholesaling, manufacturing, etc.), with the exception of truck transport, where almost five family members were employed on average.[3] I found that of the 1,242 businesses, the median number of hired employees was zero, and that the seventy-fifth percentile for number of employees was only three employees. In contrast, it was only at the ninety-first percentile that 108 businesses employed hired ten workers or more (Nonini 1983a, 136–137; table 26). These large businesses also tended to have partners, instead of being owned by individual owners. Thus a majority of the businesses surveyed in the 1979 census depended exclusively on family labor, and about two-thirds showed at least as much dependence on family labor as on the waged labor of outsiders. At the other end of the distribution, where I defined a "large" employer as one employing ten or more waged employees, only 8.7 percent of all the businesses surveyed could be said to be large.

This observation is not merely of statistical concern but of political interest as well. Non-Chinese, especially government officials like Mohamad bin Bakar and Balasingam quoted in chapter 2 and UMNO leaders, were prone to accuse Chinese of being "clannish" and "exclusive" because a large proportion of the employees they hired were Chinese. Although, as I showed above, more than four out of five hired employees in the town's Chinese-owned businesses were Chinese (83 percent), in this connection it is important to reiterate that the majority of the town's businesses—especially retailers and artisans—hired no employees at all but employed only family members, and some two-thirds employed as many family members of the owner as outsiders. Moreover, Malay-owned businesses in town employed virtually the same average number of family members (2.27) as did Chinese businesses (2.28) and both were lower than the average number of family members employed in Indian-owned firms (2.50)—an interesting finding (Nonini 1983a, calculated from 140, table 28). The conclusion is that if "clannishness" or "exclusiveness" was defined by preferential employment of family members of the owner, then both Chinese and Malays were equally guilty of the charge.

When the charge meant preferential hiring of co-ethnics for waged work, this was true for Chinese employers, but it was interesting that Malay owners also preferred to hire Chinese, for 65 percent of their waged employees were Chinese, compared to 88 percent for Chinese employers (Nonini 1983a, 134–135, table 25). Whether this was due to the greater cultural openness of Malay owners than Chinese owners to hiring those who were not coethnics, or to perceived advantages that Chinese wage workers had compared to Malay workers, or to some other cause, is not an issue that can be debated here.

My frustrations over the limitations of the 1979 census in answering these questions, however, pressed me further in the later phase of my 1978–80 research to undertake a second investigation of wealth among Bukit Mertajam's Chinese—to collect information about private limited liability companies located in Bukit Mertajam and its surrounding district of Seberang Prai Tengah through the collection and analysis of documents filed at the Penang branch of the Registrar of

Companies.[4] A variety of standardized information about such companies lay in the companies' legally required filings with the Registrar of Companies—the names and addresses of the shareholders and directors and other officers of the company, the amounts of their paid-up share capital, descriptions of the commercial activities of the companies, and details about the bank and other loans they had received. For the purposes here, I report on what my findings from a combined analysis of this database of 220 private limited liability companies and my 1979 census findings, taken together, revealed about the local Chinese mercantile elite and their "large" concentrations of property (Nonini 1983a), and about what it can tell us of the distribution of wealth among Chinese in Bukit Mertajam in the late 1970s.

I began with the owners of the 108 large businesses (with ten or more employees) found in the 1979 census. It made sense to think of the enterprises these people owned or controlled as significant "local concentrations of [wealth-generating] property" (Nonini 1983a, 181–251)—and it was the enterprises, not the people, that I first focused on. Further analysis of the limited company documents on file led me to add 63 businesses to arrive at a total of 171 local concentrations of property within the district as a whole.[5]

I discovered that 134, or about 80 percent of these 171 businesses, were owned or controlled by residents of Bukit Mertajam—they were therefore *locally* owned or controlled. Of these 134 businesses, 64 were manufacturers (in garments, foodstuffs, etc.); 27 were supermarkets, department stores, and textile wholesalers; thirteen were truck transport firms; and twelve were wholesaling enterprises (of fish, vegetables, beverages, canned goods, etc.)(Nonini 1983a, 195–196, table 29). Then, from my limited liability company data, I was able to ask of these concentrations of property: Who owned (or controlled) them?[6]

The owners and directors of these 134 businesses consisted of 294 Chinese, 7 Malays and 1 Indian—almost all men (Nonini 1983a, 198–199, table 30, 201–202). These 294 Chinese individuals formed the local mercantile elite because of the wealth-generating property they owned and controlled; they formed the core of the men of position discussed in chapters 3 and 4. Yet there was an even more select group within them. Fifty-three men out of 294 formed five enterprise syndicates that linked together 63 of the 134 businesses referred to; they did so through the directorships in these businesses they shared with one another (230–233, figs. 9(a)–9(d)). Their networked financial wealth gave them great influence in Chinese society, and several of the celebrities playing apex leadership roles in associations came from this small pool of business owners.

What of the 156 men who owned or controlled 37 (22 percent) of the 171 businesses which were *not* owned by Bukit Mertajam residents? They fell into two groups—the shareholders and directors of private limited liability companies, and the directors of publicly listed (limited liability) corporations. Among the former, 76 of these men were directors of 24 private limited liability companies and did not live in Bukit Mertajam or in the district; 65 of these men (or 85 percent of the total 76) lived in Georgetown, Kuala Lumpur, or Singapore (Nonini 1983a, 199–200). They were, I hypothesize, Chinese owners of property whose business holdings were sufficiently large and dispersed that they could afford to—indeed their status as tycoons required them as members of Malaysia's national Chinese bourgeoisie to—live in these largest cities of Malaysia where the commercial, financial, and political action was.

The identities of the other 78 directors of thirteen corporations with large operations in Bukit Mertajam were equally interesting. They served as directors of large banks and of manufacturing and real estate development corporations publicly listed on the Kuala Lumpur Stock Exchange (with substantial government equity) and of government semistatutory bodies (e.g., Urban Development Authority) (Nonini 1983a, 200–201). Almost all of the thirteen businesses they directed were among the largest 100 corporations in Malaysia (Lim 1983, 52–70). For this group, 47 out of the 78 directors were Chinese, while 22 were Malays. That 28 percent of the top executives of these thirteen corporations and government bodies were Malays was a sign of the top-down changes already underway in the ethnic composition of Malaysia's (i.e., the national) economic elite in the direction of increased concentrated wealth among Malays, and of the potential access to political power and patronage associated with it.

To conclude, approximately 300 businessmen stood out among almost 10,000 Chinese who formed the labor force of Bukit Mertajam, in a profoundly unequal distribution of wealth within this population—one in which approximately 75 percent were either hired wage or salaried workers or self-employed. These economic inequalities translated into deep social and political inequalities, as the chapters of this book demonstrate.

Finally, there were 78 extraordinarily wealthy men who lived outside of Bukit Mertajam because they were directors of thirteen of Malaysia's largest corporations, whose banking, manufacturing, housing development, and other operations played a disproportionate role in the daily lives of Bukit Mertajam residents, and as it turned out, 28 percent of these men were Bumiputras.

Notes

INTRODUCTION

1 In this book, most transcriptions provided of words or phrases in Chinese are rendered in Mandarin pinyin, except for a relative few rendered in Hokkien which are followed by an "(H)." Those rendered in Malay, if not proper names, are followed by an "(M)."

2 During the postwar period, these prohibitions on travel were effective both ways, imposed by the Malaysian government on travel to China for any Chinese under the age of fifty, and by the PRC government on travel from China to the Nanyang.

3 This changed with the Bandung Conference of 1955, but the residual effects of the discourse prevailed among Chinese in Malaysia all the same, many of whom—those residing in Singapore, Penang, and Malacca, the states forming what had been the Straits Settlements—found their right to Malaysian citizenship and its entitlements still called into question in the 1960s.

4 Vertovec and Cohen (1999, 1) point to the conceptual multiplicity of meanings of "diaspora" within various bodies of scholarship. Diasporas have been defined as (1) a kind of transnational "social morphology" in migration studies; (2) imbuing a kind of "consciousness," that is, diasporic consciousness, particularly in cultural studies; (3) referring to a certain kind of representation and "a mode of cultural reproduction," for instance, as an ethnic or religious diaspora, diasporic literature, music, drama, TV programs, and the like within media studies; (4) providing one transnational framework for the circulation of capital; and (5) a site of "political engagement" for the members of certain diasporic and exile groups.

5 Not long after the publication of Ong and Nonini's (1997) *Ungrounded Empires: The Cultural Politics of Modern Chinese Transnationalism*, I remember being gently castigated by one prominent Malaysian academic, a good friend, who expressed to me his feeling that our arguments about transnationalism and diasporas among Chinese had been fodder for such polemics.

6 The approach outlined in this section is inspired by a large and growing body of studies arising from a cultural Marxist perspective, which have demonstrated the existence of class-based forms of consciousness, values, and worldviews embedded in the practices of daily social relations in class societies. See, among others, E. P. Thompson (1963, 1978); Paul Willis (1981); June Nash (1979); Michael Taussig (1980); James C. Scott (1985); Gerald Sider (1997, 2003, 2006); Gavin A. Smith (1999); and Gerald Sider and Gavin A. Smith (1997).

7 The largest, and principal, holders of wealth in late colonial Malaya were, of course, not Asian, but the European and especially British corporations that owned the colony's largest tin mines, rubber plantations, and agency houses that held monopolies over imports into and exports from the colony (Puthucheary 1960).

8 For instance, differences in wealth and status in Malay villages between relatively large landowners and poorer wage-laborers and tenants are reflected in the ardent support by the former for UMNO; opposition to or only tepid support for UMNO, or allegiance to PAS by the latter. See Scott (1985) and Kessler (1978).

9 Throughout this book when I employ the term "Chinese society" as a gloss for the Chinese phrase *huaren shehui*, or more simply, *huashe*, I refer to a specific representation of who Chinese people are, a representation that is used within the rhetoric of local politics by Chinese elites. Unfortunately, it has also become a term appropriated in translation by positivist sociologists, anthropologists and other scholars to refer a social group "out there" with certain cultural characteristics. Not only do I *not* use the phrase in this way; this latter usage is a reification that chapter 7 seeks to deconstruct.

10 There were, of course, exceptions—women with whom I formed close and sympathetic connections, such as Mrs. Tan, with whose family I lived during 1978–80 and in 1985, and with several other women, who were married and middle-aged—and I gained crucial ethnographic insights from my interactions with each.

CHAPTER 1

1 During the Emergency, identity cards and thumb printing were not the only forms of increased surveillance of the population, which also included the increased numbering and registration of house lots and landholdings and the use of social surveys (Harper 1999, 196). Nor were Chinese workers and squatters the only targets of surveillance, which also included Indian plantation laborers, railway and port workers organized by trade unions (Stenson 1980; Ramasamy 1994; Ramachandran 1994), and Malay activists of the leftist Malay Nationalist Party (Funston 1980). But only Chinese workers and squatters, whom the authorities saw as forming the civilian "base," the "People's Movement," Min Yuen, supporting the MCP, required intensified surveillance in order to separate them from the guerrillas, and indeed such was the strategic objective of the New Village program as a whole.

2 Between 1948 and independence in 1957, the political unit was known as Federation of Malaya, or Malaya for short; after independence, it became known as Malaysia.

3 According to Sandhu (1964b, 152), "In 1948 Malaya was the biggest single repository of British overseas investment. Malaya was responsible for almost all the dollar earnings of the whole sterling bloc. More than 80 per cent of this was paid into the sterling pool in London and 'without Malaya, the sterling system . . . could not exist.'"

4 An additional constraint on Malayan wage rates was that the United States required that Malayan tin and rubber be sold to American manufacturers at a low price as a condition for its postwar reconstruction aid to Britain: this had the effect on British capitalists of placing downward pressure on wages just as demands for increased wages were accelerating.

5 So called, instead of a war, for insurance reasons!

6 Morgan (1977, 190–191) writes that "it is no exaggeration to say that the attack on the trade unions was characterized by an unparalleled ferocity, matched in European experience only by the assault of fascism on the labor movement."

7 Vasil (1971, 142–143) wrote: "Almost all the Chinese-educated [members of the MLP] are of working-class origin from the little towns and New Villages in the country. They are all educated in Chinese-medium schools, centers with a long tradition of Chinese nationalism. They are not all well-educated; most of them can afford only a few years of schooling, perhaps up to the primary level. Basically most of them, except their small number of ideologically articulate leaders, are Chinese chauvinists. Ideological extremism is only incidental. Their basic commitment is to the great fatherland China and its great culture, heritage, and language. Most of them talk in clichés and one is not certain if they understand all that they are saying or whether they are only parroting what they have been told by their leaders." In contrast, the English-educated Chinese of the MLP were "moderates" who were "cosmopolitan in outlook" and "genuinely non-communal" (Vasil 1971, 142–143).

8 Tan's (1988) study points to militant efforts from the early 1900s onward by Malay political leaders and intellectuals to associate an exclusive definition of the *bangsa Melayu*—the "Malay nation"—with the political project of a new state free from colonial rule and immigrant influence (Tan 1988, 16–21). With the postindependence rise to power of governing Malay political and Chinese economic elites, a new cultural racialization started to be institutionalized in state laws and practices: members of these elites came to agree there were essential differences between the two groups, even if they disagreed about which group was to be ranked as superior vis-à-vis the other within the mechanisms of state recognition—an uncertainty that the May 13, 1969, riots resolved decisively in favor of Malay domination. Afterward, expanding Malay elite control over the state allowed them to create an increasingly close legal identification between the bangsa Melayu, national "culture" and religion, and state policies of group preference, thus sedimenting a binary of essential group difference between Malays (and other indigenes), and nonindigenes. As Tan (1988, 21–28) points out, the corresponding term to bangsa among Chinese was *minzu*, or a "nationality" as a group; and within earlier China nationalist rhetoric equal minzu made nonexclusive claims on the state. In Malaysia after independence, the rhetoric of Chinese-led opposition political parties continued to express contentions between Malay and Chinese in terms of equal minzu with nonexclusive claims on the Malaysian state, over and against the exclusivist claims made by Malay leaders on behalf of bangsa Melayu. For this reason, in this book, when informants or sources use the English word *race* or the Chinese cognate *zhongzu*—usually in connection with political rhetoric—I gloss it as "race." Otherwise I employ the awkward concept "ethno-racial," as in "ethno-racial group." As shown in chapter 3, an informal derogatory racist label used by some Chinese for Malays—"barbarians"—cross-cut and negated the more temperate rhetoric of minzu, bangsa, and race.

9 These myths were exemplified for instance in the stereotypes set out in the social Darwinist tract *The Malay Dilemma* 1970; reprint 2008), written by Mahathir Mohamad, later to become Malaysia's prime minister for more than two decades (see Khoo 1995, 24–34).

10 Unfortunately, the only ethnography of Chinese residing in Province Wellesley during the early 1950s period of forced resettlement is the idiosyncratic study of rural Teochew vegetable farmers by William Newell (1962). Newell—having fled his rural field site in Sichuan province in western China with the rise to power of the Chinese Communist Party in 1949—appeared determined to recapitulate his study of "rural China" by avoiding the New Villages and instead found as his new field site a village located in Permatang Pau, a few miles north of Permatang Tinggi New Village—where "numbers of Chinese [were] still living freely in the open countryside outside the new villages" (Newell 1962, xxi). Even if his choice of Malayan field site may have been commendably shaped by his desire to do fieldwork outside an obvious condition of confinement, it still conveyed an essentializing sinological axiom of the period: Chinese here, Chinese there—what was the (essential) difference?

11 Not all MCP guerrillas were ethnic Chinese, but a majority were. Other guerrillas were ethnic Indian and Malay. One exception was in the eastern central region of the peninsula where the MCP's guerrilla force, the Pahang Regiment, was almost exclusively Malay (Short 1975).

12 Indians, most of whom were poor and lived in large numbers on plantations, nonetheless were, I would argue, classified as "urban," in that the British and their UMNO inheritors saw them as having no moral rights to reside in rural areas, despite the manifest dependence of rural plantations on them for labor. In this respect, their absence of a status associated with rights to land situated them, like Chinese, as "urban."

PREFACE

1 Under the Industrial Coordination Act, a government-owned enterprise could assume up to 30 percent of a company's equity outright and was entitled to use the company's profits from the equity thus taken over to pay for the shares it had acquired.

2 The largest such trustee corporations included the National Corporation (Pernas), the National Equity Corporation (Permodalan Nasional Bhd.), the National Unit Trust (Amanah Saham Nasional), and the Bumiputra Unit Trust (Amanah Saham Bumiputra).

CHAPTER 2

1 The commercial survey included all establishments that my team of enumerators and I could locate that were sited in permanent built structures, advertised their goods or services by signs, and were located within the municipal boundaries of Bukit Mertajam. As such, it excluded mobile street vendors, hawkers at coffee shops, and people operating illicit businesses. It also excluded approximately one hundred vendors who rented stalls in and behind the public wet market downtown.

2 The "workforce" of 7,203 people had two components—those who were owners of businesses and family members of owners engaged in actively operating the business (2,864 persons), and employees of these businesses (4,339 persons) (Nonini 1983a, 123).

3 Previously called Central Province Wellesley during the colonial period.

4 Teochews were the distinctive Chinese speech group whose ancestors came from the prefecture of Chaozhoufu in eastern Guangdong Province, China (Skinner 1957). More than 40 percent of Chinese in Bukit Mertajam came from this prefecture. They spoke a language, also called Teochew (M: *Chaozhouhua*) native to that region of southeastern China. Although within the same language family as Mandarin Chinese, Teochew is not intelligible to exclusively Mandarin speakers. Teochew and Hokkien (*Fujianhua* in Mandarin), a language originally spoken by migrants from the nearby Amoy and Quanzhou regions of southern Fujian Province (Skinner 1957), are mutually intelligible. A dialect of Hokkien, "Penang Hokkien," served as a vernacular lingua franca among Chinese in the Penang region.

5 People knowledgeable about the industry informed me that the number of such factories probably exceeded one hundred, if one included those the census missed or those located outside the town's boundaries but still within its metropolitan area.

6 For a favorable view of the NEP written by one of its policy architects, see Faaland et al. (1990); for more critical views, see Esman (1991), Ho (1992), and Edwards (1992).

7 The estimate is from a survey conducted in 1966. See Khoo (1966).

8 I found these additional twenty-six businesses through recording and analyzing data on limited liability companies held by the Registrar of Companies in Georgetown and Kuala Lumpur. These businesses operated outside the boundaries of Bukit Mertajam covered by my census, but within the district of Seberang Perai Tengah (Central Province Wellesley) (Nonini 1983a, 191, table 29, 196). (See the appendix for details.)

CHAPTER 3

1 *Towkay* (Hokkien)—term of address and reference people used for the male head of family businesses. I never heard the female form *towkayniu* (Bodman 1955) used for their wives—wives of towkay were called *thai-thai*, e.g., Ong thai-thai, "Mrs. Ong." A second more formal term, "merchant," *shangren*, was much less frequently used, and usually in the third-person plural, as on certain occasions such as speeches in Mandarin before association banquets.

2 In my 1978–80 fieldwork discussed here, I spoke only Mandarin and had not yet studied or learned to speak Hokkien.

3 Teh Cheok Sah (his real name) is mentioned as a leading founder, *faqiren*, of the Hanjiang Association in Hanjiang Gonghui (Dashanjiao) (Hung Kung Association, Bukit Mertajam) 1965.

4 In the legacy of British colonialism, the Malaysian Yang-dipertuan Agong (King) and sultans of each state conferred lifetime titles of nobility, analogous to "Sir" and "O.B.E." on prominent citizens and contributors to parties within the governing Barisan Nasional. These were highly coveted as signs of prestige by men of position.

5 The quote within the subhead above refers to Albert O. Hirschman's (1977) classic on the rationalization for capitalism before its emergence in Europe.

6 Of more than one thousand business establishments in the town of Bukit Mertajam in 1979 for which I have census data, the median number of outside (nonfamily) workers was zero, and about three-fourths of all establishments employed three outside workers or fewer.

7 This section epigraph is from Bodman (1955), *Spoken Amoy Hokkien*, 175. *Huanà* is a vulgar term in Hokkien derived from *fan* (M), "barbarian," with the diminutive suffix "à" added.

CHAPTER 4

1 See Nagata (1975a, 6); Fussell (2001).

2 As described in chapter 1, this New Village was the site of an infamous event during the Emergency.

3 In class terms, the aggregate effect of these practices of extracting money through a multitude of such dyadic ties was a net transfer of surplus capital from Chinese business families to the new members of the state-connected Malay capitalist and managerial class, the Melayu Baru, over the first two decades of the New Economic Policy.

4 During the recession in 1985, the ICA was amended so that the minima required for 30 percent Bumiputra equity were raised to MR$ 1,000,000 in capital and fifty employees (Crouch 1996, 208).

5 According to the assistant registrar of companies, Penang, until the mid-1970s there were only about three thousand limited liability companies whose documents were held in the Penang regional office of the Registrar of Companies, but as of 1980 this had grown to about six thousand companies on record. As a result, he said, his office was having a difficult time coping with the increase (assistant registrar of companies, personal communication).

6 Banks, they said, insisted on a public listing of accounts, which loan officers could access to determine whether in fact property which companies used as collateral for a loan (debenture) was actually free of prior claims on it by creditors.

7 The image of the *dalang*, or "puppet master," is a favorite metaphor in Malaysian public life for describing the big operators who manage politics through patronage and influence peddling from behind the scenes.

8 The irony that a measure designed to uplift Malays into small business circles actually promoted the multiplication of small Chinese firms while transforming Malay men into petty rentiers via Ali-Baba was a more or less open public secret. As a reporter in an article in the Penang newspaper, *The Star*, cited the president of the Pan-Malaysia Lorry Owners Association: "'Now, anyone [any Bumiputra] can apply to the Licensing Board for lorry permits and even non-operators can and apply and receive a permit,' said Puan Zainab. The Government should stop issuing these permits as the market is already saturated" (Ong 1985, 6).

9 State-sanctioned predation was not the only aspect of Malaysian governing logics that constrained enterprises in the petty capitalist sector to remain small and stimulated fierce competition among them, although it was by far the most important. The Malaysian

government was also committed to leaving capitalist growth relatively unregulated in certain crucial respects—for instance its laws and policies that allowed new small businesses to easily be set up, and for debtors to escape their creditors and start businesses anew (usually by leaving a locale). There was also an overall state orientation that promoted export-oriented industrialization. Thus the location of nearby factories in export processing zones in Butterworth meant that many small businesses in Bukit Mertajam profited by operating as industrial assemblers, packagers, and transporters—that is, as subcontractors—who served these factories.

CHAPTER 5

1 A sign of the place of Chinese women in the export industrialization process then underway in the export platforms of free trade zones and industrial estates were the lines of blue factory buses I observed during 1978–80, for which workers, mostly women, queued up near the Post Office downtown in the morning to take them to assembly plants for the daytime shift (see plate 6). Other buses and minibuses passed through the squatter neighborhoods near downtown and in the New Villages to collect such workers for their day of toil. Not only Chinese but also Indian and Malay women, of course, rode the factory buses to Prai and Butterworth.

2 "Dialects," *fangyen* (M), was the term used by English- or (Mandarin-) Chinese language speakers in Malaysia to refer to all Chinese speech forms spoken in Malaysia other than Mandarin, which was associated with the capacity to read and write Chinese ideographs. These "dialects," however, are what some linguists see as distinct but related Chinese languages, while other linguists follow prevailing usage in China to see them all as "dialects" of its national language (Ramsey 1987). In Bukit Mertajam, these dialects included Hokkien, or *Fujianhua* (M); Teochew, *Chaozhouhua* (M); Cantonese, *Guangdonghua* (M); Hakka, *Kejiahua* (M); Hainanese, *Hainanhua* (M); and Teochew Khek, *Chaozhou Kejiahua*. Norman (1991) sees Hokkien and Teochew as very closely related to each other (and therefore as highly mutually intelligible) and as members of the coastal southern Min language group. For that reason, when I refer to Hokkien, which was the lingua franca among non-Mandarin Chinese speakers in the Penang region, I am also referring to Teochew, spoken by some people in the district whose ancestors came from Puning County and other counties on the Guangdong Province side of the border with Fujian Province.

3 Sider (2005, 174) points to the necessity for historical anthropologists to reject "Weberian notions that power and culture, and the conjunction of power and culture (e.g., the whole concept of '*stand*'—a status grouping—and the notions of political legitimation) are forms of social order, or of social ordering, rather than names for, on the one hand, domains of chaos imposed upon daily life and, on the other, the necessary, unavoidable (and often order-creating) struggles that continually emerge within and against this chaos."

4 It was not at all uncommon when I visited towkays, especially younger men, to observe that they cultivated the long curling fingernail on the little finger of their right hands—a sign of the leisured, gentry class in late imperial and Republican China. The least physical effort would have broken it.

5 According to Cheah (1979, 42), the Ang Bin Hui "never entered the sphere of public politics, but developed along the lines of a standard secret society, and is said to have spread to all the main ports of the Straits of Malacca, including Singapore, Penang and Rangoon, in each of which it started to recruit the lower classes of the Chinese community such as street hawkers, coolies and dock laborers."

6 In the 1978 parliamentary elections in Penang, the opposition DAP gained three new seats in Parliament at the expense of the MCA and Gerakan, including the Bukit Mertajam

seat. In large part this was due to defections by parliamentary candidates from the MCA who ran as independents. In the State Assembly elections, however, the MCA and Gerakan largely held their own against the DAP in Chinese-majority assembly constituencies (Kassim 1978, 74–78).

7 In 1978–80 and in 1985, trucks had open-air cabs, no air-conditioning, often no side doors or insulation to deaden the roar and the heat of the truck engine a few feet behind which the driver and his codriver or attendant sat. Driving or even riding in the cab for long hours was exhausting, dirty, and sweaty work.

8 The distinction between using a permit and owning it was crucial since the truck permit was, far more often than not, owned by a Bumiputra, the "Ali," and was leased informally to the Chinese "Baba" who owned the truck corresponding to the permit.

9 This referred to fish and poultry hauled to early morning wholesale auctions in cities like Kuala Lumpur and towns several hundred miles to the south of Bukit Mertajam.

CHAPTER 6

1 As I stated in chapter 2, 102 Chinese owned 53 truck transport companies in Bukit Mertajam and the surrounding district, and most of the 1,100 people they employed as drivers, managers, clerks, truck attendants, and general laborers were Chinese men. Of these, 625 were long-haul truck drivers, and of these, slightly more than 550 were Chinese men (Nonini 1983a, 265–269).

2 Owners asserted that it would be easy for drivers to take, for instance, a few chickens from the several hundred baskets loaded onto a truck carrying these to distant cities or towns. It would be difficult for consigners to determine that goods were missing, for drivers could soak the baskets that the chickens were carried in in water, to make up for the weight loss due to fowl taken. There would always a ready market for such goods en route, and evidence of larceny would be promptly and enthusiastically disposed of at restaurants or at families' dinner tables.

3 All truck drivers interviewed were men (and I knew of no women who drove); all but one managing truck owner interviewed were men; all but one office clerk interviewed were men, although owners often employed daughters or wives as unpaid account clerks, or hired unrelated women to do this work.

4 This was due to the course of my 1978–80 dissertation research described in chapter 2. This study included the truck transport industry, but as my frustration with its positivist imperatives and my subjects' resistance to them grew, I started to inquire about labor-management relations specifically within this industry. These became the subject of the new research project I began in 1985, where I studied interactions between owners and clerks on one hand, and truck drivers, on the other. But in the new project, I encountered challenges of timing and spacing: verbal interactions between bosses and workers occurred in offstage areas such as loading docks and warehouses. Such interactions were fleeting, at the beginning of a driver's shift or at its end, while most of a driver's work time was spent en route, *zai bantu zhong*. In order to study these ephemeral interactions and conditions en route I decided to accompany drivers on three long-distance truck trips in 1985.

5 See the section below, "Toward an Alternative Heuristic."

6 Ibid.

7 In the narrow sense, this was money to be spent on drivers' food and drinks while en route. One informant observed, for instance, that a meal for two hungry drivers could amount to as much as MR$ 30, for fish, chicken, etc. For the two days of a trip, this would come to MR$ 60 or more. But each driver on a two-day trip to Kuala Lumpur and back would only be paid MR$ 80, so where was money for meals to come from, if not from rice-eating money?

8 Edwards and Scullion (1982, 169–181) have referred to these conflicts as contestations to define "the effort bargain."

9 Reloading was essential given Bukit Mertajam's location as a transshipment point—freight was brought back to company depots in and near the town for sorting by destination, and aggregated into the larger loads for long-distance shipment to the south and southeast.

10 I write of "time's duress" in the trucking industry in chapter 2. For another example, a trip from Bukit Mertajam to Kuala Lumpur started on the evening of Day 1, with the delivery of goods to Kuala Lumpur consignees taking place during the morning and early afternoon of Day 2, the pickup of goods from Kuala Lumpur consigners occurring during the late afternoon and early evening of Day 2, and the return to Bukit Mertajam made during the night of Day 2 and early morning hours of Day 3.

11 Informants claimed that it was only in Hokkien or Teochew, and never Mandarin, that Chinese employed "vulgar speech," *cuhua*; one lay linguist argued that it was the capacity for speakers to make puns from homonyms and near-homonyms (saying, varying by tone only) in these languages that allowed them to engage in subtle sexual double entendres.

12 The distinction between "showing manners" and "being crude" among Chinese paralleled the distinction among Malays between *kasar* (M), "vulgar," and *alus* (M), "refined," and probably derived from it. Working-class Chinese were implicitly racialized in a derogatory way within the new terms of the emergent post-NEP hegemony of Malay domination. Since a common Malay assumption was that compared to Malays who were *alus*, Chinese were *kasar*, then it could follow that the towkay/boss, being more *alus* than the worker, was in effect somewhat more "Malay" as well, while to be a working-class Chinese was to be more *kasar*, thus more "Chinese"!

13 See note 3.

CHAPTER 7

1 These amendments in 1970 to the Sedition Act prohibiting the public discussion of "sensitive" issues such as Malay special privileges, Malay (Bahasa Malaysia) as the national language, or the sovereignty of the Malay rulers were particularly effective in provoking precisely such discussion outside the public arena of the press and public assemblies. As Foucault (1978) has suggested in the case of sex, nothing does more to promote the prevalence of a certain discourse on the popular level than its formal prohibition.

2 In following the dispute, I draw heavily from articles appearing in two regional Chinese-language newspapers, from data in interviews of some of the principal participants, information provided by key informants, and personal observation in 1979 and 1980. I collected further follow-up data in 1985 and 1990.

3 "Chinese society" glosses the Chinese term *huaren shehui* used throughout the dispute.

4 Newspaper accounts referred to Chinese society in "northern Malaysia," *Beima*, and represented this space in terms of the geographic scope of news items from cities and towns within the region; in this sense, the three Chinese-language newspapers presented "northern Malaysia's Chinese society" as consisting of those Chinese residing—and reading Chinese—in the states of Penang, Kedah, and Perlis, and in the state of Perak north of Ipoh.

5 In Mandarin, *dejiaohui*.

6 The proprietors of wholesaling, retailing, transport, and industrial businesses located within the town and nearby, held important offices in these associations and groups. Members of the town's mercantile elite controlled the activities of these associations. Officers of these associations were drawn from a relatively small number of about

three hundred Chinese men who owned and operated local businesses and who knew each other on a face-to-face basis (Nonini 1983a, 228–241). Most of these men were petty property owners but a minority, the most wealthy and influential, were large employers who held the highest offices within these associations, such as chairman and secretary.

7 These are glosses for the Chinese names, which reveal more accurately the spatial provenience of members, as follows: Hokkien Association, Fujian Huiguan; Teochew Association, Hanjiang Gonghui (from the Han River in Chaozhoufu); Cantonese Association, Guanghuizhao Huiguan (from Guangzhou, Huizhou and Zhaoqingzhou prefectures); Hainanese Association, Qiongyai Tongxianghui (from Qiongzhou prefecture and Yaizhou independent department).

8 Of the twelve members of the Managing Committee, five were representatives from the Cantonese Association, three from the Hokkien Association, three from the Teochew Association, and one from the Hainanese Association.

9 Among all the speech groups of Chinese who migrated from southern and southeastern regions of China to Malaya, it was only among the Hakka ("guests" or *ke* in Mandarin) that there was no one-to-one relationship between a specific China regional native-place and a single language, since the migratory history of Hakkas within China prior to the nineteenth century led them to be widely dispersed throughout the mountainous regions of southern and southeastern China (Reinknecht 1979). These regions were already encompassed within the prefectures from which the ancestors of members of the other four native-place associations migrated to British Malaya.

10 One particularly strong source of discontent among Chinese were the frustrations meted out by the government to a nationwide campaign by Chinese associations to establish a proposed privately operated university, Merdeka University, where Mandarin was to be the principal language of instruction. This campaign had, by 1979, gone on for several years, and had been repeatedly blocked in its progress by the national government through various legal obstacles. Chinese associations sought to convene at that time to protest the recent decision by the Minister of Education that the new university would not be given a charter. See Das (1978a, 1978b, 1978c, 1978d).

11 The appearance of a spokesperson for Tang was itself noteworthy. Spoken Mandarin was the normative language of political rhetoric among Chinese in Malaysia—being taught in the Chinese-language primary language schools in Malaysia and associated in China nationalist theory with the Chinese written characters whose mastery linked one to the larger public of readers of the Chinese-language print media. However Tang was a Teochew Hakka, an older man, relatively unschooled, and unable to speak fluent Mandarin.

12 This relative ranking by prestige—in which the chair officers of an association were more highly esteemed than members of its executive board—was consistent with findings among diaspora Chinese in Thailand (Skinner 1958, 87) and was one ranking rubric within the segmentary imaginary discussed here.

13 In a subsequent discussion, Headmaster Sim told me that Soo was a "young leader" who did not understand how things worked in Chinese society in Bukit Mertajam. Sim said that although it was not publicly known, Soo had proposed that the profits coming from the rental properties and plantation owned by the temple be reinvested in yet more businesses in order to grow its wealth, rather than be returned to the temple Managing Committee to donate in its name to local schools. Sim went on to imply that rivalries over "reputation," mingyu, between members of the Managing Committee—manifested in such donations—and the requirements of the temple's nonprofit bylaws, militated against accepting this proposal.

14 Tan (1988, 27) has observed that "Sun clearly came in from the English concept of *nation*, which he translated as both *guojia* [state] or minzu [race] in Chinese. Sun equated *minzu zhuyi* with *guozu zhuyi* (ideology of a people of a *guo*) because his main concern

was to make China the sole focus of political loyalty, overriding the traditional bonds to family, clan and province. Minzu and guojia are thus merged in a nationalism defined as a 'doctrine of the state.'" Bergère and Lloyd (1998, 359) note that for Sun "racial nationalism should . . . rest upon traditional family and clan loyalties and extend these to the whole country. . . . It would be possible for the nation-state to be constructed naturally, working from the bottom upward, from the individual citizens to its central organizations. . . . Race (minzu) would find its spontaneous expression in the state *guojia*)."

15 Tan (1988) describes the controversies in the 1950s and 1960s about the meaning of minzu vis-à-vis the reigning concept of *bangsa Melayu*—"Malay race"—which Malay nationalists and their successors among UMNO leaders took as defining the ideal citizens of an independent Malayan nation. Tan also points out that although Sun identified the Chinese minzu closely with the Chinese guojia, or state, that Chinese intellectuals more frequently envisioned the possibility of more than one minzu coexisting as citizens of a certain state.

16 Skinner (1968) points to the compromised apex leader in Chinese settlements in colonial Southeast Asia who served as a broker whose actions had to satisfy both the colonial state, on one side, and the body of leaders who selected him, on the other. What Skinner failed to note, however, was that the compromises involved in bringing Chinese into agreement with the rationalities entailed in colonial governance extended far beyond the leader to encompass the larger population of urban Chinese being governed.

17 The significance of "registration" for Chinese in Malaysia needs to be seen in terms of the history of British colonial and postcolonial state practices of repression against dissident groups. See chapter 1.

18 These titles reflected an imagined feudal order of sovereignty based on loyalty to the Malay rulers, *raja*. These titles were ranked and given out to prominent citizens on the birthdays of the King, Yang-di-Pertuan Agong, and of the sultans or governor-generals of each Malaysian state. Receiving such a title, *shoufeng*, was a cause for celebration requiring that families, friends, and association leaders congratulate the recipient through placing advertisements in the Chinese-language press and fete them in a local restaurant.

19 In 1979, four of fifteen members of the the Board of Trustees of Jit Sin Independent High School were also members of the temple Managing Committee; two of the ten members of the Jit Sin National Type High School were also members.

20 Fund-raisers to find money to finance operations for residents who needed surgery or to provide for the expenses of local sports teams to travel to tournaments and donations to old-age homes and the like were perfunctory and provided little money to needy local working-class Chinese.

21 This may explain why at two crucial junctures in the dispute—its beginning and its end—the roles played by local Chinese school headmasters were pivotal. The day after Soo put forth his proposal, the headmaster of an outlying primary school provided an authoritative backing that it could have received from few other men. And the dispute was drawn to a close by the intervention and mediation of the headmaster of the town's Chinese-language national type high school. What both headmasters possessed that no other persons had was an irreproachable reputation of disinterestedness: their commitment to the welfare of the area's Chinese-language schools and their students was beyond question. That combined with the fact that both were prominent supporters of the Malaysian Chinese Association, which belonged with UMNO to the ruling coalition of the government.

22 Chinese society in the Penang region was defined territorially by those who were the readers of "local news," *difangxingwen*, and the "Penang supplement," or *Bingchengban*—who were coextensive with the population of Chinese language readers

within the circulation hinterlands of these newspapers, that is, Chinese living in Penang, northern Perak, Kedah, and Perlis.

23 At the same time, Soo's opponents claimed (via gossip, not in public speeches) that his agitation to reorganize the Managing Committee had alarmed the government—in other words, the Special Branch political police—because it threatened to create "disorder" within Chinese society concerning exactly which groups should be represented on the committee—registered ones? Any ones? They argued more publicly that his call jeopardized the committee's status as a tax-exempt entity registered solely for the purposes of worship and education.

CHAPTER 8

1 In 1985, the Industrial Coordination Act was amended so that the minimal conditions requiring 30 percent Bumiputra equity were MR$ 1 million in paid-up capital and fifty employees (Crouch 1996, 208); as the results from my commercial census discussed in chapter 2 demonstrate, all but a very few numbers of Chinese-owned businesses fell below this threshold.

2 As noted in chapter 7, these were the Hokkien, Teochew, Cantonese, and Hainanese associations.

3 From 1986 to 1997, the committee dispensed MR$ 832,000 to local kindergartens, primary, and secondary schools; provided MR$ 14,000 to various people in need of money for operations and medical services, gave out MR$ 51,000 in *angpao* to old-age pensioners on Chinese New Years; and from 1987 to 1997 awarded MR$ 174,000 in scholarships to high school and university students (Treasurer's Report and Welfare Report, in Hock Teik Cheng Sin Temple [Fudezhengshen Temple] 2007, 100–101, 124–125, 150–151).

4 See chapter 2 on the decisions parents made on which schools to send their children to, if they had the choice.

5 According to one informant, compensation was reduced from between MR$ 50,000 and MR$ 100,000 for usufruct and prior occupation to between MR$ 15,000 and MR$ 20,000.

CHAPTER 9

1 Instead of the imprecise label "middle-class," I use "propertied" or "property-owning" class, or "petty property class" as appropriate, in what follows.

2 Ethnic claims on public space were also pressed in the name of religious rights through the erection of shrines to Datuk Kong, a "Malay" god who ate no pork but was a place god protecting those working in construction sites, with their shrines often located on the shoulders of public roads. These shrines had been forcibly moved by Malaysian police and Municipal Council workers in the 1980s and 1990s.

3 One other form of public worship by Chinese, with non-Chinese, takes place at the Catholic festival of St. Anne, which takes place in late July and early August each year. Those Chinese who worship St. Anne and other Catholic saints at St. Anne's Church, about a mile east of downtown Bukit Mertajam on Jalan Kulim, enacted a form of cosmopolitical sovereignty similar to the Daoist/Buddhist forms described in this chapter. It combines the two modes of spatial appropriation described in this chapter—an influx of worshippers to the grounds of St. Anne's Church, combined, on the Saint's day, with circumambulation by Saint Anne (i.e., as her statue) and her worshippers around the grounds of the church. Unlike the case of the Daoist/Buddhist practices described in the chapter, however, its fame draws non-Chinese people from outside Bukit Mertajam—thus generating a less localized sense of solidarity.

4 See the last section of chapter 2. For each of seventeen of the twenty-three days, the members of a business organization—the vegetable vendors, the fish wholesalers, etc.—were responsible for providing the offerings on the tables before the altar of Dashiye (Podogong) and for paying the costs of the Teochew opera, or wayang, performed that day for the pleasure of Dashiye and the gods of the Fudezhengshen Temple.

5 However, descriptions of the banquets featuring celebrities and men of position who served as incense urn masters, committee members, and prestigious guests for such festivals were still being featured, as was true a decade earlier (see, e.g., "At the double celebration banquet for Sugar Cane's Shilinggong in Bukit Mertajam, [State Assemblyman] Leong Dao Seng calls on Chinese society to treasure religious freedom in developing its rights" (*Guanghua Ribao* 1992).

CHAPTER 10

1 The restriction of the mobility of working-class women to local spaces appears to be a specific Penang regional pattern, in contrast to the much-noted mobility by young women from other regions to overseas locations for labor sojourns, such as among women from the Cantonese areas of Perak state to the south (Michael Chong interview, July 12, 1997).

2 "Symbolic violence" as used by Bourdieu (1977, 1991) refers to unconscious practices of intimidation euphemized both by those who dominate and those who are dominated. It operates not so much by imperative language as by verbal insinuation, tone, tempo, and volume, and by gesture and other body language (see also Krais 1993). Symbolic violence "puts a person in his/her place."

3 As of 2001, the "I.C." itself has become the source of data for the state about the location and nature of the body of its holder by means of a recently implemented computerized data base containing files on all citizens (Thomas 2004).

4 According to Munro-Kua (1996), whereas in 1984 Chinese formed 33.2 percent of the Malaysian population and Malays 56.6 percent of population, in 1985 they made up only 25.8 percent of university admissions in Malaysia compared to 67.3 percent of admissions for Malay students. In the same year, 1985, the *majority* of Chinese Malaysian university students (59.4 percent) entered overseas universities, whereas only 20.2 percent of Malay students entered overseas universities (Munro-Kua 1996, tables 2.2 and A.6, 23, 166). In the 1990s and 2000s, the trend toward overseas university studies for Chinese continued. For instance, in 2005, when 12,802 Chinese students were admitted into Malaysian universities (Malaysia Development Plans, cited in Mukherjee 2010, 21, table 12), an estimated 36,000 "self-sponsored" students (the vast majority Chinese whose families paid their way) were enrolled in overseas universities (estimated from Ministry of Higher Education 2008).

5 For instance, truck transporters and wholesalers came to depend on the telephone and fax in daily operations.

6 The observant reader will note the discrepancy between Mr. Yap's claim that his youngest son attended Monash University and his youngest son's description of having attended the Royal Melbourne Institute of Technology. Monash University is located in Clayton, perhaps ten miles northeast of Melbourne's downtown; RMIT is located within its downtown area.

7 Chinese labor migration out of southern China to Southeast Asia is almost as longstanding as the history of European colonialism in the region (see Trocki 1997) and is voluminously documented (see Blythe 1947; Nonini 1993). Travel by Chinese laborers to work in Japan and Taiwan has been but one of many migrations worldwide by working-class Chinese in recent years. It is a process arising during the last three decades

under the conditions of flexible labor markets and labor control associated with the current phase of globalization and hegemonic decline in the West (see Harvey 1989, Nonini and Ong 1997; Friedman and Friedman 2008). For an analysis of illegal migrants from China sojourning in the United States, see Kwong (1994a, 1994b).

8 I would thus challenge Cohen's (1987, 109) generalization that "the mass of illegal workers are usually neither romantic heroes of the wild frontier, nor amateur micro-econometricians. Rather they are sad, fearful, pathetic individuals desperate to escape intolerable conditions at the periphery of the regional political economy, thrown about by forces they at first only dimly comprehend." Although my informants were neither frontier heroes nor econometricians, they were not particularly sad, fearful, or pathetic, nor "thrown about" by forces beyond their understanding.

9 This characterizes the larger pattern of Chinese laborers' migration worldwide. Kwong (1994a, 2) describes Fuzhounese migration to the United States: "There are fewer jobs [in New York City] for women, because there are fewer undocumented women. Migration from China is a planned operation of extended families, who prefer to send young males first."

10 The ringgit, the unit of Malaysian currency, varied around 2.5 to the U.S. dollar during 1991–92.

EPILOGUE

1 This by no means implies that workers who were Malaysian citizens formed a "labor aristocracy" as set out in the classical Marxism of Marx or later of Lenin. The "embourgeoisement" and privilege compared to other workers and reformism and political opportunism conveyed by this concept in the literature (Bottomore 1983) implied access to an established trade union movement and to its consolidated power, which never existed for Chinese laborers after the repressions of the Emergency.

APPENDIX

1 As to the claims of NEP supporters about Chinese wealth, "domination," and "clannishness," see the quotes of government officials and other non-Chinese given in chapter 2. These claims were also rife in the public statements of UMNO leaders in the English- and Malay-language newspapers of the 1970s and 1980s. The most articulate scholarly support for the NEP is that of Faaland et al. (2003), which carries a foreword by then prime minister Mahathir Mohamad. Among their other questionable claims, Faaland et al. (405–415) distinguish between a "Chinese economy" and a "Bumiputra economy" as if it was completely self-evident what these were. While there is no doubt that Chinese have had *on average* higher incomes and greater wealth than Malays, this dual-economy distinction finesses the central question of the overlapping powers of the corporate-state nexus driving the Malaysian economy. It completely ignores these powers (of capital accumulation, discriminatory government policy, and legal compulsion) that favor accelerated wealth accumulation among an extremely small multi-ethnic elite of political leaders and corporate owners, and have generated increasing class disparities within each ethnic group and within the Malaysian population as a whole. The effects of these powers working over time make the "averages" game of Faaland et al. largely meaningless except as a rhetorical prop for unjust social policies.

2 The observant reader will note that the bases for my 1979 commercial census and the 1980 Malaysian Population census for Bukit Mertajam were not the same. First, the years were different, 1979 versus 1980. More critically, the 1979 census enumerated employees who *worked in enterprises* located within the municipal boundaries of the town, while the 1980 population census enumerated people *residing* within those bound-

aries. Obviously, some people commuted to the town to work there, and others who lived in the town commuted to work elsewhere. Nonetheless, a good argument can be made for a large overlap in the two bases—a large majority lived and worked within the boundaries of Bukit Mertajam.

3 Because half of the twelve transport businesses found had not only headquarters in Bukit Mertajam but also branch offices in other cities and towns, it is possible that truck transport provided a greater possibility to employ additional family labor in far-away positions where owners felt that trust in handling money (e.g., office manager, collection manager) away from the personal surveillance by the owner was required.

4 During 1978 to 1980, Bukit Mertajam merchants were registering their business enterprises in increasing numbers as private limited liability companies (with the affix *Sendirian Berhad*) as distinct from the two prior prevailing forms of legal business organization—the sole proprietorship and the partnership. Informants told me that limited liability companies, unlike these two older forms, had lower effective taxation rate (probably because they were less subject to auditing by the Inland Revenue Service), and moreover, were a form of business organization where the liabilities of shareholders were limited to the amount of their paid-up capital, precisely the ostensible purpose of limited liability companies. I argue in chapter 4, however, that additional valued social goals were being met by local merchant's rush to register their enterprises as limited liability companies in these years. In the analysis that follows, private limited companies need to also be distinguished from "public limited liability companies" (with the affix *Berhad*)—which, unlike the former, were corporations that offered shares for sale to the public on the Kuala Lumpur Stock Exchange.

5 I added businesses hiring more than ten workers within the town that I had not found in the census (14); businesses hiring more than ten employees that operated outside the town boundaries but within the district—typically land-extensive enterprises like sawmills and rice and oil mills (16); businesses that hired fewer than ten employees but which had concentrated capital, like banks, finance companies, and lottery operators (13); housing development companies with concentrated capital but an undetermined number of employees (10), and other businesses, with indicative but incomplete data on employee or capital (10). My methodology is fully set out in Nonini 1983a (185–194).

6 The functions of ownership and control required separation because in the records on limited liability companies, a person could be deemed a director, hence having "control" of the business, without being an owner. In the case of the relatively modest scale of most locally owned businesses, this distinction was moot, since directors and owners completely overlapped; but in the case of companies not primarily or at all owned locally, directors were distinct from (major) owners, as in large, publicly listed limited liability companies.

References

Abu-Lughod, Lila. 1993. Writing against Culture. *In* Recapturing Anthropology: Working in the Present. R. Fox, ed. Pp. 137–162. Santa Fe, NM: School of American Research.

Agamben, Giorgio. 1998. Homo Sacer: Sovereign Power and Bare Life. D. Heller-Roazen, transl. Stanford, CA: Stanford University Press.

Ahmad, Kamis. 1978. Penang Perspective: Boom Town in the Making on the Mainland. *In* New Straits Times. Kuala Lumpur, May 8, 1978.

Alonso, A. M. 1994. The Politics of Space, Time and Substance—State Formation, Nationalism, and Ethnicity. Annual Review of Anthropology 23:379–405.

Althusser, Louis. 1971. Ideology and Ideological State Apparatuses (Notes towards an Investigation). *In* Lenin and Philosophy and Other Essays. L. Althusser, ed. Pp. 127–188. New York: Monthly Review Press.

Anderson, Benedict. 1994. Exodus. Critical Inquiry 20(2):314–327.

———. 2006. Imagined Communities: Reflections on the Origin and Spread of Nationalism. London: Verso.

Armstrong, M. Jocelyn, R. Warwick Armstrong, and K. Mulliner. 2001. Chinese Populations in Contemporary Southeast Asian Societies: Identities, Interdependence, and International Influence. Richmond, UK: Curzon.

Aronson, Ronald. 1995. After Marxism. New York: Guilford Press.

Azizan, Suzana Ariff. 2011. Enhancing Human Capital for Technological Development: A Comparative Study of a Selected Public University, a Large Local Corporation and an Industry-Public Sector Initiative in Malaysia. Ph.D. thesis, Faculty of the Parts. Wollongong, New South Wales, Australia: University of Wollongong.

Bakhtin, M. M. 1965. Rabelais and His World. Cambridge, MA: MIT Press.

———. 1981. The Dialogic Imagination: Four Essays by M. M. Bakhtin. Austin: University of Texas Press.

Barth, Fredrik. 1969. Introduction. *In* Ethnic Groups and Boundaries. F. Barth, ed. Pp. 9–38. Boston: Little, Brown.

Bechhofer, Frank, and Brian Elliot. 1981. Petty Property: The Survival of a Moral Economy. *In* The Petite Bourgeoisie: Comparative Studies of the Uneasy Stratum. F. Bechhofer and B. Elliot, eds. Pp. 182–200. New York: St. Martin's Press.

Bergère, Marie-Claire, and Janet Lloyd. 1998. Sun Yat-sen. Stanford, CA: Stanford University Press.

Bloch, Maurice, and Association of Social Anthropologists of the Commonwealth. 1975. Marxist Analyses and Social Anthropology. New York: Wiley.

Blythe, W. L. 1947. Historical Sketch of Chinese Labour in Malaya. Journal of the Malayan Branch, Royal Asiatic Society 21(1):26–28.

Bodman, Nicholas Cleaveland. 1955. Spoken Amoy Hokkien. 2 vols. Kuala Lumpur, Malaya: Government of Federation of Malaya.

Bonacich, Edna. 1973. A Theory of Middleman Minorities. American Sociological Review 38(5):583–594.

Bottomore, Tom. 1983. Labor Aristocracy. *In* A Dictionary of Marxist Thought, T. Bottomore et al., ed. P. 265. Cambridge, MA: Harvard University Press.

Bourdieu, Pierre. 1977. Outline of a Theory of Practice. Cambridge: Cambridge University Press.

——. 1984. Distinction: A Social Critique of the Judgment of Taste. Cambridge, MA: Harvard University Press.

——. 1986. The Forms of Capital. *In* Handbook of Theory and Research for the Sociology of Education. J.G. Richardson, ed. Pp. 241–258. New York: Greenwood.

——. 1991. The Production and Reproduction of Legitimate Language. *In* Language and Social Power. J. B. Thompson, ed. Pp. 43–65. Cambridge, MA: Harvard University Press.

Bowie, Alasdair. 2004. Civil Society and Democratization in Malaysia. *In* Growth and Governance in Asia. Y. Sato, ed. Pp. 193–201. Honolulu: Asia-Pacific Center for Security Studies.

Boy, Alasdair. 2004. Civil Society and Democratization in Malaysia. *In* Yoichiro Sato, ed., Growth and Governance in Asia, pp. 193–201. Honolulu: Asia-Pacific Center for Security Studies.

Butler, Judith. 1990. Gender Trouble: Feminism and the Subversion of Identity. New York: Routledge.

——. 1993. Imitation and Gender Insubordination. *In* Social Theory: The Multicultural & Classic Readings. C. Lemert, ed. Pp. 637–648. Boulder, CO: Westview Press.

Buxbaum, David C. 1966. Chinese Family Law in a Common Law Setting: A Note on the Institutional Environment and the Substantive Family Law of the Chinese in Singapore and Malaysia. Journal of Asian Studies 25(4):621–644.

Calagione, John, Doris Francis, and Daniel Nugent, eds. 1992. Workers' Expressions: Beyond Accommodation and Resistance. Albany, NY: SUNY Press.

Caldwell, Malcolm. 1977. From "Emergency" to "Independence," 1948–1957. *In* Malaya: The Making of a Neo-Colony. M. Amin and M. Caldwell, eds. Pp. 216–265. Nottingham, UK: Spokesman Books.

Castoriadis, Cornelius, and David Ames Curtis. 1997. World in Fragments: Writings on Politics, Society, Psychoanalysis, and the Imagination. Stanford, CA: Stanford University Press.

Certeau, Michel de. 1984. The Practice of Everyday Life. Berkeley: University of California Press.

Cham, B. N. 1975. Class and Communal Conflict in Malaysia. Journal of Contemporary Asia 5(4):446–461.

Chan, Kwok-bun, and Chaire Chiang. 1994. Stepping Out: The Making of Chinese Entrepreneurs. Singapore: Simon & Schuster Asia.

Cheah, Boon Kheng. 1979. The Masked Comrades: A Study of the Communist United Front in Malaya, 1945–48. Singapore: Times Books International.

——. 2003. Red Star over Malaya: Resistance and Social Conflict during and after the Japanese Occupation of Malaya, 1941–1946. Singapore: Singapore University Press National University of Singapore.

Cheu, Hock Tong. 1988. The Nine Emperor Gods: A Study of Chinese Spirit-Medium Cults. Singapore: Times Books International.

Chin, James Ung-Ho. 2006. New Chinese Leadership in Malaysia: the Contest for the MCA and Gerakan Presidency. Contemporary Southeast Asia: A Journal of International and Strategic Affairs 28(1):70–87.

Clarke, John. 2004. Changing Welfare, Changing States: New Directions in Social Policy. London: Sage.

Clifford, James. 1988. The Predicament of Culture: Twentieth-Century Ethnography, Literature, and Art. Cambridge, MA: Harvard.

——. 1992. Traveling Cultures. *In* Cultural Studies. L. Grossberg, C. Nelson, and P. Treichler, eds. Pp. 96–116. New York: Routledge Press.

——. 1995. Diasporas. Cultural Anthropology 9(3):302–338.

Clifford, James, and George E. Marcus, eds. 1986. Writing Culture: The Poetics and Politics of Ethnography. Berkeley: University of California Press.

Cohen, Robin. 1987. The New Helots: Migrants in the International Division of Labour. Aldershot, UK: Gower.

Collins, Alan. 2006. Chinese Educationalists in Malaysia—Defenders of Chinese Identity. Asian Survey 46:298–318.

Corrigan, Philip, and Derek Sayer. 1985. The Great Arch: English State Formation as Cultural Revolution. Oxford: Basil Blackwell.

Crissman, Lawrence. 1967. The Segmentary Structure of Urban Overseas Chinese Communities. Man 2(2):185–204.

Crouch, Harold. 1996. Government and Society in Malaysia. Ithaca: Cornell University Press.

Das, K. 1978a. Hussein Acts to Stop the Rot. Far Eastern Economic Review 102, 42: 12–13, October 20, 1978.

——. 1978b. The Shadow of '69 Passes Again. Far Eastern Economic Review 102, 44: 28–29, November 3, 1978.

——. 1978c. The Wisdom of the Mandarins. Far Eastern Economic Review 102, 48: 14–15, December 1, 1978.

——. 1978d. Stepping Back from the Brink. Far Eastern Economic Review 102, 49: 12–13, December 8, 1978.

Deleuze, Milles, and Felix Guattari. 1983. Anti-Oedipus: Capitalism and Schizophrenia. Minneapolis: University of Minnesota Press.

Diamond, Stanley. 1979. Toward a Marxist Anthropology: Problems and Perspectives. New York: Mouton.

Dunk, Thomas W. 1991. It's A Working Man's Town: Male Working-Class Culture in Northwestern Ontario. Montreal: McGill-Queen's University Press.

Edwards, C. 1992. (Review) Growth And Ethnic-Inequality—Malaysia New Economic-Policy, by Just Faaland, J. R. Parkinson, and R. Saniman. International Affairs 68(2):387–388.

Edwards, P. K., and Hugh Scullion, eds. 1982. The Social Organization of Industrial Conflict. Oxford: Basil Blackwell.

Edwards, Richard. 1979. Contested Terrain: The Transformation of the Workplace in the Twentieth Century. New York: Basic Books.

Elliot, Anthony. 2002. The Social Imaginary: A Critical Assessment of Castoriadis's Psychoanalytic Social Theory. American Imago 59(2):141–170.

Esman, Milton J. 1991 (Review) Growth And Ethnic-Inequality—Malaysia New Economic-Policy, by Just Faaland, J. R. Parkinson, and R. Saniman. Journal of Asian Studies 50(3):734–736.

Fabian, Johannes. 1983. Time and the Other: How Anthropology Makes Its Object. New York: Columbia University Press.

Far Eastern Economic Review. 1998. Migration: Deport and Deter: Indonesian Illegal Workers Get a Harsh Send-off from Malaysia. *In* Far Eastern Economic Review. Pp. 16–17, 20.

Ferguson, James. 1999. Expectations of Modernity Myths and Meanings of Urban Life on the Zambian Copperbelt. Berkeley: University of California Press.

Foucault, Michel. 1977. Discipline and Punish: The Birth of the Prison. New York: Vintage Books.
——. 1978. The History of Sexuality. Vol. 1. An Introduction. New York: Pantheon Books.
Fox, Richard G. 1991. For A Nearly New Culture History. *In* Recapturing Anthropology: Working in the Present. R. G. Fox, ed. Pp. 93–114. Santa Fe, New Mexico: School of American Research Press.
Freedman, Maurice. 1957. Chinese Family and Marriage in Singapore. London: Colonial Office, Colonial Research Studies, 20.
——. 1979a [1960]. The Growth of a Plural Society in Malaya. *In* The Study of Chinese Society: Essays by Maurice Freedman. G.W. Skinner, ed. Pp. 27–38. Stanford, CA: Stanford University Press.
——. 1979b. The Chinese in Southeast Asia: A Longer View. *In* The Study of Chinese Society: Essays by Maurice Freedman. G. W. Skinner, ed. Pp. 3–21. Stanford, CA: Stanford University Press.
——, 1979c. The Handling of Money: a Note on the Background to the Economic Sophistication of Overseas Chinese. *In* The Study of Chinese Society: Essays by Maurice Freedman. G.W. Skinner, ed. Pp. 22–26. Stanford, CA: Stanford University Press.
——. 1979d. Immigrants and Associations: Chinese in Nineteenth Century Singapore. *In* The Study of Chinese Society: Essays by Maurice Freedman. G.W. Skinner, ed. Pp. 61–83. Stanford, CA: Stanford University Press.
——. 1979e. An Epicycle of Cathay; or, The Southward Expansion of the Sinologists. *In* The Study of Chinese Society: Essays by Maurice Freedman. G.W. Skinner, ed. Pp. 39–57. Stanford, CA: Stanford University Press.
Friedman, Jonathan. 2008. Transnationalization, Sociopolitical Disorder, and Ethnification as Expressions of Declining Global Hegemony. *In* Historical Transformations: The Anthropology of Global Systems. K. E. Friedman and J. Friedman, eds. Pp. 203–226. Lanham, MD: Altamira/Rowman & Littlefield.
Friedman, Kajsa Ekholm, and Jonathan Friedman. 2008. Modernities, Class, and the Contradictions of Globalization. Historical Transformations: The Anthropology of Global Systems. Friedman and Friedman, eds. Lanham, MD: AltaMira/Rowman & Littlefield.
Funston, N. J. 1980. Malay Politics in Malaysia: A Study of the United Malays National Organisation and Party Islam. Kuala Lumpur: Heinemann Educational Books (Asia).
Furnivall, J. S. 1939. Netherlands India: A Study of Plural Economy. Cambridge: Cambridge University Press.
Fussell, Jim. 2001. Group Classification on National ID Cards as a Factor in Genocide and Ethnic Cleansing. New Haven, CT: Seminar Series, Yale University Genocide Studies Program and Genocidewatch.org.
Gamba, Charles. 1962. The Origins of Trade Unionism in Malaya: A Study in Colonial Labour Unrest. Singapore: Published by Donald Moore for Eastern Universities Press.
George, Cherian, Asian Media Information and Communication Center, and Wee Kim Wee School of Communication and Information. 2008. Free Markets Free Media? Reflections on the Political Economy of the Press in Asia. Singapore: Asian Media Information and Communication Centre (AMIC) and Wee Kim Wee School of Communication and Information Nanyang Technological University (WKWSCI-NTU).
Gibson-Graham, J. K. 1996. The End of Capitalism (As We Knew It). Oxford, UK: Blackwell.

------. 2006. A Postcapitalist Politics. Minneapolis: University of Minnesota Press.

Gomez, Edmund Terence. 1999. Chinese Business in Malaysia: Accumulation, Ascendance, Accommodation. Honolulu: University of Hawaii Press.

------. 2008 Enterprise Development and Interethnic Relations in Malaysia: Affirmative Action, Generational Change, and Business Partnerships. *In* Chinese Entrepreneurship in a Global Era. R. S.-K. Wong, ed., Pp. 91–116. London: Routledge.

Gomez, Edmund Terence, and Hsin-Huang Michael Hsiao, eds. 2004. Chinese Enterprise, Transnationalism, and Identity. London: Curzon/Routledge.

Gomez, Edmund Terence, and K. S. Jomo. 1997. Malaysia's Political Economy: Politics, Patronage, and Profits. Cambridge: Cambridge University Press.

Gooding-Williams, Robert. 1993. Introduction: On Being Stuck. *In* Reading Rodney King/Reading Urban Uprising. R. Gooding-Williams, ed. Pp. 1–12. New York: Routledge.

Gosling, L. A. Peter. 1983. Changing Chinese Identities in Southeast Asia: An Introductory Review. *In* The Chinese in Southeast Asia. Vol. 2. Identity, Culture, and Politics. L.A.P. Gosling and L.Y.C. Lim, eds. Pp. 1–14. Singapore: Maruzen Asia.

Gramsci, Antonio. 1971. Selections from the Prison Notebooks. Q. Hoare and G. N. Smith, transl. New York: International Publishers.

Guanghua Ribao 1978. Dashanjiao Doumugong Jiuhuangdadi xunyou shiqu; shanxin yentu mobai. (Bukit Mertajam's Doumu Temple Nine Emperor Gods travel downtown on inspection; devotees along the way kneel and worship.) Guanghua Ribao, Penang, October 10, 1978.

------. 1979a. Dashanjiao Mindang jianyi gaishan jiaotong cuoshi. (Bukit Mertajam Gerakan proposes improved traffic measures). Guanghua Ribao, Penang, September 15, 1979.

------. 1979b. Beima Loli Cheshangye Gonghui wengao fanbo Loli Siji Gonghui: qiangdiao chezhu siji youru yinchi xixi xiangguan yingai liangjie hezuo. (North Malaysian Lorry Merchants Association report refutes the Lorry Drivers Association; emphasizes that truck owners and drivers are like gums and teeth, related as close as one breath to the next, and should cooperate in a forgiving way). Guanghua Ribao, Penang, August 4, 1979.

------. 1979c. Zhengfu yi pizhun yaochiu; zhun loli tigao zaizhong, kezai jiudunzhong huowu. (The government has granted the request for an increase in overweight; nine tons of freight can be carried.) Guanghua Ribao, Penang, August 18, 1979.

------. 1979d. Chen Huangzhong sheyan weilao Weizhong wanrenyen gongzuorenyuan: Nadu Xu Pingdeng cheng Pingminhua Yiyuan shi changqi shiye, xiwang shehui rexin renshi dingli zhichi. (Tang Weetiong [pseudonym] lays out a banquet to entertain those who have worked on the Central Province Wellesley Ten-thousand Person banquet; Datuk Xu Pingdeng declares that the Pingminhua Hospital is a long-term matter, and hopes that society's enthusiastic people will support it with great strength). Guanghua Ribao, Penang, July 25, 1979.

------. 1979e. Weisheng Keshu Gonghui shiwu zhounian huiqing: Weisheng Keshu Gonghui qinghe chengli shiwu zhounian jinian, qingnianzu zhuren Xiao Mingli zai yanhuishang zhizhe huqing Dashanjiao Fudezhengshenhui zeqi tuanjie Weizhong zhuci shetuan shiming. (At the fifteenth anniversary celebration for the Province Wellesley Hakka Association: The Province Wellesley Association celebrates its establishment fifteen years ago; Youth Section Head Soo Menglai [pseudonym] at the banquet in his speech calls on the Fudezhengshen Committee to take up the mission of uniting Central Province Wellesley's Registered Associations). Guanghua Ribao, Penang, August, 1979.

——. 1979f. Wulabi Huaxiao yinyue wanhui shisanwei rexin renshi jiancai. (At the Berapit Primary School's musical evening, thirteen enthusiastic personages cut the ribbon). Guanghua Ribao, Penang, September 2, 1979.

——. 1979g. Beima Loli Cheshang Gonghui qing Zhongyuan, Cai Zhihua zhi zhengfu jing zhengshi chongjun zengjia loli zaizhong xianliang, bixu jingguo yidang shenqing, Jiaotongbu dachong you zonghui dai shenqing. (At the celebration of Zhongyuan by the North Malaysian Lorry Merchant Associations, Chua Tee Hwa [pseudonym] refers to the government's giving formal approval to an increase in weight limits; it is required that the appropriate application be made, and the Transport Ministry promises to let the association put in the applications [for others]). Guanghua Ribao, Penang, September 8, 1979.

——. 1979h. Weizhong Xiaofanshangye Gonghui yanqing chengli shisi zhounian jinian, Huizhang Zheng Ruinai bei zhengfu zai di san jingji fazhan jihua xia, neng zeng jian basha yu xiaofan zhong xin. (At the banquet celebrating the fourteenth anniversary of the founding of Province Wellesley Hawkers Association, the Head of the Association Teh Swee Nai [pseudonym] [reminds] the government that under the Third Economic Development Plan, it can increase the construction of the number of markets and hawkers' centers). Guanghua Ribao, Penang, September 11, 1979.

——. 1979i. Yao Fudezhengshen Hui chulai lingdao Dashanjiao de zhuci shetuan jianyi: Huang Xingzhi zeaize yu zhangcheng, tang xiugai jiang sangshihuo miansuodeshui quanli. (Regarding the suggestion that the Fudezhengshen Committee come out to lead Bukit Mertajam's registered associations, Ng Heng Kee [pseudonym] counters that if its bylaws are amended, this will cause the loss of giving up its tax exempt status). Guanghua Ribao, Penang, September 11, 1979.

——. 1979j. Weisheng Guanghuishao Huiguan qiuji yanhuizhong, Wei Yaji pilu Fudezhengshen Huiwu you lianghao chengjiu. (At the autumn worship banquet of Province Wellesley's Guanghuishao Huiguan, Booi Ah Keik [pseudonym] points out that the Fudezhengshen Committee's conduct has had excellent results). Guanghua Ribao, Penang, September 18, 1979.

——. 1979k. Xiao Mingli piping Huang Xingji tanhua; renwei shiying xinhuanjing shetuan keyi xiugai zhangcheng; xiwang tanxun buxuan Fudezhengshen Lishihui xinliyuan. (Soo Meng Lai [pseud.] criticizes the statement of Ng Heng Kee [pseud.]; he is of the opinion that in order to adapt to the new environment, associations can modify the bylaws; he hopes to pursue the by-election of committee members of the Fudezhengshen Managing Committee.) Guanghua Ribao, Penang, September 17, 1979, p. 5.

——. 1979l. Dashanjiao Fudezhengshen Lishihui fa wengao: Zhendui Xiao Mingli suo zhize shixiang: pouming zhenxiang yishi zhengting, qiangdiao jiang yizhao zhangcheng guiding fuzhu jiaoyu cishan shiye. (The Managing Committee of Fudezhengshen Temple publishes a report: It focuses on the matter accused [of it] by Soo Meng Lai [pseudonym], explains the true state of affairs by setting out the correct view, and emphasizes that it will act in accordance with the regulations in its bylaws to support and aid education and charity). Guanghua Ribao, Penang, September 25, 1979.

——. 1980. Dashanjiao Fudezhengshen yu Weisheng Keshu Gong Hui wuhui shijian xuangao yungshi; Shen Jiuyen zhucui zuotanhui xianyi huo jieshou. (The misunderstanding between Bukit Mertajam's Fudezhengshen and the Province Wellesley Hakka Association is declared permanently dispelled; Sim Chew Yen [pseudonym] presides over an urgent discussion and presents an argument that receives acceptance). Guanghua Ribao, Penang, January 31, 1980.

——. 1992. Dashanjiao Zheba Shilinggong shuangqing yanhui, Liang Daosheng hu huashe zhenxi congjiao ziyou fazhan quanli. (At the double celebration banquet for Sugar Cane's Shilinggong temple in Bukit Mertajam, [State Assemblyman] Leong Dao Seng calls on Chinese society to treasure religious freedom in developing its rights). Guanghua Ribao, Penang, June 29, 1992.

Gupta, Akhil, and James Ferguson. 1997. Culture, Power, Place. In Culture, Power, Place: Explorations in Critical Anthropology. A. Gupta and J. Ferguson, eds. Pp. 1–32. Durham, NC: Duke University Press.

Hall, Stuart. 1992. Cultural Studies and Its Theoretical Legacies. In Cultural Studies. L. Grossberg, C. Nelson, and P.A. Treichler, eds. Pp. 277–294. New York: Routledge.

Hanjiang Gonghui (Dashanjiao). (Hung Kung Association, Bukit Mertajam). 1965. Benhui Dagongdong AMN Zheng Shisan. (The outstanding contributions to this association by Teh Cheok Sah, AMN). In Hanjiang Gonghui Sanshiqizhounian Qingdian Tekan. (Souvenir Magazine, 37th Anniversary Celebration, Hung Kung Association of Bukit Mertajam). Bukit Mertajam, Malaysia: Hanjiang Gonghui (Dashanjiao) (Hung Kung Association, Bukit Mertajam).

Hannerz, Ulf. 1990. Cosmopolitans and Locals in World Culture. In Global Culture: Nationalism, Globalization, and Modernity. M. Featherstone, ed. Pp. 237–252. London: Sage.

Haraway, Donna. 1991. Situated Knowledges: The Science Question in Feminism and the Privilege of Partial Perspective. In Simians, Cyborgs, and Women: The Reinvention of Nature. D. Haraway, ed. Pp. 183–202. New York: Routledge.

Harper, T. N. 1999. The End of Empire and the Making of Malaya. Cambridge: Cambridge University Press.

Harvey, David. 1989. The Condition of Postmodernity. Oxford, UK: Basil Blackwell.

Hebdige, Dick. 1979. Subculture: The Meaning of Style. London: Methuen.

Heng, Pek Koon. 1996. Chinese Responses to Malay Hegemony in Peninsular Malaysia, 1957–96. Southeast Asian Studies 34(3):500–522.

Hirschman, Albert O. 1970. Exit, Voice, and Loyalty: Responses to Decline in Firms, Organizations, and States. Cambridge, Ma: Harvard University Press.

——. 1977. The Passions and the Interests: Political Arguments for Capitalism before Its Triumph. Princeton, NJ: Princeton University Press.

Hiscock, Geoff. 2000. Asia's Wealth Club: Who's Really Who in Business—The Top 100 Billionaires in Asia. London: Nicholas Brealey.

Ho, Khai Leong. 1992. Dynamics of Policymaking in Malaysia: the Formulation of the New Economic Policy and the National Development Policy. Asian Journal of Public Administration 14(2):204–227.

——. 2012. At a Crossroads: Malaysia's Coalition Politics and Chinese-based Political Parties. In Malaysian Chinese: Recent Developments and Prospects. L. Suyadinata, ed. pp. 70–85. Singapore: Institute of Southeast Asian Studies.

Hock Teik Cheng Sin Temple (Fudezhengshen Temple). 1986. Commemorative Book, 100th Anniversary. Bukit Mertajam: Bukit Mertajam Fudezhengshen Temple.

——. 2007. Dashanjiao Fudezhengshenhui yibaiershi zhounian jinian (Commemoration of the 120th anniversary of the Bukit Mertajam Fudezhengshen Temple). Bukit Mertajam: Hock Teik Cheng Sin Temple (Fudezhengshen Temple).

Hokkien Hoay Kuan, Seberang Perai. 1976. Majallah Cenderamata Jubli Emas Hokkien Hoay Kuan (Golden Anniversary Memorial Book of the Hokkien Hoay Kuan). Bukit Mertajam: Hokkien Hoay Kuan, Seberang Perai.

Holston, James. 1989. The Modernist City: An Anthropological Critique of Brasilia. Chicago: University of Chicago Press.

Hooker, M. B. 1969. The Relationship between Chinese Law and Common Law in Malaysia, Singapore, and Hong Kong. Journal of Asian Studies 28(4): 723–742.

Hsing, You-tien. 1997. Building Guanxi across the Straits: Taiwanese Capital and Local Chinese Bureaucrats. *In* Ungrounded Empires: The Cultural Politics of Modern Chinese Transnationalism. A. Ong and D. Nonini, eds. Pp. 143–166. New York: Routledge.

Jabatan Perangkaan (Department of Statistics) Malaysia. 1986. Laporan Penduduk Kawasan Pihak Berkuasa Tempatan : Umur, Keturunan, Jantina, Isirumah, Aktiviti Ekonomi, Pelajaran. (Population report for local authority areas; age, ethnicity, sex, households, economic activity, education). Kuala Lumpur: Jabatan Perangkaan (Department of Statistics) Malaysia.

Jay, Martin. 1993. Downcast Eyes: The Denigration of Vision in Twentieth-Century French Thought. Berkeley: University of California Press.

Jesudason, James V. 1999. The Resilience of One-Party Dominance in Malaysia and Singapore. *In* The Awkward Embrace: One-Party Domination and Democracy. Herman Giliomee and Charles Simkins, eds., pp. 127–172. Australia: Harwood Academic.

Jomo, K. S., and Patricia Todd. 1994. Trade Unions and the State in Peninsular Malaysia. Kuala Lumpur: Oxford University Press.

Kahn, Joel S. 1995. Culture, Multiculture, Postculture. London: Sage.

Kahn, Joel S. 2006. Other Malays: Nationalism and Cosmopolitanism in the Modern Malay World. Honolulu: Asian Studies Association of Australia in association with University of Hawaii Press.

Kahn, Joel S., and Josep R. Llobera. 1981. The Anthropology of Pre-capitalist Societies. London: Macmillan.

Kassim, Ismail. 1978. The Politics of Accommodation: An Analysis of the 1978 Malaysian General Election. Singapore: Institute of Southeast Asian Studies.

Kessler, Clive S. 1978. Islam and Politics in a Malay State, Kelantan, 1838–1969. Ithaca: Cornell University Press.

Khoo, S. H. 1966. Bukit Mertajam—A Survey. Geographica 2:n.p.

Khoo, Teik Huat. 1986. 1980 Banci Penduduk Dan Perumahan Malaysia: Laporan Penduduk Kawasan Pihak Berkuasa Tempatan: Umur Keturunan Jantina Isirumah Aktiviti Ekonomi Pelajaran. (1980 population and housing census of Malaysia: Population Report for local authority areas: age ethnicity sex households economic activity education.). T. H. Khoo, ed. Kuala Lumpur: Jabatan Perangkaan (Department of Statistics) Malaysia.

Krais, Beate. 1993. Gender and Symbolic Violence: Female Oppression in the Light of Pierre Bourdieu's Theory of Social Practice. *In* Bourdieu: Critical Perspectives. C. Calhoun, E. LiPuma, and M. Postone, eds. Pp. 156–178. Chicago: University of Chicago Press.

Kua, Kia Soong. 2008. Racial Conflict in Malaysia: Against the Official History. Race & Class 49(3): 33–53.

Kuhn, Philip A. 1997. The Homeland: Thinking about the History of Chinese Overseas. Canberra: Australian National University.

Kwong, Peter. 1994a. Wake of the Golden Venture: China's Human Traffickers. The Nation October 17:422–425.

——. 1994b. The Wages of Fear: Undocumented and Unwanted, Fuzhounese Immigrants Are Changing the Face of Chinatown. *In* Village Voice.

Laclau, Ernesto, and Chantal Mouffe. 1985. Hegemony and Socialist Strategy: Toward a Radical Democratic Politics. London: Verso.

Lee, Ching Kwan. 2007. Against the Law: Labor Protests in China's Rustbelt and Sunbelt. Berkeley: University of California Press.

Lefebvre, Henri. 1974. The Production of Space. Oxford, UK: Basil Blackwell.

Lent, John. 1976. Guided Press in Southeast Asia: National Development vs. Freedom of Expression. Buffalo: Council on International Studies, State University of New York, Buffalo.

——, ed. 1978. Broadcasting in Asia and the Pacific: A Continental Survey of Radio and Television. Philadelphia, PA: Temple University Press.

——. 1982. Newspapers in Asia: Contemporary Trends and Problems. Hong Kong: Heinemann Asia.

Lever-Tracy, Constance, David Ip, and Noel Tracy. 1996. The Chinese Diaspora and Mainland China. New York: St. Martin's Press.

Lie, John. 1994. The "Problem" of Foreign Workers in Contemporary Japan. Bulletin of Concerned Asian Scholars 26(3):3–11.

Lim, Linda Y. C., and L. A. Peter Gosling, eds. 1983. The Chinese in Southeast Asia. Singapore: Maruzen Asia.

Lim, Mah Hui. 1983. The Ownership and Control of Large Corporations in Malaysia: The Role of Chinese Businessmen. *In* The Chinese in Southeast Asia. Vol. 1. Identity, Culture and Politics. L. Y. C. Lim and L. A. P. Gosling, eds. Pp. 275–315. Singapore: Maruzen Asia.

——. 1985. Contradictions in the Development of Malay Capital: State, Accumulation, and Legitimation. Journal of Contemporary Asia 15(1):37–63.

Loh, Francis Kok Wah. 1980. Beyond the Tin Mines: The Political Economy of Chinese Squatter Farms in the Kinta New Villages, Malaysia. Ph.D. diss., Cornell University.

——. 1982. The Politics of Chinese Unity in Malaysia: Reform and Conflict in the Malaysian Chinese Association, 1971–1973. Singapore: Maruzen Asia.

——. 1988. Beyond the Tin Mines: Coolies, Squatters, and New Villagers in the Kinta Valley, Malaysia, c. 1880–1980. Singapore: Oxford University Press.

——. 2001. Where Has (Ethnic) Politics Gone? The Case of the BN Non-Malay Politicians and Political Parties. *In* The Politics of Multiculturalism: Pluralism and Citizenship in Malaysia, Singapore, and Indonesia. R. W. Hefner, ed., pp. 183–203. Honolulu: University of Hawaii Press.

Loh, Francis Kok Wah, and Boo Teik Khoo, eds. 2002. Democracy in Malaysia: Discourses and Practices. Richmond, UK: Curzon.

Loh, Francis Kok Wah, and Johan Saravannamuttu, eds. 2003. New Politics in Malaysia. Singapore: Institute of Southeast Asian Studies.

Lyotard, Jean-Francois. 1984. The Postmodern Condition: A Report on Knowledge. Minneapolis: University of Minnesota Press.

Mahathir bin Mohamad. 2008 [1970]. The Malay Dilemma: With a New Preface. Singapore: Marshall Cavendish Editions.

Malaysia, Government of. 1979. Mid-Term Review of the Third Malaysia Plan, 1976–1980. Kuala Lumpur: Government Printers Office.

Marcus, George E., and Michael M. J. Fischer, eds. 1986. Anthropology as Cultural Critique: An Experimental Moment in the Human Sciences. Chicago: University of Chicago Press.

Marx, Karl. 1963 [1852]. The Eighteenth Brumaire of Louis Bonaparte. New York: International Publishers.

——. 1976 [1867]. Capital: A Critique of Political Economy. Vol. 1. B. Fowkes, transl. New York: Penguin Books.

Marx, Karl, and Frederick Engels. 1970. The German Ideology, Part One. C.J. Arthur, ed. New York: International Publishers.

Massey, Doreen B., et al. 1999. City Worlds. London: Routledge, in association with the Open University.

Mellström, Ulf. 2003. Masculinity, Power and Technology: A Malaysian Ethnography. Aldershot, UK: Ashgate.

Miles, Lilian, and Richard Croucher. 2013. Gramsci, Counter Hegemony, and Labor Union-Civil Society Organization Coalitions in Malaysia. Journal of Contemporary Asia 43(3):413–427.

Milne, R. S., and Diane K. Mauzy. 1977. Politics and Government in Malaysia. Singapore: Federal Publications.

Ministry of Higher Education Malaysia. 2008. Jadual 5.1: Bilangan Pelajar Malaysia di Luar Negara, Jumlah, Tahun 2002–7 (Table 5.1: Number of Malaysian students overseas, total, years 2002–7), Vol. 2012.

Mintz, Sidney. 1985. Sweetness and Power: The Place of Sugar in Modern History. New York: Penguin.

Morgan, Michael. 1977. The Rise and Fall of Malayan Trade Unionism, 1945–50. In Malaya: The Making of a Neocolony. M. Amin and M. Caldwell, eds. Pp. 150–198. Nottingham, UK: Spokesman.

Mukherjee, Hena. 2010. Access to and Equity in Higher Education—Malaysia. Washington, DC: The World Bank.

Mullard, Chris, and Martin Brennan. 1978. The Malaysian Predicament: Towards a New Theoretical Frontier. Journal of Contemporary Asia 8(3):341–354.

Mulvey, Laura. 1994. Visual Pleasure and Narrative Cinema. In Movies and Methods. B. Nichols, ed. Pp. 303–315. Vol. 2. Berkeley: University of California Press.

Munro-Kua, Anne. 1996. Authoritarian Populism in Malaysia. New York: St. Martin's Press.

Nagata, Judith A. 1975a. Introduction. In Pluralism in Malaysia: Myth and Reality. A Symposium on Singapore and Malaysia. J. A. Nagata, ed. Pp. 1–16. Leiden: Brill.

——. 1975b. Perceptions of Social Inequality in Malaysia. In Pluralism in Malaysia. Nagata, ed. Pp. 113–136. Leiden: Brill.

——. 1976. The Status of Ethnicity and the Ethnicity of Status: Ethnic and Class Identity in Malaysia and Latin America. International Journal of Comparative Sociology 17(3–4):242–260.

Nash, June. 1979. We Eat the Mines and the Mines Eat Us: Dependency and Exploitation in Bolivian Tin Mines. New York: Columbia University Press.

Nelson, Cary, and Lawrence Grossberg. 1988. Marxism and the Interpretation of Culture. Urbana: University of Illinois Press.

Newell, William H. 1962. Treacherous River: A Study of Rural Chinese in North Malaya. Kuala Lumpur: University of Malaya.

Nonini, Donald M. 1979. The Mysteries of Capital Accumulation: Honoring the Gods and Gambling among Chinese in a Malaysian Market Town. In First International Symposium on Asian Studies. Vol. 3. Southeast Asia. Pp. 701–710, Hong Kong: Asian Research Service.

——. 1983a. The Chinese Community of a West Malaysian Market Town: A Study in Political Economy. Ph.D. Diss., Stanford University.

——. 1983b. The Chinese Truck Transport "Industry" of a Peninsular Malaysian Market Town. In The Chinese in Southeast Asia. Vol. 1. Ethnicity and Economic Activity. L. A. P. Gosling and L. Y. C. Lim, eds. Pp. 171–206. Singapore: Maruzen Asia.

——. 1987. Some Reflections on "Entrepreneurship" and the Chinese Community of a West Malaysian Market Town. Ethnos 52(3–4):350–367.

——. 1992. British Colonial Rule and Malay Peasant Resistance, 1900–1957. New Haven, CT: Yale University Southeast Asia Monographs 38.

———. 1993. Popular Sources of Chinese Labor Militancy in Colonial Malaya. *In* The Politics of Immigrant Workers: Labor Activism and Migration in the World Economy since 1830. C. Guerin-Gonzales and C. Strikwerda, eds. Pp. 215–244. New York: Holmes and Meier.

———. 1997. Shifting Identities, Positioned Imaginaries: Transnational Traversals and Reversals by Malaysian Chinese. *In* Ungrounded Empires: The Cultural Politics of Modern Chinese Transnationalism. A. Ong and D. Nonini, eds. Pp. 204–228. New York: Routledge.

———. 1999. The Dialectics of "Disputatiousness" and "Rice-eating Money": Class Confrontation and Gendered Imaginaries among Chinese Men in Peninsular Malaysia. American Ethnologist 26(1):46–68.

———. 2003. All Are Flexible, but Some Are More Flexible than Others: Small-Scale Chinese Businesses in Malaysia. *In* Ethnic Business: Chinese Capitalism in Southeast Asia. K. S. Jomo and B. C. Folke, eds. Pp. 73–91. Routledge/Curzon Studies in the Growth Economies of Asia. Vol. 50. New York: Routledge/Curzon.

———. 2013. Critical Structural Realism and Anthropologists' (Encounters with) Recalcitrance and Failure. Paper presented for the panel, Critical Structural Realism in the Study of Power: Building on the Work of Stephen Reyna, Annual Meeting of the American Anthropological Association, Chicago Illinois, November 22, 2013.

Nonini, Donald M., and Aihwa Ong. 1997. Introduction: Chinese Transnationalism as an Alternative Modernity, with Prefaces to Parts 1–4. *In* Ungrounded Empires: The Cultural Politics of Modern Chinese Transnationalism. A. Ong and D. Nonini, eds. Pp. 3–33, 37–38, 89–90, 167–169, 259. New York: Routledge.

Nonini, Donald M., and Arlene A. Teraoka. 1992. Class Struggle in the Squared Circle: Professional Wrestling as Working-Class Sport. *In* Dialectical Anthropology: Essays in Honor of Stanley Diamond. Vol. 2. The Politics of Culture and Creativity. C. W. Gailey, ed. Pp. 147–168. Gainesville: University Press of Florida.

Norman, Jerry. 1991. The Min Dialects in Historical Perspective. *In* Languages and Dialects of China. W. S.-Y. Wang, ed. Pp. 325–360, Journal of Chinese Linguistics, Monograph Series 3. Berkeley, CA: Project on Linguistic Analysis.

Olsen, Stephen M. 1972. The Inculcation of Economic Values in Taipei Business Families. *In* Economic Organization in Chinese Society. W. E. Willmot, ed. Pp. 261–296. Stanford, CA: Stanford.

Omohundro, John T. 1981. Chinese Merchant Families in Iloilo = [Shang chia]: Commerce and Kin in a Central Philippine City. Quezon City, Philippines: Ateneo de Manila University Press.

Ong, Aihwa. 1991. The Gender and Labor Politics of Postmodernity. Annual Review of Anthropology 20:279–309.

———. 1999. Flexible Citizenship: The Cultural Logics of Transnationality. Durham, NC: Duke University Press.

Ong, Aihwa, and Donald M. Nonini, eds. 1997. Ungrounded Empires: The Cultural Politics of Modern Chinese Transnationalism. New York: Routledge.

Ong, Hock Chuan. 1985. Fight Is Fierce in the Lorry Industry. *In* The Sunday Star. Penang, Malaysia.

Orrú, Marco, Nicole Woolsey Biggart, and Gary G. Hamilton. 1997. The Economic Organization of East Asian Capitalism. Thousand Oaks, CA: Sage.

Ortner, S. B. 1984. Theory in Anthropology since the 60s. Comparative Studies in Society and History 26(1):126–166.

Oxfeld, Ellen. 1993. Blood, Sweat, and Mahjong: Family and Enterprise in an Overseas Chinese Community. Ithaca: Cornell University Press.

Page, Helan. E. 1988. Dialogic Principles of Interactive Learning in the Ethnographic Relationship. Journal of Anthropological Research 44(2):163–181.

Pan, Lynn. 1994. Sons of the Yellow Emperor: A History of the Chinese Diaspora. New York: Kodansha International.

Peña, Devon Gerardo. 1997. The Terror of the Machine: Technology, Work, Gender, and Ecology on the U.S.-Mexico Border. Austin, TX: Center for Mexican American Studies University of Texas at Austin.

Pepinsky, Thomas B. 2009. The 2008 Malaysian Elections: An End to Ethnic Politics? Journal of East Asian Studies 9:87–120.

Pinches, Michael. 1999. Cultural Relations, Class, and the New Rich of Asia. In Culture and Privilege in Capitalist Asia. M. Pinches, ed. Pp. 1–55. London: Routledge.

Puthucheary, James. 1960. Ownership and Control in the Malayan Economy. Singapore: by D. Moore for Eastern Universities Press.

Rabinow, Paul. 1989. French Modern: Norms and Forms of the Social Environment. Cambridge, MA: MIT Press.

Ramachandran, Selvakumaran. 1994. Indian Plantation Labour in Malaysia. Kuala Lumpur: Abdul Majid for Institute of Social Analysis.

Ramasamy, Nagaih, and Chris Rowley. 2008. Trade Unions in Malaysia: Complexity of a State-Employer System. In Trade Unions in Asia: An Economic and Social Analysis, J. Benson and Y. Zhu, pp. 121–138. Milton Park, UK: Routledge.

Ramasamy, Palanisamy. 1994. Plantation Labour, Unions, Capital, and the State in Peninsular Malaysia. Kuala Lumpur: Oxford University Press.

Ramsey, S. Robert. 1987. The Languages of China. Princeton, NJ: Princeton University Press.

Redding, S. Gordon. 1990. Spirit of Chinese Capitalism. Berlin: Walter De Gruyter.

Reinknecht, Gottfried. 1979. The Hakka and Their Region. In Chinese Regionalism in West-Malaysia and Singapore. W. Moese, G. Reinknecht, and E. Schmitz-Seiber, eds. Pp. 69–93. Hamburg: Mitteilungen 77, Gesellschaft fur Natur- und Volkerkunde Ostasiens e. V.

Robison, Richard, and David S. G. Goodman, eds. 1996. The New Rich in Asia: Mobile Phones, McDonalds, and Middle-Class Revolution. London: Routledge.

Roseberry, William. 1989. Balinese Cockfights and the Seductions of Anthropology. In Anthropologies and Histories: Essays in Culture, History, and Political Economy. W. Roseberry, ed. Pp. 17–29. New Brunswick: Rutgers University Press.

Rouse, Roger. 1995. Questions of Identity: Personhood and Collectivity in Transnational Migration to the United States. Critique of Anthropology 15(4):351–380.

Ryle, Gilbert. 1949. The Concept of Mind. New York: Barnes and Noble.

Sandhu, Kernial Singh. 1964a. Emergency Resettlement in Malaya. Journal of Tropical Geography 18:157–183.

——. 1964b. The Saga of the "Squatter" in Malaya: A Preliminary Survey of the Causes, Characteristics and Consequences of the Resettlement of Rural Dwellers during the Emergency between 1948 and 1960. Journal of Southeast Asian History 5:143–177.

Scott, James C. 1985. Weapons of the Weak: Everyday Forms of Peasant Resistance. New Haven, CT: Yale University Press.

——. 1990. Domination and the Arts of Resistance: Hidden Transcripts. New Haven, CT: Yale University Press.

——. 1998. Seeing Like a State: How Certain Schemes to Improve the Human Condition Have Failed. New Haven, CT: Yale University Press.

Seddon, David. 1978. Relations of Production: Marxist Approaches to Economic Anthropology. London: Cass.

Shimada, Haruo. 1994. Japan's Guest Workers: Issues and Public Policies. New York: Columbia University Press, with University of Tokyo Press.

Short, Anthony. 1975. The Communist Insurrection in Malaya, 1948–1960. London: F. Muller.

Shukor, Rahman. 1997. Tough Times during Emergency Period. *In* New Straits Times Kuala Lumpur, Malaysia.

Siaw, Laurence K. L. 1983. Chinese Society in Rural Malaysia: A Local History of the Chinese in Titi, Jelebu. Kuala Lumpur: Oxford University Press.

Sider, Gerald M. 1997. Against Experience: The Struggles for History, Tradition and Hope among a Native American People. *In* Between History and Histories: The Making of Silences and Commemorations. Pp. 62–80. G. Silder and G. Smith, eds. Toronto: University of Toronto Press.

——. 2003. Between History and Tomorrow: Making and Breaking Everyday Life in Rural Newfoundland. Peterborough, Ontario, Canada: Broadview Press.

——. 2006. Anthropology and History: Opening Points for a New Synthesis. *In* Critical Junctions: Anthropology and History beyond the Cultural Turn. D. Kalb and H. Tak, eds. Pp. 168–176. New York: Berghahn Books.

Sider, Gerald M., and Gavin A. Smith. 1997. Between History and Histories: The Making of Silences and Commemorations. Toronto: University of Toronto Press.

Simoniya, N. A. 1961. Overseas Chinese in Southeast Asia—A Russian Study. Ithaca: Cornell University, Department of Far Eastern Studies, Southeast Asia Program, Data Papers No. 45.

Siraj, Mehrun. 1994. Women and the Law: Significant Developments in Malaysia. Law and Society Review 28(3):561–572.

Skinner, G. William. 1957. Chinese Society in Thailand: An Analytical History. Ithaca: Cornell University Press.

——. 1958. Leadership and Power in the Chinese Community in Thailand. Ithaca: Cornell.

——. 1960. Change and Persistence in Chinese Culture Overseas: A Comparison of Thailand and Jav. Singapore: Nan-yang Hsüeh Hui.

——. 1965. Marketing and Social Structure in Rural China (Parts I, II and III). Tucson, AZ: Association for Asian Studies.

——. 1968. Overseas Chinese Leadership: Paradigm for a Paradox. *In* Leadership and Authority. G. Wijeyewardene, ed. Pp. 191–207. Singapore: University of Malaya.

——. 1996. Creolized Chinese Societies in Southeast Asia. *In* Sojourners and Settlers: Histories of Southeast Asia and the Chinese. A. Reid, ed. Pp. 51–93. St. Leonards, Australia: Asian Studies Association of Australia/Allen & Unwin.

Smart, Alan. 1999. Predatory Rule and Illegal Economic Practices. *In* States and Illegal Practices. J. M. Heyman, ed. Pp. 99–128. Oxford, UK: Berg.

Smart, Alan, and Josiah McC. Heyman. 1999. Introduction. *In* States and Illegal Practices. J. M. Heyman, ed. Pp. 1–24. Oxford, UK: Berg.

Smart, Alan, and Josephine Smart. 2005. Petty Capitalists and Globalization: Flexibility, Entrepreneurship, and Economic Development. Albany: State University of New York Press.

Smart, Josephine, and Alan Smart. 1999. Personal Relations and Divergent Economies: A Case Study of Hong Kong Investment in South China. *In* Theorizing the City: The New Urban Anthropology Reader. S. M. Low, ed. Pp. 169–200. New Brunswick, NJ: Rutgers University Press.

Smith, Carol A. 1976. Regional Economic Systems: Linking Geographical Models and Socioeconomic Problems. *In* Regional Analysis: Vol. 1, Economic Systems. C. A. Smith, ed. Pp. 3–63. New York: Academic Press.

Smith, Gavin A. 1999. Confronting the Present: Towards a Politically Engaged Anthro-
    pology. Oxford, UK: Berg.
Spivak, Gyatri Chakravorty. 1987. Scattered Speculations on the Question of Value. *In*
    In Other Worlds: Essays in Cultural Politics. Pp. 154–178. New York: Methuen.
Star, The. 1992. Rise in Illegal Malaysian Workers in Taiwan. Penang, Malaysia.
Stenson, Michael R. 1970. Industrial Conflict in Malaya: Prelude to the Communist
    Revolt of 1948. New York: Oxford University Press.
———. 1980. Class, Race, and Colonialism in West Malaysia: The Indian Case. Vancou-
    ver: University of British Columbia Press.
Stockard, Janice E. 1989. Daughters of the Canton Delta: Marriage Patterns and Eco-
    nomic Strategies in South China, 1860–1930. Stanford, CA: Stanford University
    Press.
Stockwell, A. J. 1984. British Imperial Policy and Decolonization in Malaya,
    1942–1952. Journal of Imperial and Commonwealth History 13(1):68–87.
Strauch, Judith V. 1981. Chinese Village Politics in the Malaysian State. Cambridge,
    MA: Harvard University Press.
———. 1984. Women in Rural-Urban Circulation Networks: Implications for Social
    Structural Change. *In* Women in the Cities of Asia: Migration and Urban Adap-
    tation. J. T. Fawcett, S.-E. Khoo et al., eds. Pp. 60–80. Boulder, CO: Westview
    Press.
Sun, Yat-sen, Frank W. Price, and Li-ting Chen. 1953 [1927]. San Min Chu I (The three
    principles of the people). Taipei: China Cultural Service.
Tan, E. K. B. 2001. From Sojourners to Citizens: Managing the Ethnic Chinese Minor-
    ity in Indonesia and Malaysia. Ethnic and Racial Studies 24(6):949–978.
Tan, Liok Ee. 1988. The Rhetoric of Bangsa and Minzu: Community and Nation in
    Tension, the Malay Peninsula, 1900–1955. *In* Working Papers, Center of South-
    east Asian Studies, Paper No. 52. Clayton, Australia: Monash University.
Taussig, Michael T. 1980. The Devil and Commodity Fetishism in South Africa. Cha-
    pel Hill, NC: University of North Carolina Press.
Thomas, Mathews. 2004. Is Malaysia's Mykad the One Card to Rule Them All—The
    Urgent Need to Develop a Proper Legal Framework for the Protection of Per-
    sonal Information in Malaysia. Melbourne University Law Review 28(474).
Thompson, E. P. 1963. The Making of the English Working Class. New York: Vintage
    Books.
———. 1967. Time, Work-Discipline, and Industrial Capitalism. Past and Present
    38:56–97.
———. 1978. Eighteenth-Century English Society: Class Struggle without Class? Social
    History 3:133–165.
Thompson, John. 1995. The Media and Modernity: A Social Theory of the Media.
    Stanford, CA: Stanford University Press.
Toh, Kin Woon. 2003. Machang Bubok: Changes in Voting Patterns, 1995–99. *In* New
    Politics in Malaysia. F. K-W. Loh, ed. Pp. 141–157. Singapore: Institute for
    Southeast Asian Studies.
Trocki, Carl. 1997. Boundaries and Transgressions: Chinese Enterprise in Eighteenth-
    and Nineteenth-Century Southeast Asia. *In* Ungrounded Empires: The Cultural
    Politics of Modern Chinese Transnationalism. A. Ong and D. Nonini, eds.
    Pp. 61–88. New York: Routledge.
Vasil, R. K. 1971. Politics in a Plural Society: A Study of Non-communal Political Par-
    ties in West Malaysia. New York: Oxford University Press, with Australian Insti-
    tute of International Affairs.
Vertovec, Steven, and Robin Cohen. 1999. Introduction. *In* Migration, Diasporas, and
    Transnationalism. S. Vertovec and R. Cohen, eds. Pp. xiii–xxviii. International
    Library of Studies on Migration. Cheltenham, UK: Edward Elgar.

Von Vorys, Karl. 1975. Democracy without Consensus: Communalism and Political Stability in Malaysia. Princeton, NJ: Princeton University Press.

Wang, Gungwu. 1981. Community and Nation: Essays on Southeast Asia and the Chinese. Singapore: Heinemann Educational Books Asia and Asian Studies Association of Australia.

———. 1991. Among Non-Chinese. Daedalus 120(2):135–158.

———. 2000. The Chinese Overseas: From Earthbound China to the Quest for Autonomy. Cambridge, MA: Harvard University Press.

Weidenbaum, Murray L., and Samuel Hughes. 1996. The Bamboo Network: How Expatriate Chinese Entrepreneurs Are Creating a New Economic Superpower in Asia. New York: Martin Kessler Books.

Weiss, Meredith. 2013. Malaysia's 13th General Elections: Same Result, Different Outcome. Asian Survey 53(6):1135–1158.

Weston, Kath. 1990. Production as Means, Production as Metaphor: Women's Struggle to Enter the Trades. In Uncertain Terms: Negotiating Gender in American Culture. F. Ginsburg and A. L. Tsing, eds. Pp. 137–151. Boston: Beacon Press.

Whitley, Richard. 1992. Business Systems in East Asia: Firms, Markets, and Societies. London: Sage.

Williams, B. F. 1989. A Class Act—Anthropology and the Race to Nation across Ethnic Terrain. Annual Review of Anthropology 18:401–444.

Williams, Raymond. 1977. Marxism and Literature. Oxford, UK: Oxford University Press.

Willis, Paul. 1981. Learning to Labor: How Working Class Kids Get Working-Class Jobs. New York: Columbia University Press.

Willmott, Donald E. 1960. The Chinese of Semarang: a Changing Minority Community in Indonesia. Ithaca: Cornell University Press.

Willmott, W. E. 1967. The Chinese in Cambodia. Vancouver: University of British Columbia Publications Center.

———. 1970. The Political Structure of the Chinese Community in Cambodia. London: Athlone Press.

Winichakul, Thongchai. 1994. Siam Mapped: A History of the Geo-Body of a Nation. Honolulu: University of Hawaii Press.

Wittgenstein, Ludwig. 1933. Tractatus Logico-philosophicus. Reprinted, with a few corrections. New York: Harcourt Brace.

———. 1958. Philosophical Investigations. G. E. M. Anscombe, transl. Cambridge: Cambridge University Press.

Wolf, Eric. 1982. Europe and the People without History. Berkeley: University of California Press.

Wong, Chin Huat. 2009. MCA's Irrelevant Civil War. In The Nut Graph. Available at http://www.thenutgraph.com/mcas-irrelevant-civil-war/print.

Wong, Raymond Sin-Kwok, ed. 2008. Chinese Entrepreneurship in a Global Era. London: Routledge.

Wu, Baijia. 1985. Jianzhu Baogao: Dashanjiao Fudezhengshen Miao Chengli Baizhounian; Jinian ji Xinhuisuo Chengqingdian Tekan (Building Report: Special Supplement to commemorate the 100th anniversary of the Bukit Mertajam Fudezhengshen Temple and of the celebration of the opening of the new committee hall). Xingbin Ribao, Penang, September 15, 1995.

Xingbin Ribao. 1978. Fanma Loli Cheshangzonghui zhuxi chengqing: Loli mingqi zaifei zhangjia meidun buyu erjiao, liyou wujiagaozhang kaixiaoda yu renwei zunan. (Chairman of the Pan-Malaysian Lorry Merchant's Association clarifies: lorry transport charges beginning next year will go up no more than twenty cents; justification is high expenses due to price increases and man-made obstacles.) Xingbin Ribao, Penang, December 31, 1978.

——. 1979a. Dashanjiao zuori kaishi qingzhu Yulanshenghui; yilian yenxi shiqitian. (Bukit Mertajam yesterday started the celebration of Yulanshenghui; opera will be performed for seventeen consecutive days.) Xingbin Ribao, Penang, August 28, 1979.

——. 1979b. Beima Loli Siji Gonghui wengao zhendui loli yunzai chaozhong, jing jiaguo zai siji shenshang, hu quanye tuanjie zhengqie shen liyi. (Northern Malaysian Lorry Drivers Association aims at lorry transport overloads when the blame falls on the driver, and calls on everyone to unite to strive urgently for their [drivers'] benefit). Xingbin Ribao, Penang, January 9, 1979.

——. 1979c. Beima Loli Cheshang Gong Hui wei jiaqiang zuzhi, sheli Jipo fenhui. (North Malaysian Lorry Merchants Association, in order to strengthen its organization, establishes a Kuala Lumpur branch). Xingbin Ribao, Penang, February 21, 1979.

——. 1979d. Beima Loli Siji Gonghui fabiao wengao huxu Fanma Loli Chezhu Zonghui Beima Cheshang Gonghui guanzhu yueshu shuxia chezhu huiyuan buyao zhishi siji yunzai chaozong. (North Malaysian Lorry Drivers Association publishes a report calling on the Pan-Malaysian Lorry Owners Association and the North Malaysian Lorry Merchant Association to take care to restrain their owner members to not instigate drivers to carry overloads). Xingbin Ribao, Penang, March 13, 1979.

——. 1979e. Beima Loli Siji Gonghui fabiao wengao judian bochi Beima Loli Cheshang Gonghui. (The North Malaysian Lorry Drivers Association refutes the North Malaysian Lorry Merchants Association point by point). Xingbin Ribao, Penang, August 15, 1979.

——. 1980a. Beimai Loli Siji Gonghui wuyue yiri changnian dahui jiangshang loli siji miandui wenti. (The North Malaysian Lorry Drivers Association holds its annual meeting on May 1 to discuss problems facing truck drivers). Penang.

——. 1980b. Dashanjiao Zheba Shilinggong dingqi qing Lushanshigong ji zhongshen baodan qianqiu. (Shilinggong Temple in sugar cane, Bukit Mertajam, schedules the celebration of the birthday of Lushanshigong and numerous gods.) Penang, July 3, 1980.

Xingzhou Ribao. 1992. Tong shi tianya tiaofeijiren. (All are faraway airplane jumpers). Petaling Jaya, Malaysia.

——. 2007. Dashanjiao saomiao: Weisheng boai julebu juan jin sanqian yu silianzong. (Bukit Mertajam scan: Fraternal Club of Province Wellesley donates almost three thousand to charitable friendship association.) Sidebar. Petaling Jaya, June 26, 2007.

Xu, Wurong (Hsü Wu-Jung). 1951. Malaiya Chaoqiao Yinxiangji. (Notes on impressions of Teochews in Malaya). Singapore: Nanyang Bookstore Company.

Yao, Souchou. 1987. The Fetish of Relationships: Chinese Business Transactions in Singapore. Sojourn 2(1):89–111.

——. 2002. Confucian Capitalism: Discourse, Practice and the Myth of Chinese Enterprise. London: Routledge Curzon.

Yeung, Henry Wai-Chung. 2004. Chinese Capitalism in a Global Era: Towards Hybrid Capitalism. New York: Routledge.

Yeung, Henry Wai-Chung, and Kris Olds, eds. 2000. Globalization of Chinese Business Firms. New York: St. Martin's Press.

Yong, K. H. 2006. Silences in History and Nation-State: Reluctant Accounts of the Cold War in Sarawak. American Ethnologist 33(3):462–473.

Index

economic growth, 73, 215, 218, 222–27
passim, 237, 287, 313–14n9; conventional
wisdom, 2, 6. *See also* industrial growth
economic recession. *See* recession
economy, moral. *See* moral economy
education, 72, 91, 204–5; classical, 4, 90, 129,
130, 166, 204, 238; women's, 270. *See also*
higher education; high schools; primary
schools; technical institutes
elections, 122, 138, 143, 148, 187, 215, 222–26
passim, 314–15n6
elite. *See* upper class
embodied pedagogies, 20, 24, 133, 172–74
Emergency, 1948–60. *See* Malayan Emergency,
1948–60
emigration, 184, 244. *See also* labor sojourns
Engels, Friedrich, 174
English language, 54, 91, 238
English-language schools and universities, 205,
224, 238, 267, 268, 271
ethnically discriminatory quotas. *See* quotas,
ethnically discriminatory
ethnicity, 9–19 passim, 38, 47, 166, 216, 260;
coffee shop sorting by, 246; on identity card,
27. *See also* alliances, cross-ethnic
ethnic violence, 72. *See also* riots: Kuala
Lumpur, 1969
eviction, 124, 229, 240–42 passim
expatriation, 52, 267, 285. *See also*
transnational mobility and traversal
export-oriented industrialization, 54, 67,
73–74, 136, 215, 222–27 passim, 235, 236,
287, 313–14n9
export processing zones, 122, 127, 223, 224,
247, 263, 288, 289; Penang state, 54, 74, 259,
314n9; transportation, 314n1

Faaland, Just, 321n1
Fabian, Johannes, 174
factories and factory work, 63–66, 288, 289,
294–95, 303–4; transportation, 223, 314n1.
See also export processing zones; garment
industry
family businesses and labor, 77, 84, 93–94, 268,
274, 301, 304
farmers, Malay. *See* Malay farmers
feminist theory, 7–8, 18, 132
Ferguson, James, 18–19
Festival of the Hungry Ghosts
(Yulanshenghui), 78–81, 131, 134, 252–55
festivals. *See* Catholic festivals; Daoist/
Buddhist festivals
feudal titles. *See* titles of nobility

films and video, 237, 259, 260, 264, 281
financial crisis, 213, 215, 218–19, 223–27
passim, 264, 287, 289
fish trade, 61, 62, 68, 103, 105, 144–45, 168, 171
food industry and trade, 61, 62, 67, 68, 76,
89, 98; city square use, 240; role in Daoist
festival, 80; transportation in, 143, 144–45,
168, 170; tributary relations in, 113. *See also*
seafood industry
forced relocation and resettlement. *See*
displacement of squatters; displacement of
working class; eviction; New Villages
foreign investment, 54, 223, 227, 236; in China,
298, 299
Foucault, Michel, 39, 316n1; governmentality,
203–7 passim
Freedman, Maurice, 9, 10, 16, 125
free trade zones (FTZs). *See* export processing
zones
Fudezhengshen Temple, 79, 85, 185–86, 209,
239, 252–55 passim, 259
Fudezhengshen Temple Managing Committee,
186–208 passim, 234–38 passim, 296, 298,
317n8, 317n13, 319n23
fugitive spaces, 227–33, 243–61
fund-raising, 199, 228, 238, 292, 296–97, 319n3
Furnivall, J. S., 9, 10

Gamba, Charles, 30, 35, 137
gambling, 63, 119, 227, 228, 278, 280; as leisure
activity, 138, 181, 232
gangster stereotype of truck drivers, 69, 70, 135
garment industry, 7, 63–66, 80, 131, 298, 299
gender, 7–9, 13, 20, 22, 75, 126, 133, 265–66;
in health care, 292; in migration to United
States, 321n9; in transnational reversals, 277;
in trucking industry, 169, 177–84 passim.
See also masculinism; patriarchy
gendered space, 179–80, 229–33, 245, 320n1
General Labor Unions (GLUs), 32, 34, 35, 36
Gerakan Party, 74, 102, 108, 124, 144, 146,
224–26 passim, 240; election of 1978,
314–15n6; elites' connections to, 203, 217,
236, 287; in National Front, 5, 46, 52, 216,
222, 287; Penang state, 215, 224, 226, 287;
314–15n6; waning influence, 215, 237
German Ideology (Marx and Engels), 174
"getting by" (phrase), 82, 83, 90–93 passim,
114, 230, 237, 249, 295
globalization, 213–24 passim, 243, 258, 259,
264, 276, 284–87 passim, 298–300 passim,
320–21n7; education and, 267, 274–75;
shipping industry, 236